THE ROME THAT DID NOT FALL

THE ROME THAT DID NOT FALL

The Survival of the East in the Fifth Century

Stephen Williams and Gerard Friell

London and New York

First published 1999
by Routledge
11 New Fetter Lane, London EC4P 4EE

Simultaneously published in the USA and Canada
by Routledge
29 West 35th Street, New York, NY 10001

Typeset in Garamond by Routledge
Printed and bound in Great Britain by Biddles Ltd,
Guildford and King's Lynn

British Library Cataloguing in Publication Data
A catalogue record for this book is available from the British Library

Library of Congress Cataloging in Publication Data
Williams, Stephen
The Rome that did not fall: the survival of the East in the fifth century/
Stephen Williams and Gerard Friell.
Includes bibliographical references and index.
1. Byzantine Empire – History – To 527. 2. Rome –
History – Empire, 284–476. 3. Emperors – Rome.
4. Emperors – Byzantine Empire. 5. Rome – History –
Germanic Invasions, 3rd–6th centuries. I. Friell, Gerard. II. Title.
DF555.W55 1999
98–22745 CIP
949.5´013–dc21

ISBN 0–415–15403–0

The subjects of the Byzantine empire, who assume and dishonour the names both of Greeks and Romans, present a dead uniformity of abject vices, which are neither softened by the weakness of humanity nor animated by the vigour of memorable crimes.

(Edward Gibbon, *Decline and Fall*, ch. 48)

All the historians who have discussed the decline and fall of the Roman empire have been Westerners. Their eyes have been fixed on the collapse of Roman authority in the Western parts and the evolution of the medieval Western European world. They have tended to forget, or to brush aside, one very important fact, that the Roman Empire, though it may have declined, did not fall in the fifth century nor indeed for another thousand years. During the fifth century while the Western parts were being parcelled out into a group of barbarian kingdoms, the East stood its ground.

(A.H.M. Jones, *Later Roman Empire*, conclusion)

For the ruler of Byzantium, the unshakable assurance that his State represented Civilisation itself, islanded in the midst of barbarism, justified any means that might be found necessary for its preservation; while the proud consciousness of his double title to world dominion – heir of the universal Roman Empire and Vicegerent of God himself – enabled him to meet his enemies at the gate, when capital and Empire seemed irretrievably doomed, and turn back the tide of imminent destruction. Ruinous schemes of reconquest and reckless extravagance in Court expenditure were the obvious consequences of the imperial ideal; but what the latter-day realist condemns as the incorrigible irredentism of the Byzantine Emperors was not merely the useless memory of vanished Roman glories. It was the outcome of a confidence that the Empire was fulfilling a divine commission; that its claim to rule was based on the will of the Christian God.

(H. St L.B. Moss, in Baynes and Moss, *Byzantium*)

CONTENTS

CONTENTS

ILLUSTRATIONS

Figures

Maps

Table

ACKNOWLEDGEMENTS

We thank especially Jim Crow for his information on the continuing archaeological project on the Anastasian Wall and its hinterland. Ramsay MacMullen's early suggestions on the book are appreciated. The late, sadly missed, Herbert Jarmany read the early and central chapters, and made thoughtful and helpful comments. We are indebted to Teresa Friell for extremely skilful help in scanning and translating a great deal of the text from one system to another. Michael Embree and Stephen Nelson added useful if controversial comments. Perhaps these reminded us that the concerns of late Roman history still have some links with the concerns of the present day.

S.W.
G.F.

LIST OF ABBREVIATIONS

CAH	*Cambridge Ancient History*
Chron. Min.	*Chronica Minora*
Chron. Pasch.	*Chronicon Paschale*
CJ	*Codex Justinianus*
C. Th.	*Codex Theodosianus*
ERFP	Blockley, *East Roman Foreign Policy*
FCHLRE	Blockley, *Fragmentary Classicising Historians of the Later Roman Empire*
Fr.	*Fragments*
GRBS	*Greek, Roman and Byzantine Studies*
JRA	*Journal of Roman Archaeology*
JRS	*Journal of Roman Studies*
LRE	Jones, *Later Roman Empire*
PLRE	*Prosopography of the Later Roman Empire*
Procopius I–VIII	*History of the Wars (Bellum Persicum/Vandalicum/Gothicum) Buildings (de Aedificiis)*
SH	*Secret History (Anecdota)*

INTRODUCTION

The Late Roman empire, with its great baggage of accumulated traditions, was much given to face-saving legal fictions. At the end of AD 476, an embassy in the name of the Senate of Rome arrived at Constantinople seeking audience with the Eastern Roman emperor, Zeno. Everyone knew that it came, not from the Senate but from the barbarian warlord, Odovacer, who by killing off his rivals had made himself the real ruler of Italy. This was only what a succession of similar warlords, Roman and barbarian, had done before him: holding the titles of supreme military commander (*Magister Utriusque Militiae*) and ruling through pliant and impotent emperors whom they had come to set up and dispose of at their convenience.

Now Odovacer had taken the final logical step, of deposing the latest boy emperor, Romulus Augustulus, without even going through the charade of setting up a successor. It had not even been necessary to kill him: the youth had obediently abdicated and retired on a pension to his family's estates in Campania. His very name had been a humiliating nickname, mockingly echoing the legendary founder and restorer of Rome. The Senate's message respectfully proposed that it was no longer necessary to have a separate emperor in the West, and that henceforth Zeno alone should rule the whole empire. They brought with them all the imperial insignia of diadem, purple and gold robes and much else, which they solemnly presented to Zeno. In return, they requested that Odovacar, whom they had chosen for his military and political wisdom, be recognised by Zeno as his loyal administrator of the diocese of Italy and be given the rank of 'Patrician' – the polite title legitimising what had come to be recognised in the West as military dictatorship.

This maintained the threadbare supposition that the Romans still ruled an empire from the Atlantic to the Euphrates, and that the many barbarian kings, warriors and settlers in the West were federate 'allies', supporting the empire and subject to Roman overlordship. In fact, the Western empire had been dismembered in the previous fifty years and replaced by a mosaic of new, warlike Germanic kingdoms: Franks, Burgundians, Visigoths, Vandals, Saxons and others, often at war with each other, living easily or uneasily side

1

by side with the Roman people and nobility in the former provinces. Odovacer was already using the title *Rex* – the first king of the Romans since the Tarquins were expelled and the Republic founded in 509 BC.

Still, Odovacer badly needed recognition from Zeno if he could get it, because the Eastern empire, centred on Constantinople, was still acknowledged as the source of legitimacy and even vaguely feared. There, powerful Roman emperors still truly ruled, something unseen in the West for eighty years, and could still send effective armies and fleets to intervene in western Europe, which they had done on several occasions.

The ambivalent replies of Zeno need not concern us at this point. The whole episode, so significant to later historians, excited barely a ripple of interest at the time. Most striking is the contrast between the two halves of what had been the old Roman empire: the Latin West and the Greek East. Both faced similar military and political crises at the beginning of the turbulent fifth century. Yet somehow the East, despite the ravages of the Goths, and then Attila and the Huns, despite barbarian inroads, weak or immature emperors and dangerous intrigues around the throne, had survived and was consolidating its power. The West had gone under. In less than a century, Byzantine armies would be reconquering the lost provinces of Africa, Italy and southern Spain.

In this book, we attempt to trace and explain the many causal strands by which this remarkable achievement came about.

Part 1

SEPARATION

1

CRISIS AND PARTITION

Theodosius I, the last single Roman emperor ever to rule the whole of both the Eastern and Western halves of the empire, was preoccupied for much of his difficult reign with reaching and sustaining an accommodation with the Goths within his territories. This was forced upon him after the crushing defeat of the Romans under emperor Valens by the Visigoths at Adrianople (Edirne in modern Turkey) in 378. About two-thirds of the available Eastern Roman field army was wiped out, and their emperor with it; the strategic balance had shifted against the empire.[1] There was no longer any practical military way of expelling the Visigoths from imperial territories, whatever ignorant patriotic opinion might say. There was nowhere else for them to go, since the newly arrived Huns had expelled them from their traditional homelands north of the Danube, except for a minority who had migrated to Transylvania and others who remained as subjects of their Hun conquerors.[2]

After a few minor victories, mainly achieved by starving the Visigoths of supplies, Theodosius brought them to a treaty in 382. It was the best that could be had in the circumstances, but nonetheless altered permanently the power relations between Romans and barbarians. They were settled as treaty 'allies' (*foederati*) in Moesia (northern Bulgaria), accepting the emperor as overlord and obliged to supply forces to him on demand. In the military emergencies, a similar settlement had been negotiated by the Western emperor Gratian with the Ostrogoths and Huns in Pannonia (western Hungary) from which they could no longer be excluded.

Of course, the Romans had many treaties with allied tribes immediately bordering their frontiers; they had taken in many barbarian peoples as disarmed settlers, mainly from the Germanic tribes, and Romanised German troops were a large component of the army, including many of its top commanders. But the treaty of 382 was a distinctly new departure, and both sides knew it. Imperial propaganda papered over the details and presented it merely as continuing traditional practices. 'Which is better,' demanded the panegyric of Themistius, 'to fill Thrace with corpses or with farmers? With graves or with people?'[3] In reality, the Visigoths were now a foreign nation in arms *within* the empire's territories under their own chieftains, not a settlement subject to Roman administration. Their soldiers were not integrated into the Roman command structure as barbarians had always been before, but fought as separate allied armies for specific campaigns under their own tribal leaders.

Still, the treaty held more or less successfully, with some strains, for the next twelve years, and Theodosius hoped it would not prove a precedent. He cultivated the Goths assiduously, impressing them with the power and wealth of Rome, promoting their nobles in his service, and generally persuading them of the advantages of peace and friendship. The aged Gothic king Athanaric, finally forced to make his peace with the once-hated Romans, was dazzled by the power, splendour and wealth of Constantinople, and his magnificent reception there, as he was clearly intended to be.[4]

Theodosius no doubt hoped that, given time, the Visigoths could be peacefully assimilated and their national identity diluted, as so many others had been. The policy was rational and had some success: many Gothic nobles responded, like Athanaric. But it depended heavily on Theodosius' own personal and diplomatic qualities, and the Gothic leaders saw the treaty in their own traditional way as a personal pact between rulers, which might or might not be renewed. Certainly the policy of accommodation was unpopular in the Greek East, where many people heartily detested the Goths: because of the plundering and ravaging of their lands, because of their uncouth customs, because their Christianity was Arian, not Orthodox, or simply because they were 'barbarians', that is non-Hellenic.

Theodosius' reign was punctuated by two costly civil wars, which depleted the already overstretched armies of the time. They illustrated only too well the near-impossibility of a single man ruling effectively over the whole of the beleaguered empire, and the wisdom of the customary dual rule of East and West. Originally, he had ruled the East only: the West was ruled by his colleague Gratian, who had appointed him after the disaster of Adrianople, and the two had co-operated closely and fraternally. But in 383, shortly after the treaty with the Visigoths, Gratian was overthrown and murdered in a military coup, originating in Britain and led by the general Magnus Maximus with the strong support of most of the army. Before Theodosius was in any position to intervene – even if he wanted to – Maximus had secure control of Britain, Spain and Gaul up to the Alps. He had been elected emperor by the army and accepted by the civil bureaucracy, and immediately put out peace feelers to Theodosius, promising coexistence: they were both Spaniards and old military colleagues, and Maximus hoped he could come to an agreement. His coins and official portraiture showed the two of them as brother-emperors.

Theodosius withheld recognition but made no immediate move against Maximus, which would have been a great military gamble at that time. Gratian's younger brother, the twelve-year old boy Valentinian II, was still alive and recognised as the legitimate Western emperor at Milan, with his mother Justina acting as de facto regent. Maximus ruled his portion of the empire competently, defended the Rhine frontier and was generally popular. Theodosius had no great wish for war, but felt he could not abandon the legitimate dynasty of Valentinian I to which he owed his own elevation. For several years there was an uneasy truce, interpreted in different ways by the influential groups of either side. Cautious unofficial embassies were exchanged, exploring the possibilities of accommodation, but they came to nothing.

The decision was made in 387, when Maximus suddenly invaded across the Alps and occupied Italy, against little resistance. The boy emperor, his mother and the court at Milan fled to the East to seek protection and military support from Theodosius. He chose to support them and, being recently widowed, joined himself to the Valentinianic dynasty by marrying the sister of Gratian and Valentinian, Galla. The other part of the alliance was a commitment to civil war against Maximus. In a lightning campaign in 388, he launched a double attack on the West, took Maximus off guard, defeated him utterly in a set battle near modern Lubljiana, then captured and executed him. The Western senatorial aristocracy rushed to make their peace with Theodosius, which was easily done: there were no reprisals, and he genuinely impressed them with his clemency, his urbanity and warm, easy manner, just as he had impressed his former Gothic enemies.

Yet in the longer term his victory was a strangely hollow one. He had done his duty to the dynasty of Valentinian and crushed Maximus, but he now had two growing sons of his own, Arcadius and Honorius. Like every successful emperor he was a dynast, and he clearly intended that they should eventually succeed him on the thrones of East and West when the time came. He had little enthusiasm for restoring the seventeen-year old Valentinian II as emperor of the West, and in fact he was restored in name only.

Here, dynastic ambitions and the demands of political and military realism pulled in opposite directions. It was obvious that the West, facing enormous pressure from barbarian tribes along the whole of the Rhine and upper Danube, needed a strong and warlike military emperor. Maximus had been this. Honorius was still a young child, and Valentinian was quite inexperienced. Theodosius therefore appointed what amounted to a guardian for him, in the shape of his trusted general Arbogast, who became the supreme military commander in the West. Because of his barbarian origin he could not aspire to the throne as Maximus had done, but he wielded far greater power than any general, appointing officials and issuing instructions in the name of Valentinian II – as Theodosius in distant Constantinople intended he should.

Arbogast used his power well, governed from the imperial capital of Trier and defended the Rhine frontier vigorously, but he could not solve the awkward problem of the boy emperor. Valentinian felt humiliated, a puppet emperor only, prisoner in his own palace. He sent despairing messages to

Theodosius for help; he attempted in vain to dismiss Arbogast. Finally, in 392, he was found hanged in his own quarters. Arbogast claimed it was suicide, and it probably was, but this was not believed in the East. Once again, Theodosius vacillated. He was not sufficiently interested in the problems of the West, yet could not ignore them. Arbogast protested his loyalty, but his own authority was in suspension without a legitimate emperor and the West was officially rulerless. Receiving no instructions or assurances from Theodosius, after three months he set up his own emperor to rule through, a civil official Eugenius, and once again sought friendship with Constantinople. Once again, Theodosius, thinking primarily of his own dynasty, plunged into the hazard of another civil war. In 394, at the battle of the Frigidus on the border of Italy, Arbogast and Eugenius were defeated after heavy losses on both sides. Especially heavy were the losses among Theodosius' Visigothic allies, who fought loyally in the front line under their chieftain Alaric. This they resented: the Romans, they suspected, much preferred to shed Gothic blood than their own. They may also have wondered why they were fighting in the emperor's own civil quarrels, instead of against foreign enemies such as the Huns.

Very soon after this victory, in January 395, Theodosius died suddenly at Milan. Almost all the circumstances were ominous. The main part of the empire's total field army was in the West. Theodosius' two sons, Arcadius and Honorius, heirs to the twin thrones of East and West respectively, were inept and immature youths aged eighteen and ten (indeed, Honorius verged on mental backwardness). Real power devolved on Theodosius' trusted general and son-in-law Stilicho, who for the moment commanded the combined armies. But as a semi-barbarian (his father had been a Vandal commander in Roman service) he could not aspire to the throne in his own right, even had he wanted to. With some legitimacy he claimed to have been appointed 'guardian' of the two imperial children and, as regent, claimed all the delegated powers of the late emperor. In fact, there was no legal office of regent in Roman law, and his claim was based narrowly on an unwritten, unwitnessed 'bequest' by Theodosius on his deathbed. But it was strongly upheld by bishop Ambrose of Milan in his funeral oration, and Stilicho's authority was generally accepted in the West by the army, the civil bureaucracy and of course, the boy emperor Honorius, to whom he betrothed his own daughter.[5]

Stilicho was an energetic and capable ruler, wholly devoted to the interests of the empire as he saw them, but his constitutional position was always an anomaly, just as Arbogast's had been. He was supreme military commander of cavalry and infantry in the West (*Comes et Magister Utriusque Militiae*), and quickly brought the other top commanders and their staffs under his direct control. Based on his guardianship and marriage link with the imperial family (*parentela*) he made appointments and issued laws, but only in the emperor's name. When the emperor came of age, or even came

8

under a rival influence, what then? He expected to inherit all the authority of Theodosius, but from the beginning his claims were utterly rejected in the East, especially by the Praetorian Prefect Rufinus, who managed the young emperor Arcadius and was himself the de facto ruler at Constantinople.[6] A rift opened, which was never completely healed.

The disgruntled Visigoths were returned to their allotted homelands in Thrace, which in their absence were being raided by their enemies the Huns. They quickly proclaimed their chieftain Alaric king, and began a plundering migration well beyond their assigned territory, at one stage threatening Constantinople. The Eastern government, effectively controlled by Rufinus, had no adequate forces to stop them, and was forced to buy them off with subsidies and promises. The intrigues between East and West allowed Alaric to enhance his position. What he wanted was both larger and richer lands to settle his people, and also the post of a top Roman military commander (*Magister Militum*), which had been firmly refused by Theodosius.

The intrigues and conflicts between the effective governments of East and West (not the helpless boy emperors) were to continue destructively for the next thirteen years. On the peremptory command of Constantinople, the Eastern portion of the army was dutifully returned, but on its arrival its Gothic commander Gainas, allegedly acting on Stilicho's secret orders, assassinated Rufinus in a blatantly public killing under the eyes of the emperor himself. The Prefect had accompanied the young emperor to greet the returning army on the great parade field of the Hebdomon immediately outside the city. As he greeted or inspected the troops their ranks quietly encircled Rufinus, and he and his Hun bodyguard were cut to pieces. The violence of the act may have shocked the emperor and others, but it was widely popular as Rufinus was detested by almost all classes: by the military because of his bloody purges and assassinations; by the civil rulers because he was a Gaul by origin and seen as an outsider; and by the population because of his rapacious confiscations and taxation. According to Claudian, his head was joyfully carried through the city on a spear.[7]

But if Gainas had ever expected to take Rufinus' place as the leading man in the East, as Stilicho was in the West, he was quickly thwarted. In place of Rufinus, the eunuch Chamberlain Eutropius became the new power behind the throne and defied Stilicho as before, with the support of the other civil ministers. They were glad to be rid of Rufinus, but had no intention of letting a powerful general become dominant. Gainas retained his position, but was denied the command and rank of *Magister Militum* which, after loyal service to Theodosius, he expected as his due.[8]

Stilicho confronted and defeated Alaric and the Visigoths in several engagements, but never decisively. After the costly civil war of 394, the defection of the Visigoths and the return of the Eastern portion of the army, Stilicho was now operating with the last substantial Roman field armies available in the West, which had to be kept in being at all costs. Apart from border garrisons, often composed of barbarians granted frontier lands and expected to defend them, these forces, numbering perhaps 60,000 at most, were all that existed to protect the heartlands of Gaul and Italy, as well as the more outlying provinces of Britain, Spain, Raetia, Noricum and Pannonia.[9] Stilicho could not now afford a victory over Alaric that involved heavy troop losses. Despite conscription, recruitment of Roman provincials was becoming increasingly difficult: landowners were reluctant to part with scarce manpower, and connived with their equally reluctant peasants to avoid the draft, often substituting a cash payment which could be used to hire barbarian troops. As a leader well qualified to handle barbarians, Stilicho no doubt hoped to pressurise Alaric back to his earlier alliance and use his military strength once again in Roman service.

Stilicho's propaganda, specifically against Eutropius, left no doubt that he still claimed authority over the Eastern boy emperor too. The Eastern government had begun to fear him as a military threat. When his campaign against Alaric led him to land an army temporarily in Greece, which was part of the Eastern half, Eutropius used the pretext to officialise the whole simmering conflict and have Stilicho declared a public enemy, a usurper and rebel against legitimate authority. In the circumstances, this was tanta-mount to a declaration of war. Eutropius encouraged the Count of Africa, Gildo, to revolt against Stilicho and throttle the Italian grain supply. Stilicho sent an expedition to Africa which quickly suppressed Gildo, but Eutropius' next move was to grant Alaric the post he coveted – *Magister Militum* in eastern Illyricum (Yugoslavia) – hoping to turn his menace west-wards again.

This was another sharp tilt in the Gothic–Roman power balance. Other 'barbarian' generals – Stilicho, Bauto, Fravitta – were firmly Roman in their loyalties, serving the legitimate emperor, and having broken all ties with their native peoples, as their military fathers had done before them. But Alaric was a Gothic king first and foremost, and a Roman commander only for the prestige and opportunities it offered – a large subsidy with legal access to the wealth and resources of Illyricum, and especially its arms facto-ries. There was now no chance of weaning him back to the restricted treaty of 382. He was a third power centre who could play off East and West to his advantage. Equally dangerous was the open example he provided: what he had done, other barbarian leaders could do too.

Eutropius was determined to thwart the political ambitions of the mili-tary. By 398 he had eliminated several leading generals in a series of treason trials and was justly hated in military circles. Although he tried to deal with foreign dangers by diplomatic means, raiding by the Huns into imperial territory now required a military response. Instead of entrusting the command to any of Arcadius' generals Eutropius assumed it himself and, to general surprise, was successful; at all events, the Huns retreated. Perhaps dazzled by this success, Eutropius made the political error of assuming a consulship; almost no rewards or recognition went to the other commanders or the troops. Worse, the spectacle of a eunuch occupying the ancient dignity of a consulship outraged senatorial opinion and almost everyone else, and Stilicho's propaganda exploited it to the full. ('O shame in heaven and earth! Our cities behold an old woman decked in a consul's robe....Was it for this that Horatio kept the bridge, and Mucius braved the flames?')[10]

In the year of his consulship the Gothic general Tribigild led a revolt among the Ostrogoths, who had been settled ten years earlier in Phrygia (Mesopotamia), and who had served in the campaign against the Huns. Like Alaric's Goths, they felt cheated of the due rewards for their military service. They were less than an organised army – unlike the Visigoths – but under Tribigild they spread considerable fear in the easterly provinces.[11] Eutropius sent two forces to deal with them: federate Gothic troops under Gainas (the Gothic commander whom he mistrusted), and regular troops under Leo (a protégé of his, with little military ability). At this point Gainas was probably still loyal to the empire, but it was loyalty towards Stilicho in the West, whose agent he was widely believed to be; and Stilicho was a public enemy. His increasingly isolated position, his resentment of being denied promotion and the deadly antagonisms between him and Eutropius soon led him into desperate intrigues well out of his political depth.

The revolt of the Ostrogoths, added to the unpopularity of Alaric's military appointment, caused an angry anti-Gothic, anti-barbarian protest at Constantinople in 399, which was immediately echoed in a far wider movement in the city and countryside. Synesius of Cyrene, a philosophical-literary figure, delivered an address heavily criticising the policies of the emperor, which he would not have dared to do had he not been assured of strong backing among the aristocratic governing classes. He was, in fact, the stalking horse of a growing political faction. His oration *de Regno* is a lecture on the true nature of kingship, couched in an idealised Hellenic setting. A king (emperor, *Basileus*), he declares, should be vigorously taking the field at the head of his army, not trapped in the enervating life of the palace with its luxuries, false ceremonials and plots. Citizens alone should bear arms. The state's soldiers, as Plato taught, should be its watchdogs, not wolves in the fold. But our armies are full of barbarian wolves, who give advice even in the council chamber. The accommodating policies of Theodosius were a mistake, born not of weakness but of a misplaced generosity to the barbarians. But wolves and sheep, barbarians and civilised men, cannot mix: their union is unnatural. The shepherd cannot tame the cubs of wolves. Barbarians should either be expelled to their own territories or used by Greeks as helots to till our lands.[12]

As a political programme, this was about as realistic as a rabid English newspaper urging that we invade France in the tradition of Henry V. Since the third century, the Roman army had depended on a steady influx of Germanic 'barbarian' fighting men – the only question being how and on what terms they were deployed. The aristocratic party knew this very well, but its point was to raise a patriotic, anti-barbarian flag, and the popular response was quick in coming. We may conjecture what loyal Frankish, Gothic or Sarmatian officers thought of this, not to mention the empress Eudoxia, daughter of the general Bauto and herself part-Frankish by birth.[13]

As a Goth, largely in command of Goths, Gainas' loyalties wavered, or perhaps he sensed new opportunities. Leo's forces were defeated by Tribigild's Ostrogoths. Sent to suppress them, Gainas temporised, while groups of the local populations attacked the bands of Ostrogoths and inflicted great losses on them. Then, impulsively, Gainas joined forces with the rebel Tribigild and demanded from the emperor and government a negotiated settlement with the rebels, the rank of *Magister* for himself, and the removal of Eutropius. All were agreed. Together the two marched on Constantinople with dominating force. Eutropius was removed, followed by several other anti-Gothic, anti-Stilicho ministers (Aurelian, Saturninus and John) whose lives were protected by the intercession of bishop John Chrysostom. Only Eutropius was executed, on Gainas' insistence.

Gainas and his motley Gothic army occupied Constantinople and he ruled, increasingly by force, for several months. He eliminated Tribigild and attempted clumsily to do, but in reverse, what Alaric had done – combine the authority of Roman commander with the leadership of tribal Goths. But it is one thing to command an army in the field, and another to use the army to govern a great metropolis, every section of whose population is bitterly hostile. The regular armies had been dispersed and were for the moment without leadership.

Having achieved nothing, and feeling the army's support ebbing away, Gainas abruptly abandoned the city, but his withdrawal of troops was so clumsy that the population were able to trap many of them inside the city in loose order and, despite their arms, massacre them. With the emperor's public approval as many as 7,000 of Gainas' troops and their families were butchered, including some who had taken refuge in a church. The patriotic party returned to power, and Gainas was declared a public enemy. He began to plunder Thrace to support his remaining forces, but the local populations shut their city gates against him and the dwindling, demoralised army retreated to the Hellespont, hoping to cross back to Asia. There they were caught by a small, but disciplined regular force under the loyal Gothic *Magister*, Fravitta, and cut to pieces. Gainas and his remaining forces then fled desperately across the Danube, where the Hun king Uldin promptly killed him and sent his head as a diplomatic present to the emperor Arcadius at Constantinople. A monumental column was erected in the Forum of Arcadius with a continuous narrative frieze relating the defeat of Gainas and the expulsion of the Goths from Constantinople.[14]

Fravitta was rewarded with a consulship, but he too was later convicted on a trumped-up treason charge and executed.[15] With Alaric holding the balance in Illyricum, the strongest possible signals went out from the new rulers at Constantinople that his Visigoths would meet the most determined resistance from the army and civil populations if he tried to move eastwards again; the implication being that he should try his fortunes elsewhere. The East now enjoyed a period of comparative peace and stability, with a competent civil government under the effective leadership of the Praetorian Prefect Eutychianus, and after him, Anthemius. But relations with Stilicho in the West were still implacably hostile.[16]

Alaric tried to invade Italy, but was again repulsed by Stilicho near Verona. The insecurity led Stilicho to remove the seat of the imperial court from Milan, which had been chosen as a commanding centre close to the frontiers, to Ravenna, which was a safe coastal refuge away from the main military routes and protected by great tidal marshes. In 405, a new influx of people from beyond the Danube invaded Italy through Noricum under their warlord Radagaisus. Alaric stood idle, but Stilicho's army inflicted a crushing defeat on Radagaisus at Fiesole, capturing Radagaisus and executing him, and incorporating many of the prisoners into his own forces.

Yet, the victory, militarily decisive, had been at a quite crippling cost. Stilicho had been forced to assemble this army very rapidly, when military manpower was becoming extremely scarce. He had recruited large numbers of Hun mercenaries, and been forced to strip the critical Rhine frontier of the most effective troops, which had meant making whatever ad hoc 'treaties' he could with the opposing German tribes, invariably ceding control of territory and hoping that this would buy stability at least for a time. In the last resort, the defence of Italy itself took precedence over the defence of Gaul. Theodosius' federate strategy had begun to unravel, no longer under Roman military control except for a barely disguised, orderly retreat.

At the end of 406, sensing a rare opportunity, a great conglomeration of barbarian tribes – Suevi, Vandals and Alans – crossed the frozen Rhine into Gaul, overcame the resistance of the Frankish federates, and could never again be dislodged. This great invasion was the beginning of Stilicho's decline from power, as his strategic problems multiplied beyond control. In the beleaguered north, whose population felt abandoned, a rebel general Constantine had proclaimed himself emperor in Britain and crossed to Gaul with widespread support. Stilicho still tried vainly to reach an agreement with Alaric, hoping to use him to put down the usurper and regain Gaul. Alaric's financial price was growing ever higher, and when Stilicho approached the Senate to raise the money, it was bitterly resented. Most of the senators had extensive lands in Gaul as well as Italy, and murmured that Stilicho was in league with Alaric, a fellow-barbarian; now they were being asked by a Vandal military dictator to pay a Visigothic plunderer to crush a Roman patriot trying to defend Gaul. 'It is a treaty of slavery', proclaimed one, who then discreetly went to ground.[17]

The sudden death of the Eastern emperor Arcadius in 408 led Stilicho to his fatal mistake. He rashly revived his old, futile ambition of marching east to become the legitimate protector of the new child-emperor Theodosius II, thus uniting East and West again – a project that was by now quixotic. Once away from the Court and Honorius, his enemies pounced: he was arrested on imperial orders and executed without the slightest pretence of a trial. Many of his followers were tortured to death to reveal his supposed treasonable conspiracy, but nothing was discovered.[18] The senatorial nobles, whose huge evasion of their tax liabilities was a contributory factor to the Western crisis, damned Stilicho as a barbarian traitor, a wolf in the fold – a view even some modern historians have taken. But whatever his errors he was a loyal Roman, attempting to defend the West against forces too powerful and complex for him. After him there continued the territorial fragmentation of Roman Europe which none of his successors was able to prevent.[19]

The prolonged and damaging split between Eastern and Western governments in 395 to 408 would not have occurred had the two brother emperors at Milan and Constantinople been adult, effective rulers instead of ciphers. In the past, imperial colleagues in East and West had quarrelled and even fought each other, but this had always been understood as an interruption to the normal state of things, and the outcome was a renewed unity and co-operation. Either emperor would normally come to the other's aid in serious difficulties, such as major invasions or rebellions, and the most important decisions of the empire would, at least publicly, be made and proclaimed jointly.

In the reigns of Honorius and Arcadius power was in the hands of deputies who deeply mistrusted each other, whose authority was open to challenge and whose position could be undermined. The external and internal barbarian pressures were more urgent than ever, and each side took whatever immediate regional measures it could to cope with them. Eutropius naturally enough seized the opportunity to induce Alaric to move westward; Stilicho had little choice but to strip the Rhine frontier beyond the danger point in order to save Italy. No doubt, the conflict was intensified by Stilicho's sincere, but stubborn insistence that the will of the dead Theodosius entitled him to protectorship over both boy emperors. But the suspicions of the East and the instability of the regency there in any case thwarted genuine co-operation between the effective rulers. After Rufinus' murder, Eutropius looked for an excuse to break off relations with Stilicho and tried to unseat him. After him, the Eastern Prefect Anthemius, it is strongly suspected, intrigued with the Italian senators to help topple Stilicho when the opportunity offered. The overall result was that for a long period East and West were openly manoeuvring against each other like separate states, providing great opportunities for barbarians such as Alaric to exploit. Although there would again be formal reconciliation between the two thrones and capitals, the chronically difficult conditions of the fifth century prevented the older relationship from ever being fully restored.

2

THE FOURTH-CENTURY BACKGROUND

The administrative division of the empire into East and West, corresponding to the Greek and Latin halves, dated back at least to the late third century, when the empire painfully emerged from over fifty years of chronic disorder. Repeated barbarian invasions, civil wars and ungovernable armies had all but wrecked the empire as a single political unit. The causes of the great tribal movements southward and westward are still argued over, but by about 240 the empire was faced by a great arc of hostile tribes pressing along the whole length of the Rhine and Danube frontiers. Added to this was a resurgent Persia, under the new, aggressive Sassanid dynasty, intent on conquering Rome's eastern provinces.

In this changed world situation, one fixed imperial centre could not possibly defend every threatened area and its citizens. Frontiers were breached repeatedly, provinces pillaged and fought over. The loyalties of the legions and the insecure provincials gravitated towards one strong regional commander, who could pay them and defend them, away from a distant Roman emperor, who could not. With the breakdown of dynastic continuity and the rise of the Praetorian Guard as casual emperor-makers, generals with their regional armies were tempted, or forced by their troops, to declare themselves emperors, either of the whole empire or secure sections of it. Gaul, Britain and Egypt all seceded at some period. The sheer time and cost of moving, supplying and paying armies over thousands of miles, only to fight one another for mastery, made these rivalries very destructive to the fabric of the state. Much provincial administration was eroded, the currency suffered uncontrolled inflation, many areas fell back on a barter economy, and troops were paid crudely in kind, requisitioned from the areas they passed through in a manner akin to plunder. Between 235 and 284 there were fifteen 'legitimate' emperors and many other usurpers, mostly elected by armies in the field and then murdered in turn by the same armies in favour of a rival candidate.[1]

Diocletian, elected by the Eastern army in 284, had no son, and had to experiment with alternative arrangements from the beginning. He ended the disorders by the expedient of, in effect, anticipating rebellion by legally adopting and appointing a trusted colleague, Maximian, as co-emperor in the West, while he himself ruled the East. It was later formalised into a more complex system of four emperors, bound by marriage ties into an artificial adoptive dynasty. The two senior emperors, the *Augusti*, adopted younger military colleagues, the *Caesares*, by marriage, signalling legitimate imperial powers and the eventual right of succession.

The empire was too large, its enemies too many to be ruled from one centre by one emperor. Rome ceased to be the effective political capital and was largely ignored. The new crude, patriotic soldier-emperors had to be continually on the move with their armies (and governments) close to the frontiers. Trier, Milan, Aquileia, Sirmium, Salonica, Nicomedia, Antioch; all became the effective capitals, as the whole apparatus of imperial court, ministries, military headquarters and accompanying throng of soldiers, officials and their supporting populations settled in and around them preparing for next year's campaign. As a result of all this, and a great increase in the size of the armies, backed by conscription, major defensive wars could now be fought and won on several frontiers simultaneously – something hardly ever achieved or indeed demanded before. By about 300, Roman armies were everywhere victorious: on the Rhine, the Danube, in Britain and Africa, and in the crushing defeat of Persia.[2]

After Diocletian's principled retirement in 305, his artificial tetrarchic dynasty fell apart in a new round of civil wars whose ultimate victor was Constantine. But Diocletian's other great reforms of almost every area of the state were continued and refined by Constantine, and proved extremely durable: together they amounted to a new militaristic form of empire, centralised, hierarchic and, as far as possible, regimented. Constantine separated military and civil chains of authority and reorganised the armies. He abolished the Praetorian Guard and the old legionary system, replacing it with two types of force: highly mobile and flexible field forces (*Comitatenses*) and static border garrisons (*Limitanei*). He also introduced a new command structure and professional officer training cadres (*Candidati*), which now allowed trusted and capable officers of Germanic ('barbarian') origins to reach the topmost commands – the newly created Marshals: *Magister Peditum, Magister Equitum*, Master of Infantry and Master of Cavalry.[3]

Under the strong military emperors Aurelian, Diocletian and Constantine the symbolic status of the emperor himself (*Augustus*) was deliberately elevated to near-godlike status, mainly as a device to overawe the volatile armies. The previously despised Oriental trappings of monarchy – diadem, jewelled robes, elaborate court ceremonial and public ritual – were all pressed into service. The figure of the emperor was no longer the civic *Princeps* of Augustus, nor yet the first among the military leaders, but now *Dominus*, despotic lord over soldier and civilian alike. All these trends went against the civic traditions of the earlier empire, epitomised by the sentiments of the senatorial and equestrian nobility. The soldier-emperors were all of comparatively lowly provincial origins, almost exclusively from the Danube regions, and favoured their own countrymen or colleagues in filling the upper military and civil ruling strata according to merit and professionalism as they saw it.

After Diocletian's cruel and futile persecutions, Constantine adopted Christianity as the most favoured religion, hoping it would help to unify the empire. He naturally became supreme head of the church, as the emperor had always been of the old state religion. He also made the historic decision to establish a permanent new capital for his empire at Byzantium on the Bosporus, the strategic city commanding communications between Europe and Asia, whose defences had so impressed him in his final civil war. This was to be the new Rome, and no expense was spared on it. Among many other things, it was an acknowledgement that the eastern, Hellenic provinces were the stronger in wealth, cities and population.

Constantine ruled essentially alone after 324, but his successors soon rediscovered the lesson that the empire was too vast to be ruled by one man from one centre. Henceforth, with a few short exceptions, collegial rule was to be the norm, usually between imperial kinsmen ruling East and West respectively. The usual capitals were Milan and Constantinople, but emperors also made use of other imperial centres such as Trier, Salonica and Antioch. Though geographically distinct, the two halves were in no sense conceived of as separate states. All laws carried the names of both emperors and usually ran throughout the whole empire. On the death of one emperor, the other had the automatic right to proclaim a successor. Emperors could and did transfer troops and resources, and come to each other's aid, at least until 395.

A further stabilising factor was the greater background of loyalty to an established dynasty. The House of Constantine ruled jointly or exclusively for seventy years (293 to 363) and soldiers and subjects fully expected the purple to pass to male blood relations – even though the loose constitutional theory still allowed the army to 'elect' an emperor from among themselves, as they had elected Diocletian in 284. There were periodic civil wars for the throne in the fourth century, which were very costly in money and manpower, but dynastic loyalties and the collegial principle prevented these episodes from collapsing into the prolonged anarchy of the third.

The most dangerous enemies were the tribes threatening the 1,500-mile Rhine and Danube frontiers, from the Low Countries to the Black Sea, now amalgamated into larger, loose federations: Saxons, Franks, Alemanni, Burgundians, Quadi, Vandals, Sarmatians, Tervingi (Visigoths), Greuthungi (Ostrogoths) and others. They wanted plunder, lands, or both. Although their total numbers were not the myriads they were once believed to be, they were all warrior societies, like Zulus or Highlanders, in which every free man bore arms and considered war his main or only business. Compared with Roman and Hellenic urban societies they could put a far larger proportion of their total populations into the field.

Diocletian and Constantine had invested heavily in elaborate frontier defences – chains of forts, strongpoint cities, military roads, border garrisons. These were also bases for aggressive campaigns deep into barbarian territory, to ensure Roman ascendancy beyond the formal frontiers. This was backed by active diplomacy: treaties were made with tribes to guard a portion of frontier against other tribes, or fight them, or supply men for the Roman army, in return for subsidies, Roman military help and guarantees of their territory, or sometimes land within the empire for settlement. It made excellent sense to recruit barbarians into the armies, and allow controlled immigration and settlements (*Laeti*). This safety valve defused an external threat, got deserted land under cultivation again, and brought the warlike energies of the tribes into the service of the empire. Without continual barbarian recruitment, the enlarged armies could not have been kept up to strength. By about 350 a large proportion of the army, perhaps a quarter, was of distant or recent barbarian origin, but decidedly Roman in status and loyalties.[4]

Nonetheless, treaties with the external tribes could easily be broken, and the frontier system was enormously expensive to maintain. War was continuous, and the cost of the armies – over 500,000 men, at least on paper – was by far the largest element in the now crushing burden of taxation. However, the frontiers held for most of the fourth century, under vigorous military emperors such as Constantius, Julian and Valentinian. The original global threat, emanating from widespread tribal movements, had been generally contained.

After 376, quite new strategic problems arose which completely disrupted the frontier system along the eastern Danube. This was the westward movement of the Huns, Altaic steppe pastoralists, the first wave of the 'horse peoples' who would later upset large areas of the settled world for many centuries. Their main economic base was not so much agricultural land as herds, they could move easily over very great distances, and employed superb cavalry tactics that hardly any other army could match. During the 370s they progressively displaced the Germanic Tervingi and Greuthungi (henceforth, Visigoths and Ostrogoths) from their lands in the whole of the Dnieper-Ukraine-Moldavian regions. The Visigoths, in desperation, petitioned the Eastern emperor Valens for settlement land within the empire on the usual terms, which was agreed.

The unexpected scale of the immigration proved unmanageable. The immigrants were not disarmed, and local Roman exploitation and incompetence led to a revolt. They were finally brought to the fateful battle of Adrianople on 9 August 378 and inflicted a shattering defeat on the Romans, the effects of which could never be reversed. Two-thirds of the eastern field army, perhaps 15,000 men, including the emperor Valens himself, were wiped out. The eastern European provinces from Greece to Constantinople were virtually defenceless. In this emergency, the Western emperor Gratian hurriedly adopted the general Theodosius as his co-emperor in the East, to save what he could. This led to the treaty of 382, establishing the Visigoths as a distinct allied nation in arms on Roman territory.[5]

It was against this background that the two halves of the empire came apart after Theodosius' death in 395. In a time of great danger and instability caused by Alaric and the wandering nation of Visigoths, and with the imperial armies gravely weakened by the recent civil war, co-operation between the two governments was more necessary than ever. Instead, there followed a period of bitter cold war between them, during which the West, whose resources were already dangerously low, underwent a series of calamities from which it never recovered.

3

FORTUNES OF EAST AND WEST

The great political events of 408 – the sudden death of Arcadius in the East and the violent overthrow of Stilicho in the West – had very different sequels for their respective governments. Officially, however, there was the publicly proclaimed reconciliation and formal unity of the two thrones, signalled by the shared consulship of Honorius and the child emperor Theodosius II in 409.

In the West, the situation deteriorated from tottering instability to near-anarchy. Parts of Gaul were overrun by new barbarian invasions. Burgundians were established west of the Rhine. Alans, Vandals and Suevi sacked many cities before migrating and plundering southwards to the Pyrenees, and thence into Spain.[1] Almost the only core of Roman military authority was in the hands of the usurper Constantine in Gaul, who was technically in rebellion against Honorius at Ravenna. In Italy, following Stilicho's murder and the bloody purge of his supporters, there was a violent anti-barbarian backlash among the Roman part of the army. Some tens of thousands of Stilicho's Gothic troops, in danger of being massacred with their families, deserted en masse to join Alaric.[2] There was now no adequate military force to resist or even deter him. No new commander arose to fill the central role of Stilicho. One candidate was the entirely loyal Gothic general Sarus, who had avoided the purge, was deeply hostile to Alaric, and aspired to Stilicho's old position. He was the most capable general available and, despite his origins, probably the best military hope against Alaric: but he was passed over. Instead the Master of Offices, Olympius, secured the appointment of two new *Magistri* in place of Stilicho's unified command, but they were mere placemen who did nothing and soon disappeared into obscurity.[3]

The menace of Alaric destabilised the Court, and only served to fuel its incessant, futile intrigues. Its policy towards him swung wildly from appeasement to haughty defiance, and back again. His own peace proposals might possibly have settled his Visigoths in Pannonia, but they were rejected. Solemn undertakings to him over hostages were not fulfilled, yet no measures were taken for military defence. By the last months of 408, with Honorius and his Court in Ravenna and half-minded to escape by sea,

Alaric's army had advanced, plundering, through Italy, camped outside Rome, and cut off its supplies from the port of Ostia.[4]

Famine quickly sapped resistance. Vague proposals to arm the citizens came to nothing, and thousands of barbarian slaves deserted to the Goths. No relief force came from the emperor at Ravenna. Vindictively, Stilicho's widow Serena, despite being of imperial family, was executed on the flimsy suspicion of having contact with Alaric. It is said that the City Prefect Pompeianus even tried to revive the ancient pagan sacrifices on the Capitol, abolished for the last thirty years: but that no-one could be found to perform the rites.[5]

Alaric's aim was not to capture Rome but put pressure on the government of Honorius at Ravenna to give him what he wanted – land for settlement, and a top military command which would extend and legitimise his power within the Western empire. He agreed to lower his price for raising the blockade: 5,000 pounds of gold and 30,000 of silver. The incomes of many individual senators were quite enough to assemble this money, but they largely evaded their contributions – to the point where the authorities had to strip the gold from public statues to raise the sum. Alaric duly withdrew his forces into Tuscany, but kept control of the roads to Rome. Representatives of the Senate had already gone to Ravenna to secure Honorius' agreement to a full peace treaty.

Alaric was dangerous and destructive, but hardly the terrible scourge of God that later legend tended to paint. The Visigoths had no homeland to return to, and they had a constant food supply problem without Roman support. They were outsiders, as Arian Christians as well as barbarians. They wanted land for permanent settlement, and Alaric had his eye on the old provinces of Noricum and Pannonia (Austria and western Hungary), which by now were largely ruined by invasions, and which were Roman in little else but name.

This might possibly have been the basis of a tolerable peace, in the face of the government's military helplessness. Many advisers at Honorius' court urged this course, but their view never prevailed long enough to become a consistent policy. After initially agreeing to the terms of a treaty, Honorius delayed, refused to ratify the treaty, then clumsily violated it by sending a small force of 6,000 men to relieve Rome; they were intercepted and cut to pieces. Alaric nonetheless sent a new embassy to Ravenna to negotiate, and in the meantime his brother-in-law Athaulf arrived in Italy with fresh troops. Another swing of policy now occurred at Ravenna. Olympius and his adherents were ousted from leading positions and Olympius' place taken by Jovius, the new Praetorian Prefect of Italy, who was an old associate of Stilicho and Alaric. He now proposed a peace conference at Ariminum.[6]

Alaric responded readily, but now with higher demands: he wanted the provinces of Noricum, Venetia and Dalmatia for his people, plus a regular subsidy of gold and supplies. Jovius proposed that Alaric also be given the high Roman military position, *Magister Utriusque Militiae*, commanding general of cavalry and infantry. At this point Honorius majestically refused, in the most disdainful terms. Enraged, Alaric threatened to sack Rome. Honorius declared war, emboldened by a promise of 10,000 hired Hun troops from the Illyrican provinces. Few if any arrived, and seem to have made no difference to the military equation. Alaric then tried again, demanding only Noricum, plus reasonable corn supplies. His new kingdom, he proclaimed, would act as an allied buffer against the new threats from beyond the frontier.[7]

There are many exemplars of inept diplomacy in history, but that of Honorius and his ministers in the years 408 to 410, makes George III's policy towards the American colonies appear almost statesmanlike by comparison. Every opportunity was thrown away, every difficult situation transformed into a worse one. For reasons that are baffling, Alaric's latest and more modest demands were refused, and Jovius and Honorius both swore a solemn oath of war to the death against him. Again he marched on Rome and blockaded it, and the Senate offered negotiation. Since it was now evident that Honorius at Ravenna cared little about the plight of Rome, Alaric decided to set up an alternative puppet emperor at Rome who would give him what he wanted. Priscus Attalus, the new Prefect of the City, was elevated to the purple and did what he could to bring the nobility of Rome over to his side against Honorius.[8] Alaric was granted the command of Master of Infantry, and his brother-in-law Athaulf, Count of the Domestic Cavalry Troops.[9]

The policy was more difficult than Alaric expected, and he made several blunders. Africa, the vital granary of Italy, remained loyal to Honorius and threatened to blockade supplies to Rome. Alaric's Visigothic army, with the figurehead emperor Attalus, now besieged Ravenna, where the terrified Honorius offered to share imperial power. But Attalus insisted on his complete abdication. Jovius now changed sides again back to Alaric, and Honorius prepared to escape by sea to the East. He was saved by a small but timely force despatched from the East by the Prefect Anthemius. It was only about 4,000 men, but enough to hold the huge marshes around Ravenna against an investing army. Alaric withdrew again, turning his attention to the urgent problem of the African grain supply. Attalus had sent a small armed delegation to Carthage to persuade or threaten Heraclian, Count of Africa, to raise the blockade. It was repulsed, its leader Constans killed, and Rome soon felt the pinch of famine again.[10] Alaric naturally wanted to send a full army to recapture the province, but Attalus and the Senate, in a sudden display of independence and pride, opposed the indecent despatch of a *barbarian* army against what was still a Roman province – just as they had opposed sending Alaric against the Gallic usurper Constantine.

The followers of Attalus began to shift their allegiance back to Honorius. The friction between Alaric and his puppet emperor now erupted into the open. In frustration, Alaric stripped Attalus of the purple (though sparing his life) and put out new peace feelers to Honorius, recognising him again as sole legitimate emperor. The two met personally a few miles outside Ravenna in July 410. Alaric clearly needed a settlement as much as Honorius did and, despite his volatile temperament, this was perhaps the eventual opportunity for a durable peace. After all, later events were to show that a settlement with the Visigothic nation was possible. At this point there appeared Sarus, Alaric's old Gothic enemy, who had been denied the military promotion he believed he deserved, and who certainly did not want Alaric reconciled with Honorius and given a high military position. With his troops at Picenum, he launched a sudden attack on Alaric's camp, intending to wreck the peace process. He succeeded.[11] Suspecting the collusion of Honorius, Alaric angrily broke off negotiations and for the third and last time marched on Rome. On 24 August 410, he forced the Salarian Gate – helped by treachery, some said – and his troops sacked and pillaged the city for three days.[12]

News of the sack of Rome, which had not been taken by an army for eight centuries, reverberated around the world in a brutal demonstration of how helpless the Western empire had become. It was a moral, psychological shock rather than a great strategic turning point. The horrors of the sack, in a city already reduced by famine, extortion and siege, have been generally exaggerated. It was not at all like Attila's later sack of some of the great Eastern cities. There were few shocking atrocities. Having looted most of what was easily available (but spared many churches) and taken many captives, including the emperor's sister Galla Placidia, Alaric withdrew south to Campania. He failed to take Naples and, reverting to his earlier plans, prepared a full-scale invasion fleet to capture Africa. It was wrecked in the straits of Messina, and shortly after this Alaric was suddenly taken ill and died.[13]

It was the symbolic humiliation of the sack, far more than any concrete damage, which stunned the imaginations of this and later generations. In a culture that tended to see history as great cyclical epochs rather than continuity, this had all the signs of the end of an era. As foretold, an Age of Gold had been followed by an Age of Silver, and eventually an Age of Iron and Rust. Pagan traditionalists blamed the calamity on the abandonment of the old religion. As Horace had said, 'So long as you obey the gods, you will rule.' For over a thousand years Jupiter and his pantheon had protected Rome, given her world domination and saved her again and again from calamities. Yet, less than a century after their worship had ended, had come this unthinkable disaster. The most memorable Christian reply to this charge was Augustine's apocalyptic *City of God*. With echoes of his Manichean past, he says there are two eternally opposing cities: the Heavenly City of God, created by angels; and the perishable City of Earth, created by the rebellion of fallen angels. The epochs of history correspond to the six days of Creation, and we are now living in the last, sixth epoch, after which the City of God will hold sway.

Even to many Christians this was uncompromisingly fatalist and other-worldly: the survival of the Roman state and order, a value universally unquestioned, was considered unimportant, irrelevant, compared with the eternal bliss which the chosen few would enjoy in the City of God after the perishable earthly dunghill had passed away. These ideas were only faintly echoed in the East. Some pagans, still followed by the historian Zosimus many years later, repeated the stock accusation that Rome's disasters were the result of neglecting the old gods. But Christian opponents had no need at all to reply in the desperate manner of Augustine, in view of the mani-festly greater security and prosperity of the Christian East.

In the East during these years, after the Gainas crisis was past, the posi-tion was far more secure. There was a growing Hun presence north of the Danube, severe raiding from the mountain Isaurians in Asia Minor, and a disruption of the capital's grain supply from Egypt, but none of this bore comparison with the perilous state of things in the West. Constantinople and the heartland provinces were not threatened, and there were still great resources of armies and money to be deployed. After Arcadius' unexpected death, at the age of only thirty-one, the accession of his seven-year-old son Theodosius II went off smoothly, thanks to the strong loyalty to the dynasty, but also to the careful management of a capable and undisputed regent in the person of the Praetorian Prefect Anthemius.[14]

Superficially, his position in relation to the child monarch might have seemed similar to Rufinus and Eutropius before him, but Anthemius had several solid advantages over them. There was no hostile conspiracy trying to thwart him from the West. The removal of Stilicho, which he probably had a hand in, ushered in a return of cordial relations between the two thrones, although in practice Constantinople could not or would not do much to help Ravenna. It was a strategic fact that Eutropius in the East had bought off the threat of Alaric and his Visigothic 'allies', by exporting him westwards. At home, with the fall of Gainas and the massacres and expulsions of 399 to 401, the East had brutally rid itself of what it saw as its Gothic challenge. The explosive anti-barbarian feelings of the popular Greek mobs had allowed a traditionalist, patriotic faction of aristocrats, ministers and offi-cials led by Anthemius to secure a dominant position in the government. They effectively reversed all Theodosius I's policies of accommodation with the Visigoths and, like Rufinus and Eutropius, attempted to keep control securely in civilian hands – even to the extent of weakening the armies to a degree, as a result of which they did not provide military aid to the West on any scale.

Despite popular feeling after Gainas there was no large-scale purge of Goths in the armies. What measures were taken were minimal and cosmetic. There was, it appears, at least a tinge of official guilt over the massacre of 7,000 Goths in Constantinople, since the episode is pointedly omitted from the detailed narrative scenes on the column of Arcadius. Even at the height of the crisis, the proportion of troops of Gothic origin in the regular armies was probably under a quarter, and many of these remained loyal throughout. Gothic regulars were counterbalanced by Romans, and federate troops by Huns and Alans. Goths were edged out of the higher commands for a period of over ten years. The downfall of the loyal Gothic *Magister* Fravitta, who had defeated Gainas and received a consulship for it, may well have been a court power struggle rather than part of a deliberate purge. At all events, by the early 420s Gothic *Magistri* again appear, whose careers must have spanned the period of maximum hostility.

Anthemius was no upstart, relying precariously on imperial favour and a narrow base of protégés. He came from a distinguished Egyptian family of administrators: his grandfather Philip had risen to become Praetorian Prefect to the emperor Constantius II. He had served Theodosius I on the embassy to Persia, and under Arcadius became Finance Minister (*Comes Sacrarum Largitionum*), then Master of Offices (*Magister Officiorum*), and finally in 405, Praetorian Prefect for the Orient, the senior Prefect and second in authority only to the emperor. He and his family epitomised the new Constantinian aristocracy of service rather than noble birth. It was a powerful class of administrators with a common classical education, professional skill and experience, and careers which depended heavily on the imperial government – as distinct from the Italian senatorial nobility, amongst whom the top posts were mostly seen as simply part of the traditional family honours system.

To call Anthemius head of a party would be misleadingly rigid, but he was prominent among a loose tendency of cultured, like-minded men such as John, Aurelian, Saturninus and their many friends. They favoured a strong imperial monarch rooted in the civic institutions, the preservation of traditional Roman and Hellenic values alongside Christianity, a check on powerful generals, diplomacy in preference to war if possible, and less reliance on barbarians. The extravagant diatribes of Synesius against the Gothic wolf in the fold, calling for patriotic renewal and cleansing did not accurately represent their views. But if they were not so unrealistic as to hope to expel 'barbarians', at least they were concerned to prevent any one group from dominating, and to avoid new settlements of federate 'allies'.

Anthemius had other qualities that had been blatantly lacking in Rufinus and Eutropius. He was honest and public-spirited, devoted to the interests of the state as he saw them, not just his own aggrandisement. Naturally, he had high ambitions for himself and his wide network of family and clients, but they were the proper ambitions of a dedicated mandarin, not an adventurer. (His son Flavius Isidorus was Proconsul of Asia and later, City Prefect of Constantinople.) His integrity, combined with his attested statesmanship, good judgement and willingness to consult and take advice, gave him a wider base of supporters than previous Prefects had enjoyed. By itself this would not have guaranteed him a dominant position with the emperor Arcadius, had the formidable empress Eudoxia[15] still been a force in the government. But in 404, she had died of a miscarriage and soon afterwards Anthemius had moved into the top position, holding the consulship for 405 and confidently gathering the reins of power into his hands. The next year he received the title 'Patrician', the highest honorific status that could be conferred on a leading minister or general, but without the military-dictatorial connotations it was to acquire in the West.

He had thus been the trusted protector and adviser to Arcadius for three years, and easily transferred this influence to the new child emperor. An almost unique law in the name of Theodosius II explicitly authorised Anthemius to deal with all provincial affairs as he saw fit, and simply present his decisions for the imperial signature.[16] Equally significant, and altogether exceptional, is the fact that he was to hold the Praetorian Prefecture for nearly ten years – an almost unheard-of tenure. Synesius summed up the Eastern regime quite simply: 'The times belong to Anthemius.'[17]

On the face of it, the continued unquestioning loyalty to the Theodosian dynasty in both halves of the empire may seem remarkable, considering the quality of those who comprised it. None of the males succeeding to the purple inherited even a trace of Theodosius I's imperial qualities. None was given any apprenticeship in war or statecraft, and both Honorius and Theodosius II ascended the throne as children. Indeed, it is doubtful whether an apprenticeship would have done much for them. Honorius, as we have said, seems to have verged on mental backwardness. A century earlier Theodosius I's sons would probably have been immediately overthrown and replaced by the nearest powerful general, but long periods of dynastic rule had buttressed their position. Now, through an accretion of accident and intention, the apparent emasculation of the boy emperors altered the workings of imperial authority without wrecking dynastic continuity. They became even more encased in the jewelled shell of the palace and its controlling rituals, including the strong and popular pieties of the Church. They continued to be the carefully nurtured symbols of central authority, but an authority routinely wielded on their behalf by the ministers of the Court who had most to gain by preserving the situation. In the East it was further stabilised by a contrasting succession of vigorous and capable dynastic women – Eudoxia, Pulcheria, Eudocia – whose influence filled much of the gap vacated by the feeble males, who functioned as ministers in all but name, and helped to keep real power in the orbit of the palace. Factional personal disputes could be fought out within the constraining frame of palace and capital.

Only if military force or massive popular violence at Constantinople came directly into play, as they had done in the crisis of 399 to 400, might the government, and with it the throne, be seriously threatened. As recently as

403–4 there had been popular riots in favour of bishop John Chrysostom, who had been exiled for insulting the empress Eudoxia. The palace had been threatened, troops had attacked the mob and killed many, and at one stage the Great Church had been set on fire, damaging the Senate house and palace. This was a sharp reminder, if one were needed, of certain limits to the emperor's power in the capital. In the Hippodrome, which held about 80,000 people for the adored chariot races, the mobs could and did make their collective sentiments very clear with impunity. Only a small number of palace troops (*scholae*) were permanently stationed in Constantinople (the main Praesental armies being billeted in the surrounding territory), and these were not always enough to put down serious riots involving large numbers. But of course, having the Praesental armies or a portion of them in the capital itself would be a far greater anxiety to the civil government.

In 408, the delay in grain supplies from Alexandria to Constantinople led to bread riots, in which the house of Monaxius, the City Prefect, was burnt down.[18] Alternative grain supplies were quickly re-routed from other areas, and the whole organisation of supply and distribution overhauled. Once the disturbances were over Monaxius instituted a central reserve fund, supplied partly from senatorial contributions, to buy grain quickly in emergencies. Anthemius took the responsibility for the Egyptian grain convoys away from the shipowners (*navicularii*) and transferred it to the naval supply system.[19] The governor of the staging-post of Karpathos was made responsible for the convoys, together with the Prefects of Egypt and Constantinople. A seven-year programme of building warships and supply ships was later begun.

The Hun king, Uldin, now overlord of the peoples beyond the lower Danube frontier, had long fished in Roman waters. He had obliged Arcadius by beheading Gainas, and had helped Stilicho to his victory over Radagaisus, but he could equally be a menace who had to be bribed and placated into good behaviour. He now invaded Thrace with his subject hordes, capturing the city of Castra Martis and pillaged the surrounding territories. Roman forces in the region were temporarily unable to stop him, and attempts to negotiate were rebuffed contemptuously. Yet, like other invaders before him, Uldin could assemble a large aggressive host, but had much greater difficulty holding it together and provisioning it, especially if food supplies were withdrawn into the fortified cities. The Romans were able to lure many of Uldin's non-Hunnic subject chieftains, such as the Sciri, away from their allegiance, no doubt with ample gold and further promises. The invasion was soon divided and dominated by force and diplomacy, and the Romans were able to counterattack. Uldin and his core of Huns, after suffering severe losses, had to retreat back across the Danube. The remainder seen to have been divided and reduced piecemeal, and after various agreements many were settled on Roman territory, not as tribal units but distributed to landowners as tenant farmers, *coloni*.[20] They were not drafted into the armies, and emphatically not given any form of federate status.

A different kind of threat was not met successfully. For a long period the Taurus mountain region of Cilicia, in Asia Minor (Isauria), had been the base of a small but very warlike brigand people. They mounted such serious raids into the surrounding countryside and cities that a special military command had been set up to deal with them, with forts, guard posts and about 2,000 *limitanei*. They were, in fact, considered barbarians, and the cordon around them an internal frontier.[21] It only contained them intermittently, and in 404, after particularly dangerous raiding, a special expedition was mounted against them under Arbazaicus, himself distantly Isaurian in origin. Initially he drove them back to their mountains, but rather than follow up this success he then came to a deal with them for a portion of their plunder. Called to account by Constantinople, he was able to evade prosecution, it was said, by presents to the empress Eudoxia. Thereafter Isaurian raiding continued sporadically, and the Isaurians themselves were later to become, for a short period, a faction in imperial politics.

To deal effectively with future threats in the Balkans it was important to have a stable peace on the Persian frontier which would release many of the troops that would otherwise be stationed there. The long-standing issues between the two empires were, traditionally, agreed trading routes and monopolies; frontier fortifications and the military balance; respective influence or control of the buffer-states, especially Armenia; and, latterly, the position of religious minorities such as Christians or Zoroastrians in each other's territories. A series of embassies, promoted by Anthemius, from the emperor to the Persian King Yezdegerd I, succeeded in establishing and preserving good relations, with frequent diplomatic exchanges.

These were certainly helped by Marutha, the bishop of Sophanene in Armenia, whose medical skills providentially cured Yezdegerd's son when the Magian healers had been unsuccessful. This not only helped the position of Christians within Persian territories, but also led to a closer diplomatic relationship between the two thrones. Over the next years, agreements were reached on most of the contentious points. Christian churches in Persian territories were tolerated and protected, provided they did not proselytise; they became a lawful body under the bishop of the Persian capital Ctesiphon. It was a sensitive matter, but helped by the informal offices of the Syriac Christian churches, whose communities had an anchorage in both empires and who had the greatest stake in peaceful relations. The Roman empire would reciprocate for Magians and Zoroastrians. An agreement was renewed, whereby the cost of defence of the remote Caspian Gates should be shared. This was an important strategic pass through the Caucasus mountains, through which raiders such as the Huns could threaten both Persian and Roman empires. As the most vulnerable of the two, Persia had already built a fortress at Viraparakh, but Roman contributions to its considerable cost were slow in coming. Perhaps in redress for this, international trade, with its revenues but also its great potential for spying, was confined to

Callinicum, Nisibis and Artaxata to net Persian advantage. However, the peace treaties held at least until 420, after Yezdegerd was dead and Anthemius had left office.[22]

The Hun invasion had been foiled by money and diplomacy as much as by direct military strength, and Anthemius immediately took measures against a recurrence. The Danube barrier itself was strengthened by establishing a new fleet of 250 fighting vessels, such as had successfully repulsed an attempted Ostrogothic invasion in 386.[23] The affected areas of Thrace were relieved with special food supplies, and all the strategic cities had their walls strengthened, their citizens being drafted into corvée labour for the task. But the greatest enterprise of all, and of truly historic proportions, was the decision to construct a completely new belt of landward defences to Constantinople, taking in the expanding suburbs of the city and nearly doubling its area.

The land walls of Anthemius, also called the walls of Theodosius, still impress today as one of the world's great monuments of military architecture. They extended nearly four miles, from the Sea of Marmora to the Blachernai region on the Golden Horn. In its final form, it comprised a 60-foot (18-metre) moat, then a line of outer walls with forward bastions at intervals of 60 to 80 yards (55 to 73 metres). Behind them rose a far higher inner wall with a series of projecting artillery towers over 60 feet (18 metres) high, covering the spaces between the bastions of the outer wall, so that every approach could be dominated by a field of fire. Properly manned and equipped, these walls were as near impregnable as anything could be. In the next thousand years, they were to withstand sieges and assaults by every enemy, except for the so-called Fourth Crusade of 1204, which succeeded by treachery. Only the advent of heavy siege cannon in the fifteenth century would finally end their effectiveness.[24]

It has also been suggested that a subsidiary motive of Anthemius was to guard against a repetition of the 399 crisis, when Gainas' army had occupied Constantinople, and dominated emperor and government by force. The walls were also a physical and psychological barrier separating the civilian government from the Praesental armies outside, making it more difficult for them to impose their will on it.

Anthemius was removed from the scene by 414, either by palace politics or by death. The dominant influence over the boy emperor was now his sister Pulcheria.[25] Although only a year older than him (fourteen), she was far more mature, ambitious and forceful. Her conflict with Anthemius began early. It seems very likely that Anthemius, with his own great reputation, family prestige and extremely wide network of clan influence (two Prefects from the same family) aimed at an alliance with the imperial family, a quite natural step which had been achieved by both Stilicho and Rufinus. Pulcheria herself was approaching marriageable age, as were her two slightly younger sisters. A marriage to one of Anthemius' younger relations was a distinct possibility.

Pulcheria would have none of it. Already she had taken charge of affairs within the palace in a domineering manner, and persuaded her brother to dismiss the Chamberlain Antiochus. A marriage alliance would open up the palace to a new direct male political influence with the figure of Anthemius more powerful than ever. She therefore publicly and ostentatiously vowed herself to perpetual virginity with all the extravagance of youth, and persuaded her sisters to do the same, dedicating a gold and jewelled altar inscribed with her vow in the Great Church of Constantinople.[26] As effective head of the imperial household, she personally took charge of the emperor's education in manners, imperial deportment and most importantly, religion.

With Anthemius removed, such was the hold of Pulcheria over her brother that, against all protocol, she procured for herself the imperial title *Augusta*, hitherto accorded only to the consort of the emperor.[27] Soon government policies began to change. In place of an urbane Hellenic-Christian ethos came a piously Orthodox regime inspired by the palace. Churches were founded, relics eagerly collected, religious foundations endowed, Jews persecuted and pagans barred from public office. Synagogues, unlike the old pagan temples, had previously been respected and protected by law from Christian mobs: now, a new law forbade the building of new synagogues and, in as many words, condoned their destruction, 'in desert places, if it can be done without riots'.[28]

At Alexandria, always a riot-prone city, the Patriarch Cyril, taking his cue from this, led violent attacks on the Jews and their synagogues, against the strong opposition of the Prefect of Egypt, Orestes. Then a mob of Cyril's lay brethren or 'hospital attendants' (*Parabalani*) publicly attacked the famous woman philosopher, Hypatia, dragged her into a church, violated and murdered her, tearing her body to pieces. There was an official investigation, but the crime went unpunished. Initially measures were taken to curb the *Parabalani*, but soon a new imperial instruction actually confirmed Cyril's authority over these dangerous street thugs.[29]

Pulcheria also broke with the anti-Gothic, anti-militarist bias of the previous administration. Despite their Arianism in religion, Gothic and Alan generals once again occupied top commands in the tradition of Theodosius I. Plintha, a Goth, not only held the consulship for 419 but occupied a Praesental *Magister* post for over twenty years. He was related by marriage to the Alan Ardaburius, who came to prominence soon after this.[30] Like other ambitious political families, these generals came to form a distinct military grouping, linked by dynastic ties. But like Fravitta and others before him, and in contrast to Gainas and Alaric, they were solely Roman military leaders, members of the Roman ruling class whose careers had been in the army and whose tribal identities had been left behind. In any case, since the Visigothic migration and settlement in the West there was no bloc of Gothic federates in the East on which to base external support, even had they wished it. Among the five *Magistri*, they were normally balanced by native Roman appointees.

30

Before long the ultra-pious character of the regime, with its intolerance and uncompromising universalist claims, began to put cordial relations with Persia under strain, and the hostility was reciprocated. Perceiving the change of mood, some Christian communities in Persian domains became restive under the constraints of mutual toleration: the Zoroastrian priesthood demanded measures against them. In an attempt at mediation, the Persian bishop of Ctesiphon, Yablaha, came to Constantinople as an official envoy of the king, but was made to undergo an examination of his faith – hardly a helpful diplomatic gesture. Then, in 419 a Christian bishop in Khuzestan, Abdaa, destroyed a fire-altar of the official state religion, and was executed together with others. The following year Yezdegerd died, or perhaps was assassinated, and his son Vahram V was determined to be a more correct Zoroastrian Persian king, ending the tolerant measures of his father. Christian refugees began arriving at Constantinople, where the mood was enthusiastic for a crusade. The emperor, in the words of one chronicler, 'was ready to do anything for Christianity'.[31]

Persia was invaded in 421 in a double offensive. Anatolius, a Roman, invaded Persian Armenia from the north, while Ardaburius advanced into Mesopotamia. Anatolius joined with Armenian rebels and made progress, while Ardaburius defeated a Persian army and besieged the great Persian fortress city of Nisibis (Nusaybin).[32] An Arab attack on Syria was heavily defeated. The arrival of Vahram's main army forced Ardaburius to raise the siege of Nisibis, but the Persians made no further headway. In 422, news of a new Hun invasion into Thrace gave a check to the Roman impetus, and from then on it was only a matter of time and careful exchanges before negotiations were in progress, leading to a peace settlement.

Both sides claimed victory to their respective peoples, but in fact, it was very much the *status quo ante*. The Persians still held Nisibis and did not cede any territory. Both sides agreed to build no new fortifications on the borders and to refrain from dealing with each other's Arab allies. Rome agreed to end its support for the Armenian rebels. Both agreed once again to tolerate each other's religious minorities. Pulcheria's pious regime seized on this clause as a great victory for Christianity: and indeed the balance was strongly in Roman favour, since Christians in Persian regions were far more numerous and substantial than Zoroastrians in the Roman sphere.[33] Wisely, the Christian community in Persia now decided to separate itself from the church of the Roman empire, and appeals to this church for jurisdiction or support were to be ended. It thus freed itself from the ebb and flow of Roman religious politics and, as far as possible, from suspicion of being a foreign fifth column.

The war had been generally inconclusive, but the fact that the two sophisticated monarchies could readily adjust their interests in a treaty which had a good chance of holding, indicated that stability could generally be attained on the Euphrates frontier. The true cost of the war to the empire had been the transfer of so many units from the Balkan regions. Despite Anthemius' earlier defensive measures, with insufficient field troops facing the new Hun king, Rua, he was able to penetrate deep into Thrace and even briefly menace Constantinople. He had to be bought off by a treaty, which promised him 350 pounds of gold annually (a small sum by East Roman standards), plus favourable arrangements over ransom of prisoners, and access to Roman markets. The Huns were quiet after this, but it had been a more serious invasion than Uldin's, and cast a shadow over the future security of the Danube provinces.[34] Anthemius' priorities of peace with Persia and strong defence on the Danube had been clearly vindicated.

Figure 1 Obelisk of the emperor Theodosius I at the Hippodrome in Constantinople, erected in 390. He was the last emperor to rule a united empire of East and West.

Source: The Conway Library, Courtauld Institute of Art

Note: Reproduced by kind permission of A.M.M. Bryer

Figures 2 and 3 The twin guardian spirits personifying the old capital and the new: Rome and Constantinople. Ivory diptych, fifth century.

Source: Kunsthistorisches Museum, Vienna

Figure 4 The Western emperor Honorius, during whose feeble reign the disintegration of the West began.

Source: Aosta Cathedral Treasury; Archivi Alinari/Anderson

Figure 5 Flavius Stilicho, guardian of Honorius and first of the military dictators or
generalissimos, who dominated Western emperors during the fifth century.
On his right, his wife Serena, niece of Theodosius I, and their son
Eucherius.

Source: Monza Cathedral Treasury; Archivi Alinari/Anderson

Figure 6 The victory column of Arcadius at Constantinople, now lost, celebrating the historic expulsion of the Goths from the city in 400.

Source: Freshfield Album, Column of Arcadius (Trinity MS 0.17.2.f.12)

Note: Reproduced courtesy of the Masters and Fellows of Trinity College Cambridge

Figure 7 The defensive land walls of Constantinople, built by the Prefect Anthemius in 405–14. They were to survive every attempt at assault until 1204. The bastions are modern restorations.

Note: Photograph: Tony Wilmott

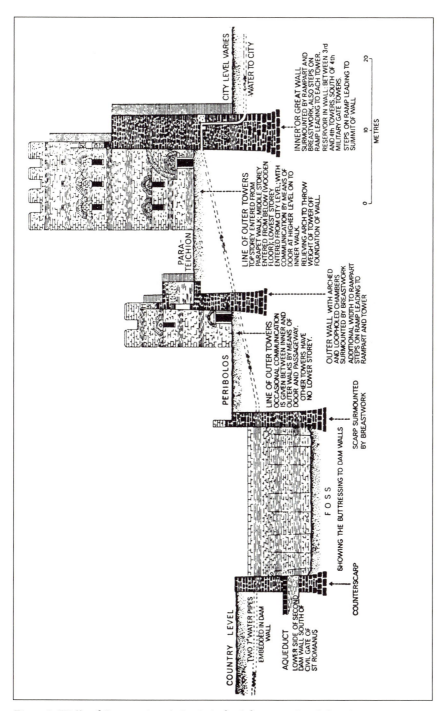

Figure 8 Walls of Constantinople in their final form, sectional drawing.
Source: Steven Runciman, *The Fall of Constantinople*, Cambridge 1965.

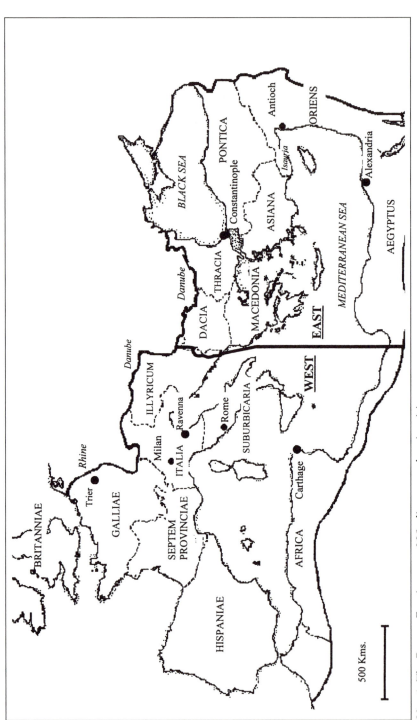

Map 1 The Roman Empire c. AD 395: dioceses and major cities.

4

THE WESTERN WARLORDS

After Alaric's death, it was possible to think of retrieving the imperial position in Gaul. An army under capable commanders, Constantius, a Roman, and Ulfila, a Goth, finally reduced the rebel Constantine at Arles after a long siege, and put an end to his separatist state, which had included Spain.[1] His uncertain rule had allowed the Vandals, Alans and Sueves to cross the Pyrenees and occupy areas of the Spanish provinces. Athaulf succeeded Alaric to the kingship of the Visigoths, and abandoned the project of invading Africa and that of occupying Italy entirely. Instead, he led his forces and their families northward into Gaul, where they occupied the fertile region between Bordeaux and Narbonne. Galla Placidia, the emperor's sister, went with him as his imperial prisoner, treated honourably.

Athaulf appears as a more predictable ruler than Alaric, well aware of the advantages of a settlement with the empire. He obliged Honorius by crushing two short-lived usurpers, Sebastian and Jovinus, in Gaul, and then demanded supplies for his people and land in Gaul for a permanent federate settlement, in return for which he would restore Galla Placidia. Honorius was unable to provide the supplies, and Athaulf therefore occupied Narbonensis and Aquitaine.

His next bold move, which alienated Honorius and traditionalist opinion, was to marry Placidia, without resistance on her part – independently of political calculation, there had sprung up a strong attraction between them.[2] She was a spirited, imaginative woman and used the new relationship to persuade Athaulf to a permanently pro-Roman policy. Far from seeing her position as being in disgraceful barbarian captivity, she adopted the role of Roman ambassador and mediator with the Gothic allies. Their first son was named Theodosius after his imperial grandfather. Athaulf is credited with a famous vision of a future state, very obviously scripted by Placidia:

> At first I wanted to erase the Roman name and convert all Roman territory into a Gothic empire. I longed for Romania to become Gothia, and Athaulf to be what Caesar Augustus had been. But long experience has taught me that the ungoverned wildness of the

> Goths will never submit to laws, and that without laws a state is not
> a state. Therefore I have more prudently chosen the different glory of
> reviving the Roman name with Gothic vigour, and I hope to be
> acknowledged by posterity as the initiator of a Roman restoration.[3]

Idealised though this is, it would be wrong to dismiss it as pure sentiment.
The attitudes of many Germanic rulers, who had been in close relationship
with the empire for many years, had become more complex, and Athaulf (if
he actually said it) would not be the last to seek an accommodation which
included Germanic military kingship and Roman institutions.

In the West, Honorius' general, Constantius, who had ended the separatist regime in Gaul, soon became the supreme military figure. He
combined the Praesental commands of infantry and cavalry, dominating
emperor and government, and filling a very similar role to Stilicho before
him (Stilicho's murderer, Olympius, he had already executed). Although
there were other *Magistri* in the West, Stilicho had secured the all-important
change that the senior Praesental commander – first himself and now
Constantius – directly appointed all their subordinate commanders and officials, giving him military supremacy. He had no claim to guardianship of
the emperor (who was now twenty-six, though no more effective a ruler) but
his unique position was distinguished by the revived title of Patrician,
(signifying far more than it did in the East), and later, a third consulship,
both of which now came to imply a special relationship with the emperor.[4]

A lasting alliance with the Visigoths was in fact impeded by Placidia's
marriage to Athaulf, which Honorius still regarded as barbarian captivity – a
view Constantius strongly shared, having designs on her himself. He made
war on the Visigoths and drove them into Spain, but Athaulf was assassinated
in 415, and soon afterwards Constantius was able to negotiate with his
successor Wallia the return of Placidia.[5] The Visigoths were fully fed and
supplied, and on Rome's behalf Wallia attacked and defeated the Vandals,
Alans and Sueves who were ravaging Spain.[6] In return for this service, the
Visigoths, the largest barbarian nation in Roman territory, were granted
extensive, permanent lands in Aquitaine, including the cities of Toulouse and
Bordeaux. Their kings were recognised as federate allies of the empire, bound
to defend their territory in the interests of the empire as well as their own, and
supply forces as requested. Under a dual arrangement, which became a model
for others, the Roman proprietors retained a third of their former lands, and
the native population continued to be subject to Roman law and administration.[7] In this way, both sides were able to represent the treaty as successful.
The Visigoths at last acquired a proper kingdom, while the emperor, though
forfeiting the tax revenues, had powerful allies who would (hopefully)
contribute to his military resources and the defence of Gaul.

Constantius, who made a similar allied settlement with the Burgundians
west of the Rhine, readily accepted the realities of the position, recognising

that the Germanic presence in the West was permanent, and had to be integrated into alliances as far as possible.[8] They had become the main reservoir of military force, and wherever he could, Constantius manipulated barbarians to fight other barbarians, conserving scarce regular Roman manpower. It was, of course, impossible and even undesirable to exclude Germans from high military command, despite many of them maintaining their tribal links in a way that had been strictly forbidden a generation earlier. They were excellent commanders and he employed them readily, reserving for himself the position of commander-in-chief. In reality, however, his military position was one of commanding directly the modest remaining regular army and the hired federate units, while merely managing and balancing the military potential of the different tribal allies.

Constantius had achieved, by 418, a settlement that was probably the best that could be had, and which restored some peace and order to the war-torn regions of Gaul and Spain after a decade of confusion and insecurity. A loosely federated Roman-German polity was possible in the West, and it continued for a time through an adroit balance of power. But the natural ambitions of the new kingdoms, their overall military preponderance and indispensability as sources of soldiers, could not be checked by any direct Roman coercive means. There was only the appeal to their treaty obligations and their own supposedly larger interests, the offers of advantages and concessions, and their residual awe for Rome and civilisation, of which they vaguely wanted to be a part.

Constantius achieved his political and personal desire in 417, and married Galla Placidia, despite her reluctance.[9] He thus established his proper tie with the imperial family, as Stilicho had done, and shortly afterwards the couple had a son, significantly named Valentinian, after Placidia's grandfather, the great emperor Valentinian I.[10] Her dynastic hopes now focused on this imperial child, since her brother Honorius was both childless and useless.

Whether or not it sprung from her persuasion, Constantius, unlike Stilicho a Roman by birth, in 421 took the logical step and had himself raised legitimately to Augustus, as Constantius III, co-emperor with Honorius in the West.[11] Galla Placidia automatically became Augusta. It was perhaps a testimony to Honorius' feebleness that he was persuaded to accept an imperial colleague in the same realm, an arrangement that had not existed since Diocletian's Tetrarchy. But at least it put the supreme commander and real head of government on the throne, finally ending the split rulership that had weakened the West for so long.

And yet, most strangely, the move seemed a failure. Constantius' elevation was pointedly not recognised at Constantinople by Placidia's imperial niece and nephew, possibly because they resented the intrusion, or feared a new Stilicho figure and a danger to their dynasty in the West. Yet Constantius had no obvious reason to be hostile to Constantinople, had no other family, and every reason to protect the imperial family into which he had married. According to Olympiodorus, Constantius found palace life at Ravenna, with its irksome and empty ceremonials, frustrating and depressing. So widely had the centres of real and titular government diverged that this is hardly surprising. Yet Constantius must have known this very well, and had it in his power to change it. However that may be, after six months as emperor, while planning retaliatory measures against the East, he suddenly fell sick and died. Poison was rumoured, as usual.

This was to be the last serious chance of reuniting real military and civil power with imperial authority under a single warlike, capable and legitimate emperor. Even at this stage it might have enabled Constantius III to halt, if not actually reverse, the continual erosion of Roman power in favour of the new Germanic kingdoms. Henceforth, Galla Placidia Augusta struggled both to control her brother Honorius and to thwart new generals who might aspire to the military dictator role of Stilicho and Constantius. Like Pulcheria, she enjoyed power and was quite prepared to rule the West as regent if she could. But even apart from the constitutional problems, the West badly and obviously needed a strong Roman military figure. From many points of view her best option might well have been to select and marry such a protector: but with her, as with Pulcheria, larger strategic interests of State were either subordinate to, or not distinguished from, interests of family. Fierce and exclusive dynastic loyalties shut off other fruitful improvisations for which Rome was famous, and which might have had a different outcome.

Soon, court plots estranged Placidia from Honorius and finally led her to seek refuge at Constantinople with her infant son. Honorius himself died in 423 after the most inglorious reign for a century. Immediately into the power vacuum moved a new military figure – the *Magister Militum* Castinus, who set up his own puppet emperor, an obscure civil servant called John.[12] Castinus himself, significantly, aspired not to the imperial purple, but instead to that familiar dominant role enjoyed by Stilicho, and for most of the time by Constantius, and which was now becoming institutionalised: the formal title Patrician, the special imperial connection, and the position itself, which we might call military dictator and which O'Flynn has aptly named 'generalissimo'.

Even more than with Constantius, Theodosius and Pulcheria were once again adamant that only a member of the House of Theodosius, enjoying God's protection, could properly occupy either throne. Without hesitation, the placatory envoys of John were banished and the East prepared for war on behalf of Placidia and her infant son. The price was the transfer of certain provinces – Dalmatia and part of Pannonia – to the Eastern government, and a promised future marriage alliance between Valentinian III and an imperial cousin in the East. Constantinople, which would not send serious military help when the Visigoths trampled through Italy, was now ready for a major invasion simply to preserve its dynasty and influence in the West, but would otherwise leave the West to face its grave barbarian problems on its own.

The invasion was commanded by the Alan *Magister*, Ardaburius, who had fought well against Persia, and his half-Gothic son Aspar. Alarmed at the news, John despatched to Pannonia one of his senior officers, Aetius, to engage the largest possible force of Hun mercenaries on his side. Aetius was uniquely qualified for this, having been brought up among the Huns as a hostage, and having cultivated a long, unrivalled relationship with their kings.[13] After some blunders and mishaps, in which several rebel commanders defected, the Eastern generals captured John, who was taken to Aquileia and publicly mutilated and tortured before being executed, to Placidia's great satisfaction. Castinus' forces melted away and he disappeared. Galla Placidia was recognised as regent and her son crowned Valentinian III.[14]

Publicly it seemed a victory for the East, an affirmation that the empire was after all one, ruled by a single dynasty at Ravenna and Constantinople. But the victory settled little or nothing as the realities of fragmenting power in the West re-emerged. Aetius returned from Pannonia with a powerful army, allegedly of 60,000 Huns. Too late to help John and naturally detested by Placidia, he was nonetheless in some position to name his terms. Before the Huns were sent home, a very costly business, Aetius had to be pardoned and his services accepted, though Placidia tried to concede as little as possible. In 425, Aetius was given a major military command, not in Italy but Gaul, where the Roman regular army had been drastically weakened over the last two decades. As a first-class general, adept at dealing with barbarians, he consolidated his position there, defended Roman territory by war and diplomacy against the encroachments of Visigoths, Burgundians and Franks, and always carefully nurtured his special relationship with the Huns, whose forces he depended on.

For ten years or more, Galla Placidia ruled the Western empire as far as anyone did. Determined to preserve the throne for her son, she carefully played the top military commanders off against one another: Aetius in Gaul, Felix in Italy and Boniface in Africa.[15] Of these, Aetius had the greatest military reputation. It was not until his rivals had been violently removed, and he himself once again brought a decisive force of Huns into the balance, that he finally occupied the generalissimo position of Stilicho and Constantius, commanding and ruling in the name of the youth Valentinian III. But although he secured the titles of Patrician and 'Protector' of Valentinian and Pulcheria, he had none of the relationship with the imperial family that his predecessors had enjoyed. They hated him but reluctantly had to put up with him.[16]

Aetius' military achievements in Gaul had depended heavily on his Hun allies as well as his own astute diplomacy, and tended to mask actual Roman weakness. The ceding of so much territory, with its former tax yields and recruitment potential, had reduced even further the native Roman components of the armies. Added to this was the great reluctance of landowners to part with peasant manpower through conscription, preferring to commute it to a gold payment where it could not be evaded in some other way. In contrast, this gold could immediately hire willing and capable barbarian warriors from societies where warfare was still the normal male way of life. A distinctly Roman regular field army, commanded, officered, trained and paid in the old way, was now only one force among many, and by about 430 it was too precious to be risked unless this was unavoidable. The real fighting was done almost entirely by barbarian units or tribal forces under one or other contract.

5

A CHANGING STATE

The ascendancy of Pulcheria and her religious regime did not seriously weaken the government, but it changed the character of the imperial court, and gradually gave the imperial authority an altered image to the world.

Anthemius was replaced as Prefect of the East by the aged Aurelian to advertise a certain continuity, but in practice the many adherents of Anthemius, his family and clients were dropped from office one by one, and Aurelian lasted only until 416. There was not the violence that had accompanied the removal of Rufinus and Eutropius. No new Praetorian Prefect held office as long as Anthemius had done, but the new Master of Offices, Helion, was an ally of Pulcheria and lasted thirteen years.[1] Anthemius' loose party fell back into the large pool of competent administrators that made up the senatorial mandarinate, and others were promoted to fill its place. The only loss resulted from the zealous attempt to remove pagans from the government and army by the law of 415,[2] which led in turn to an unseemly auctioning of jobs that was even cruder and more extortionate than the usual practice. As Eunapius complains, in the time of Pulcheria high office could be bought by all kinds of vulgar outsiders, and the usual qualifications – previous experience, intellectual and literary merit, membership of the mandarin aristocracy – were no longer enough to guarantee promotion.[3]

Pagan opinion and writing were not legally penalised, but in public affairs the atmosphere was putting them more on the defensive. The ban was generally effective at least in the short term, as Eunapius testified, except for those who prudently became baptised. A decade later a more liberal Prefect obtained from Theodosius a law to remind his subjects that Jews and pagans who obeyed the law and 'lived quietly' were protected in person and property against violence.[4] Yet pagans are still found in the government service as late as the sixth century.

Aelia Pulcheria herself, though doubtless sincere in her religious belief, was no cloistered nun. Her public vow of virginity which she extended to her sisters, was also, as we saw, a device to exclude external male influence from the imperial family, much in the way Elizabeth I continually avoided marriage. She was a highly intelligent, astute politician in the mould of her mother Eudoxia, and from an early age understood power and liked exercising it. As so often in the century, we see frustrated female political talents breaking their confining mould at a time when the imperial males were proving hopelessly incompetent and, as the women saw it, would throw away all the rightful dynastic power and authority to manipulators and adventurers unless they were stopped. Eudoxia had managed her husband Arcadius with great shrewdness. In the West, Galla Placidia, after two political marriages, ruled virtually alone until her son came of age. These women filled a power vacuum. Of course they could not personally direct armies or issue laws so long as there existed a male on the throne, but they could guide and manipulate him into wise policies, always of course in the larger interests of the imperial dynasty, in which their whole position was anchored.

This indeed was the point. The one unalienable function of imperial women, on which their dignity and influence depended, was to bear male imperial children. Pulcheria's great innovation was to forswear marriage and childbearing in favour of unrivalled influence over her brother. To retain this she needed a new kind of legitimacy, and found it in extreme Orthodox piety. The brilliant, cultivated salon of courtiers, politicians and aristocratic women which her mother Eudoxia had maintained, making the palace the focus of Constantinople society, was firmly ended. Instead she and her sisters kept apart, fasted, chanted antiphons and read scriptures at appointed hours of the day, and their company was holy monks and learned priests. All the customary female adornments of gorgeous clothes, jewellery, cosmetics and stylish idleness were conspicuously discarded in favour of household and charitable activities. The palace now resembled a convent. From her own personal fortune, Pulcheria founded churches, monasteries and hospitals, and purchased many holy relics.[5] The young emperor, a timid bookish youth by temperament, was drawn into this orbit. Pulcheria took personal charge of his education, which included not just the classics and a large portion of biblical and Christian texts, but also imperial manners and external demeanour: how an emperor should conduct himself on the ceremonial occasions when he appeared in public, received ministers or ambassadors, or presided over the Consistory. By all accounts, this was no easy task for such a shy and retiring monarch as Theodosius.[6]

As she browbeat her brother into making the desired appointments, or admonished him for signing state papers without even reading them, her power was fully recognised among the ruling circles.[7] Though only a year older than him, Pucheria was acknowledged as the emperor's guardian (*epitropos*), and official ceremonial and iconography presented her imperial authority (*basileia*) alongside that of her brother, as in the grouped portrait busts in the Senate house. In the wider population she enjoyed awe and admiration as 'the Orthodox one', and palace propaganda claimed that the crusading 'victory' over Persia in 421–2 was the result not just of the successful generals but also of Pulcheria's piety in dedicating her virginity to Christ, and in her boundless holy works of charity.

The influence of women behind or sharing the throne was not at all new, nor of course was the dignity and rank of Augusta. What was novel was Pulcheria's refusal to accept the well-defined maternal place of imperial females and instead to advance, step by step, the idea of an independent female imperium or *basileia*. One of her subtler devices was to promote earnestly the popular cult of the Mother of God, *Theotokos*, until that figure possessed a glory and power second only to Christ himself. Mary the Blessed Virgin, by miraculously giving birth to the Divinity, had expunged the sin of Eve which all womankind had inherited – or so the theory went, eloquently expounded by bishops such as Eusebius and Proclus. By analogy, Pulcheria who had dedicated her sex and her childbearing gift to Christ, was mystically reliving the virgin dignity of the unblemished Mary, the New Eve. To oppose her independent imperium on the mere grounds that she was a woman was to risk insulting the Mother of God herself, whom the mob revered and for whom it was ready to riot.[8]

The *Theotokos* doctrine and cult had much opposition, which later came to a head in the person of Nestorius, the intemperate bishop of Constantinople. He had already upset the political-religious balance in Constantinople by trying to take over a 'heretical' Arian church, which, like others, had been specifically reserved for the Gothic soldiers, including their powerful generals. Like John Chrysostom, he wanted to put women back in their place. Against other theologians, such as Apollinaris, he insisted that the human and divine natures of Christ were distinct. Mary was the mother of the human Jesus in swaddling clothes – *not* the mother of God. There were angry public clashes with Pulcheria. On Easter Sunday, he forbade her to take her habitual communion with her brother in the Sanctuary of the Great Church, from which he insisted women and lay persons were excluded. 'Have I not given birth to God?', she demanded. 'You have given birth to Satan!' was his damning reply. After this, partisans eagerly gathered on both sides.[9]

Pulcheria had already found an ally in the dangerous Patriarch Cyril of Alexandria, orchestrator of riots and pogroms, who argued that the two natures of Christ were inseparably joined in a 'hypostatic' union, that his human nature had no independent existence, and that since Mary bore his human flesh she was the Mother of God. Violent disputes and anathemas blew up between the two sees, until Theodosius was persuaded to call a General Council to debate and decide the whole question at Ephesus in 431. Publicly, he himself stood apart from the debate, other than insisting that it should avoid religious innovations. But the evidence suggests that, for once in opposition to his sister, he wanted and expected Nestorius to be vindicated. Instead, Cyril arrived with fifty bishops and his notorious street fighters (supposedly comforters of the sick) who gathered around them a violent mob of monks, thugs and city riffraff, and took the proceedings by storm. Nestorius, who had to be guarded by soldiers, bitterly described the scene: 'Everything they did was a cause of amazement and fear. They blocked up the streets so that everyone was intimidated, and they dominated the scene, lying around drunk and shouting obscenities.'[10]

Nestorius was deposed, with the connivance of Pulcheria. At first Theodosius wanted to reject the decision, but then John of Antioch arrived and convened a counter-Council, which claimed to depose both Patriarchs, and adopted a compromise formula of 'the unconfused union of two natures'. By this time the mobs of Constantinople too were demonstrating for Pulcheria and against Nestorius, aided by widespread bribery by Cyril's allies: 'Mary the Virgin deposed Nestorius!…Many years to Pulcheria! Many years to the Orthodox One!'[11] Pulcheria's final victory was to pressurise Theodosius into allowing Cyril to return to his Patriarchate.

The time of Pulcheria saw a further step in the process of spiritualising the imperial power which had been going on since Constantine and Christianity. Theodosius I had had a great sense of theatre and ceremonial, and when the occasion demanded – especially when it came to impressing barbarians – he could present himself as a glittering, godlike monarch on a plane above all others. Equally he could mix with all ranks of his subjects and most of all, he commanded armies personally in war, as every emperor had done for almost two centuries. But his sons and grandsons had no military skills at all, little political sense and almost nothing of his wider sociability. It suited the civil ministers such as Anthemius, and after him Pulcheria, to keep these obviously ineffective monarchs largely confined to the palace as impressive icons with rarity value, while they ran the business of government in their names. However, the emperor was traditionally and universally expected to lead the armies, just as he was expected to issue laws. Even if the real fighting was done by his generals, he should still be among the army, at least seemingly directing strategy. The army itself expected this, and although the civil bureaucracy undoubtedly preferred an unwarlike monarch confined to his capital, the military role was still an undeniable part of what an emperor should be. As Synesius had challenged the emperor Arcadius: 'The emperor is an artisan of war: how can he learn to use his tools if he does not mix with his soldiers?'[12]

Pulcheria's response to the problem was once again mystical rather than concrete. The emperor *did* lead the armies to victory – by his piety and holiness (aided, of course, by his sister). As the vicar of God on earth his prayers and offerings counted far more than any mere subject, and were the real guarantee of the state's divine favour and protection. When the war against Persia was about to be launched, Theodosius sent to the archbishop of Jerusalem a gold cross studded with jewels, ordering it to be erected on the mount of Golgotha. Christ's victory over death would give Theodosius victory over his enemies. On coins the traditional Roman victory symbols were now combined with a jewelled cross. On the great parade ground of the Hebdomon a new victory column was erected, crowned by a statue of Theodosius. The inscription extols him as victorious commander-in-chief *through the vows of his sisters*.[13]

In an age that fervently believed in the heavenly powers, this was more than just pious fiction, and represented a certain shift away from Roman traditions. The feminisation of the dynasty tended to pietise the monarchy. It enhanced the sacral character of the emperor, which might compensate for an unwarlike nature, and was thus an influence for stability. It reaffirmed the supremacy of emperor over bishop, and it began to close the earlier gap between secular military values and the Christian virtues. Christ, his Holy Mother and the saints aided the army just as Jupiter and Hercules had once done, and their power gave it the strength of several legions. No longer was Christianity cloistered and indifferent to Roman patriotism, war and battles. On victory monuments, angels were depicted fighting on the Roman side. Soon the figure of the soldier-saint would become a popular one. Pulcheria herself founded a church in the capital to 'Our Lady Giver of Victory'.

Although no soldier or statesman, Theodosius was a scholar in his pious way: he was reputed to know the scriptures by heart, and collected a considerable library. He also did a great deal to encourage learning, especially law and history. It was in his reign that both pagan and Christian historians, becoming impressed by the contrasting fortunes of East and West which they were witnessing as contemporaries, began to write distinct Eastern histories in which they began to assume that Constantinople, not Rome, was the natural, immovable centre of the world. Four ecclesiastical historians, Sozomen, Socrates, Theodoret and Philostorgius, covered the period from Constantine I to their own day, the middle of Theodosius II's reign. Usually it could be risky to publish a history of one's own times, which might cast judgement on a reigning emperor or even more, his powerful ministers. But, with due discretion, the histories were written nonetheless. The Christian writers saw themselves as continuing Eusebius' unrivalled *Historia Ecclesiastica*, written at the turn of the fourth century, which vividly describes the persecutions of Diocletian and Galerius, the final triumph of Constantine, and the rebirth of the empire under God's protection.

It was by no means a Christian monopoly. The underlying coexistence, with the classical culture that educated Christians admired and shared, could not be swept away by monks and bigots. In the polished classes at least, pagan Hellenic scholars still had a place. Theodosius was pulled in different directions. As a pious Christian, he was always uneasy about the continued existence of pagans, but as a responsible ruler, he was also reluctant to violate traditional legality and custom. Christian pressure caused him to ban the Neoplatonist Porphyry's classic *Against the Christians*, but this was an exception. Indeed, it is remarkable to find Zosimus, towards the very end of the century, still pouring forth conventional pagan invective on the whole conversion of the state to Christianity, which he considered an unmitigated disaster. Two pagan historians also published during Theodosius' reign. Eunapius of Sardis covered events from about 270 to 404, while Olympiodorus of Thebes described the years from 408 to 425. Both the Christian Sozomen and the pagan Olympiodorus dedicated their histories to Theodosius.[14]

The significant point is that for the emperor and for the Christian historians, as for Eusebius, the period beginning with Constantine I represented a distinct historical era. Although of course the empire was still one, both pagans and Christians were impressed by the strength and prosperity of Constantinople and the Eastern half compared with the turmoil and sufferings of the West, including of course the apocalyptic sack of Rome. It could not but foster some sense of the distinctness of the East, and its ability to survive indefinitely even if the old Rome perished. To many Christians this success was clear evidence of the divine favour and protection accorded to their pious, Orthodox emperors and state.

In the same spirit, Theodosius founded a university at Constantinople, intending it as a Christian centre of higher learning to counterbalance the older Athens and Alexandria, which were still respected centres of traditional Hellenism. Teaching was divided nearly equally between Latin and Greek, and the main subjects were classics, rhetoric and law, with a smaller proportion of philosophy. In fact, the character of the institution was closer to the professional law school at Bierut, than the speculative academies of Athens, still teaching the spirit of Plato, Aristotle and Plotinus. It offered the essential equipment for the typical Christian gentleman-mandarin portrayed by Sozomon, who naturally aspired to a career in the great bureaucracy.[15]

The last attempt to bring any order to the burgeoning body of Roman law had been made in the time of Diocletian, who had retired in 305 after issuing an enormous number of legal decisions on almost every subject. Two jurists, Gregorian and Hermogenian, had compiled carefully organised collections of the important imperial legal decisions going back to the time of Hadrian, and these had proved so useful that they had become semi-official works.[16] Although emperors were the sole source of legislation and its final interpreters, Roman law predated the emperors and required them to rule through it. The great body of law was civil and private, concerning property, contracts, marriage, personal rights and status. It had accumulated over centuries, but it lacked a clear, formal mechanism of repeal. A new law on some matter was simply superimposed on that of an earlier emperor and took precedence over it, but the earlier law was not definitely debarred from being cited in a civil case. To abolish it entirely would have been a kind of insult to the proper memory and honour due to an earlier emperor, akin to defacing his statues or erasing his name from inscriptions.

Since Diocletian, a sprawling profusion of new imperial legislation of all kinds had been pouring forth in the reigns of Constantine, Constantius,

Julian, Valentinian, Valens, Theodosius, Honorius and Arcadius. This was in the form of edicts and constitutions (general laws and statements of principle, usually addressed to the Praetorian Prefect or other high magistrate); decretals (legal rulings made personally by the emperor in public court); consultations (legal rulings in response to judges' queries from lower courts); and then the huge mass of rescripts (particular interpretations of points of law in reply to individual petitions). There were incomplete and competing collections of many of these decisions, which replicated and often contradicted one another, so that courts could be in genuine confusion about what the law actually said, and lawyers could invariably cite precedents which nobody was in a position to reject as spurious.

Probably at the instigation of his then Praetorian Prefect, Antiochus, in 429, Theodosius appointed a commission (headed by Antiochus), to produce a definitive, authoritative compilation of the laws. He wanted to go further and codify all Roman law on a consistent and coherent basis, building on the articulated principles of the earlier jurists such as Ulpian and Papinian, but this more ambitious task had to wait for Justinian in the following century.[17]

Nonetheless, the compilation of sixteen books, published in 438, was a considerable advance. Only those decisions since 312 that appeared in the Theodosian Code could henceforth be cited as valid law, including new ones which might be added. (Here too the reign of Constantine I was taken as a watershed.) For all earlier law, only the collections compiled under Diocletian were recognised as valid and authentic. Legal decisions were grouped according to subject and chronological date, obsolete laws dropped and contradictions removed as far as possible. The Theodosian Code was an important step in reducing the unwieldy accumulation of many centuries of legislation into a logical and principled form. The imperial preamble boasts:

> Having swept away a cloud of volumes on which many wasted their
> lives and explained nothing in the end, we establish a compendious
> knowledge of the imperial constitutions since the time of the divine
> Constantine....None of the older emperors, however, has been
> deprived of their immortality; the name of no author of a constitu-
> tion has fallen to the ground; rather, they enjoy a borrowed light
> since their august decrees are associated with us.[18]

The Code was published as an authentic and complete record of imperial legislation in both East and West, naturally issued in the joint names of Theodosius II and Valentinian III, asserting the unity of the empire. But in fact it had long been accepted practice that an emperor's legal decisions normally applied only in that portion of the empire he actually ruled, and the principle was now explicitly acknowledged for future decisions. Only those new laws, or Novels, officially communicated by one emperor to the other and promulgated by him, were to run in both East and West.[19]

In foreign affairs, things were less successful. The Huns' breach of Anthemius' Danube defensive system in 422 should have alerted Constantinople to a growing problem in that quarter, but this does not seem to have been appreciated. It had, after all, occurred when the bulk of the armies were away fighting Persia and, after doing some damage, the Huns had withdrawn again. In any case, a new challenge arose after 429, which greatly altered the balance of forces in the Mediterranean. The new Vandal king, Gaiseric, whose people were settled in Baetica (Andalusia) together with the Alans, succeeded where Alaric had failed in the great ambition of invading Roman Africa.[20]

This was primarily a Western crisis, into which the East was drawn only belatedly when it seemed the whole of Africa as far as Carthage might be lost. It arose from yet another power struggle in the West, described in the previous chapter. The Count of Africa, Boniface, attempted, as others had done before him, to secure the rich African provinces as his own independent power-base from which he could defy Aetius. Civil war erupted. After initial failure, a loyal, largely Gothic army under Aetius' commander, Sigisvult, invaded Africa, took Carthage and Hippo, and provoked the desperate Boniface into enlisting Gaiseric's Vandals to his aid. This was the great opportunity Gaiseric wanted. Obligingly supplied with Roman ships, he transported virtually the whole Vandal and Alan army and people across to Africa in May 429. The total numbers are reliably reported as 80,000.[21]

Boniface had intended to allot them the westernmost Mauretanian provinces for settlement, but once established in force Gaiseric held the initiative, and had no intention of confining his new kingdom to these limits. He invaded eastwards, deliberately spreading terror among the civilian populations to drive them out of their lands. Only in 431, when he was besieging Hippo – the siege in which Augustine died – did the East come to the assistance of the West by despatching a military expedition under the *Magister Militum*, Aspar.[22] It was defeated in battle by the Vandals, lost Hippo, but managed to hold Carthage and Cirta. Soon afterwards, the Hun king, Rua, renewed hostilities on the Danube, threatening to invade again.

This dangerous pattern of multiple military commitment was to be repeated. Generals and ministers were slowly, no doubt reluctantly, having to recognise that it was now near-impossible to fight and win wars on more than one frontier simultaneously. Effective fighting armies took time to assemble and even longer to transport to a distant war area. This was immensely more difficult and costly if armies had to be transported overseas, as was only too evident in the expeditions against Vandal Africa, described in later chapters, whose costs were to prove near-crippling. The Theodosian organisation of the army under five independent top commands had been a rational response to challenges on different frontiers, as well as a mainstay of political stability. Yet it meant that even at full strength and efficiency, which was not always the case, only perhaps a fifth of the East's full fighting resources were immediately available against an enemy threat at any one time. Low-level attacks such as Arab raiding could usually be dealt with locally, but serious invasions could not. The *limitanei* could hold their positions in defensive strong-points and hamper an invasion, but not defeat it in battle. To do this required a main field army. The two Praesental army groups represented a strong mobile reserve, but even so it was hardly practical to deploy more than two field armies – one regional, one Praesental – in any campaign without creating dangerous weaknesses elsewhere.

The Persians, and now the Huns, were aware of large-scale Roman troop transfers and knew how to take maximum advantage of them. Here diplomacy had to supplement military strength. Events had shown that it was worthwhile making considerable concessions to Persia for the sake of peace in that theatre, which allowed troops to be moved elsewhere. The fact that a Roman army could usually defeat a Persian one in a set battle, or at any rate hold the Euphrates frontier securely, led some contemporaries to criticise emperors for seeming to give too much away in peace treaties. With their imaginations fixed in victorious wars in the traditional fashion, they failed to realise that the main threat of a hostile Persia was no longer that it would conquer Roman provinces, but that it tied down large forces when they were needed elsewhere. Fortunately, diplomatic relations with Persia were enlightened and usually fruitful. The Persians were increasingly preoccupied with the Hephthalite steppe people on their northern borders, and the empire took careful advantage of this fact, especially when Persia requested financial help in dealing with this 'common enemy', as they presented it.

An East Roman army was still present in Africa until 435 when a treaty was signed. The empire was in a poor position to contest the Hun threat from the north. Rua angrily protested against Roman reception of Hun 'fugitives' – that is, Hun nobles and warriors who had defied his authority by coming over to the Romans – and he threatened to invade as he had done years before. An exchange of embassies was agreed, the Roman side being led by the Praesental *Magister* Plintha, now the senior Gothic general, who was determined to handle all negotiations. Before he and his mission had reached the Huns, Rua suddenly died. The kingship passed to the royal brothers Bleda and Attila, who strongly pressed Rua's demands and were ready for war; fighting may actually have broken out. Plintha was able to defuse the situation by agreeing at Margus to a new treaty more favourable to the Huns. All 'fugitives' would be returned, the annual subsidy would be doubled (perhaps reflecting the new dual kingship), safe markets established for the Huns, and – more overtly humiliating for Roman prestige – Rome would make no alliances with anyone at war with the Huns.[23] Some of the Hun nobles who were returned were Attila's domestic enemies. As an arrogant gesture towards the Romans, on delivery they were promptly impaled without even waiting to take them back to Hunnic territory. But the treaty at least removed the main threat of a new Hun invasion, and Rome could turn to other foreign problems while Bleda and Attila consolidated their dominion over the other tribes north of the Danube.

In Africa, a tolerable treaty was negotiated with Gaiseric, but again conceding more than had originally been intended. It was not with Constantinople but with the Western emperor Valentinian III, and granted the Vandals not just Mauretania but part of Numidia too.[24] Hippo, though almost deserted, was reoccupied and Gaiseric agreed to pay an annual subsidy to the Romans. The stance was thus maintained that Gaiseric's African kingdom was a federate ally of the Western empire. Roman power itself was concentrated in the strategic city of Carthage and the provinces of Byzacena, Africa Proconsularis and Tripolitana (Tunisia and northwest Libya). In Italy Aetius recognised only too clearly the fragile balance of power and did all he could to placate the new kingdom. Gaiseric, a shrewd statesman as well as a formidable military ruler, also understood the balance of forces and concealed for the time being his ambition to take as much of Roman Africa as he could.

The military power of the East had come, belatedly, to the aid of the West to save it from disaster. Only the imminent threat of losing Carthage, the commercial and political capital of Africa and the naval key to the whole western Mediterranean, had prompted Constantinople to act. Eastern military intervention was certainly welcome but, in contrast to the days of Theodosius I, it could not be relied on and could no longer be in sufficient strength to be decisive and lasting.

Figure 9 The mausoleum of Galla Placidia in Ravenna. She married the Visigothic King Athaulf, and then the generalissimo Constantius, later the emperor Constantius III. For over a decade she was the effective ruler of the West.

Source: The Conway Library, Courtauld Institute of Art

Figure 10 Valentinian III, son of Galla Placidia and ineffective Western emperor
during the invasions of Attila. After murdering his great general Aetius
he was himself murdered in revenge in 455.

Source: Musée du Louvre

Note: © Photo RMN – Chuzeville

Figure 11 Theodosius II, 408–50. Though personally unworldly, he was managed
by other strong figures. His main achievement was the codification of the
law in 429–38.

Note: © The British Museum

Figure 12 Pulcheria Augusta, the forceful sister of Theodosius II who dominated
the Eastern government and initiated a period of fervent Orthodox piety.

Note: © The British Museum

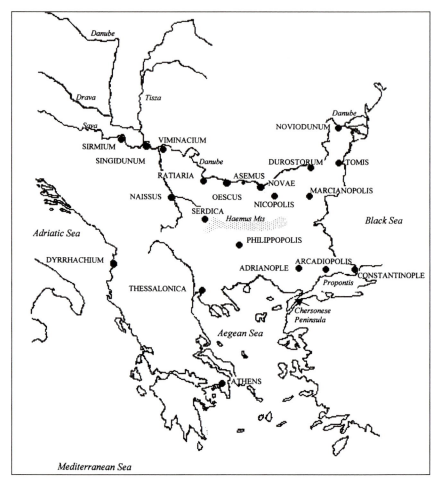

Map 2 The Balkans: major cities.

Part 2

ON THE DEFENSIVE

6

THE SHOCK OF ATTILA

In the winter of 439 to 440 the Eastern empire's relations with the Huns were not of the highest priority. The Huns were still nominally governed by the terms of the treaty of Margus, agreed with the two young royal brothers Bleda and Attila five years earlier.[1] True, this was a somewhat humiliating treaty. But with the deteriorating situation in Africa it was preferable to the direct invasion which King Rua had threatened – and which had been avoided only by his timely death. It was seen as the clear intervention of God against the pagan enemy, as prophesied in Ezekiel.[2]

In any case, the terms of the treaty did not have to be taken entirely seriously – or so Theodosius' ministers advised. In the first year or two a token of compliance had been made: some important Hun fugitives were returned, and the first stipulated payments of gold duly delivered. But Hun military manpower in the empire was by now a valuable commodity, and there had never been any intention of giving it up. The repatriation of Huns soon dwindled, and the flow of gold simply stopped. Bleda and Attila were preoccupied with consolidating their hold over the subject tribes, and unable to do much about it in the immediate future. The Danube was guarded by its river fleet, the frontier forts and cities now fully manned, and the armies of Thrace and Illyricum intact. The land walls around Constantinople had been supplemented by sea fortifications against possible naval attack. Theodosius and his government could feel reasonably secure. They simply had not yet discovered what new kind of enemy they were dealing with.[3]

They did not, perhaps, appreciate the scale and seriousness of all the changes that had been taking place in the great areas north of the Danube since Uldin's time. No longer were the Hun raiding expeditions those of loose, transient tribal conglomerations, lacking political cohesion and easy to fragment. Hun overlordship of settled agricultural peoples – primarily the Goths – had now given them a regular food supply that could support larger forces for longer periods. They enjoyed acknowledged superiority in cavalry warfare, with their unmatched speed of movement, manoeuvre and concentration of force, and their lethal archery assaults using the powerful composite bow.[4] This could secure them enough plunder to reward more

63

warriors, and, in turn, compel wider allegiance and so mount greater expeditions. So long as the Hun king was politically competent and victorious in war, he could not only hold together the Hun, Alan, Goth, Gepid and other groupings more firmly, but elevate himself and his family to a dynastic position distinctly above the other nobles.

The persistent demands by Rua, and now Attila, for the return of Hun 'captives' or 'fugitives' were first of all a determination to eliminate all opponents or rivals which Roman diplomacy might exploit. More ambitiously, it amounted to a claim of sovereignty over all those independent tribes and subtribes who had preferred military service with the empire under their own chieftains – primarily Huns, but other groups too, whose main body beyond the Danube acknowledged Hun overlordship. It did not take great penetration to see, in the Hun wars, conquests and alliances among remote regions and peoples, something more than just the ebb and flow of endless fighting among barbarians. There was now a growing ambition on the part of the dominant royal houses to gather forcibly and under one rule, in the Caspian, Don, Dneiper, Dacian and Pannonian regions, as many as possible of the disparate groups of Huns and their subjects.

There is still some obscurity about the origins and nature of the Huns before they encountered Roman civilisation in the late fourth century – their relation to other nomad pastoralists, their economy, level of technology and social structure. It is now broadly agreed that, like other pastoralists, their economy was not self-sufficient, and not some intermediate stage between hunter-gatherers and farmers, but depended on coexisting with agricultural peoples. Their own basis of wealth might be herds rather than land, but they needed a constant supply of cereals and other agricultural produce. It is also very possible that their technical production skills were more advanced than classical and many modern writers have assumed, and also that they had the beginnings of a stratified society of nobles. Almost certainly their political organisation underwent a rapid change in contact with the Roman empire. But to Roman eyes they first appeared as ugly and dangerous savages at the lower level of barbarism, without houses, farming or laws, dressed in skins, eating roots and raw flesh, and living in the saddle. Most impressive was their superb horsemanship and ease of movement over enormous distances. Such is the fearsome picture portrayed by Ammianus, describing the tribal movements of the 370s. Well before Attila, the Huns and Alans were highly valued mercenary cavalry, serving in the armies of Theodosius I, Stilicho and of course, Aetius; but attitudes towards them had softened little. They were still 'people...but little known...dwelling beyond the Maeotic Sea [Sea of Azov] near the ice-bound ocean, [who] exceeded every degree of savagery'.[5]

Far more alarming than the Huns, was the shattering news from Africa, in 439, that the Vandal king, Gaiseric had broken the earlier treaty and taken Carthage. The new Vandal kingdom in Africa had been accepted only reluctantly and with the greatest apprehension by the Western government because there had simply been no alternative; and now their fears were being realised. Carthage was the greatest harbour in the western Mediterranean, with shipyards, dockyards and all the facilities to service a fleet. With Carthage in his hands, Gaiseric could not only block the grain lifeline to Italy, but, his piratical fleet could now also attack the Italian coasts, where there was no longer an effective navy to stop them. Soon there came reports that he was preparing to do just that. Rome, Naples and the coasts were put in a state of defence, and Aetius was summoned with the army to Italy from Gaul. Unlike other barbarian troubles in the West, this blow clearly menaced the East as well, though less directly. Vandal fleets might now challenge Roman naval control of the eastern Mediterranean for the first time in centuries. The nervous atmosphere was heightened by rumours that a Vandal fleet had already appeared off Rhodes.

Faced with common danger, the East responded vigorously this time to Ravenna's urgent pleas for help.[6] It was decided to mount a major military and naval expedition, and a ringing announcement of this, intended to reassure the fears of Italy, was issued by Valentinian. Troops were assembled from all over the East, and a great invasion fleet fitted out. The command was given to the generals Areobindus, Ansila and Germanus.[7] The armada prepared to sail early in 441 to halt Gaiseric, recapture Carthage and reassert crumbling Roman authority in Africa.

Almost immediately, the strain on military reserves was tested seriously by an unexpected Persian attack on Roman Armenia by King Yezdegerd II, in violation of the recent treaty. The government was nonetheless firmly committed to the African war as its first priority, and the forces on the Euphrates frontier would have to make do with whatever strength they had. Meanwhile Gaiseric had taken the initiative and launched his fleet, but instead of attacking the Italian mainland directly he landed on Sicily and besieged several cities. In the event, Persia found itself menaced in turn by an invasion of the Hephthalites (the so-called White Huns) from the Caspian region, and its Armenian thrust soon lost impetus. The imperial generals Aspar and Anatolius were easily able to negotiate a truce.[8]

The Eastern armada duly sailed, and Gaiseric prudently raised his sieges in Sicily and withdrew his forces and fleet to Africa. The arrival of the expedition unopposed in Sicilian waters put great heart into the Italian defenders and government. The first objective of the war, it seemed, had been achieved. More difficult was what to do next. The great army and fleet could not simply sit around in Sicily indefinitely, but would have to mount a serious invasion of Africa soon, where the Vandals would be waiting for them. But where, and when? It was at this stage of argument and indecision that the second blow fell on the Eastern homeland, and this time it came from Attila.[9]

The transfer of troops for the African war was too good an opportunity for Attila to miss, and so the particular provocations and excuses that led to his first invasion are perhaps unimportant. In one version, some Huns made an unprovoked attack on a small Roman town north of the Danube, an agreed trading post. When imperial representatives ventured to protest against this violation of the treaty, they were met in turn with Attila's indignant list of their own side's violations, all justified complaints: the failure to return Hun captives, to pay the agreed sums of gold, and in addition the spoilation of some sacred Hun graves by the bishop of Margus, the very city where the treaty had been solemnised. The imperial envoys had no adequate replies, if indeed any replies would have mattered. Negotiations were broken off, and they could only await anxiously what Attila might do next.[10]

It seems there were virtually no Roman field armies at all in the Balkan area, and even the garrisons of the Danube strong-point cities – Sirmium, Singidunum, Viminacium, Ratiaria – had been thinned to a dangerous level to supply the African expedition. The Romans knew how formidable the Huns could be in a battle on the open plain, but Theodosius' military advisers had perhaps calculated that, in the last resort, and in this mountainous region, the skilfully fortified strong-points could hold out even with a small force against nomadic raiders who lacked the siegecraft to capture them. If so, they were soon rudely undeceived.

Without further ado Attila crossed the Danube with his warriors close to the junction with the Morava river, to the east of Singidunum (Belgrade). Evading or brushing aside what river fleet still operated, they besieged and soon captured the city of Viminacium (Kastolacz) despite its defences, then sacked and pillaged it thoroughly. When all possible booty had been plundered or destroyed, and all the surviving inhabitants led off enslaved, Attila methodically burnt and demolished the remaining city – walls, bastions, basilicas, theatres, churches, markets, houses.[11] Almost nothing remained of it at all, until Justinian built a new city on the site when the empire expanded again a century later. Even the city's treasury, hastily buried during the siege, was never recovered until archaeologists unearthed a great coin hoard in the twentieth century.[12]

The fate of Viminacium struck a new level of fear into the civilian population of the western Danube, and the message communicated itself to Constantinople. Roman cities had been lost and pillaged before, but not completely obliterated. The Huns were despised for having no understanding or use for cities. Now that was being terribly demonstrated. Attila had enough sophisticated siege engineering skills in his service, captive or hired, to breach or scale the walls that civilisation had built against him and his kind, and then ruin them.[13]

Theodosius' government was sufficiently alarmed to recall the great dilatory army still sitting in Sicily, where its predations on the population had made it increasingly resented. Moving this unwieldy assembly back by sea to its Eastern bases was not to be accomplished quickly, and in the meantime Attila did not stop with Viminacium. His ferocious forces now moved on nearby Margus, which offered no resistance and opened its gates, perhaps betrayed by its guilty bishop, fearing local retribution. But it suffered the same fate as Viminacium – sack, pillage, enslavement of its people, then wrecking. It was never rebuilt.[14] Then followed the fort of Constantia, directly across the river.[15] Driving west along the Danube valley, Attila next took and reduced Singidunum (Belgrade).[16] The last and greatest disaster was Sirmium itself. This great, populous city, once an imperial capital, was still the pivot of East–West military communication, as well as the keystone of the Danube defence system. Though not completely razed, it was wrecked thoroughly. In terms of imperial prestige and strategic importance its loss was every bit as grave as Carthage.[17] Today there remain only the ruins at Mitrovica.

We can deduce, but cannot easily imagine (unless we ourselves have lived through similar times), the state of mind of the civil populations of the Danube frontier regions Attila passed through. If these savages could pull down the strongest walls, if they did not stop until they had taken or destroyed everything, if they were deaf to all supplication, where was there refuge or hope? The emperor's soldiers did not protect them – had even God and His Holy Mother deserted them?

Warfare and movement came to a halt with the approach of winter, as it always did. Somehow, Aspar, by now the East's foremost military commander, succeeded in negotiating a one-year truce with Attila. Its causes and terms are obscure.[18] Attila was quite glutted with booty and captives, and his hordes returned in bloated triumph to their home territories beyond the Danube. He had caused enormous damage materially, morally and strategically, tearing a great hole in the Danube frontier system and striking fear into the empire. No longer would these Romans dare to deal casually with him, a great king and conqueror, as if he were some ignorant paltry chieftain to be fobbed off with trinkets and promises.

His direct zone of destruction in 441 did not reach further south than the Danube cities, although there had been nothing to bar his way. In contrast to the Goths, Franks, Vandals, Alemmani, Burgundians and other tribal invaders, the nomadic Huns had little interest in capturing fixed territory for settlement. Their aim was to dominate peoples and conscript their fighting men, and their immediate and obvious goal was plunder on the largest possible scale: gold, silver, jewellery, ornaments, metalware, furnishings, cloth, plate, weaponry and movable goods of all kinds, including horses, livestock and slaves, skilled or unskilled, male or female, drudge or concubine. To a martial, but materially impoverished, steppe society, these splendid spoils of war were the currency that would reward and bind the Hun nobles, the subject aristocracies and their followers all down the strata of domination. What Attila, at the top of this social pyramid, wanted was not conspicuous wealth but peerless glory and power, despotic monarchy such as no nomadic king had ever enjoyed before. Even the ambassadors of the emperor must be seen to kneel and offer tribute, returning his rightful subjects to him, seeking his permission to make war on third parties, acknowledging his overlordship. Among his own richly attired nobles, with their silks and golden goblets, Attila alone, in inverted ostentation, sat above them in traditional rough Hunnic dress with his wooden drinking cup.[19]

He was conscious of being an outstanding leader of his people, in contrast to his elder brother Bleda. Attila commanded a larger federation of tribes than any of his predecessors, and had dramatically demonstrated his greater prowess and dazzling success. He and they had changed a tribe of poor warrior pastoralists into rulers of a super-national empire of peoples, militarily irresistible and commanding all the wealth they wanted. He also commanded the special skills of others, from Latin secretaries to Greek siege engineers, and was able to recruit and reward this talent handsomely. After these spectacular victories his ambitions could only expand.

Attila's ambitions took a new shape. In the Roman areas he had ravaged, he had no interest in capturing either territory or cities for his own use, and no plan to allow the subject areas limited recovery, which he might then exploit afresh. The cities and their communications were simply obstacles to him, potential pockets of Roman resistance or interference. His response was to ruin them or make them unusable, creating a new wilderness which he could dominate at long range. To Roman eyes it must have seemed the very opposite of civilisation as they understood it – almost as if cities were an affront to Attila, and he destroyed them just because he was able to. Similarly, his own royal authority was not a traditional institution defined by conventions of legitimacy and obligation, but a personal power which had to be displayed directly. His naked ability to have someone instantly crucified, or alternatively laden with gold, was not a blemish on his kingship but its essential character. Personal power and political position were not distinguished. Attila's prestige and glory consisted in unending victory in war, with all its tangible spoils, and he went to war to enhance his glory.[20]

The one-year truce skilfully negotiated by Aspar gave the empire a badly needed breathing space, but Aspar must have been under no illusions that it was just as much in Hun interests as in Roman ones. Attila was probably surprised at the extent of his own success. At all events, bound by the seasonal pattern of Hun raiding, he needed to transport the great quantities of plunder to his home base in triumph with his elite warriors, and to reassert his fierce authority over the subordinate tribes.

The imperial armies were slowly transported back from Sicily. The great and costly expedition had achieved nothing beyond merely deterring the Vandals from the Italian mainland. Against a dispiriting background of Roman withdrawal, yet another feeble treaty was negotiated with Gaiseric, who had every interest in drawing out the negotiations as long as he could. The treaty was ratified in 442, and left Gaiseric in control of Carthage as well as reallocating the provinces of Africa entirely to Vandal advantage.

Only the more impoverished provinces – Mauretania and part of Numidia – were left to the Western empire, and these henceforth existed almost on sufferance. The grain supply to Italy was not cut off, but it was now in practice a foreign import. Gaiseric agreed to pay an annual 'tribute', probably in grain. In this state of Western Roman weakness, Aetius took great care not to give Gaiseric any pretext for further aggression, and attempted to seal the treaty by arranging a marriage between the emperor's daughter, Eudocia, (when she should come of age) and Gaiseric's son, Huneric, who was sent to Italy in a pledge of good faith. Gaiseric, triumphant, dated his new calendar from his capture of Carthage on 19 October 439. The enlarged Vandal kingdom, officially titled Kingdom of the Vandals and Alans, was now formally recognised by Ravenna as a federate 'ally' on a par with the Visigoth and Burgundian kingdoms in Gaul.[21]

Even more than these other burgeoning Germanic states, the Vandal kingdom of Africa was the work of one ruler: Gaiseric. Shrewd, ruthless and consistently successful militarily, he was to enjoy a very long reign of almost fifty years, and seized every opportunity to improve his position. He had several important advantages. There were no other barbarian peoples as competing neighbours except the native Mauri, who caused only intermittent trouble. After 439 Roman military force could only engage him from overseas, with all the delays and risks of naval invasion, which he could oppose at sea. In barely ten years he had forced the Romans into two major treaties which confirmed his control of virtually all of former Roman Africa.

In his original expansion from western Mauretania he had terrorised the Roman ruling population into flight, but by the capture of Carthage and the treaty of 442 accommodation was reached with the Roman landowners. Some of them migrated to the non-Vandal regions, or even to Italy or the East, but many stayed. The mass of the peasantry barely noticed the change of rulers, except for their Arian religion. Barbarian nobles of the three ruling groups – Asdings, Silings and Alans – took over large landholdings, and extensive tax-free allotments were granted to the warriors. But considerable arable areas were still left to the Roman aristocracy, whose original landed wealth had been so great that even after 442 they enjoyed a measure of prosperity and the social rank attached to it. Throughout the century of Vandal rule they continued to occupy municipal offices and perform civic functions. Despite periodic persecutions of Catholics by the Arian Vandals, there was continued coexistence, much as in Visigoth Aquitaine and for similar reasons. The newcomers were neither numerous nor sophisticated enough to replace Roman culture and institutions with new ones, except in royal and military matters. At Carthage and other cities the circus, amphitheatre, basilicas, baths, public squares and suburban villas still carried on in their way of life, and new churches and basilicas were built. Most of the former levels of prosperity continued in Gaiseric's reign.[22]

With the main armies returning to the East, Theodosius seems to have been persuaded easily into false confidence by his intimate courtiers. They represented the disastrous events of 441 as an exceptional setback to the normal order of things made possible only by the temporary absence of Roman armies and not to be repeated. From the distant vantage point of Constantinople it was tempting for the emperor to view the destruction of the Danube cities as exceptional. Yet the sack of such a vital strong-point as Sirmium and the alarming evidence of Attila's new-found siege abilities should have prevented any such mood. The main military advisers, Aspar and Areobindus, who knew the Huns well and would sooner or later have to fight Attila, no doubt took a less sanguine view. But they were not now among the innermost circle of confidants, and if they advised caution it went unheeded.[23]

The truce came to an end early in 443, and Attila with his army announced his conditions for peace, which were not unexpected or unreasonable from his new position. He insisted on the immediate return of all Hun 'fugitives' from Roman territory, and prompt payment of all the agreed gold tribute due to him. Any delay or procrastination, and they now knew what to expect. But Theodosius was persuaded that he was now in a stronger bargaining position. His envoys refused to hand back the Huns in question, but offered to continue the talks towards a mutually acceptable settlement.[24] Affronted, Attila moved like lightning, sacking Ratiaria (Archar in modern Bulgaria), the base for the Danube river fleet, then thrusting south-west down the military highway to Naissus (Nis) which was likewise stormed and sacked. The chronicler Priscus of Panium gives a vivid description of the well-organised assault on Naissus, in which siege towers with protected archers, battering rams and, finally, scaling ladders were used. The attack by several siege towers and rams simultaneously at different points on the wall finally overcame the defences and the Huns broke into the city. Both these key cities, Ratiaria and Naissus, were also main arms factories (*fabricae*) and it is likely that the Huns took not just the stores of manufactured weapons but also their skilled workers, who could look for favourable conditions from their new masters. Several years later, when the historian Priscus travelled through it, Naissus was still ruined and deserted except for a few sick people being cared for in Christian hostels.[25]

We do not know if all these cities were properly garrisoned and defended, whether they fell to assault or if some were handed over in treachery or despair. What is most striking is the speed and direction of Attila's offensive compared with that of 441. This time he swept hundreds of miles along the main military artery of the empire, directly towards the Bosporus and Constantinople itself. From Naissus he quickly captured Serdica (Sofia), then Philippopolis (Plovdiv). Aspar and Areobindus, commanding the field armies in the Balkans were either caught off-balance by this advance, or deliberately decided to place themselves blocking the advance to Constantinople.

Their forces finally met Attila in the easternmost part of Thrace not far from Constantinople itself. We have no details, except that in several battles they were outmanoeuvred and defeated. By swift movements the Huns reached the sea north and south of Constantinople, cutting off the retreating Roman forces' communication with the city and confining them helplessly in the small peninsula of the Chersonesus (Gallipoli).[26] The one local victory over the Huns was not by the regular army at all, but by a spirited citizen militia from the small city of Asemus on the Danube (near modern Pleven in Bulgaria). They were able to ambush a strong but unwieldy force of Huns who were already cluttered with their booty and captives, defeat them and rescue the Roman prisoners.[27]

With the remnant of the main Roman army immobilised, Attila's forces drew nearer to Constantinople itself and made their menacing point by capturing the small fortress of Athyras, barely twenty miles from the city. The atmosphere was nervous enough for the emperor and his palace household to withdraw from the capital into Asia Minor, but Attila did not attempt to assault Constantinople. Instead he turned south and finished the war by a last battle which broke the remaining Roman army. Defeated and humiliated, Theodosius, from his place of safety, could only sue for peace again. Anatolius, the general who had negotiated the truce with Persia a year earlier, was now given the thankless task of arranging a new peace with Attila.

With the armies cut to pieces, and the whole of the European provinces defenceless, Anatolius had no bargaining position at all. He informed Theodosius that he would be unable to refuse any of Attila's terms. The posture of negotiation between equals, which had brought on the king's wrath so recently, could not now be contemplated. The terms were heavy, but not impossible: immediate delivery of all Huns in Roman custody; no fugitives to be received in future; immediate payment of all arrears of gold, calculated at 6,000 pounds (432,000 solidi), and the annual tribute to be trebled to 2,100 pounds of gold. The ransom of Roman prisoners was raised to 12 solidi per head. Finally, the men of Asemus were to be surrendered with all their Hun prisoners and liberated Roman prisoners. The Hun army would remain on Roman territory until all demands were met in full. Their negotiator was Scotta, one of Attila's leading nobles, who made very clear their readiness to resume war at any time, and came in person to Constantinople to oversee Roman compliance.

Once again Attila's main desire was for gold, Hun rebels and fighting men, and this time there was no tardiness in meeting his demands. All the gold was paid and many Huns delivered up. But it was explained that those who had adamantly refused to return to Attila's domains had been massacred by their Roman captors. Whether this was true or part of an evasive fabrication we do not know, nor what kind of numbers were involved. However, Scotta seems to have accepted the account and, surprisingly, shown no particular objection to this Roman action. Attila may have intended to kill them in any case. After a frustrating correspondence with the citizens of Asemus, who had no intention of being handed over to the Huns, and who moreover massacred nearly all the Hun prisoners, Attila no longer insisted on this condition, to Anatolius' great relief. The new treaty was concluded late in 443.[28]

For the next four years Attila remained north of the Danube, while the empire struggled to repair the ravages he had caused its European provinces, but he did not leave the empire alone. All kinds of embassies were sent to Constantinople, to monitor compliance with the treaty, to raise minor issues, and on any other pretext. Diplomatic courtesy required that ambassadors always had to be presented with rich gifts, and the envoys of Attila blatantly exploited this custom like children in a sweetshop, with their king's encouragement. The annual sum of 2,100 pounds of gold was many times the subsidies paid to other potential enemies. This, together with the costs of the Persian and African wars, meant that for the first time the Eastern imperial treasury began to feel some financial strain.[29]

This was accentuated by a particularly harsh winter in 442–3, which had brought many areas close to starvation. The Praetorian Prefect of the East introduced two special tax measures which were deeply resented by the senatorial classes.[30] A special levy of gold was imposed, and in addition a large proportion of the tax rebates allowed by previous emperors was cancelled, and the arrears now demanded. These proved enough to meet Attila's demands, and by the next year the government was able to promise its citizens that it would not repeat the second measure.[31] Despite all the extra costs of Attila's invasions in physical destruction and the loss of revenues, as well as the great expense of the abortive African expedition, the huge resources of Asia Minor, Syria and Egypt, almost untouched by war, could still manage to absorb them.

This was in striking contrast with the position in the West. With the great loss of tax revenues from Africa, and much of Gaul and Spain, the government faced near-bankruptcy, as the emperor Valentinian officially admitted in a legal pronouncement of 444.[32] He cites the need to raise recruits for the armies, but confesses that the revenues are not enough to pay and equip the existing forces, let alone new ones. As a natural consequence, the regular Roman component of the Western armies, as against allied Germanic forces, mercenaries, federate formations, or tribal groups rewarded by territorial control for their services, had shrunk even further. The loyalties of all these forces had to be negotiated, but at least they were readily available.

There were other differences apart from the East's greater and more secure tax base. The financial ministers at Constantinople were more able and willing to keep a grip on the wealthier classes – principally their own broad senatorial class – despite all the protests, bribery and evasions. As members of the new mandarinate, the ministers' career prospects were not so tied to the purses of the very rich. The Prefect Antiochus and those who followed him in the years after 430 made many determined attacks on senatorial tax evasions. Emergency taxes were firmly imposed on those classes able to pay, not on the wider population. This did not happen in the West, where the great senatorial clans of Italy and Gaul still connived incestuously with the fiscal officials to escape the bulk of the taxes on their vast estates, as they had done for generations. Belated imperial attempts to stop these abuses after 440 made only a small difference.

Despite their disappointing performance against Attila, the top army commands were not reorganised or purged. By now the Gothic military faction was probably too well entrenched, and in any case Theodosius was far from being a warlike emperor. Encased within his near-monastic palace where he sang psalms with his pious sisters, fasted twice a week and occupied himself with devotional works, the good man even shrank from necessary capital punishments – which did not prevent a number of unjust executions in his name. He had no understanding of military affairs and no liking for them. His immediate and absorbing concerns at this time were, quite literally, domestic. Always a pliant figure, he was invariably managed by others who naturally schemed and manoeuvred for dominant influence.

For most of the reign this role had been filled by his divisive, overbearing sister Pulcheria who, as we saw, had secured for herself the supreme female rank of Augusta. Vowed to perpetual virginity, she cultivated public piety and holiness ('the Orthodox One'), managed bishops and many other appointments, and had great popular support among the Orthodox plebs of Constantinople. She continued to promote assiduously the new cult of the Mother of God, *Theotokos*, a figure of supreme female power and protection, second only to Christ himself.[33]

The bride Pulcheria had selected for her brother Theodosius was the eloquent and cultured Athenais who had adopted the name Aelia Eudocia on marriage.[34] From the beginning it was a highly artificial situation of, in effect, two empresses, and perhaps it was inevitable that she would sooner or later come into conflict with Pulcheria. Eudocia was spirited enough, and she had gained great prestige by going on pilgrimage to Jerusalem, but was at a permanent disadvantage in having so far failed to produce a male heir – the one sound foundation for a capable Augusta's influence.[35] Until now the rivalry had been confined within the imperial family, but by about 441 a more insidious influence arose in the shape of the eunuch Chrysaphius Ztommas, an official of the bedchamber who was in daily contact with Theodosius. He achieved his intimate confidence, and found Theodosius easy to manipulate.[36]

Chrysaphius attempted, through Eudocia, to undermine Pulcheria's dominant influence over the emperor. She demanded that Pulcheria's own separate imperial court and Chamberlain should instead be assigned to her, the imperial consort and the true empress, but Theodosius refused: 'I will not dismiss my sister, who governs well, with skill and piety.'[37] Finally Chrysaphius succeeded when Eudocia insisted, on a different tack, that since her sister-in-law had embraced the holy ascetic life she should properly be ordained a deaconess and withdraw from worldly affairs. Somehow the emperor was persuaded by this pious argument where other considerations had failed.[38] Pulcheria, realising she had been outflanked, avoided the shackles of ordination by withdrawing voluntarily from the palace, with her household, to the palace of the Hebdomon in the suburbs of Constantinople.

Unsuspecting, Eudocia was preparing her own downfall. Within a year Chrysaphius, playing a very dangerous game, had poisoned her husband's mind against her by creating suspicions of her adultery with Paulinus, formally the Master of Offices, a long-standing personal friend of Theodosius and an intimate of the imperial couple.[39] On the face of it the accusation seems very unlikely, and both denied it vigorously. But Theodosius, perhaps as unworldly in these matters as in war and statecraft, was prepared to believe it: Chrysaphius aroused in him not only jealousy and affront, but the even greater fear that the adulterous couple were plotting to assassinate and supplant him. Still protesting her innocence – which she did up to her death – Eudocia, amid wide public sympathy, departed for Jerusalem and further holy works, and never returned. She had not formally been convicted in any way, and retained her title of Augusta and the household that went with it. Paulinus was exiled to Cappodocia and was soon afterwards executed on orders from the palace.[40] For the next six years Chrysaphius' influence over the emperor was dominant and widely feared among Constantinople's ruling classes.

Outside the vicious atmosphere of the inner palace, ministers and generals carried on competently to limit the damage of Attila's invasions. Finances were brought under control. The Master of Offices, Nomus, who wielded wide powers as one of Chrysaphius' supporters, was ordered to rebuild some of the forts along the western Danube frontier. The order was probably part of a general instruction to strengthen and improve the discipline of the static *limitanei* garrisons on all the frontiers, not just the Danube. They were not to be summoned away from their military duties, and their units were to be brought up to strength, properly paid and properly drilled.[41]

The City Prefect of Constantinople, Cyrus, one of Eudocia's earlier protégés, had already strengthened the Anthemian land fortifications by a belt of sea walls. Cyrus was a very popular and devoted Prefect. As well as building the Baths of Achilles and a *Theotokos* church, he provided the city's first street lighting and – himself a literary figure – secured the very great innovation that valid wills and judicial decisions could now be in Greek, the vernacular language, instead of Latin.[42] The crowds cheered his praises in the Hippodrome, but such a level of open popularity was dangerous, suggesting a rival focus of loyalty to the palace and dynasty. Chrysaphius sowed suitable suspicions in the emperor's ear, and Cyrus was dropped from the Prefecture. He was exiled, forcibly ordained and sent as bishop to the remote and hostile town of Cotyaeum in Phrygia, where a turbulent congregation had already murdered several previous incumbents. But Cyrus survived and surfaced again at the capital after the death of Theodosius.

However, Chrysaphius' machinations did not generally damage the military leaders. Aspar and his colleagues personally survived the defeats by Attila, and now had to rebuild the armies while time permitted. Although Aspar was regarded as probably the foremost and most experienced commander of his day, and although Areobindus was formally part of the government as a Praesental general, they were now outside the inner sanctum of decisions where Chrysaphius alone held sway. Whether this was by choice or necessity, it served them in good stead. The demilitarisation of the imperial court and government over the past thirty years had allowed them to grow into something of a force apart, so long as they took great care not to appear to threaten the dynasty in any way. They formed a distinct faction, which was often cemented by marriage ties. Both Aspar and Areobindus held their commands for long periods despite setbacks and defeats. Aspar, of Alan-Gothic parentage, had risen to prominence under his loyal and distinguished father Ardaburius, who had defeated the Persians and later the Western usurper John, and installed the legitimate emperor Valentinian III on the Western throne. The new *Magister* Arnegisclus was a member of the faction.

The earlier hostility to Gothic military leaders had not lasted long. The firm rejection of large Gothic federate settlements had paradoxically cleared the way in the longer run for the new Gothic military elite to re-emerge, but on a more restricted basis. Unlike Alaric and Tribigild they could not base their power in any way on settlements of armed Gothic 'allies' in the empire. The sole basis of their authority was once more what it had always been for Germanic generals in the fourth century – they were loyal, capable and indispensable Roman military leaders whose 'barbarian' origins prevented them from aspiring to the throne themselves. They enjoyed political leverage, but it was institutionalised and based on their indispensability to the state, not on their command of armed violence. The fact that the East's main barbarian threat was now the Huns further underlined their usefulness, since Goths hated and feared the Huns even more than the Romans did. A certain balance between Germans and Romans was preserved in the multiple commands of the five army groups.

This again was in strong contrast to the position in the West, where the top military commands had in practice always been concentrated in very few hands. By now effective government, such as it was, had become thoroughly militarised in the figure of a single dominant army commander or generalissimo, quite separate from the emperors Honorius and Valentinian and the palace ministers around them. Aetius ruled not because of any supposed guardianship role in the imperial family, but because he could control the largest block of military force, based on his backbone of Huns and other troops personally loyal to him alone. With this he could just about manage and balance the other Germanic allies settled within the empire. Aetius himself, frequently on the move and always in the midst of his army, made civil and military appointments, concluded treaties and even issued laws in the emperor's name. Embassies had begun to address themselves to him directly, not Valentinian. At Ravenna there was merely a court, not a government. Both Galla Placidia and Valentinian personally detested Aetius, but had to put up with him as long as he controlled the army.[43]

On the Eastern frontier, Persia still had not withdrawn its forces and the earlier truce had not been converted into a negotiated treaty. There was raiding in Armenia from a migratory people, the Tzanni, around the eastern Black Sea coast, and in Asia Minor from the particularly troublesome Isaurian mountain peoples. None of this was more than a nuisance to the government, but it tied down forces. A series of other disasters sapped confidence at Constantinople. Following the severe winter and near-famine of 442 to 443, there were tremendous storms and flooding in large areas of the neighbouring province of Bithynia, in which whole towns were lost. A plague spread through the crowded districts of the capital, accentuated by a temporary collapse of the city's food supplies; mobs rioted and many were killed. Each of these misfortunes could of course be coped with singly, but together they suggested a gloomy pattern of divine disfavour and a sense of impending ills to come.[44]

We know little of Attila's actions in this period, except that in about 445 he at last murdered his brother Bleda and incorporated all his followers and vassals directly under his own rule.[45] Roman embassies continued to make their way to him in the interior of his territories somewhere north of the middle Danube to which he had now moved. There is every reason to suppose that he was continuing to extend his domination over the disparate groups of Huns and subordinate tribes, and continuing his diplomatic moves towards the Western empire. Nominally, he still supported Aetius, in the West, against the Visigoths and the strong peasant rebel forces, the Bagaudae. Several years earlier Hun forces had obliged Aetius by crushing the Burgundians.[46] But after Aetius' lieutenant Litorius had recklessly led Hun mercenaries into a disastrous defeat by the Visigoths near Toulouse, Attila pointedly sent no more Hun forces to Aetius' army, of which they had always been the backbone.

The vague foreboding at Constantinople turned into serious alarm when the news came at the end of 446 that Attila was preparing to invade again. His reasons are unknown – it was certainly not because of the slowness of the Eastern government to fulfil the earlier treaty conditions.[47] His motives are perhaps as obscure as his reasons for leaving the East unmolested for so long. But now he was massing even greater forces than in 441, including larger hosts of subject warriors, such as the Goths under Valamir and the Gepids under Ardaric, who now crossed the Danube and poured into the Eastern provinces of Moesia and Scythia.[48]

7

RESISTANCE AND RECOVERY

The Roman armies were prepared for Attila, and based at Marcianople (near modern Varna). They were commanded by Arnegisclus, even though he shared the shadow of defeat by Attila in 443.[1] He decided this time to deploy his army as a single concentrated mobile force, and seek out the enemy in a single set battle where he would be neither cramped in movement nor split into separate components. He had learnt from the earlier debacle in which the Roman forces had been trapped uselessly, and reduced piecemeal, unable to offer any protection at all, to Constantinople. A single great battle with all his strength, skilfully chosen and commanded, might just break Attila or at least cripple him – nothing else would. The city at least had its great belt of walls, more formidable than any other defended fortress, which Attila had threatened but not attempted to assault as he had done so many others. The recent invasions had confirmed, as always, the pivotal importance of the Bosporus and Constantinople. As long as this great gate was kept firmly shut no barbarian invasion from the West – unless they took the very long route through the Caucasus – could penetrate into the heartland of Anatolia, Asia and the Oriental provinces where the bulk of the empire's great resources of wealth lay.[2]

But at the end of January 447 there came a catastrophe so appalling that it could only mean that God had turned his face against the empire. The whole region of the eastern Mediterranean has always been particularly prone to earthquakes, being one of the friction and potential collision areas between the enormous tectonic plates that make up the earth's cool outer crust. Their terrifying power, violence and suddenness, against which men were utterly helpless, naturally led people to see them as acts of divine wrath, traditionally by Poseidon the earth-shaker. Also, there had long been scientific curiosity about them, as we see in one of Ammianus' long digressions in his histories, where he discusses the plausible theory that they are the products of great subterranean water pressures.[3] In this Christian epoch, they were commonly regarded as God's punishment for human wickedness. An earlier earthquake in 438 had shaken Constantinople without doing much damage, but the divine warning and need for general atonement had so impressed people that it resulted in a pious annual procession to the Hebdomon.[4]

The series of shocks which now hit the Eastern provinces was incomparably greater, the worst in living memory. Evagrius believed, quite plausibly, that they were the worst the city had ever experienced. Beginning on 26 January 447 and continuing for about four months afterwards, earthquakes and the consequent floods ravaged Thrace, the Cyclades, the Hellespont and other areas, with great destruction and loss of life. At Constantinople many buildings were torn apart, people were crushed and buried, but by far the most terrible, a whole section of the great land walls collapsed, including, we are told, fifty-seven towers.[5] The city was appalled as never before at the prospect now facing it. At this time of supreme peril, with Attila's hosts about to invade, perhaps already on the move, God had chosen to smite his people, to shatter in pieces their one great shield. What could possibly save them now from the fate of Sirmium, Naissus and the other cities?[6]

After the first few days, shattered nerves recovered. Attila was still hundreds of miles away and in his path stood a powerful Roman army. Perhaps indeed, God had chosen to test them, to demonstrate that in him and his Holy Mother alone was their true refuge and strength, surer than any walls? This time the emperor Theodosius emerged from the palace and assisted in the defence of the empire in the one way he knew how. He led a great penitential procession in person, barefoot like the ten thousand others with hymns, icons and relics, to the Hebdomon where a solemn service of repentance was held. Personal despair became channelled into collective supplication and spiritual hope.

The Praetorian Prefect Constantinus, his officials and soldiers quickly mobilised the city's manpower to clear the moats of rubble and rebuild the wall.[7] A drastic corvée was imposed, and all available citizens pressed into service. The well-established Blue and Green factions of chariot supporters in the Hippodrome in their semi-official organisations provided the basis of a chain of command. In the meantime, the *Magister Militum* of the Orient, the Isaurian Zeno, had been urgently ordered to Constantinople with a strong force to manage the city's defence.[8]

Soon the great combined force of Arnegisclus, which probably included the field armies of Illyricum, Thrace and the Praesentals, moved out from Marcianople westwards, and finally met Attila's host near the river Utus (Vid), northwest of modern Bulgaria. Unfortunately, we have almost no details of the battle, which must have been a great and bloody collision. Again, the Romans were defeated, but only after a fiercely contested battle in which Arnegisclus himself died, fighting on bravely after his horse had been killed under him.[9] The evidence suggests that this time Attila met stiffer opposition and suffered heavier losses than hitherto. He had been mauled, not defeated. His forces, though diminished, were still masters of the field and once more had much of the Balkans open to them. They soon pressed on and took Marcianople.

By the end of March, after frantic efforts, Constantinople's great land walls had been fully repaired with towers, gates and moats as before. An inscription, still surviving on the walls today, commemorates Constantinus' achievement: 'not even Pallas could have built it faster or better'.[10] Zeno's Isaurian troops prepared to man the fortifications, with all their archers, artillery, defensive engines and organised support for supply, reinforcement and rapid repairs. Faced with these preparations, Attila once again did not try to assault the city. He had already suffered severe losses. But as if in frustration or compensation, he ravaged the Balkans even more completely than before: Thrace, Illyricum, Moesia, Dacia were all plundered terribly, and this time the Huns moved south into Greece. The government and army did almost nothing to help the populations. 'Attila ground nearly all Europe to dust,' writes Marcellinus. In Thrace, records Callinicus, 'there was so much slaughter and bloodshed that no-one could number the dead. They sacked churches and monasteries and slew the monks and virgins....They so devastated Thrace that it will never rise again as before.'[11]

Though immediately protected by the city's defences, Theodosius' government, dominated by Chrysaphius and his supporter Nomus the Master of Offices, felt they had no choice but to negotiate Attila's withdrawal once more (although others were now questioning this). This time Attila demanded not just the usual tribute but the relinquishing of territory. A whole belt of country south of the Danube was to be permanently evacuated by the Romans. Perhaps because it was due south of Attila's own capital, it was to extend from Singidunum to Novae along the Danube, then five days' journey southward in depth, a total area of about 30,000 square miles. Several provinces or parts of provinces with their cities and populations would have to be abandoned, and the new frontier would run through Naissus, which Attila had sacked in 442. He did not want to acquire this land as conqueror and occupier but, in the same way as his wrecking of the key cities, to alter the Balkan military geography and free it completely of Roman obstacles. He had repeatedly penetrated the Danube frontier, but it was still a natural barrier that could be fortified again as soon as he withdrew, costing him effort and warriors in the future: better to abolish it completely. If in future he might extend his ambitions farther afield – and perhaps he was already toying with the idea – he needed to secure his rear, and this alteration would achieve that.

These conditions were again agreed in a new, abject treaty in 448. For the first time some opposition to the continuing policy of appeasement was provoked. Priscus of Panium regarded it as a shameful capitulation, bleeding the empire's wealth with ever-growing tribute, openly advertising Roman weakness and inviting other barbarians to similar extortions.[12] This feeling became centred on the new military commander in Constantinople: Zeno.

His defensive measures during the crisis had certainly raised the morale of the emperor and people, although they had not been put to the test of an assault. His prestige with Theodosius was sufficient to gain him a consulship for 448, but equally important was the palpable presence of a strong force of Isaurian troops in the capital itself, which normally contained only a few units of palace guards. Though legally Roman subjects, these were uncouth aliens amongst the Greek population, and solidly loyal to their commander. With the main Praesental armies still recovering from the battle of the Utus, the Isaurians were for the present in a pivotal position.

Zeno did not deliberately flex these muscles but, being for the present unassailable, he probably became the voice of many in the senatorial classes who hated Chrysaphius and hated paying the endless tribute to Attila, but had not dared speak openly. The appearance of an opponent with the ear of the emperor whom Chrysaphius could not neutralise in his usual way, propelled him into an atypically rash and dangerous plot to retrieve the fortunes of the empire and himself in a single stroke. If our source, Priscus, is to be believed, Chrysaphius now set in motion a conspiracy to have Attila assassinated by one of his own intimates. It misfired badly.[13]

Chrysaphius supposedly suborned Edeco, one of Attila's close lieutenants, who was at Constantinople on one of the many embassies. Chrysaphius promised him riches beyond his dreams if he could contrive to kill Attila on his return. He duly returned with these secret instructions as part of a larger delegation to Attila in 449. Our source, Priscus, actually accompanied the delegation in a minor capacity, travelling many weeks in unfamiliar lands to reach the presence of Attila. He provides a wealth of interesting detail of the manners of the Huns and the ceremonials at Attila's court, seen through Greek eyes.

Attila's residence was somewhere between the Danube and the Tisza – a royal village dominated by an ornately carved wooden palace, with towers and a surrounding stockade.[14] The delegation encountered several other envoys, including those from the Western emperor Valentinian III. After much delay and procrastination with intermediaries they were granted audience with Attila and invited to his banquet, where they were courteously treated according to Hun custom, and excused the all-night sessions of drinking and singing. The offers of women to share their beds were politely declined. Each man was allotted his own cup-bearer and each saluted the king with his wine in order of precedence before sitting down. Others ate off golden plates and drank from gold and silver cups, but Attila alone, at the centre of all, ostentatiously ate and drank from plain wood. He clearly relished the role of arbiter of nations, equal or superior to Roman emperors, as attested by the constant flow of embassies and gifts to him. The Greek and Roman secretaries, through whom he communicated, were much in evidence. His tone was measured and reasonable, but he never lost an occasion to point out his own irresistible power, and how he was able to take any

Roman city he chose. Several times in the long conversation he threatened war over what he felt was an insult to him, such as the matter of finding a Roman wife for his secretary Constantius. On their return, the delegation witnessed a Hun prisoner, allegedly a Roman spy, being impaled.[15]

On the details of the plot to kill Attila, Priscus is less plausible. Indeed, it seems to have been so clumsily managed that it is scarcely credible Chrysaphius should have instigated such an amateurish attempt. At all events, it was betrayed to Attila quite early on. He seems to have had some amusement at the expense of the embassy, but his clear and concrete demand to Theodosius was that the minister Chrysaphius be punished with death. Priscus tells the story that he sent back one of his Roman secretaries, Orestes, with the bag that had held the bribe of gold, instructing him to demand of Chrysaphius in the emperor's presence whether he recognised it.[16]

Attila's moods changed quickly, but the impression is given that he was actually beginning to lose interest in the Eastern empire, or at least to see it less as an area to plunder than as a source of indefinite extortion. Territories could be ravaged and wasted only once or twice, and would not easily replace their wealth after that; whereas Constantinople could be squeezed annually. Attila made much of demanding that only the very highest ranking Roman ambassadors should be sent to him, refusing to treat with lesser officials. Given the guaranteed flow of imperial gold rather than the haphazard plunder of war, it was necessary for him to see and present himself as victor, Lord of all Nations, with the bejewelled ministers of East and West placing their tribute submissively at his feet.

With Chrysaphius and his clumsy plot so discredited at Constantinople, Zeno pressed his advantage, and the dispute reached a more open and poisonous stage. Chrysaphius' head was demanded as the simple price of peace with Attila, and many voices no doubt breathed Amen. Yet such was the extraordinary hold he still had over Theodosius that against the odds, Chrysaphius escaped. Quickly he arranged a new embassy to Attila led by Anatolius and Nomus, both of highest rank and diplomatic skills and men with whom Attila was willing to deal. They were to do all they could to soothe his anger and induce him to abide by the treaty of 448, assisted by lavish gifts and a personal sum of gold from Chrysaphius.[17]

Chrysaphius was saved perhaps less by his own skills than by Attila's waywardness. For all his ambition and astuteness, his personal despotism allowed no checks to his impulsive swings of mood, which had frequently changed long before his envoys had completed their journeys with his latest demands. Within a year of the abortive attempt on his life, the ambassadors were astonished to find him in a most conciliatory frame of mind, and the mission succeeded far beyond expectations.

Attila agreed to abide by the conditions of 448. Further, he would make no more demands for the return of Hun or subject fugitives, provided the Romans no longer harboured them. Perhaps he now felt that the purpose of these demands had been served. Even more generously, he was prepared to drop the demand for a huge belt of Balkan territory to be evacuated by the Romans. The question of Chrysaphius' punishment was also dropped. Rarely can diplomatic success have been achieved so easily. Chrysaphius was redeemed. Theodosius now began to fear that Zeno might plot a revolt against him.[18]

Attila's change of front is surprising, but it is probably a mistake to look for subtle motives in every move he made. There is the appearance of arbitrary whim in all his dealings, and this shows repeatedly in his obsessive concern with trivial or personal matters that are soon forgotten again. Sometimes these are deliberate tactical pinpricks to worry his opponents, but not always. In 443, over the question of Asemus, he gets distracted from the whole issue by the search for two captive Roman children who might be exchanged for two Hun prisoners in Roman hands. Then there is the paltry affair of some gold plate from the sack of Sirmium being held by the banker Silvanus, which actually causes him to threaten war. Like many other new rulers, he was no doubt so sensitive about his dignity that he conflated large issues with small. There seems some reason why he should have been in a giving vein in 450, but not why he should have given so much, so readily.

By this time if not well before, Attila had become interested in Western Europe as a new field for his adventures, since there was no longer much more to be gained by plundering the wasted Danube lands, and an effortless gold subsidy was flowing to him from the Eastern government. It was a tacit admission that Constantinople was an effective barrier again his further eastward expansion. Having decided to move westwards, it made sense for him to safeguard his rear by leaving the Eastern empire in a docile mood.

His reasons for invading the territory of the Western empire have been lengthily debated. We can discount the romantic incident of the Western princess, Honoria, sister of Valentinian III, who had been plotting against her brother and had as a result been forced by him into a loathsome marriage. She appealed to Attila to rescue her, and sent him her signet ring. Attila made great display of his new role of her betrothed and chivalrous saviour, even demanding half the Western empire as her dowry: but it was only an excuse for him to intervene in the West as he had already decided to do.[19] He did not do it, as Priscus claims, to oblige the Vandal king, Gaiseric, who was casting around for allies against his enemies the Visigoths.[20] Nor, as some modern historians seem to have supposed, did he dream of ruling a great land empire from the Don to the Atlantic.

By 450, there were more warrior nations behind Attila's banner than ever before, and he could not hold them together for long without doing something with them. His charismatic kingdom, inherently unstable, depended on a continual dynamic of victory, power and glory to support his authority and bind the allegiances of so many subgroups. Glory was his overriding desire, and the actual shape of it was secondary. The confused politics of the fragmented Western empire offered beckoning opportunities for greater glory, and Attila's westward expansion should be seen in this light, rather than as a rational plan of territorial conquest. The great difference between shaking the earth and actually ruling it was not steadily focused in his mind.

In the West, good relations with the Huns were a cornerstone of all Aetius' policy, since it was on them that his military power had always been squarely based. Until recently, he had been on friendly terms with Attila, as with his predecessors. His own son Carpilio had spent some time as a guest-hostage at Attila's court, as had Aetius himself. He persuaded the Western government to send Attila gifts and gold payments, and to grant him the rank of *Magister Militum* – by now a titular honour which was often bestowed by the West on friendly barbarian rulers, carrying with it a generous subsidy. But now this relationship began to be called in question. Ever since Attila's troops had suffered a severe mauling from a numerically superior army of Visigoths, he had stopped lending mercenaries to Aetius.

Perhaps Aetius' position as a powerful Western warlord of Huns and other warriors had in any case become intolerable to Attila, who could not accept such a rival. He knew of the latent animosity the emperor felt for Aetius, and early in 450 he wrote imperiously to Ravenna that he intended to march against the empire's enemies, the Visigothic kingdom of Toulouse, and that he would do so as the ally of Valentinian; he had no quarrel with the Western empire, he declared. This announcement pointedly ignored and excluded Aetius, the actual ruler, who had to conclude that Attila was trying to drive a wedge between him and the emperor, perhaps even vaguely hoping to replace him as supreme commander and 'protector' of the Western empire.[21]

While these new clouds were gathering, in July 450, at Constantinople, Theodosius was suddenly thrown from his horse and suffered a fatal spinal injury.[22] He took two agonising days to die, but in that time events moved rapidly. In the East he was the last male of the Theodosian line, whose members had ruled for seventy years and, however personally wanting, he had always relied on the long-ingrained loyalty to the dynasty. No-one present had ever experienced a dynastic vacuum and all the destabilising forces this might unleash.

The last complete dynastic break had been the death of Julian in battle in 363. After a false start, the general Valentinian had been elected emperor by the army in the field. Of course, in pure legal theory, the legitimate successor was Valentinian III in the West, but everyone knew this to be unrealistic. Influential figures that had remained in the background while Chrysaphius had held the stage now emerged. If Zeno was in the capital, we do not hear of him directly, but the subsequent change of policy suggests his influence at least, and he was accorded the rank of Patrician the following year.

First to emerge was the venerable Augusta Pulcheria, long starved of power in her semi-convent atmosphere in the Hebdomon. Her dynastic status was of great importance but her position ambivalent. As a woman she could not rule alone in her own right: unlike Galla Placidia in the West, she had no imperial son in whose name she could exercise power. Yet, such was her prestige that for almost a month she acted as provisional monarch. One of her first, widely popular, acts was to execute Chrysaphius.[23]

There remained the Army, with its traditional prescriptive right of election. But there was now no need, and no opportunity, for an army in the field to proclaim its favoured candidate; nor was there any need for military force to flex its muscles. Flavius Ardabur Aspar, the senior *Magister* of long standing and acknowledged leader of the influential Gothic military faction, could answer for most of the army leaders. His power was also acknowledged by the senatorial nobility, of whom he was a leading member, having held a consulship. As a Goth he could not safely aspire to the purple himself. He therefore selected, in some consultation with other parties, a trusted former officer of his: an aged tribune called Marcian, a Thracian by origin who had served for many years as his *domesticus*, or household commander. He arranged a formal marriage between Marcian and Pulcheria, her vow of virginity notwithstanding. Whatever the artificiality of the contract it was approved by all those who counted. A most improbable account was put around that Theodosius had nominated Marcian on his deathbed.

Shortly after the marriage Marcian was proclaimed emperor and saluted by the troops at the Hebdomon with all ceremony. Pulcheria herself crowned him with the diadem and the purple robe. Coronation by a female was an act almost without precedent, but which clearly called on every strand of dynastic sentiment and loyalty that could be mustered.[24] In retrospect, it was an important achievement. Army, dynasty and civil authority in the capital had all co-operated responsibly in an orderly transfer of *imperium*, and advertised its full legitimacy to soldiers and people.

Marcian was obviously a safe candidate, and largely the creature of other forces, notably Aspar, whose son Ardaburius was immediately promised promotion to *Magister Militum* for the Orient. All this did not matter provided they acted competently and in concert, as a wider government of the main ruling groups. In fact, Marcian was not the mere cipher he might have been, and within the realistic constraints he ruled well, even though much of his energy was taken up with the ecclesiastical attempt to reverse the crypto-Monophysite decisions of the recent Council of Ephesus.

The immediate new departure was a dramatic reversal of the policy towards Attila, disregarding all the concessions he had recently made. Marcian boldly announced that he was repudiating all the recent treaties: there would be no more gold subsidies. If Attila remained at peace, the emperor would give him 'gifts', but if he chose war, he would be met by armies as strong as his own.[25]

This brave change of front was indeed a risk, but not entirely uncalculated. The new regime knew that Attila and his hordes were already well advanced in preparation for a great Western expedition, with all its unknown eventualities. They had seen him twice stopped in his tracks by the walls of Constantinople, and they knew how popular the policy would be with the senatorial classes. Yet, it was a risk all the same, which a more timid government would not have taken. It is as if Marcian, Pulcheria and the ministers, in their first joyous flourish, were so eager to reverse everything Chrysaphius had stood for, so imbued with shame and frustration by the years of appeasement, that they rushed into a defiantly patriotic stance without carefully reckoning all the consequences.

Attila reacted angrily but did not alter his larger plans, as Marcian and Aspar had correctly calculated. He loudly demanded his gold tribute, promising that on his return from Western Europe he would deal with Marcian. Then in the spring of 451 he led his huge multinational horde westward from their assembly zone in Pannonia, to 'assist' the emperor Valentinian against his Visigothic enemies. The emperor had not, of course, asked for such assistance, and needed it as little as the plague. Already Attila's clumsy machinations had managed to multiply the enemies facing him. A serious split had occurred over the royal succession of the Ripuarian Franks settled in the northern Rhine area. Of the two rival heirs to the throne, the elder appealed to Attila for an alliance, while the younger had turned to Aetius and the Romans. Both Aetius and Valentinian, casting around urgently for allies, accepted him readily, plying him with gifts and promises, and the great majority of Franks swore allegiance to him and rejected his pro-Hun brother.[26] Attila was now committed to war, not just with the Visigoths but with the Franks and Romans too. The crude attempt to alienate Aetius from his emperor had not succeeded, but on the contrary had driven them closer together.

The story of Attila's great rampage through the Western provinces has been told many times. Once it had become clear by 450 that a breach with Attila was unavoidable, Aetius' position had become desperate. Deprived of the Hun alliance and his own Hun soldiers, detested by the emperor and the Augusta Galla Placidia, he had been in serious danger of becoming politically and militarily isolated. However, he was able to exploit all the careful alliances he had forged and the personal authority he had established over many years in settling the various groups of barbarians in Gaul: Visigoths, Franks, Burgundians, Alans and others. With great skill and energy he called on the old loyalties and present interests, and managed to persuade most of them to abandon any short-term policy of neutrality or waiting on events, and join in a great alliance against the common invader who threatened them all. The most delicate but urgent task was to bring over the Visigoths, his traditional enemies but the most powerful single force. Helped by well-chosen intermediaries, Aetius nonetheless succeeded. Considering all the mutual antagonisms and suspicions of these nations, not least the Romans, it was a triumph of diplomacy, outclassing Attila's blundering efforts. Perhaps only Aetius, with his unrivalled knowledge of the barbarians and great personal reputation among them all, could have done it.[27]

Attila's total force was very large: frightened contemporaries or colourful narrators put it at the fantastic figure of half a million, but it was certainly the largest expedition he had ever mounted, capable of causing untold destruction to an already fragmented Gaul. It called into being an artificially united front to oppose it. Both sides were unusual coalitions of various nationalities, with some waverers and some peoples fighting on both sides, or pretending to. Attila's forces included Gepids, Alans, Sciri, Heruli, Rugians, some Franks and Burgundians, as well as a large force of Ostrogoths under their three chieftains, Valamir, Vidimir and Theodemir. The motley force of Aetius included the Visigoths under their king, Theoderic, Ripuarian Franks, Salian Franks, Burgundians, Alans, Saxons and even the Celtic Armoricans who had broken away from the empire.[28] The strictly Roman field army under Aetius' direct command was larger than any other individual contingent except for the Visigoths. Both numbered perhaps 20,000. The whole great army, approximately 60,000 strong, was at least temporarily in the service of the Roman empire.

After sacking Metz but failing to take Orleans, Attila gave battle in June 451 at a location in northeast Gaul still uncertain but vaguely called the Catalaunian plains (*locus Mauriacus*). It was a huge and bloody collision involving possibly over 100,000 troops in all, an enormous number for this time. There were great losses on both sides, especially among the Visigoths whose king, Theoderic, was killed. This was seen by some as exemplifying the traditional Roman policy of letting barbarians slaughter other barbarians while Roman legions were conserved. By nightfall, neither side was in clear possession of the field.

Next day the previously undefeated Attila was entrenched behind his laager of wagons. He was reported to have built a great funeral pyre of all his finest trophies, and was prepared to die magnificently on it rather than face defeat and possible capture by his enemies.[29] They did not attack him. Aetius could not afford the losses and uncertainties of another great clash, but for Attila a very costly battle that produced neither victory nor plunder was tantamount to a defeat – the first he had suffered, and proportionately damaging to his hitherto undented prestige. Attila's forces retreated back to the Hungarian plain.

Aetius quickly dismissed most of the allied contingents back to their home territories, a decision for which he has been heavily criticised, then and now. In fact, the Visigoths, lacking a king, were about to leave in any case. It was alleged, from a safe distance, that Aetius was in a position to destroy Attila completely but instead deliberately allowed him to withdraw, wishing to preserve the Hun power and, despite everything, even wean it back to an alliance as he had done before, and which he still needed.[30] Very much the same had been murmured against Stilicho in a similar situation.

Aetius was indeed walking a tightrope, an even more difficult one then Stilicho had walked. He had to keep himself militarily indispensable to the empire by defeating its enemies, but since today's enemy could be tomorrow's ally, to defeat any one of them too completely could upset the fine balance of forces that kept him in power. As always, he had to compensate for actual Roman weakness by levering one barbarian nation against another, as others had done before him. It is most likely that after this great battle he felt unable to destroy Attila's army. Even had he been able to, the result would have been in effect a great overweening victory for the Visigoths, not the Romans. Yet at the same time, to keep his barbarian coalition assembled in arms for any time once the immediate threat was past would have put very unwelcome strains on his leadership.[31]

By any account, however, he made serious errors at this point, obviously believing that a chastened Attila could at least be kept at arm's length from the West for the immediate future. It was a shock to him when the very next spring the Huns advanced westward a second time, now into a virtually undefended Italy. Aetius had few troops there. His power base was in Gaul. The invasion was very destructive as usual, but Attila's aims are unclear, beyond the need for continuous war and the desire to revenge himself on the Romans. After a prolonged and difficult siege the great imperial city of Aquileia, the gateway to Italy near modern Trieste, was captured, sacked, pillaged and ruined in the same manner as Sirmium.[32] All the prestige Aetius had gained the previous year was lost overnight.

The horde then spread over the north Italian plain, taking Milan and other cities, plundering but not destroying them. Aetius could menace Attila's rear and his communications, but little more. There was serious alarm that Attila would go on to sack Rome, as Alaric had done, but far more destructively. Physically nothing barred his way: Rome's walled defences were weaker than many of the cities he had taken. It was even claimed that Aetius advised the emperor to flee to the relative safety of Gaul, but this may have been the invention of his enemies.[33]

Although he had the ample plunder of Aquileia and Milan, Attila's position was nonetheless distinctly weaker than it had been. His total forces were seriously depleted, yet he had failed to establish a dominant position for himself in the West. Neither half of the empire had paid him any gold subsidy for two years, and his ability to reward his followers was diminishing. Most important, his own home base territories in the Hungarian-Carpathian basin were not secure. He had issued bloodthirsty warnings to Marcian and ordered some punitive raids into East Roman territory, but the new emperor had not only remained defiant but actually taken the offensive. Calling in aid the prayers of the bishops assembled for the Council of Chalcedon, Marcian's forces attacked across the Danube and, perhaps helped by subject peoples ripe for revolt, inflicted a defeat on the Huns remaining there.[34]

Added to this, the north Italian countryside was still suffering from the famine of the previous year, and provisioning the Hun armies was becoming a serious problem which no amount of plundered wealth could solve. With famine came its brother, plague: already the first cases were appearing in Attila's ranks. It was at this opportune moment, while the Huns were still north of the Apennines, that the Western government offered to open negotiations, with the object of building Attila a golden bridge out of Italy. The delegation was led in person by Bishop Leo of Rome, and the church naturally ascribed the successful outcome to his spiritual authority, aided by the miraculous appearance of the holy saints Peter and Paul. In fact, Attila was already looking for a way of withdrawing with what he still had.[35]

Doubtless with bribes, gifts and supplies Attila retreated again north of the Danube, without having secured any formal treaty or achieving anything beyond destruction, and still threatening that he would return. By previous standards, the expedition had been almost as great a failure as the invasion of Gaul, and the loyalties of his subject groups were already under strain. Regaining his base territory he could do nothing else but plan new wars to retain his authority, and he soon issued a declaration of war to Constantinople: next spring, he declared, he would invade the empire and enslave its inhabitants. Marcian and Aspar prepared to resist, not without anxiety.

The East's policy of spirited resistance had its rationale. After the events of 447 they probably calculated that any treaties with Attila were worth little, and that so long as he lived and ruled there was little point in trying to reclaim and rebuild the ruined Danube provinces, only to have them plundered again as soon as there was any modest recovery. Better to rely on the strong barrier of Constantinople. In ten years, approximately six tons of gold had been found to pay Attila – better use it to pay and equip their own armies, or buy barbarian allies. The Hun invasions had demonstrated very clearly that, provided Constantinople was firmly held and the wealthy Asiatic and Oriental provinces secure, it was possible to lose control of the European provinces temporarily without mortal damage to the empire. Sooner or later the invaders could be expelled or would withdraw, and these regions could be reclaimed. Fortunately perhaps, the policy of defiance was not put to the test, because in 453 there came the dramatic news that Attila had unexpectedly died.

He had been celebrating his wedding with yet another of his many brides, and drank himself insensible before collapsing in the nuptial tent. In the morning, he was found dead beside the weeping and terrified girl, either from haemorrhage or alcoholic suffocation. The warriors, it is reported, slashed their faces in howling grief and prepared a splendid barbaric funeral. The finest horsemen galloped around the silk-tented bier to invigorate the spirit of the dead hero. Singing long and soulful dirges, they placed the body in three successive coffins of gold, silver and iron, and buried it in a great barrow with his weapons and captured treasures. Finally, all those who had carried out the burial were themselves slain, to conceal forever the hero's resting place.[36]

The Roman world, and Marcian in particular, breathed a collective sigh of relief, deliverance, and thanksgiving. The single great threat that had dominated Constantinople's foreign policy for twelve years was suddenly lifted with the drunken choking of one man's breath. The East waited and watched eagerly for the confusion and fragmentation which must surely follow among Attila's former empire, hoping to take full advantage of the radically changed situation.

The dissolution was not long in coming; indeed, it was almost explosive. No other Hun leader existed with anything approaching the stature of Attila, nor were there any clear rules of succession in this agglomeration of a kingdom. No one is certain how many sons Attila had in all, but without any precedent, the more powerful ones simply divided the polity between them — warriors, peoples and herds, with their associated territories. Soon they were fighting each other, and it was clear that the huge concerted campaigns Attila had mounted were beyond their capacity, unless and until one of the brothers was able to conquer the others. But there was no time for that before revolts broke out among the subject peoples, who suddenly became aware of their rulers' disunity.[37]

It began with an isolated rebellion of the Ostrogoths under Valamir, but before long — within a year of Attila's death — large areas of the plains territories north of the Danube were embroiled in a confusion of war, upheaval and movement on a scale that had not been seen since the Huns had first arrived in the region nearly a century before. Here suddenly was a golden diplomatic opportunity for the Eastern empire to divide and manipulate its neighbours, perhaps even to rearrange the barbarian peoples on its northern frontier to its own liking. Already many of them were seeking settlement lands of military service in the empire, as they had done before Attila. It was a chance that might not come again.

Marcian almost certainly reached an agreement with Ardaric, king of the Gepids, previously one of Attila's close advisers, who was able to assemble and sustain a coalition of Rugians, Sciri, Heruli and others against their Hun overlords. It is very likely that Roman gold helped to cement this alliance. It finally bore fruit at a great battle on the river Nedao in Pannonia some time in 455, where the alliance met a combined army of Huns and overwhelmed it, killing Attila's eldest son Ellac.[38] After this defeat the Huns were still a force, but would never again achieve the unity and dominance of Attila's time. The main Hun survivors from the river Nedao retreated eastwards towards the Carpathians. Other fragmented bodies, their larger tribal organisation broken, were accepted as warriors into the empire. Soon afterwards, several of the other surviving sons of Attila rallied and launched a new war against their former subjects, Valamir's Ostrogoths, who had liberated themselves first, then stayed aloof from Ardaric's coalition.[39] The Huns attacked one portion of the Ostrogoths in Pannonia, hoping to defeat them before the rest could mobilise to their aid, but the result was yet another great Hun defeat. The survivors sought refuge in the Theiss-Danube area, with Roman agreement.[40]

With their military and financial resources, and their knowledge of the Germanic and steppe peoples, Marcian's government and those succeeding him worked to improve the empire's position in every direction. The devastated areas were settled with many groups of Attila's former subject peoples whom he had forcibly confined north of the Danube: Rugians in eastern Thrace, Sciri in Lower Moesia and Scythia, Gepids in Dacia, and others. Many of these were in fact *foederati* settlements of varying size. It was not possible to restore the Balkan provinces to their previous position and recreate the firm, preclusive Danube barrier that had existed before Attila. The old distinction between *laeti* (controlled, unarmed settlements under Roman administration) and *foederati*, had been eroded, and the arrangements were no doubt negotiated in an ad hoc way.

In Pannonia proper, the Ostrogothic kingdom of Valamir had re-established itself after defeating and expelling the Huns. Though nominally a province of the West, most of it had long ceased to be Roman in reality. By accepting the Ostrogoths as federate allies, Marcian was merely acknowledging an established fact. Nevertheless the empire was in a strong bargaining position and was the overall gainer. Compared with the nightmare of Attila, there was now a bloc of more or less reliable, more or less manageable allied peoples south of the Danube who were all hostile to the Huns, who might function as checks on one another and who could be induced by the appropriate gifts, subsidies and treaties into serving the larger defensive interests of the Eastern empire.[41]

All these peoples, as well as many remnants of the Huns, now provided a willing supply of troops for the Roman armies, which the treasury had ample means to pay. They were engaged either as direct recruits, or as agreed conscripts from the new settlers, mercenary formations or allied forces under treaty. The Ostrogothic kingdom of Valamir was the source of large numbers of allied troops. Another group of Ostrogoths under Triarius was settled in Thrace as federates, but not as a recognised kingdom. These two groups were to revive old political challenges in the next reign.

The momentous death of Attila did not have the same favourable consequences in the West. Instead, it led indirectly, by a series of costly blunders, to new political disasters. Aetius' position had already been weakened by the invasion of Italy. The dramatic removal of the whole Hunnic threat after 453 made him appear dispensable at last, after thirty years of power. This situation was accentuated by a change of policy from the Visigoths, whose new king, Theoderic, now sought alliance and friendship with the emperor. Undermined, Aetius was assassinated by the timidly vengeful Valentinian in

September 454. According to most sources, he was actually cut down in the palace by Valentinian himself.[42] 'You have cut off your right hand with your left,' one courtier is alleged to have told him. Less than a year later Aetius' own adherents avenged their patron by murdering Valentinian while he was exercising on the Campus Martius in Rome, putting an end to the male line of the Theodosian dynasty in the West. Political chaos followed, with two ephemeral emperors and no concentrated military power centre.

With the one strong warlord ('the last of the Romans', as Procopius later called him) removed from Italy, the Vandal king, Gaiseric, who had prudently kept to his own African domains while Aetius ruled, now calmly sailed with his fleet to Ostia where he declared his intention of sacking Rome. As a Christian he agreed with Bishop Leo that there would be no bloodshed; but in return his army spent two weeks systematically removing from the city every possible item of value, from the statues even down to the copper on the roofs, and loading it on to their ships, later to adorn the city of Carthage.[43] Rome began to resemble the decayed shell it would be in the Middle Ages. Among the thousands of captives taken back to Africa were the empress Eudoxia and her two daughters Eudocia and Placidia.

With the dynasty effectively ended and the generalissimo dead, Italy and the West entered a further stage of confusion and disintegration. Aetius had held together a Western Roman polity of sorts with the slender resources and stratagems available to him, including whatever potency the symbols of the Roman name still possessed. But his authority had been based on the personal loyalties of strong blocs of Roman and barbarian troops, most prominently, for most of his career, the Huns. It was not at all institutionalised: the next aspiring supreme commander could not inherit it, but would have to find his own, equally personal power base. In a sense, all Aetius' patriotic efforts had ultimately served only to delay and disguise a process of unravelling that could not now be stopped. After these events it became brutally clear just how diminished Roman power really was, and for how little the emperor really counted. The next generalissimo, Ricimer, was a barbarian who cynically set up and demolished figurehead emperors at will.

Attila's myth has been that of the great conqueror in the league of Genghis Khan and Tamurlaine. Even in our century Hungarian and Romanian boys are named after him. He caused great destruction but did not establish anything, certainly not an 'empire' in the minimal sense of a coherent polity with rational aims and methods of exploitation, and the means of sustaining and renewing itself. Nor is there much evidence that he aimed at anything like this. His power was personal and charismatic, and would almost certainly have disappeared with him in the same way even had he ruled many more years.

He has been seen by many as the forerunner of the great nomadic cavalry empires, the 'horse peoples', particularly the Mongols who smashed so destructively through the Russian states and so many others in the thirteenth century. But after the initial phase of destruction the Mongols consolidated into a tributary empire with its great economy of force at a distance, based on their remote Caspian capital at Sarai. The subject peoples and cities were left to continue their agrarian life with a limited autonomy, provided they paid annual tribute to Sarai and accepted its political jurisdiction. The powerful sanction was that of a terrible Mongol army returning to punish disobedient subjects in the earlier frightful manner, but the viability of the Mongol empire depended on this sanction having to be used rarely. Attila could not achieve this because he never subdued either half of the Roman empire, because he never escaped from the bloody dynamic in which war was an end in itself, and because he never created a structure that could outlast his death.

With the ending of the Hun menace and of the Theodosian dynasty, the Roman East entered on a new period in which different kinds of problems, dangers and opportunities were to be experienced. It had undergone subtle changes since the time of Theodosius I and, perhaps even reluctantly, become more conscious of its increasing distance – in power, position, manner of government and overall fortunes – from the struggling West. At this point it is useful to stand back temporarily from the narrative sequence and examine the East's overall resources, in the widest sense of that term.

Part 3

THE RESOURCES

8

MILITARY DEVELOPMENTS,
EAST AND WEST

The Roman army was the keystone of the empire: it was the guarantor of its survival in the face of its many enemies, the main driving force for both consumption and distribution in the economy, and the ultimate arbiter of the imperial succession itself. It was the single most important constituent of the Roman state.

This study is primarily concerned with the survival of the Eastern half of the empire, but as in other areas it is important to appreciate the character and development of the Eastern army through comparison with that of the Western empire. At the beginning of our period, on the death of Theodosius I in 395, the armies of East and West were similar in character and numerical strength, although with different command structures. By the end of it, on the death of Anastasius in 518, the Western army had ceased to exist, along with the state it had supported. In the East, after many wars, emergencies and reverses, the army had survived and been strengthened, providing the basis for the ambitious wars of reconquest by Justinian in the sixth century.

What is clear from this study is that the overall size, basic organisation, composition and effectiveness of the Eastern Roman army did not fundamentally change from that created by Theodosius I between 379 and 395, and inherited by Arcadius, to that bequeathed by Anastasius to Justinian. The Western army, however, underwent rapid and catastrophic change.[1]

In 395, Arcadius became sole ruler in the East, and Honorius succeeded in the West. The armies of both East and West were currently based in the West following the defeat of the usurper Eugenius, and were temporarily under the united control of Stilicho. When he bowed to pressure from Arcadius and his advisers, and returned the army of the East to its home territories, it was the force which had been successful in two civil wars inside six years that marched home leaving the defeated West behind. The two armies were very much the creation of Theodosius I at this point – the Eastern having been rebuilt after the disaster of Adrianople, together with a revised command structure; and the Western having twice been defeated in battle by him, and its forces restructured to the benefit of the East.

97

The Eastern army had been badly depleted, of both officers and men, in the Adrianople disaster of 378. Theodosius had recruited heavily, from both Roman and barbarian sources, to fill the ranks, and had moved units from elsewhere to plug the gaps in the Balkan provinces. In the short term, this led to a weakening of the army, but it could be corrected over time by competent military leadership if the pressure on the East allowed. Campaigning after Adrianople did much to develop and strengthen the army, along with troops and officers sent from the West, and the avoidance of major conflicts until 388 provided time for recruitment and training in the medium term.

The West did not suffer unduly in these years. However, the defeat of the usurper Maximus in 388 by Theodosius not only damaged the losing Western army, but also resulted in the transfer of a proportion of the Western forces, adopted as a second Praesental army for the East. A shift of some 20,000 men from West to East is implied by this readjustment, leaving the Western army significantly smaller (*c.* 250,000 at most, as compared with 300,000 in the East).[2]

Both in the aftermath of Adrianople and for his civil wars, Theodosius called on as many barbarian irregular forces as he could muster. Initially, these were assorted barbarian groups, along with allies from the Caucasus region, but later they included the main strength of the Goths settled under treaty, who contributed a reputed 20,000 men to his army in 394. Huns were also used to great effect in this latter campaign. The difference between these groups was that the Huns and others generally seem to have returned to their home territories outside the empire after a particular campaign, while the Goths returned to their allocated territory inside the empire. These campaigns emphasise the importance of readily available barbarian additions to basic manpower levels in times of stress for the standard complement and for usual levels of recruitment.[3]

In both East and West there is little evidence for permanent barbarian units (federates) recruited as a standard addition to regular forces at this stage. Barbarians were either recruited individually, trained, equipped and disciplined to fill gaps in the ranks of regular units, or participated en bloc as allies under their own leaders (under treaty obligations, or for pay and loot, or both) in temporary campaign armies.

While it is difficult to identify the exact numbers of barbarians within the army, a substantial proportion (perhaps a quarter) of known individuals of all ranks were of barbarian origin throughout the fourth and fifth centuries. This proportion would obviously rise to nearer 100 per cent of enlisted men in newly recruited units raised from barbarians under treaties or other arrangements. It is a proportion which seems remarkably consistent across time and ranks, although it does not tell us how many of these 'barbarians' were in fact from outside the empire, rather than recruited as individuals or small groups from within the Roman provinces. What it does indicate is that a very significant proportion of the army had some sort of barbarian origin, This does not indicate any tendency to unreliability. From the earliest references to barbarian recruitment their value was recognised: 'The barbarian farmer pays taxes. What is more, if he is called up for military service he hurries up, is improved by the discipline and is proud to serve under the name of soldier.'[4]

Under Constantine, in the early fourth century, the command of the army lay with one or two senior generals, the *Magistri*, directly below the emperor. When the imperial power was later shared, each ruler had *Magistri* in command of his army, with junior officers commanding regional detachments of the field army. Theodosius developed a fairly flat command structure below himself as supreme commander in the East. There were separate army groups on the eastern frontier, in the Balkans and around Constantinople, but the arrangements for command of his campaign army in 394 imply that he had not completed his review of the high military offices at his death, although the basic structure was in place.

In the East the wider command base, involving several roughly equal status generals, was distinct from the structure Theodosius clearly envisaged in the West, of a single dominant military/political appointee. The previous history of regency encouraged by Theodosius in the West emphasised his interest in maintaining close control over the hierarchy there through such an appointment, and Stilicho was intended to fulfil that role for him after 394. Gildo, in command of the African territories, had similar titles and theoretical powers to Stilicho, but without the clear distinction of marriage and other personal ties to the imperial dynasty. Stilicho was not given total authority, but a pre-eminent position.[5]

The regular army consisted of two components: the mobile field armies (*comitatenses*), grouped into several regional bodies, and the garrison armies based mainly along the frontiers (*limitanei*). At the end of the fourth century, there were distinctions of pay, privilege and status between these grades. However, units of *limitanei* often fought well where needed, formed part of campaign armies based on their territories, and were occasionally raised to the field armies. They should not necessarily be seen as second-rate troops. In fact, their role as garrisons was to be vital to the security of the provinces during the barbarian invasions that were to hit the empire over the next century and a half. Approximately two-thirds of the forces of both East and West consisted of *limitanei*.

In addition, during the periods of relative peace which prevailed on the frontiers at times, the *limitanei* were responsible for the day-to-day work of policing the borders: collecting information on barbarian movements and intentions, controlling routine movements between the empire and the *barbaricum*, and generally maintaining the peace. This customs and policing role was essential in providing a level of security for provincial economies, maintaining internal security (banditry was a serious and endemic problem in some areas), controlling trade – there were prohibitions on transferring certain goods, such as weaponry, to the barbarians, and taxes to be collected on the proceeds of legitimate commerce – and constantly patrolling to emphasise the authority of the empire and its control.[6]

There are numerous references to the recruitment of Roman provincials into the army in the fourth and fifth centuries. Most of the relevant legislation dates to periods of crisis or rebuilding, but to presume that conscription applied at these times only is unlikely; there would have been little need for new legislation when there were no problems. Hereditary obligations to join up, in force since Diocletian, along with a regular levy of new recruits was the apparent norm, although on occasion, especially in the West, a cash levy was collected rather than recruits. This system would probably have sufficed to provide the army with its minimum annual requirement for some 25,000 to 30,000 men (enough to replace retirements through age, though not significant casualties), but was clearly inadequate at times of stress. Additional recruits would have been difficult to raise from the established system, and they would require training and dispersal as necessary. It was far quicker, and probably cheaper, to recruit from barbarian sources to fill the ranks of regular units or to serve as federates. This was particularly true of cavalry units, which required additional skills and had high establishment costs. It would seem that at this stage (395) that there was no general manpower crisis, but the flexibility to meet urgent needs did not exist and led to general and occasionally mass employment of barbarians.

The size of the army is a crucial question. Only by grasping the scale of resources available can we assess the skill and success of those using them through the fifth and early sixth centuries. The major source for the late fourth/early fifth century army is the *Notitia Dignitatum*, an incomplete administrative document listing units, commands and stations, which has survived in a confused and confusing state. The answer is slightly more straightforward for the East than the West, since the *Notitia* lists for Eastern provinces seem to represent a fairly fixed point in time around the start of Arcadius' reign. The lists for the West seem to have been revised in a more or less haphazard way down to late in the reign of Honorius, probably in the 420s. However, with a certain amount of reasoned reconstruction we can make comparisons between the army of the East and its less fortunate Western counterpart, both in 395 and later.[7]

There is a problem in trying to read back from the lists for the Western army in the 420s, a time when many units had been lost, others upgraded from the *limitanei* to the *comitatenses*, and territories abandoned, to a point before all this had happened. However, in 395 the army of the West consisted of approximately 250,000 men in total, divided into 80,000 *comitatenses* and 170,000 *limitanei*. The main field armies were based in Italy and Gaul (around 25,000 men in each), with smaller groups in Illyricum, Africa and elsewhere. We have to assume that the West would have been in poorer shape than the recently victorious Eastern army, and probably these figures represent an overly positive picture of the Western army. This may explain why Stilicho was obliged to recruit so heavily before each of his campaigns.

The Rhine and upper Danube frontiers were held by *limitanei* garrisons of some 60,000 each, with another 20,000 or so in both Britain and Africa. The strongest individual provincial contingents were 15,000 to 20,000 strong and held the Illyricum-middle Rhine area, with smaller groups based in the other Gaulish provinces. Although these groups were of great importance in the general security of the frontier provinces, they were of limited value in major campaigns fought deep inside the empire. The West was stretched, with limited flexibility for reinforcement of other areas by the main Praesental army in Italy, which was required to face threats to Italy itself. The West had to defend a very attenuated European territory with only 60,000 men in field armies, and no real strategic reserve.

The overall level of cavalry was much lower in the West than the East, amounting to only 12 per cent of total regular manpower. There was a significant lack of regular cavalry in the field armies of Italy (only 12 per cent) and Illyricum (none), where there was considerable barbarian settlement, including groups renowned for their cavalry. Under Stilicho, their federate cavalry was heavily relied on, and it may be that he extended, rather than initiated, the pattern.

In addition, the Western army had been following a pattern of barbarian recruitment into the regular ranks and use of allied contingents throughout the fourth century. The field armies required strengthening for major campaigns despite continuing regular recruitment. The focus of attention on campaigns involving Italy and Illyricum encouraged a reliance on treaty arrangements to maintain peace on the lower Rhine, most of which involved territorial and/or financial considerations in return for barbarian compliance and the promise of fighting men.[8]

Although the *Notitia* in its Western lists shows infantry units under the command of the *Magister Peditum*, and cavalry under the *Magister Equitum*, it is clear that from the beginning Stilicho was supreme commander, generally referred to as *Comes et Magister Utriusque Militiae*. Although some of the *Magistri Equitum* from this period are known, they are always junior figures, acting as subordinate commanders to Stilicho and his successors. A resulting advantage which Stilicho enjoyed over his Eastern counterparts was that when he wanted to raise troops, or needed to issues legislation or make strategic decisions, he could do so almost unchallenged.

Stilicho used his position to try to institutionalise his exceptional authority, establishing the subordination of his companion *Magistri Equitum* and appointing his own men, seconded on an annual basis, to run the *officia* of all junior military commanders. This is emphasised in the *Notitia*, where the *Magister Peditum* has the direct command of all *Comites* and *Duces*. The pattern was continued by all of his significant successors.

Stilicho had to face a series of crises in the West, which placed strains on the army at his disposal and the recruitment system. In 395, with a combined force from East and West, Stilicho could defeat Alaric. After returning the Eastern armies, he had to recruit heavily while campaigning against the Franks on the Rhine. He was successful, imposing chosen rulers on the defeated tribes, and used the opportunity to fill the ranks. Recruiting continued for his initially successful campaign in 396/7 against Alaric. These recruiting drives, although bringing in barbarians in considerable numbers, seem to have been intended to strengthen the regular army. At this stage barbarians employed as federates seem to have been mainly used to provide cavalry for the field army. With full control of the forces available, Stilicho was generally successful in these three campaigns, showing that the Western army could still function effectively when well led.

Stilicho continued to campaign on the frontiers, being in Raetia in 401 when Alaric invaded Italy. Stilicho transferred troops from the British and Gaulish armies to repel this threat, as well as raising an exceptional levy of recruits, and these contingents are likely to have remained with the army of Italy rather than returned to their earlier bases.

By the time of Radagaisus' invasion in 405/6, Stilicho had resorted to mass recruitment of barbarians as federates, not regulars. The invading horde, reportedly between 100,000 and 400,000 strong, must have numbered many tens of thousands. Stilicho deployed thirty regular units (perhaps 15,000 to 20,000 men) along with his barbarians, and smashed Radagaisus' forces at Faesulae, after which 12,000 *optimates* (noble warriors/retainers) were taken into service as federates. Many of these federate troops would have owed their service, and primary allegiance, to the commander who recruited and paid them.[9]

Stilicho's army suffered substantial casualties in constant campaigning and in several major battles, and he had few good recruiting grounds from which to replace losses on this scale (Italy had long ceased to be a good recruitment base). There was also very little time to train and deploy new regulars in the constant warfare of the period. The special levy of recruits in 407 was commuted to gold, given the emergency situation. The general trend of the regular part of his forces was therefore sharply downwards, with an increasing need to rely on quickly available and cheaper barbarian troops.[10]

Beset on all sides after the collapse of the Rhine frontier and the usurpation of Constantine in 407, Stilicho simply did not have the resources to defend Italy (never mind carry the battle to Alaric and the East) and face the new threats in the northwest. The Gaulish army had either disintegrated or gone over to the usurper, and the field of conflict had now moved from the frontier to deep within the provinces, where the surviving *limitanei* were of limited value. Stilicho was left with an apparently equally Roman and barbarian army based in Italy, which was perhaps 40,000 strong at most. On the murder of Stilicho and his son in 408, the federate element of this army, deprived of the patron responsible for their recruitment who held their loyalty, defected to Alaric. The West was left with perhaps 20,000 men in each of the Italian and Gaulish armies, to face all barbarian threats, and each other in civil war.[11]

The extensive use of barbarian federates and allies was the only recourse in times of urgent need. Federate units arose from the personalised nature of recruiting, the lack of regular recruits and training time, and the constant campaigning pressures which required forces permanently in being rather than serving for limited durations as before. The charismatic nature of military leadership led to the emergence of personal followings or body-guards, originally elite regular troops (*bucellarii*). These groups soon embraced barbarians from the federates, who had a strong tradition of following warlords as personal retainers. It was clear that barbarians in all these guises were now essential for the Western army to campaign successfully.[12]

A comparison of units known before 395 and those surviving in the 420s suggests that the Western *comitatenses* had lost over half their strength in the intervening years under Stilicho and his successors. Attempts to repair this damage had been made, partly through genuinely new recruitment but mainly through the paper exercise of upgrading *limitanei* to the status of *comitatenses* (45,000 men were redesignated in this way).

The damage to the *limitanei* had also been on a massive scale: at least 40,000 men, roughly one-third of their strength, had been lost over a period of twenty to twenty-five years. This loss was most apparent in Gaul, where only a handful of units survived to be listed in the *limitanei* in the 420s. It would seem that the garrison army of Gaul almost disappeared during the civil wars and barbarian invasions between 406 and 418. The field army was cut in half, and although restored to a notional 34,000 men only about one-third of that number were survivors of the earlier *comitatenses*. The army of Italy survived in better condition. After Stilicho's execution it was not really deployed against the Goths, and so avoided major losses. It seems to have had very few transfers from the *limitanei* to keep it up to strength, which was now notionally 28,500.

Illyricum had seen only slightly more reinforcement, but in Africa almost the entire frontier army had been upgraded on paper. Britain and Armorica (Brittany) had effectively seceded from the empire. Their forces, such as survived, could no longer be counted as part of the Roman army. There were also a few thousand troops in Spain trying to control the barbarian groups who had crossed the Pyrenees.[13]

In these circumstances, barbarian troops were essential complements to the limited regular armies. After Stilicho, Constantius established a new relationship with the Visigoths following their move from Italy. They fought other barbarian groups in Spain with great success, wiping out one Vandal tribe and defeating the Alans, until finally settled by Constantius in

Gaul. It seems that the Visigoths were the strongest of the barbarian groups, other than the Huns. Constantius also tried to reach accommodations with the other barbarian peoples who had invaded Spain, but with little success. Huns were used extensively as allies, first by Stilicho, and then in increasing numbers until Aetius came to rely on them from the late 420s onwards.

Both Constantius and Aetius enjoyed considerable success against the range of their enemies, but wherever possible the fighting was done by one group of allies against another who were temporarily in dispute. There was only one major Roman field army available for mobile campaigns, and it was too valuable to risk unless there was no other choice. The army of Gaul was preoccupied with Armorican revolts, Frankish expansion, and disputes with Burgundians, Visigoths and others, and could not provide support elsewhere. Despite paper numbers it never effectively recovered from the losses of the early decades of the fifth century.

By the 430s many Western provinces had been lost or ceded to barbarian groups. The final blows came with the loss of most of Africa to the Vandals between 428 and 442, removing the wealthiest and most productive area of the empire from its chain of support. It was after this loss that Valentinian III complained that he could not afford to pay his existing soldiers, much less recruit any more. Despite this, some regular recruitment continued. The very fact that recognisable Roman army units survived into the later part of the century demonstrates that gaps were filled, either by routine conscription too common to feature in our sources, or by hereditary service and similar means.[14]

In 451, the last great field battle of the Roman army in the West was fought against Attila. The many allied groups formed the larger part of the army. The coalition had been put together by Aetius, and so was still Roman led, and the Roman army was probably larger than any of the others, except perhaps for the Visigothic contingent. Aetius could not assemble the whole Roman army, but could still deploy the equivalent of a field army, perhaps about 20,000 men. The Visigothic kingdom could field a matching force, and between Goths and Romans a collection of several other peoples held the centre: there may have been 50,000 to 60,000 facing Attila in total.

The murder of Aetius shortly afterwards had a similar effect on his forces as that of Stilicho half a century earlier: disaffection in the army but not leading to a mass departure this time. Instead, there was fragmentation, with some generals, especially Marcellinus in Illyricum, refusing to recognise central authority, and others seeking to seize it. A further bout of civil wars, involving Visigothic forces, resulted in Majorian's brief reign from 457 to 461. He had access to an army that allowed him to campaign in Gaul and Spain with some success, and to contemplate, but not achieve, a reconquest of Vandal Africa.

Increasingly, with small regional armies under their own generals, the outlook of the surviving Roman forces was becoming localised. There were independent groups in Illyricum, Gaul, Spain and Italy, and no military or political force strong enough to reunite them. They were becoming more of a localised militia and garrison force, whereas mobile troops were increasingly raised and maintained as barbarian federates. Such forces could operate effectively on occasion, as witnessed by the victories of Ricimer and Marcellinus over the Vandals, but the gap was growing between a regular paid army and an essentially mercenary force held together by strong leadership and expectations of reward. It is likely that the last recognisably Roman field army that fought in the West was that which came from the East with Anthemius when he became emperor in 467. It can only have been a few thousand strong.

There was still sufficient money in the Western treasury to put two million solidi into the great expedition of 468 against the Vandals (see Chapter 12). If Procopius' figure of 100,000 men participating in the campaign army is accurate, then the West might have been contributing up to 20,000. Although some of these might represent Anthemius' Eastern troops, the bulk were probably paid federates. Ricimer (and Odovacer, his successor as the last barbarian generalissimo) led a federate army of Italy which might have been about 20,000 strong.

Although most of the Western army melted away, there were a few survivors. The last claim to legitimacy in the West rested with Julius Nepos, who had been emperor briefly from 473 to 475. After being forced from Italy, Nepos retired to his family heartland in Dalmatia with limited forces, where he held on until final defeat in 482.

After Gaul had been partitioned by Visigoths, Burgundians, Franks and Armoricans, Syagrius, the son of the last regional *Magister Militum*, Aegidius, ruled a Roman people and territory in north-central Gaul as *Rex Romanorum* and leader of the surviving army. This independent province held out until annexed by the Franks under Clovis in 486, ten years after the deposition of the last emperor of the West.[15]

There is one more survival, however, reported by Procopius as persisting to his own time (writing in the 550s):

> Now other Roman soldiers, also, had been stationed at the frontiers of Gaul to serve as guards. And these soldiers, having no means of returning to Rome, and at the same time being unwilling to yield to their enemy who were Arians, gave themselves, together with their military standards and the land which they had long been guarding for the Romans, to the Arborychi and Germans [Armoricans and Franks]; and they handed down to their offspring all the customs of their fathers, which were thus preserved, and this people has held them in sufficient reverence to guard them even up to my time. For even at the present day they are clearly recognised as belonging to the legions to which they were assigned when they

served in ancient times, and they always carry their own standards when they enter battle, and always follow the customs of their fathers. And they preserve the dress of the Romans in every particular, even as regards their shoes.[16]

The Eastern army followed a very different pattern of development. Except for its command structure, it was initially very similar to the army in the West. Their divergence was due to factors of politics, geography and economics as much as success or failure in war.

In 395, the *comitatenses*, the five mobile field army groups in the East under the *Magistri*, were all of a broadly similar size and composition. Based on the lists of the *Notitia*, they were structured as shown in Table 1.

Strategically, this breaks down into 42,000 troops in the Balkan sector, with some 300 miles of frontier, and 20,000 facing the Persians (the smaller-scale raiding which characterised most Arab threats would mainly have been dealt with by the *limitanei* of those provinces). A strategic reserve of 42,000 was based around Constantinople and available to reinforce any sector when needed, or augment it to form a campaign army for offensive action. The balance of threat would seem to have been perceived as coming from the Danubian barbarians, and this is borne out by our historical sources. Relations with Persia were carried out at a fairly sophisticated diplomatic level, and the chances of a large-scale and completely unexpected attack from that quarter were slight; any major war should have taken place in circumstances allowing the Praesental forces to support the resident army of the Orient quickly.

The *limitanei* were dispersed in the frontier provinces in groups (each under the provincial military command of a *Dux limitis*) according to the geography of the area and the nature of the threat faced. In the East, this resulted in commands ranging from 9,000 troops (Syria, Scythia) to 25,000 (Egypt). The total number of troops in these formations amounted to 195,500 men, with 45,500 in the Balkan provinces, 88,500 on the eastern frontiers, and 61,000 in Egypt and the other eastern African provinces. There were a further 2,000 in garrison in the troubled 'internal frontier' area of Isauria, in the mountains of Asia Minor.[17]

Table 1 Structure of the five mobile field army groups in the East

Army Group	Praesental I	Praesental II	Thrace	Illyricum	Orient	Total
Infantry	15,000	15,000	21,000	16,500	15,000	82,500
Cavalry	6,000 (29%)	6,000 (29%)	3,500 (14%)	1,000 (6%)	5,000 (25%)	21,500 (21%)
Total Numbers	21,000	21,000	24,500	17,500	20,000	104,000

The frontier forces contained the remnants of the earlier imperial frontier units (*cohortes*, *alae*, frontier legionary detachments), and some more recent additions. The proportion of cavalry in these forces seems to have been about 50 per cent of the total number of troops, and at first sight this looks like the often reported bias of the later Roman and Byzantine army towards cavalry; but this is not the case. It needs to be seen against the role of the *limitanei* (involving much mobile patrolling, for which cavalry would generally be more effective). There was a much lower proportion of cavalry in the field armies, who could easily have recruited more costly cavalry if they were really preferred to infantry. The breakdown of these figures by province also indicates that in the more open frontier zones (Arabia, Palestine, the Euphrates) cavalry could be predominant, often representing 60 to 70 per cent of the total, whereas in the European provinces, or in more mountainous regions, the proportion was much lower (*c.* 40 per cent in the Balkans, and in Isauria the garrison was all infantry).

This pattern also reflected the nature of the opponents the army faced, with mounted raiders being more common in the Persian and Arab frontier regions. It is also clear that this was a long-established pattern, with the second-century Roman forces in the East also containing a very high proportion of cavalry. An increase in total cavalry numbers during the fourth century partly reflects the overall growth in the army from Diocletian, and also a strengthening of the Danube frontier army with cavalry after losses in Constantine's Sarmatian wars.[18]

Cavalry were obviously considered to be of growing importance during the fourth century, but not – as often assumed – as part of the field armies to face Gothic and other hordes in combat. Their most important function was as part of the policing of lower-level threats to provincial security; they were not a replacement for the traditional Roman reliance on well-trained, good quality infantry as the mainstay of the field army.

Following the Theodosian settlement after Adrianople, Goths formed the most important single group of barbarians in the East. The main groups were settled by treaty in the Danubian frontier provinces, in return for which they were to supply troops to fight, under their own leaders, alongside Roman campaign armies. There were also other smaller Germanic and Gothic groups, Huns settled in Thrace, and substantial allied contingents supplied by the client states of the western Caucasus and from Armenia.

One other allied barbarian group was comprised of Arab forces on the eastern frontier. Recent archaeological work has suggested that the strongest period of fortification and garrison on the *Limes Arabicus* was in the fourth and fifth centuries. We have numerous references to raiding of settled areas by Arab tribes from the desert, and especially from the Arabian peninsula, but there is evidence of fort building and a regular army presence to counter it. Despite this, there were occasions when strong tribes could force their way into the margins of the provinces, and the government responded by recognising one dominant group as imperial allies – granting them recognition, subsidies and status in return for their alliance against Persia and her allied Arab tribes when called upon, and for their prevention of similar invasions by other tribes, in which they had a vested interest.[19]

The army which Stilicho returned to the East in 395 consisted of numerous barbarian allies, who had been part of the campaign against Eugenius in 394, as well as the regular armies of Thrace, Illyricum and one of the Praesental forces. The other Praesental army, effectively under the command of Rufinus as Theodosius' regent during his absence on campaign, and the army of the Orient facing the Persian frontier, completed the field forces of the East.

Between the army's return under Gainas to assassinate Rufinus, and Gainas' attempt to seize power in 400, little changed. A more permanent administrative command structure was established to formalise the five-fold division of forces and commands, but there were few changes in the composition of the army overall. Due to Theodosius' own presence in the East prior to 394, and the more dispersed nature of power around him, no single figure dominated matters as much as Stilicho in the West. Prefects and other civil officers also held military authority at times, as part of a wider court circle of high officers of state, including the *Magistri*.

In the East, the military structure now consisted of two *Magistri* in command of the Praesental armies attendant on the emperor (one of whom in practice always seems to have been acknowledged as senior), and other *Magistri* in command of the armies in Illyricum, Thrace and the Orient. Although there were grades of seniority, no one general commanded the authority to dominate the whole military establishment at this stage. The two Praesental armies, although based in the region of Constantinople, did not form a permanently resident force in the city (although some troops, especially in transit, might be billeted there at times).

Perhaps the most significant fact is that the army was ineffective during this period: there was no attempt to contain or defeat Alaric (or for that matter, Stilicho) by direct force, and the campaign against Tribigild was a shambles. Most of these problems must be attributed to the divided civil and military factors struggling for supremacy. The army, heavily recruited from Germanic, especially Gothic, groups, may have been unreliable against other Goths, but it seems more likely that there was not the clear military leadership to take decisions and follow them through.

The ascendancy of civil government led to a policy of appeasement, rather than one which permitted the military to flex its muscles. The removal of several senior military commanders in a series of treason trials demonstrated a suspicion of the army by the civil powers, and this must have weakened the command structure while alienating the military in general. This was a trend which began early, possibly under Rufinus, and was accelerated rapidly under Eutropius: he disposed of generals who had been favoured by Theodosius, and refused to reward even those who had brought him to power.

The defeat of the Gainas revolt (see Chapter 1) by a coalition of military and civil figures, and the populace, resulted in a quite different position from that which followed the post-Stilicho crisis in the West. The authority of the imperial power was reinforced, even if exercised by a varying group of officials, and there was no direct or perceived need for a single strong military figure to face the threats to the state. Having decided to recognise Alaric and divert his attentions to the West, the East did not face any other serious military threats that might demand the attentions of such a dictatorial power.

This is exemplified by the treatment of Fravitta, who, despite his victory over Gainas and his subsequent consulship, was accused of treason and executed before 404. It is often asserted that the Eastern government, following the Gainas crisis, pursued a policy of purging Goths from the army and, in particular, from the high commands. However, there were as many Roman generals removed from office between 395 and 403 as those of barbarian origin. There is an absence of any recognisably Gothic or Germanic names among the *Magistri* in the first decade or so of the fifth century. Of the few whose names we have, there are five Romans, two Persians and an Armenian, to cover a period of almost twenty years. However, most of these known *Magistri* are from the eastern command, which was almost always given to an Oriental or Roman in all periods.[20]

The notable careers of several generals of barbarian origin must have begun during this period, in the last years of Arcadius or the early part of the reign of Theodosius II. Plintha was *Magister Militum* in 418, consul in 419, and was still an important figure when last mentioned in 434. Ardaburius was *Magister Praesentalis* against the Persians in 421, commanded the expedition against the usurper John in the West up to 425, and was consul in 427 when he was last mentioned. He may have been directly succeeded by his son, Aspar, who was certainly in a Praesental post by 431, when he commanded the expedition against the Vandals in Africa. He also held it during the Vandal and Persian wars in 441. Aspar was in this position of power for at least forty, and perhaps forty-four years.

By the appointment of Apollonius to succeed Areobindus as *Magister Praesentalis* in 443, we see the first Roman incumbent for twenty years known to our records. The preponderance of barbarian *Magistri* continued in the Thracian and Illyrican commands, with John (the Vandal), Arnegisclus and Agintheus all holding office in the 440s. However, for the same period we have Procopius, Dionysius, Anatolius and Zeno as *Magistri* in the Orient, demonstrating a clear distinction: Germanic generals usually held the European posts, sharing the Praesental commands with Romans, and Romans or Oriental officers commanded the army of the Orient.

An idea of the importance of Gothic troops, as opposed to commanders, is given by the crisis of 400. There was insufficient central authority to prevent a powerful general from recruiting directly at the start of the fifth century. In this way, Gainas had acquired a strong force of federate Goths and others, loyal in the main to him personally. He may have had a total force of some 30,000 at the height of his power, a force mainly composed of his federates, but also including regular troops and a disparate following of rebellious slaves, peasants, etc. who had joined with Tribigild's rebellion. It is not necessary, however, to imagine from this episode that more than 20 to 25 per cent at most (and probably rather less) of the Eastern army – including the federate troops – were of Gothic origin.[21]

After the loss of federate Goths, the East seems to have survived with much smaller barbarian contingents, although it continued to recruit individuals into regular units. This was not a radical departure; rather, the unprecedented semi-permanent mass recruitment of Goths by Gainas had been the departure, and the East now returned to the usual pattern of calling on barbarian groups for campaigns, and of only using smaller numbers on a more frequent basis. Huns were sent to Cyrenaica in 412, possibly from those settled in Thrace, but given the frequent complaints of later Hunnic leaders about fugitives from north of the Danube being accepted by the empire, it is possible that other groups were also used. It may be significant that the general use of Isaurian 'barbarians' (in the sense of non-regular, but technically Roman troops) dates from the 440s, when Hunnic control over their subjects was more secure and federates from north of the Danube were no longer available in numbers.

It is possible that under Arcadius there was a tendency to allow the army to run down in size. This cannot have been significant: to do so would have required a deliberate decision not to recruit/conscript as normal, for which we have no evidence. There are references to conscription in the 390s (the latest surviving legislation for the annual levy of recruits), but few from the fifth century. However, there are literary references to recruits, and volunteers, throughout the period, and we must presume that the absence of legislation indicates a lack of problems with the system rather than the lack of a system itself. This may be explained by limited pressures: no major losses on campaign, no significant threats requiring strengthening of units, and no ambitious generals seeking personal military power. We must presume that the regular forces remained much as set out in the *Notitia*, albeit at a low establishment level, as was normal in any peacetime army.[22]

Concern for the well-being of the army was demonstrated at several points. In 406 and 409 there was legislation for the issuing of rations to soldiers' families, which may have made service more attractive to citizens. The developing power of the *Magister Officiorum* can be seen in some of the legislative changes which occur, and which also illustrate the continuing relevance of the *limitanei*. In 423, 'outsiders' were prohibited from occupying the lands allocated to support the frontier forts, which should only be held by their garrisons. A general concern for the efficiency of these troops is clear from the order issued by Anatolius, *Magister* in the Orient, in 438, ordering that no-one was to distract the soldiers from their military duties. In 443, Nomus, the *Magister Officiorum*, was given administrative control of all *limitanei* in the East. He ordered that all units should be brought up to full strength, paid in full, and that they be drilled daily. Apart from any direct improvement in their abilities this may have brought about, the central administration may have helped to limit the potential for abuse of the *limitanei* and their pay system by their superiors. This law also prohibited the alienation of *agri limitanei*, the military lands which were tended by the frontier garrisons free of charge for their own profit and support. This was an additional component of their support, since they continued to receive their pay and drill as regular soldiers. In addition to this care shown for the maintenance of the *limitanei*, the participation of the *comitatenses* in several major campaigns (Africa, Persia, Italy, and repeatedly against the Huns) and the survival of many units to appear in records of the sixth century suggest that the basic organisation and complement of the field armies persisted through the fifth century.[23]

The first serious challenge to the Eastern army after Gainas came with the invasion of Thrace in 408 by a force under Hunnic leadership, but composed of a mixed grouping of subject peoples as well as the dominant Hunnic tribes. Although an imperial victory was achieved partly by political means (sowing division and conflict among the enemy, probably with bribery as the main tool), the Roman army was still capable and confident enough to take the field and the initiative, and be successful. An important pointer to the health of the army at this stage is that large numbers of Sciri, who were taken as prisoners of war, were dispersed as individual colonists to farm the land over a large region. There was no need to base them in a frontier area as a block source of warriors, or to recruit them individually into the army. Recruitment and army strength were not problems.

Apart from this Hunnic incursion, the main security threat during the first twenty years of the fifth century seems to have been internal, from the Isaurians. Their raids were very extensive, reaching even into Syria; a new military command had to be created in 413 to deal specifically with them (the *Comes Dioceseos Ponticae*), and many cities in Asia Minor received permanent garrisons for the first time.

Following the success against the Huns in 408, the Eastern army went on to some further success in several wars, notably against Persia (twice, in 421/2 and 441/2), and against John the usurper in the West. It also mounted two unsuccessful expeditions against the Vandals. Between 431 and 434 Aspar led an Eastern expedition against Vandal expansion in Africa, but was seriously defeated. In the Vandal wars we start to see a pattern developing in which the army was unable to face war on two fronts at once. There was also considerable opportunism on the part of the enemies of the empire, suggesting that their intelligence gathering was at least as effective, and probably more so, than that of the Romans.[24]

After a series of cities had been taken by Attila in 441, the main field armies faced the Huns in open battle for the first time. Commanded by Aspar, Areobindus and Arnegisclus (indicating both Praesental armies and that of Thrace), the Romans lost a series of battles and the war of manoeuvre: they were forced into the Chersonese peninsula and cut off from Constantinople, and finally defeated again there. From the accounts, it seems that there was no single decisive encounter, with the whole army being destroyed; rather, a failure to match the mobility of the Huns, or bring them to battle in conditions favourable to the Roman army.

When Attila invaded in 447, the army went out again to face the Huns near Marcianople. Defeat in 443 had not determined the empire against open battle, although the field command had passed to Arnegisclus. He was defeated and killed, but not before inflicting serious casualties on the Huns. Despite being master of the military situation there was no move by Attila against Constantinople, and an attack on Greece was halted at Thermopylae. Although the army had lost again, it is possible that the victory achieved by Attila had been at significant cost: within two years a treaty had been concluded which reversed some of the more onerous conditions previously enforced on the empire. In 451, a Hun raid in Illyricum was defeated by Ardaburius, Aspar's son, and by 452 (admittedly after Attila's defeat by Aetius), the empire was confident enough to take the initiative and attack Hunnic territory north of the Danube.

The collapse of Attila's empire on his death in 453 provided both opportunities and problems for Marcian. He settled large numbers of the dispersing barbarian subject tribes in the Balkans. This extensive pattern of settlement was partly a considered policy response to the newly independent barbarians, and had far-reaching consequences. There was a steady reconsolidation of the Balkan provinces, and archaeological evidence points to the reoccupation and refortification of both cities and military bases (often in practice the same thing) after the devastation of the Attila years.[25]

Under Leo (see Chapter 12), the Gothic and other barbarian groups began to flex their muscles, but initially only against each other. Political struggles at court were reflected in the series of appointments to senior military posts, in which Aspar and his family, other Germanic generals (such as Anagast, son of Arnegisclus who had fought Attila, and Jordanes, son of John, the earlier Vandal *Magister* of Thrace) and the Isaurian faction all competed for influence. The military high command seems to have become a political prize, argued over by various factions in the face of an emperor who was neither so weak that he could be totally dominated, nor strong enough to take complete control himself. Leo may well have encouraged this position so that no faction could dominate, but the situation only bred confusion and competition in place of a community of interest in the stability of government.

Leo did carry through a number of initiatives, but these amounted to limited restructuring rather than extensive or considered reforms. He reorganised the frontier commands in the Orient, breaking them down into a series of smaller sectors along most of their length, and establishing new commands against the Isaurian raiders in the interior; and he mounted the great campaign of 468 against the Vandals. The Vandal campaign was a massive undertaking, which involved an army of 100,000 men and a huge fleet crewed by 300,000 to transport them to their objective.[26]

Around 80 per cent of the manpower, and the costs, came from the Eastern empire, and even its financial resources were exhausted by this level of expenditure, which was double the annual establishment costs of the entire army. The economic and military infrastructure had been in good condition, supporting one of the biggest military expeditions ever mounted by the empire. Unfortunately, the dramatic failure of the expedition damaged the army almost as much as the economy.

Although the surviving armies continued to perform adequately when well led, as when Anagast defeated Dengizich, son of Attila, in 469, developing factionalism clearly weakened central authority and encouraged the emergence of a military threat from the Goths. When Aspar and his elder son were murdered by Leo, leadership of those opposed to the Isaurians and other factions was seized as an opportunity by Gothic leaders who may already have held significant military commands. With the murder of Aspar, a mainstay of political stability was removed: although he had clearly sought personal and dynastic advancement, he had not resorted to direct military force to achieve it. The Isaurians, Leo's relatives and especially the Goths had no such compunctions, and armies became part of the power struggles at court again. One consequence was that Roman military power was splintered into the competing factions, and the ill-led armies with their confused loyalties could not effectively maintain opposition to the Goths.

Despite the fact that Aspar's successor, Zeno, was later to remove the independent power of the Goths from the equation in the East, their methods reveal much about the structure and strength of his army. When Theoderic Strabo, leading his Ostrogothic federates, demanded the command of the Praesental armies he was seeking a seat at the table where real decisions were made. He could already dominate militarily outside Constantinople through his own Gothic army. Similarly, his demand for command of two units of the imperial guard, the *scholae*, was a bid for a status position within the Roman hierarchy at court. The payments he demanded suggest that he commanded a Gothic army of 13,000 men and, when later combined with the army of the Pannonian Gothic leader, Theoderic the Amal, the joint Gothic forces numbered over 20,000.

This suggests why political status appointments were so significant, apart from the money they brought with them: both Gothic leaders could dominate the immediate military picture, with a force equivalent to a Roman field army, but they could not tackle the whole military force of the empire in combat. Additional political leverage was required to ensure that the Goths did not face a united Roman opposition, and to assist in the accommodation they sought with the empire all along. Gothic interests remained much the same as always: secure territory, with plentiful supplies of food and money to maintain their followers, although their leaders may also have become interested in the status and political games played out at court.[27]

It has been suggested that Zeno may have been responsible for some significant reforms to the army, but it is difficult to see where in his troubled reign there was sufficient time to implement any considered changes. One change which is identifiable is recorded for 472, when legislation insisted that the *probatoria* (enrolment papers) of all soldiers should no longer be issued by the offices of the *Duces* and *Magistri* as previously, but only directly by the emperor. This falls into a pattern of increasing centralisation of authority over the army, bringing soldiers' appointments under the same control as other imperial posts. The reform should also be seen against the background of rivalry and competition for the throne that marked Zeno's reign, and may reflect concern about local rather than imperial loyalties being cultivated.[28]

By contrast, under Anastasius' lengthy reign (491–518) there was the opportunity for considerable administrative reform. This was also a period where the army saw major action, not only against a range of foreign opponents, but also in civil wars. These conflicts provide an opportunity to measure the success of the changes Anastasius made to the army, and to assess the legacy for his successors.

The first challenge faced by Anastasius was that posed by the long-running Isaurian problem. The Praesental armies were sent against them, along with federate Gothic and Hunnic forces. This very considerable force demonstrates that from the outset of his reign Anastasius was in complete control of the army. A decisive battle was fought at Cotyaeum in Phrygia, where the main military might of the Isaurians was destroyed, followed by progressive siege campaigns. These showed a thoroughness of purpose and a competence in the field which demonstrated the authority and efficiency of imperial command and military purpose in the new reign.

Many Isaurians were transplanted to Thrace in the aftermath of this war, and they continued to serve in numbers in the army, whether recruited from there or from their original homeland, but not in high commands. Despite the departure of Theoderic and his federates for Italy in 488, there were still Gothic warriors available to the Roman army. The presence of Huns is also significant, since their former territories north of the Danube were now being conquered by the Bulgars, a similar type of military opponent to the Huns. This changing pattern was similar in ways to the early fifth century, when different Hun groups were free to take service with the Roman army. They continued to be a frequent addition to Roman forces into the middle of the sixth century, either as individual recruits or as small federate bands.[29]

Despite their success against the Isaurians (or perhaps because they were distracted by that conflict) the armies were not successful against the Bulgars. In 493, the *Magister Militum* of Thrace, Julian, was killed in battle against them. We have no evidence for a major military disaster at this point, however, and there is no further mention of conflict with the Bulgars until 499, when a much more serious defeat was suffered. Aristus, *Magister Militum* of Illyricum, lost 4,000 men from his army of 15,000 facing a Bulgar invasion. This was a major defeat involving a full field army. It may be significant that the Roman army with the smallest proportion of cavalry (Illyricum) lost decisively to an enemy force based on mobile light cavalry, but in any case it seems to have determined the empire against similar direct confrontation for some time. When the Bulgars again raided in force in 502 (when a major Persian war threatened in the East) they were not opposed by a field army, but by a reversion to the policy of holding fortified garrison points in cities and military bases.[30]

The threat posed by the Sassanid Persian empire was of a different nature and order. The Persians maintained a standing army, with a command structure (even if held by the hereditary nobility), military bases and frontier defensive systems manned by regular troops. In 502 Shah Khavad I launched a successful invasion of the East. The war of 502 to 506 provides us with details of the size of the Roman army at this point. The invasion was in overwhelming force, and as always the Praesental armies were required to face it; the army of the Orient could not resist on its own. The empire temporarily lost Theodosiopolis, Martyropolis, and Amida, after an eighty-day siege. In 503, Anastasius sent the two Praesental armies (totalling 40,000 men) to join the army of the Orient, which deployed 12,000 men. Celer, the *Magister Officiorum*, also set out from Constantinople with a force, which included some of the imperial guards units. This was said to be the largest army ever assembled on the eastern frontier, and exceptional efforts were made to supply it and keep it in the field. The city of Edessa was turned into a huge bakery, supplying rations for at least 50,000 men.[31]

The Persians apparently had an army of roughly equal size, and in 503 no significant progress was made. Khavad only retired from Roman territory, after heavily defeating two of the Roman divisions in separate battles, because of an invasion of Persia by Hephtalites. The lack of Roman success was partly due to the difficulty of co-ordinating such a huge army, and in 504 Anastasius appointed Celer to overall command, with five subordinate generals. He also received reinforcements.[32]

In addition to the regular army there were Gothic and other federates from Europe, and Lazicans from east of the Black Sea, adding to the size of the Roman army. In 504 this force defeated the Persians in several engagements, re-took Amida and invaded the Persian heartland in Mesopotamia. This huge effort had brought into play over half of the total field forces of the empire – over 50,000 regulars (perhaps as many as 80,000 at the high point) from a total of probably less than 100,000 following defeats in the Balkans. It is clear, however, that the empire retained the ability to deploy and support an army on this scale, with the same command structure and organisation as that of the army of the early fifth century.

Fortification was a major concern for Anastasius. Although most attention has been focused on Justinian's later efforts, many of these were refortifications or additions to cities or forts built or fortified by Anastasius. This picture is now being expanded by archaeological evidence for building in many of the Danubian frontier fortifications under Anastasius, and military developments in eastern frontier fortifications well into the sixth century. The Long Walls, one day's march west of Constantinople, are the clearest example of this emphasis on defence, marking a major investment in both their construction and subsequent manning of them an outer defence for the capital. This was not a simple policy of retrenchment, but part of a larger programme of investment in military defence in the face of considerable threats. The army was also reinforced, along with the built defences of the empire.[33]

Anastasius was responsible for very significant military reforms. In 498, he largely replaced issues of rations and equipment with cash payments, making military service a more attractive option for volunteer recruits. After 511, he again increased basic pay by translating the five-yearly donative marking his accession into annual payments. In 512, he banned the practice (standard since Diocletian) of branding recruits to identify them and prevent desertion, presumably on the basis that it was no longer a sufficient problem to warrant such treatment. Military service certainly became popular, with Justinian later being able to raise a complete new army of Armenia, 15,000 strong, to the *comitatenses* without any recruitment problems.[34]

One further element in the army that should be considered is the imperial guards division. This was organised as cavalry units 500 strong, known as *scholae*, of which there were seven in the East and five in the West. These elite troops provided the imperial bodyguard on campaign, and formed one of the few bodies of troops based in Constantinople throughout most of our period. A select group of forty chosen from their number, and known as *candidati*, were the immediate personal guard around the emperor. This group, along with the tribunes commanding the individual *scholae*, were very influential at court, and the power and status of these positions was much sought after. Many individuals from the *scholae* were absent from the capital and served as imperial agents, carrying out missions in the provinces; this situation arose after the emperors ceased to participate in field campaigns personally. Administratively, the *scholae* were under the authority of the *Magister Officiorum* (not the *Magistri Militum*), but in practical terms they were under the command of the *Comes Domesticorum*, the emperor's personal military chief-of-staff. By the reign of Zeno, they had become almost entirely ceremonial troops, although they continued to play a very significant role in the politics of the court and had a say in the appointment of new emperors when dynastic continuity faltered. As a result of the political factionalism of Leo's reign a new bodyguard, the *Excubitores*, was appointed in the mid-460s. Although only 300 strong they quickly became the senior elite detachment through imperial favouritism, and played important parts as representatives of the emperor. By the early sixth century they had overtaken the *scholae* as kingmakers.[35]

There is no indication from the command or other structures of the armies deployed by Anastasius (or indeed those later used by Justinian in his Persian and Vandal wars) that there had been any significant change to the nature of the late Roman army. Many units are known to have survived from their listing in the *Notitia* until the sixth century, and the policies of fortification and pay enhancement carried through by Anastasius are in keeping with many earlier traditions. The balance of infantry to cavalry was still at least 2:1 in campaign armies of the sixth century, and there seems to be little evidence of change to the basic form and structure of the army, or its methods of combat, from those of the army inherited by Arcadius at the end of the fourth century.

Anastasius built on the existing structure and its strengths without radical innovation. His reform of the terms of service in the army created the conditions in which the empire could defend itself against threats from the north and the east, and also go on the offensive. Anastasius had managed to put the finances of the empire onto a sound footing through an efficient reform of the taxation system, and he deployed the resulting wealth in bolstering the defences of the empire, both in manpower and fortifications. He left Justinian a legacy of a well-defended empire, with a strong and well-resourced army, and a full treasury to pay it.

9

IMPERIAL WEALTH AND EXPENDITURE

Cities were recognised in the classical world as the principal demonstrations of public wealth and sophistication. They were, unlike most modern cities, expressions of wealth rather than the source of it, and reflected the economic background and aspirations of their regions. The standard administrative unit of the empire, the *civitas*, was a territory administered by an urban centre. There were, of course, many other population centres such as small towns, market centres, villages, *vici* which formed around military bases, and so on.[1]

The East had always been much more urbanised, inheriting a strong Hellenic and Hellenistic legacy that had not been matched in the West, especially north of the Alps and Pyrenees. The Eastern cities flourished during the fifth and sixth centuries, despite some decline in places due to localised insecurity. However, in the West there was a general pattern of decline in the extent and urban functions of many cities, with a few exceptions in more secure areas.

In Gaul and Britain there was little change from the number of pre-conquest tribal territories to later *civitates*; cities developed as administrative centres, but wealth was not expressed through a more general urban development. Even Africa, the most urbanised part of the West, had only fifty-three cities under the early empire, and a few added later as colonies. Many other local population centres developed in Africa, often with bishops and some other trappings of civic life, but most were not substantial urban centres. In Italy the number of towns extended to several hundred, but again only a proportion of these were cities in the full sense of centres of local government, administration and an economic life beyond localised cultivation. The total number of cities in the West can only have run to a few hundred.

By contrast, in the Eastern empire over 1,000 cities are referred to. Anatolia, the eastern frontier provinces and Egypt were the most urbanised regions, although there were also over 200 cities in the fertile lowlands of Greece, Macedonia and Thrace. The urban hinterlands were very extensively and intensively exploited agriculturally, and the cities themselves reflected this through investment in public works and other expressions of civic well-being. After the mid-third century there was an apparent general decline in public building and inscriptions. However, flourishing urban life in the fifth and sixth centuries has been revealed archaeologically, even where we have limited historical references for the continuity of urban life and prosperity in this period.[2]

Economic and cultural life generally prospered in the cities of the East. There was official encouragement of the city level of government through the *honorati*, the major public figures such as bishops, city corn-buyers, etc. who came to take on most of the former curial duties. Cities were at least as likely to prosper under their patronage as in earlier periods. One-third of local tax revenues, and one-third of the rents from civic lands, were given back to cities by central government to spend on public works, buildings, defences, teachers, policing, etc., and so there was considerable value to having urban status. Any surplus over the fixed taxation remained with the city, and so there was an incentive for effective and positive financial management of the revenues of each urban area by these important local figures; this also helped to guarantee that tax targets were met, and the state received its due revenues.

There is limited evidence for the sort of shrinkage in urban populations, areas and defences in the East to mirror the decay exhibited in many Western cities during the fifth century. In the West, cities such as Arles and Marseilles, which show signs of robust economic, religious and political activity, were exceptions in this period. Many others were reduced from their fullest extent and shrank to defended refuges, with parts of former urban areas given over to agriculture or burial. Honorius, and later Valentinian III and Majorian, issued directions to return *curiales* and *collegiati* to their cities, since many had fled to rural estates to avoid obligations, or if they were craftsmen, had become peasants since they could not make a living in the cities. The flight of wealthy senators, followed by the lower ranks who shouldered the burdens of civic office, diminished the tax base and unbalanced the economic viability on which tradesmen and craftsmen relied. With their markets replaced by self-sufficiency on rural estates the economy of the cities went into sharp decline. These indications of urban decline are common in the West, but there was no equivalent contemporary legislation in the East, suggesting that it was not afflicted to the same extent by these problems.[3]

The relative lack of urbanisation in the West does not represent the whole economic picture. The balance of agricultural production was very significant. Some 95 per cent of total imperial revenue in this period was derived from taxation of the land; only 5 per cent was a result of taxation on trade and industry. This is not to deny the importance of trade: it was of great concern to the empire, and efforts were made to secure and expand the opportunities for trade, especially through the Red Sea corridor and across

119

the Euphrates line with Persia and the east. In certain status and exotic goods trade was enormously important, and provided the wealth of some areas with specialised interests (such as those concerned with the traffic in spices and aromatics with Yemen and other areas beyond the Red Sea; significantly the major trade opportunities were geographically in the East). The importance of this balance is not in the value that the empire and its inhabitants accorded to these items and to trade in them, but in the levels of taxable wealth that the empire could exploit and deploy to achieve its aims. For the empire as a whole, just like the great magnates of East and West, agricultural land was the most important and productive asset.[4]

The importance of the two major elements of the empire – agriculture and military effort – was summed up in this way:

> For there are two occupations that we consider most necessary to the stability and permanence of the nation: agriculture, which supports and increases the soldiers; and military service, which maintains and protects the farmers. And we consider these two occupations to take precedence over all the others.[5]

Some Western provinces were very productive agriculturally, and contributed large surpluses of goods and taxes to imperial coffers, especially in Africa. Great estates, whether imperially controlled or in private hands, became a notable feature of the late Roman landscape, with grandiose villas at their centres. The nobles prospered, but this reflected a concern with personal wealth and expressions of it, not a more widely based level of prosperity. There were also some signs of agricultural decline in the West, such as disaffected and dispossessed peasants, and abandoned farmland, but towards the end of the fourth century the state generally still had sufficient taxable resources to carry out its tasks, maintaining an army roughly equal to that of the East.[6]

There was considerable regional variation in the relative and absolute wealth of the various dioceses and provinces of the Eastern empire, including a clear difference in the exploitable wealth and assets of the European and Asiatic regions. The Balkan provinces contained limited areas of fertile, exploitable agricultural land, mainly in the coastal and low-lying plains of Thrace, Macedonia, Thessaly and more restricted pockets around the classical cities of Greece. The other major region of low-lying agricultural land was the Danube flood plain, the use of which was distorted by the presence of armies in garrison and external threats to the security of the region.

Some 75 to 80 per cent of the Balkan peninsula consisted of largely unexploited mountain terrain, which was sparsely inhabited until modern times. Almost all of this area was forested, with rough seasonal pasture its main agricultural value. Its only wealth lay in timber, and occasional precious metal deposits. The former was significant in the coastal region of Dalmatia, but elsewhere was only locally useful due to transport difficulties. The mineral assets were exploited, but this did not lead to a significant tax base beyond the minerals themselves. The population seems to have been mainly a dispersed one, based on locally subsistent mixed farming. However, there was room for expansion, as the settlement of large numbers of barbarians at various times demonstrates; the feeding of federate groups could easily be achieved by the region under imperial direction, even if they could not manage to feed themselves by living off the land. At times of significant barbarian disruption the Balkan provinces could have problems feeding themselves and their resident armies, and in paying taxes. On such occasions as the great Hunnic and Bulgar raids taxes had to be remitted and supplies brought in, but in normal circumstances the region could function as a profitable part of the empire, sustaining itself and making a net contribution to imperial funds.

Cities were almost all confined to the Black Sea and Greek coasts. The exception to this was the network of fortress cities along the Danube corridor, and along the major roads connecting the frontier with the hinterland and East with West. However, these were always fairly limited in numbers compared to those in the agriculturally wealthy regions to the southeast. Apart from an early Roman phase of veteran colony foundation there was very little new urbanism introduced throughout the Roman period other than the occasional favouritism shown to their birthplaces by new emperors. Overall, a level of urbanism well below that of the Asiatic provinces was the standard pattern in the Balkan peninsula. In the two provinces of Thrace and Dacia Ripensis there are over 450 villages or similar sized settlements known from archaeological and documentary sources. This suggests a large, but dispersed and non-urbanised population suitable for manpower recruitment and localised economic activity, but not major generators of agricultural or trading surpluses to cull for taxation.

Anatolia formed a geographical contrast. It consisted of a relatively wealthy agricultural coastal plain, with a concentration of cities around the west and south coasts especially, and a fairly barren inner steppe or plateau split by very inhospitable mountain ranges. The plains supported the full range of agriculture, but the uplands were restricted to limited areas of arable with the majority of land given over to rough grazing.

From the fourth to the sixth centuries this region was not seriously affected by warfare. The lack of conflict, large markets in Constantinople and other cities, and the operation of the public transport system across the main routes through Anatolia combined to encourage the extension of exploitation of the landscape until at least the mid-sixth century. The operation of the heavy public post system (*cursus publicus*) was especially important in the inland areas of Anatolia, and other regions remote from large markets. Initially it provided the means of transporting goods to markets or to fulfil tax in kind requirements. Later, produce from these regions was sold direct to the post, both supplying it with its requirements and providing cash for producers to pay taxes while avoiding the ruinous costs of long-distance land transport.[7]

In Syria and Palestine, in addition to evidence of urban prosperity, there was a very strong village settlement pattern in the fifth and sixth centuries. Much of the exploitation focused on olive cultivation, but all forms of agriculture featured in the regional economy. Settlement and agricultural development in the Golan, the Negev and other parts of Palestine reached a peak in the late fifth and early sixth centuries, with irrigation schemes bringing new land into productive use. A similar pattern can be seen in an expansion of settlement into the limestone uplands of northern Syria: the hills east of Antioch saw the development of a similar village pattern, based apparently on olive cultivation in smaller areas of fertile soil which had not previously been thought worth the effort.

Long periods of peace in this region encouraged expansion, and inscriptions and other archaeological evidence point to a wealth and confidence in the fifth and early sixth centuries. The presence of very considerable garrison forces throughout the eastern provinces also encouraged the local economy. Investment in new land was considerable, with olives in particular requiring a long period of establishment before any returns were gained. This suggests a confident, longer-term development of the agricultural economy rather than a short-term response to particular circumstances. The extent of this pattern across most of the East also suggests that we are looking at an economy in long-term growth, and not at localised developments.

These villages were not just small agglomerations of rural settlers. Some included a range of civic buildings such as churches, baths, roads, markets, etc. They were not planned or planted settlements, but developed naturally over a period of time. They were mainly distinguished from small towns by their lack of independent civic government rather than by the scale or wealth of the settlements themselves. Well-built stone houses were common, and the presence of churches or monastic establishments may indicate an alternative form of local leadership from the usual civic pattern. We can also see this happening in the cities, where bishops were increasingly taking on many of the roles previously exercised by *curiales*.[8]

Egypt was the major source of wealth in the East. It was the single most important producer in agricultural terms, mainly arable. Some surviving figures for agricultural activity show over 90 per cent of cultivated land devoted to arable production, with the remainder split between vineyards, orchards and other limited activities. Consequently it was the wealthiest area in terms of the tax yield it produced. It was also hugely important as the source of grain for distribution to the citizens of Constantinople, who were prone to riot at any sign of a delay in the food dole. The Nile delta was divided into numerous city territories, generally with very fertile and productive hinterlands, with the exception of Alexandria which was one of the very few cities in antiquity to survive on its position as an urban centre rather than the focus of a territory.

Egypt was free from significant military threats from the late third century until the beginning of the seventh. Despite this, we should not assume all land was exploited equally: there are references to land going out of agricultural production in Egypt as well as in more threatened parts of the empire, although here the reasons seem to be mainly economic rather than military in origin.[9]

This analysis of agricultural wealth into the main four regions of the East indicates that their relative importance in production was as follows: the Balkans were least important in terms of significant surpluses; Anatolia and the Orient were both wealthy in equal measure; and Egypt was by far the most important, contributing perhaps a third of the total production of the East.

The area of the Eastern empire that was the only significant drain on both tax and agricultural production was the capital. On its foundation Constantine had allocated a grain dole for 80,000 inhabitants, but by the fifth century it is likely that its population had risen to around 500,000. The only other cities in the East that rivalled it were Antioch and Alexandria, although they were significantly smaller in population terms. Rome had been the greatest city of the empire, with perhaps up to one million inhabitants at its peak (in a period when the total population of Roman Britain may have been of the order of two million), but the calamities of the fifth century gradually reduced this level so that it may not have been significantly greater than that of Constantinople, if at all.[10]

Constantinople had a huge distorting effect on the economy of the whole East, not just its immediate hinterland. It is estimated that one-third of the total production of the East went to sustain the capital and the imperial bureaucracy which it housed; significantly that is the proportion of total production which Egypt was responsible for, demonstrating the vital role which it played. Egypt provided the equivalent of 800,000 solidi in grain for the feeding of Constantinople, and at least as much again in cash as taxation, suggesting that Egypt alone could support the whole apparatus of the capital, from feeding the population to funding the administration of the empire. The loss of Egypt would be a disaster, as the empire was later to discover.

Population, settlement density and site numbers all seem to have been on the increase across the East, with the possible exception of the Balkans. The patterns described above indicate a growing population that both required new land to farm and provided the outlets for the resulting produce. Sufficient wealth was generated for a high standard of private and public building: many churches were built across the East, replacing other forms of public building as expressions of wealth and patronage. The view that the peasantry and lower classes were suffering and declining as a result of oppressive taxation and other impositions does not seem to be supported by the growing archaeological evidence for a flourishing economy in the East.

Barbarian threats and manpower availability are only part of the picture when we assess the state of the economy, and warn against a simple view of abandoned farmland (*agri deserti*). Much of this land may have fallen into a category where the legislative and taxation thrust was attempting to force expansion of agriculture, or at least maintain it, in areas which would simply not be considered profitable enough to merit the investment of time, money and effort required to exploit them. We may be seeing, in the repeated legislation tying local populations to the land, a failing struggle to keep the agricultural – and therefore taxation – base as high as possible, and certainly above the level which would normally be sustainable in market terms. There may also have been problems in enforcing full cultivation of public or imperial lands which lacked the incentive of private owners to maximise their productivity.

There is other evidence for the imperial government attempting to maintain the viability of cities and agricultural lands. Engineering operations to protect cities from periodic catastrophic flooding or to improve their surrounding territories were undertaken by Anastasius and Justinian. Most of the difficulties referred to were episodic violent weather extremes, usually resulting in flash-flooding and loss of agricultural land through erosion. Conversely this created new areas of potentially rich land down-hill and down-river, but this was usually marshy and could only be opened up for agriculture by large-scale (i.e. state-led) drainage and other schemes. Most of this happened in Anatolia, with little evidence from the Balkans; this may reflect weather patterns, but it may also have had a basis in the over-exploitation of agricultural lands in Anatolia, leading to the conditions in which the soil was more vulnerable to erosion.

Overall, even in the concerned reigns of Anastasius and Justinian, there was probably a net loss of good agricultural lands in Anatolia (and on a more localised scale elsewhere). The works carried out indicate an imperial concern for the economic well-being of wealthy parts of the empire. Partly this may have been the expression of public beneficence expected from and practised by a good emperor, but it may well also have reflected an appreciation of the value of these productive communities to imperial finances.[11]

Wealth, whether personal or imperial, was usually expressed in terms of gold, either by weight or as coinage. Despite the collection of revenue in kind for long periods, the currency was very important as the main mechanism for the flow of imperial revenue and expenditure. The Constantinian introduction of the gold *solidus*, at seventy-two to the pound of weight, had established a secure basis for the coinage, and it was the foundation of all imperial coinage (and that of the barbarian successor kingdoms in the West) for several centuries. By the end of the fifth century silver had become essentially a ceremonial issue, and was acknowledged as bullion by weight, not as coinage.[12]

Copper coinage had mainly been put into circulation through the annual payment of the army in this medium, and through the buying of gold with copper by the state to meet its own needs. During the fourth century the importance of payment in kind, through the issues of rations, weapons, uniforms, etc., gradually increased, and the value of the copper-based salary declined through inflationary pressures (the state continually put copper into circulation as payment, but collected none in taxation – a well-recognised inflationary mechanism now, but not in a period when the value of a coin was thought to be intrinsically linked to its weight). Annual pay for the soldiers, then an insignificant part of their total remuneration, ended in the late fourth century, and by the start of the fifth century there was little copper minted in the West. The East soon followed this trend.[13]

During the fifth century the gradual commutation of taxation from goods to gold meant that the state no longer needed copper issues to buy gold solidi for its own purposes, and so lost much of its interest in them. Occasional attempts to limit the inflationary spiral of the copper coinage do, however, suggest some recognition of the problem and the difficulties it created for the general population, even if this was not recognition of the mechanisms behind the problem. The mint at Rome continued to produce copper, but Honorius legislated to reduce the denominations issued; only the smallest, the *nummus*, survived, at a rate of 7,200 to the *solidus*. This was the basis of copper coinage in both East and West throughout most of the fifth century, despite short-lived modifications by Theodosius II, Leo and Zeno.

Anastasius was responsible for the successful reform of the copper coinage of the East, but this was clearly based on an earlier successful reform in the West. In Ostrogothic Italy and Vandal Africa large copper issues, called the *follis* and based on multiples of the *nummus* (in Italy, forty *nummi* to the *follis*), were introduced along with fractional denominations (at twenty, ten and five *nummi*). In 498 John the Paphlagonian, Anastasius' *Comes sacrarum largitionum*, introduced a parallel series to this, but struck at half the weight of the Italian series. This was revised to double weight issues in 512, and remained generally stable until the middle of the sixth century. The inflationary mechanisms had not completely disappeared, but the major elements had gone and this reform was strongly appreciated by the general population. No attempt, however, was made to copy the silver issues which had also been re-introduced in the Western kingdoms; this may have been due to a greater stability in the relative valuation of Eastern copper coinage to gold issues.

The basis for introduction and circulation of coinage was state revenue, and expenditure of it. The army was the largest expense, but another major role was played by the public post. This was a huge network of staging-posts, collection points for goods and taxes, administrative centres, etc., and was probably second only to the army as an economic mechanism. The third mechanism was the flow of payments through the bureaucracy into the wider pattern of circulation and back to the treasuries in taxation. Only in the most urbanised and densely populated areas was trade a significant element in the currency cycle, from minting, through distribution to tax collection and re-minting. Much local taxation was collected by cities from their hinterlands in kind.

During the fourth century most imperial taxation had been translated into requisitions in kind. This began to change again early in the fifth century in the West, but more slowly in the East. By the 420s most of the tax assessment of Africa was in gold, rather than in kind, possibly as a result of a greater need for money to pay the surviving armies in Europe, instead of goods which exceeded the requirements of the garrison in Africa and were expensive to transport. In Italy, along with the rest of the West, the land tax was commuted to gold by 458 at the latest, despite the presence of the main field army in garrison; this suggests that pay was now entirely in gold/silver, and not in issues of rations, etc.

A comprehensive change to taxation in gold did not occur in the East until Anastasius, and he was careful to specify the circumstances in which requirements levied in kind should still be used to supply the army where possible. Tax was assessed in kind, but then translated into gold at a combination of fixed rates and locally variable prices. As a former administrative official Anastasius seems to have taken a very close and detailed interest in the workings of the taxation system, and surrounded himself with able advisers. The basis for taxation was kept under review, with returns of ration strengths of units required, pay monitored, and fees within the command structure controlled (soldiers paid a fraction of their remuneration as a 'fee' to their officers), all so that the annual indiction could be accurately assessed and revenue controlled. The troubles of previous reigns may have limited the financial reviews possible earlier in the fifth century, but Anastasius does seem to have taken a deliberate and long-term approach to regulation and modification of the whole tax, revenue and expenditure system. The resulting financial well-being of the Eastern empire was not accidental, and can largely be attributed to the good management carried out during his long reign.

By the early fifth century the standard annual tax level brought in a surplus; most emperors managed to form a reserve, and tax levels were occasionally reduced. In 424 Theodosius II reduced the taxes of Achaia to one-third of their previous level, and those for the rest of the Macedonian diocese to one-half. This seems to have been a permanent reduction, still being recorded as such under Justinian. Although he was prudent in the remission of taxation in general, Anastasius also displayed generosity (and the success of his taxation policy in general) in reducing the most oppressive assessment for land taxation, the *capitatio*, or poll tax. This was levied on all individuals regardless of the extent of their property, weighing most heavily on the rural poor; the *capitatio* was reduced in Asiana and Pontica by 25 per cent of its former level in 513, and our sources claim that Anastasius wanted to go on and abolish it altogether.[14]

The gathering of the land tax was a twice or three times yearly affair, mainly in autumn and spring, to allow the gathering and sale of crops to raise the payments. This seasonal basis for personal and public funds meant that the empire suffered a liquidity problem: unless significant surpluses had been put aside in earlier years it was extremely difficult to raise large sums in the short term. This had led to emergency measures, such as the melting down of statues and other treasures, raising loans from the church, adulteration of the silver coinage or – most unpopularly – raising emergency taxes over and above the land tax. Part of the unpopularity may well have originated in the difficulties involved in paying when the wealth of the individuals involved may also have been dependent on seasonal incomes.

The role of the Praetorian Prefect of the East was very significant. As the main financial and legal officer his role in gathering and holding revenue became increasingly important. Most of the tax yield (from the land taxes) flowed into his own treasury, rather than that of the *sacrarum largitionum* (who collected taxation from gold and silver mines, revenues from the imperial estates, and the precious metal taxes in general). By the time of the Vandal expedition in 468 half of the campaign funding came from the praetorian treasury.

There were also non-land-based taxes on the senatorial and curial classes, and on trade (of all kinds, including prostitution). The tax that seems to have hit hardest was the *chrysargon*, or *collatio lustralis*, imposed on all trade and industrial activities. This was represented by contemporaries as an extremely harsh tax, but it seems to have raised quite insignificant amounts in relation to land taxation, and was abolished by Anastasius. Anastasius also introduced a new office of tax supervisor, the *vindex*. These officials had authority over each city to manage their revenues and expenditure and to monitor the work of the tax collector in each area. The measure was deeply resented by the cities, but was part of a general pattern of regulation of fees paid to officials at all levels (within the army as well as the civil bureaucracy) and control of exemptions from and exploitation of the taxation system.

The equivalent taxes on *curiales* and senators were progressively less onerous. The curial tax, the *aurum coronarium*, seems to have been a fairly severe periodic imposition on a class that was in gradual decline, especially in the West. The occasional senatorial tax, *aurum oblaticium*, was supplemented by an annual property tax, the *collatio glebalis*, which was levied at different rates on four different grades of the senatorial order. The *glebalis* tax was abandoned by the end of Marcian's reign. There was also an occasional levy on the *honorati*, holders of honorary titles of *comes* and above, which was intended to supply horses and recruits for the army. It was usually commuted to gold, and was only levied in extreme circumstances, such as the wars under Stilicho.

The most extreme demand ever on either senatorial order was for 216,000 solidi from the entire Western senate, the equivalent of less than one senatorial annual income, and this was exceptionally high. The whole basis of the social hierarchy was that status brought privilege, and that privilege enabled the avoidance of obligations, essentially economic dues, which the masses were to be left to bear. This meant that the part of the population most able to pay for imperial functions, and responsible for implementing them, was likely to avoid paying most of the taxation required to do so. This position was exaggerated in the West by the holding of senior offices by those with little interest in pursuing taxation vigorously.

Olympiodorus records that wealthy Roman senatorial households had annual incomes of 288,000 solidi, plus revenues in kind which yielded the equivalent of one-third more again. Although there had always been very wealthy senatorial families in the West, the divergence between the majority of the order and a group of super-rich became more extreme during the fourth century. Marriage alliances between families, the exploitation of senior offices for profit, and advantages gained from the losses of lesser nobility in the many wars all enabled the accumulation of ever greater fortunes and land-holdings into fewer hands. Even a medium-grade Roman household could anticipate an income of 72,000 to 108,000 solidi. Lesser households still had incomes of 25,000 to 40,000 solidi.

At the upper end of personal expenditure we know of Western nobles paying vast sums for games to celebrate their own or family preferment as magistrates. Symmachus, a prominent social and literary figure, although not of the wealthiest class, is known to have spent 144,000 solidi to celebrate the occasion of his son's praetorship. Maximus spent 288,000 solidi for his son's games in 411. Such spending was non-productive, being intended to demonstrate wealth and status through conspicuous display; the empire did not really benefit. Later in the East, under Marcian, expenditure by office holders was specifically redirected from this sort of display to more functional targets: rather than games they were expected to pay for the upkeep of the aqueducts of Constantinople.

Although this great wealth was not usually liquid, lying in land and other goods, it does represent a huge difference from the individual wealth of Eastern figures. A lesser Roman household had the income of the wealthiest groups in Constantinople. The highest-ranking figures in the Eastern senate, the consuls, could expect an income of about 72,000 solidi a year, and a law of Zeno fixed the fee payable by recipients of this honour at only 100 pounds of gold, or 7,200 solidi. In contrast to the huge figures paid for games at Rome, the highest sum we know paid at Constantinople by a Praetor to celebrate his appointment was 1,000 pounds of silver, i.e. only 4,000 solidi. Games in Constantinople are generally recorded as costing amounts in silver, as opposed to gold in the West. When the *aurum oblaticium* was collected, the Roman senate paid 3,000 pounds in gold, and the senate of Constantinople paid the same weight, but in silver (about one-eighteenth of the sum paid in the West).[15]

There were senators in the East who were not wealthy: individuals turned down the preferment of senatorial rank due to their inability to pay the taxes which would arise from it. The chief clerks of the public and private treasuries were acknowledged as meriting senatorial rank through tenure of their offices. However, in 428, after petitioning and failing to secure exemption from the *collatio glebalis*, the senatorial property tax, they renounced the honour only a few years after obtaining it. This was not entirely new: in 393 Theodosius had created a fourth tier of the senatorial order which was only obliged to pay seven solidi per annum for the *follis* (as the tax was commonly known), and beyond this permitted the option of renouncing the rank and with it the obligation to even this level of payment. Many of these poorer senators were those who had achieved distinction as a result of their service, either as officers from the lower military ranks, or as decurions or retired civil servants. Entry to the senatorial order was a much more open possibility in the East, where service was rewarded in this way, than in the West where offices were frequently occupied by those who already held such rank, and were only fulfilling a status-led career as a sideline from their already prominent social position. Wealth, professional careers and status were therefore much more widely spread in the East, with a resultant identification of the interests of the state with those of the individuals, in contrast with the detached elitism of the Western aristocracy.

In the East a much more responsible approach to taxation of the higher orders in society was followed than in the West, with better management even where remissions of taxation were agreed. Arrears of taxation were often written off, but in very different circumstances in East and West. In 414 arrears going back to 368 were written off in the East, since it was very unlikely that they could be successfully retrieved; similarly, bad debts were written off in 433, when those of 408–28 were abandoned. However, when pressed financially by Hunnic demands in 430, Antiochus, the Praetorian Prefect, attacked such privileges, which tended to be to the advantage of the wealthy who could defer payments until they were no longer pursued; the poor had to pay up or suffer more immediate consequences. He reclaimed one-third of all rebates agreed since 395, and reduced the level of all rebates agreed since 378. In 443 another round of rebates was reclaimed at the same time as a specific levy in gold on senators; a storm of protest followed and the new measures were abandoned in 444, but the earlier measures of Antiochus were confirmed. In contrast in the West, when Valentinian III married in 438, he remitted all arrears up to 436, and again in 450 he remitted all arrears up to 447, under senatorial pressure. Majorian was later even more generous in remitting past taxes as he desperately sought senatorial support. In the East, tax arrears were enforced when the Hun pressures demanded; in the West, arrears were remitted in a state of even greater military emergency.[16]

In the mid-fifth-century financial crisis of the Western empire, when land taxes were in sharp decline, attempts were made to maintain revenue in other ways: in 444 Valentinian III introduced a new sales tax, the *siliquaticum*, a twenty-fourth of the value of goods sold. Prior to this, in 440 and 441, Maximus, the Praetorian Prefect of Italy, cancelled various exemptions which were being used as tax avoidance measures (such as buying imperial lands, which were tax free to the emperor, and still claiming the exemptions), and abolished other exemptions from *munera sordida* – the duties to share in public works: '[it is] essential for all to share in repair of military roads, manufacturing of arms, rebuilding of fortifications, production of military supplies and defence of the empire'.[17] It is unlikely that this had much impact on the Western senatorial class.

In the East, the exemptions for those who had acquired imperial lands were abolished as early as 424 and, despite pressures in several reigns, there were no significant new taxes introduced on a permanent basis. Occasional emergency measures were taken to meet specific needs (such as Hunnic subsidies), but it was not until Justinian that any significant new tax was imposed.

The levels of corruption, officially sanctioned or not, which skimmed off a proportion of the taxes actually gathered, were also radically different in East and West. In 458 in Italy the perquisite for tax officials was regulated at two solidi per *iugum* of land assessed; at the end of the fifth century in the East the same benefit was fixed (by Anastasius, as part of his general programme of control of these official 'fees') at one *siliqua*, or one forty-eighth of the Western level. Majorian had increased the level of fees in the West so that they stood at sixty times the Eastern rate. It is no surprise that, when this figure is compared to the standard tax valuation of seven solidi per *iugum*, the costs of collection amounted to at least 25 per cent of total notional revenue in the West.[18]

The total Eastern imperial income derived from these resources is uncertain. Estimates range from an annual income of five million solidi to well over 10 million. Total land tax revenue each year might be in the order of three or four million solidi, although one figure suggests Egypt alone paid over 2.5 million solidi in gold. Added to this would be the value of the other, non-land taxes in gold, plus those in goods, such as the grain levy for Constantinople and elsewhere (there was still considerable collection in kind in major garrison areas, such as Thrace and Pontica, to feed the armies), plus the imperial estate rents and other income from customs dues, etc. Given the balance of contributions to the Vandal expedition of 468 from the different treasuries, we should double the figure above to reach a total revenue figure for the East, i.e. some seven to eight million solidi as a minimum, and potentially some three to four million more.[19]

The generally steady nature and pattern of taxation throughout our period indicate that sources of revenue were fairly constant, and by implication so was the amount raised. There may have been a slow and steady climb, due to a gradually growing population and agricultural base, but the potential revenues available to any one emperor were probably not very significantly different from reign to reign.

Marcian left a reserve of over seven million solidi after only seven years in power, although some of that may have been derived from his own inheritance from Theodosius II. This was achieved in a period of considerable turmoil, although he did not have to pay the high levels of subsidy to the Huns that had afflicted Theodosius II in his later years. Specific tax measures had been introduced by Theodosius II, in the face of strong senatorial opposition, to meet the demands of the Huns, suggesting that there was a limited surplus in the system following the African expeditions and other conflicts. Marcian did resort to melting down statues to raise urgently needed funds, but the figures suggests that even under pressure from barbarians, and after carrying on several wars including costly overseas campaigns, the East was steadily accumulating a small surplus in the early and mid-fifth century. However, the nature of most revenue as a seasonally derived land tax made the immediate raising of large amounts difficult.

Leo managed almost to bankrupt the empire with his extravagantly wasteful Vandal expedition, costing some 7.4 million solidi. The 'extra' cost of the expedition over normal pay, etc., may have doubled the military budget. There were severe financial exactions, including confiscations of property, to try to meet costs in the aftermath of this debacle. It took a long time to recover any sort of reserve after this, especially given the additional demands faced by Leo and Zeno from the Isaurians and the two Gothic groups for cash subsidies. Zeno began the systematic sale of offices in an attempt to raise funds, charging 100 pounds of gold (7,200 solidi) for a consulship. Despite these pressures both emperors did manage to meet their various financial obligations, and so – with some extreme measures – the budget could still be balanced and current costs covered by revenue.[20]

Anastasius accumulated a reserve of twenty-three million solidi over twenty-seven years, despite three major wars and considerable other expenditure, such as a major building programme on cities and other fortifications. This suggests an average surplus of at least one million over standard expenditure per annum. Although we have already mentioned the efficiency of the Anastasian tax system, this figure demonstrates the strength of the tax base and the ability of the East to pay its way even while increasing expenditure on military affairs.

In contrast, the West received much lower total revenues. The wealthiest area, the African provinces, suffered from disturbances and loss of agricultural productivity in the late fourth and early fifth centuries (between one-third and one-half of imperial estate lands were written off as unproductive under Honorius), and so even before the Vandal conquest revenue from Africa as a whole may have been in decline. Africa also provided the main grain supply to Rome. However, in an insecure military situation, or with a disrupted economy, the marginal lands or those most threatened would have been the first to go out of productive use, and so the total decline in wealth generated may be less than this figure suggests at first sight. The loss of the wealthiest parts of Roman Africa to the Vandals in 442 may have cost the West something in the order of one million solidi, or 20 to 30 per cent of its total revenue.

Italy and Illyricum were much less fertile and productive than Africa, and even when Britain, Gaul and Spain were added the West must always have relied on a lower taxable base than the East. Together with Africa these regions were subject to repeated attacks, or lost to rebellion and barbarian settlement during the fifth century, and as a result the West had to remit much of the notional tax yield of its provinces. After Alaric's invasions, Italy only paid one-fifth of its usual assessment in 413; in 418, parts of Italy had this further reduced to one-seventh or one-ninth. Following the Vandal attacks in Africa and Sicily these provinces' taxes were remitted to one-eighth and one-seventh in the 440s. There must have been similar remissions for other devastated areas, such as Spain and Gaul. Together with the loss of Africa, these reductions in revenue may have amounted to 40 or 50 per cent of available Western resources at times. Given the expanding population and economy in the East throughout the fifth century and this period of great disruption in the West, the difference between their resources must have been growing rapidly. By the time of Leo's great expedition in 468 the West could only contribute two million solidi to the costs, against the 7.4 million spent by the East.[21]

A final consideration on the revenue available to successive emperors is that the theoretical total must have rarely, if ever, been achieved. Across such large territories the potential for natural disasters, civil or barbarian conflicts and simple failures in the system of collection and transit must have had some effect, either singly or in combination, in most years. Although there was undoubtedly much corrupt abstraction of revenues, in addition to the officially recognised perks payable throughout the bureaucratic system, simple collection problems probably had as much of an effect on the resources of the empire. However, despite troubles and corruption, the tax base of the Eastern empire was sufficient to withstand these difficulties and still yield a surplus in all but the most violent or incompetent of reigns. The West was faced by all these problems almost continuously in the fifth century, but it was still only in the 440s that its revenue seems to have collapsed almost completely, at which point Valentinian III complained that he could not even feed and equip his existing army, never mind recruit additional forces.[22]

There are numerous estimates of the cost of maintaining the late Roman army in the East, ranging from one or two million solidi a year to as much as seven or eight million. The lower figures do not include the high costs of expenditure on shipbuilding, campaign pay supplements and transport, fortifications, etc., but all agree that the greatest expenditure of the state was obviously the army. This was also a contemporary view, and an unpopular one: 'Enormous expenditure on military matters which afflicts the financial system'; 'ship-building, wall-building, and above all expenditure on the soldiers: for in this way each year most of the public revenues are consumed'.[23]

Since the army was the greatest element of imperial expenditure, an accurate estimate of its real costs would provide us with a more powerful indication of overall imperial state finance. Treadgold's important analysis provides a framework for us to do this, and we therefore go into a more detailed breakdown of military costs for the rest of this chapter.

The major element in army costs was in paying and equipping it. To provide comparisons for army pay is difficult, but we have some indications of both the costs of living and of the incomes of other professions. Figures from Egypt mention a skilled carpenter earning sixteen solidi a year, and a caulker earning eighteen; Procopius refers to the whores of Constantinople earning a bare living wage of around four solidi a year, which is in interesting counterpoint to the later reluctance of Gregory the Great to pay as much as two solidi for the maintenance of nuns in Rome, attributing the extravagance to the higher cost of living in the great city. Anastasius allowed six solidi a year for each monk of a monastery that he founded, but as an imperial foundation we should expect it to be well provided for. We may take a general figure of one or two solidi a year as a minimum subsistence level for an individual, without any accommodation costs (soldiers, and probably their families, were, of course, provided with accommodation). It is also worth noting that soldiers often had slaves, who cost as much as ten solidi, and so were not among the poorest professions.[24]

The regular pay of the army had deteriorated in value during the fourth century. This problem was dealt with by providing food, uniforms and weapons as payments in kind (earlier, soldiers were responsible for 'buying' their supplies out of their pay), but this left soldiers at the mercy of the official issue for the quality of items, and removed any possibility of supplementing pay by being careful or frugal with the official issue. Accessional donatives were paid unfailingly at the beginning of every reign. It would have been dangerous to do otherwise, and during the fourth century these came to be paid in precious metal rather than worthless copper (five solidi and a pound of silver, equivalent to another four or five solidi); a quinquennial donative of five solidi was also paid to each soldier. Even so, this element of pay can only have represented about two solidi a year on average.

In 375 it seems that the cost of full uniform (all kit, excluding arms) for a soldier was six solidi, with a further small increase in 396. Not all kit would need to be replaced on an annual basis, and so the element of pay replaced by these issues was much less than this figure in any one year. Arms were also issued, but again presumably on an occasional, at need, basis. In the fifth century, and probably also in the fourth, the annual ration for a soldier was worth some four solidi (with slight regional price variations). After the introduction of these allowances, and the precious metal donatives, payment in cash and in kind can only have amounted to the equivalent of some eight to ten solidi. Therefore, even after taking into account the notional value of the issues in kind, the remuneration of soldiers was low at the start of the fourth century, and declined with the currency thereafter, until stabilised through the issues in kind and donatives later in the century.

Gratian had started to pay some frontier troops in gold, and the process was accelerated under Theodosius. Matching changes were made to taxation systems, more rapidly in the West than the East: by 400 the levy of horses was replaced by a gold tax, which allowed the army to buy good horses rather than accept those which the imperial levy system could extract from the suppliers. By 406 Arcadius ordered that rations in kind would be supplied to *comitatenses* in garrison points; those on mobile duties and all *limitanei* were to be paid in cash (the latter may reflect the move towards self-supply or maintenance by cultivation of military lands by the frontier troops). However, in 409 specific reference was made to payment of frontier troops in Palestine in gold suggesting that the practice was still not universal.

Pay, based on donatives and issues in kind, amounted to ten solidi at most by the end of the fourth century. One clear way to increase this would have been to make the elements representing uniform and weapons annual, rather than occasional payments. This could only realistically be done after commuting the payments to cash, since a soldier would have little interest in accumulating repeated issues of clothing and arms. Such a move would best be attributed to an emperor with strong cash reserves and income, and a tax system that was based on gold revenue rather than in kind. The organisation of such reforms also suggests a lengthy reign, with considerable administrative interests. All these point to Anastasius as the most likely author of the reforms, and the subsequent rise in pay and conditions of service in the Eastern army.

Commutation of pay into gold happened earlier in the West, certainly by the reign of Valentinian III. The benefit to troops there would have lain in the greater potential to accumulate savings from cash payments rather than issues in kind. It seems unlikely that the pay of Western soldiers was actually increased, other than through this mechanism. There was no equivalent respite from military and financial pressures in the West to match the opportunity which Anastasius later had to reform on a grand scale.

Procopius suggests that Justinian was responsible for ending the quinquennial donative. However, he was concerned in the *Secret History* to show Justinian in the worst possible light, and the fact that the donative was not paid after 518 does not necessarily mean that it was abolished at that point.

Given the freedom with which large numbers of troops were recruited it is unlikely that conditions of service deteriorated, and so any change must have been both earlier (under Anastasius) and not detrimental to the prospects of recruits. Anastasius, similarly, seems to have had no problems in recruiting and paying a large and loyal Roman army, and so any change in the payment regime must have been neutral at worst, and potentially beneficial for the soldiery. We have a detailed description of the distribution of the quinquennial donative paid by Anastasius in 511, but no later references to the practice:

> And on the 29th the king assembled all the commanders of the forces and all the officers of the scholares and the patricians, and he said to them, 'According to my regular custom I wish to give a donative.' For so it had been his practice to give it once in 5 years ever since he became king, at the same time requiring oaths from all the Romans to the effect that they would not act treacherously against the kingdom. But on this occasion he required them to take the oath in the following manner: A copy of the Gospel being placed for them, they went in and received the 5 denarii [sic; = solidi] each, and they swore as follows: 'By this law of God and by the words which are written in it, we will contend with all our might for the true faith and for the kingdom, and we will not act treacherously either against the truth or the king.' In this manner, indeed, he required them to take the oath, because he heard that Macedonius [Patriarch of Constantinople] was trying to raise a rebellion against him. On 30th July the king gave a largesse to the whole army.[25]

This reflects the pattern of personal payments to senior figures by the emperor himself, and the general distribution of the same donative by imperial representatives in the regions to the army in general. Although annual pay was distributed through the local command structure, the donatives, representing loyalty payments from the emperor himself, were dispensed by imperial representatives despatched especially for the purpose, thereby emphasising the direct link from the common soldiery to their supreme general (and paymaster), the emperor himself.

During the fifth century a ration (*annona*) had been valued at four solidi, but it stood at five in the sixth. It is possible that Anastasius dispensed with the quinquennial donative after 511, and paid it annually as a one-solidus addition to basic pay. Significantly, in the following year (512) Anastasius legislated to end the tattooing or branding of new recruits to the army, which had been introduced under Diocletian to deal with desertion. Army service was obviously now less unattractive. Justinian was later able to dispense with the hereditary compulsion for soldiers' sons to serve in the army, and had no difficulties with native Roman recruitment.

It is unlikely that this popularity had been achieved with only the addition of one solidus to the figure of eight to ten paid in the fourth century. If the same rate of five solidi to the annona was also used for the commutation of arms and uniform issues, and those issues were made annual, then they would have represented a ten solidi a year payment, much more than the likely costs of supplying the uniform and arms themselves. This would still value the total remuneration at only fifteen solidi a year – a very significant increase, but not the twenty that seem to have been the case. One explanation is that the field army, to which these rates apply, were paid two annona, i.e. eight, and after the reform ten, solidi, rather than the five which we know the *limitanei* received; this could reflect either their higher status, or the element which the *limitanei* were supposed to obtain from cultivation of military lands. Another similar explanation is that the second 'ration' was intended to support the soldier's family. Arcadius, in 406, legislated for the issuing of rations to military families, and Theodosius II shortly after laid out a table of what these entitlements were. This family payment had been suspended by Valentinian I (and probably Theodosius I in the East), and this must have been a significant drop in conditions of service while it was in force. It may also have been reinstated in the West under Stilicho.[26]

The result is that from Arcadius onwards field army pay was the equivalent of twelve to fourteen solidi, and remained at this level through the fifth century. For some troops this was enhanced by a move towards paying this amount in gold rather than issues in kind. However, it seems clear that a significant change took place when most payment was commuted into gold in the East under Anastasius, who must have been responsible for increasing field army pay by around 50 per cent (from fourteen to twenty solidi). With these various entitlements translated into generous equivalents in gold it is easy to see the popularity of military service in the first half of the sixth century.

The pay of the *limitanei* does not seem to have changed. In 534, clerical staff in the African frontier army received only five solidi, and they were on military rates of pay. Justinian went further than this, first suspending the pay of the *limitanei* on the eastern frontier after the Persian war was concluded in 532, and then abolishing it entirely in 545. The basic pay of five solidi was not a living wage for a soldier and his family, and had not been for at least a century and a half; military lands were allocated for their cultivation, and many pursued other careers to supplement their incomes. However, they obviously continued to function up until the reconquest of Africa at least, when Justinian thought it worthwhile to re-establish them in defence of the new province. It would seem that their demise as an effective force post-dates this, and must surely relate to the suspension and then abolition of even this low level of pay. Justinian saved a huge sum of money by this move, but the speed and extent of the collapse of the eastern frontiers, both when Persia invaded in 540 and later, may have been a result of this measure.[27]

Taking the pay rates suggested above, and the probable size of the army, it is likely that the total pay bill was rising constantly from the third century to the reign of Justinian, reaching a peak early in his reign before declining as a result of his decision to suspend the pay of the *limitanei*. However, this does not represent the total cost of maintaining and deploying the army: there was heavy expenditure on fortifications, transport, campaign pay and rations and other costs. Additional allowances for officers higher rates of pay, cavalry and their allowances, etc. also have to be taken into account.

Total army costs during most of the fifth century may have been around 4 to 4.5 million solidi, with a significant rise to 5.5 million under Anastasius. The new armies recruited by Justinian would have raised this to over six million solidi, but he later saved over one million solidi by abolishing the pay of the *limitanei*. Comparisons with earlier periods are almost impossible due to the difficulty in equating later pay in gold with earlier figures in kind, or in the copper coinage. It does, however, seem clear that the army was relatively better paid in the first half of the sixth century than at any time since the early empire.[28]

Although paying the army was the single greatest expense for the empire, there were other significant calls on its revenue. Payments were made to barbarians, and to Persia, to buy peace on the frontiers. In 506, as part of the peace with Persia, Anastasius agreed to pay 39,600 solidi each year in subsidies. Justinian was later to agree to a payment of 792,000 solidi to buy the 'Perpetual Peace' with Persia. The only long-term barbarian subsidies which the Eastern empire had to pay were those to the Huns, and at their most severe under Attila the annual payments were only 2,100 pounds of gold (151,200 solidi).

In contrast, the West sometimes faced huge demands with a much lower income to meet them. In 408, 4,000 pounds of gold (288,000 solidi) was needed to buy off Alaric, and the following year this increased to 5,000 pounds of gold (360,000 solidi), 30,000 pounds of silver (120,000 solidi) and costly luxury goods such as silk and pepper. However, there are accounts of individual ransoms of up to 30,000 solidi being paid by families, and the burden on the empire should be seen in that light. The wealth was undoubtedly there in the West to meet these sorts of demands, but not enough of it was reaching the imperial treasury.

Ransoms were also paid in the East, both for prominent individuals and for ordinary captives taken in raids. Anastasius paid 9,000 pounds of gold (648,000 solidi) for the ransom of his nephew and chief general, Hypatius, from Vitalian during their civil war. He also paid 1,000 pounds of gold (72,000 solidi) to ransom prisoners taken in Bulgar raids in 517. His generosity extended to other circumstances: after the Persian war, in 505, he gave 2,000 pounds of gold (144,000 solidi) for rebuilding in the province of Mesopotamia; Amida was relieved of all taxation for a period of seven years so that it could recover after its siege; and Edessa had its taxes reduced by 50 per cent. Taxation was also remitted in many cases of natural disaster, such as earthquakes (in 527, Justin I sent 324,000 solidi for rebuilding in Antioch after an earthquake), and so imperial revenues were clearly sufficient to allow flexibility in collection.

There was also a huge amount of building work carried out under Anastasius. The costs of his fortification programme must have been higher than those of any of his fifth century predecessors, especially for the major fortress cities on the Persian frontier and the new Long Wall of Thrace. Justinian continued this trend, and added a hugely expensive programme of church building, exemplified by the great church of the empire, Hagia Sophia. Here, the sum of 4,000 pounds of gold (288,000 solidi) were spent on building during one year, and the construction took six years in total.[29]

The army was the largest cost, but the whole bureaucratic structure of government also consumed a significant part of state revenue. The imperial administration is claimed to have cost 720,000 solidi, and with the costs of provincial government added the total costs of running the empire must have been in excess of one million solidi. The grain dole for Constantinople consumed the equivalent of another 800,000 solidi, bringing the identifiable non-military costs up to about two million solidi. The public post was another major cost (Justinian thought it worth saving money by abolishing much of it), but we have no real figures on which to base an estimate of its consumption of revenue. All we can say is that, with the post, subsidies and bribes, public works and dispensations, well over two million solidi (three to four million?) went on non-military expenditure. All these costs to the treasury, either as direct outflows or reductions in inflows, demonstrate a level of 'expenditure' which was clearly supportable without excessive strain.[30]

When the military and other expenses are added, and the flexibility which allowed accumulation of a surplus at up to one million solidi a year, it seems that the total revenue of the East under Anastasius must have been at least nine million solidi in the early sixth century. Military and other expenditure would have been generally lower in the fifth century and earlier, but was matched by revenue; Justinian's expenditure seems to have been significantly higher than Anastasius', and despite savings on the *limitanei* his spending was insupportable in the longer term. Justinian is said to have spent the whole treasury inherited from Anastasius early in his own reign. Thereafter his costs were met from revenue, due to strict enforcement of taxation, and some exceptional measures: land tax was increased by a small amount, offices and monopolies on the supplies of certain goods were sold, and the public post was drastically curtailed. This last measure was a disaster for the economic viability of much of inland Anatolia.

In the West, imperial revenues declined along with the economic condition of several parts of the empire. Much of this was clearly due to barbarian inroads, but other factors played a part and individuals seem to have maintained their incomes much more successfully than the state. The army had been badly damaged during the extensive wars of Honorius' reign, but its decline and subsequent inability to recover its own strength or lost territory may have been as much a result of a lack of available funds as military problems. Maintaining the Western army as the equal of the East in the late fourth century must have been a strain on funds, given the lower revenue base. There can have been little flexibility to expand, or even maintain recruitment, or to mount expensive major campaigns after the loss of so much of the revenue base of the West during the first half of the fifth century.

By the mid-fifth century, the West clearly had the army it could afford rather than the one it wanted or needed. This helps to explain the prominence and importance of 'allies' (such as those Aetius used so successfully, needing no training and probably bringing their own weapons and equipment with them), who were cheaper than regular troops and occasionally fought for free if their interests happened to coincide with those of the empire.

The Roman economic system as a whole always had very limited flexibility for response to changed circumstances. There was a generally fixed agricultural base for wealth, and taxation at rates that could not readily be changed without serious disruption to the system. Adulteration of the coinage was a frequent recourse, but it led to inflation and chaos. Fixed assets, such as gold statues, furniture, etc., could be put back into circulation as emergency measures, but only once.

One major change, which came about mainly during the fifth century, was the change from taxation in kind to a gold-based system. This made the accumulation of a surplus easier, and facilitated the direction of imperial expenditure towards particular objectives. The success in stabilising Roman army recruitment, and the deployment of it in a series of major wars under Anastasius and Justinian, testify to the efficacy of this move.

The main difference in the East was between cautious – not necessarily peaceful – rulers who could defend the empire and still accumulate a surplus, and those spendthrifts who could inherit a huge treasury, and the same tax base, and still manage to leave the empire bankrupt at the end of their reign. What seems clear is that the revenue of the Eastern empire was adequate to cover expenditure at almost all times, with occasional crises being the result of either short-term demands which could not be met from immediately available liquid resources (such as payments to Attila in the 440s), or exceptional expenditure (such as Leo's African expedition).

This was despite a steady increase in the total expenditure on the army (the greatest cost), the administration, and on public works. Contrary to widespread modern assumptions, all this was *not* achieved by squeezing the tax base ever harder, as the continuing prosperity of most of the East demonstrates. It must have been partly due to a growing economic base, but this can only have had a gradual effect and cannot account for the rate of increase at certain times. The real answer is that the costs were well administered, with peculation kept under control and a competent series of managers running economic affairs. These were usually the Praetorian Prefects, or the *comites* of the treasury, but the greatest period of success saw these figures combined with an emperor who was similarly dedicated and talented: Anastasius.

10

CENTRALISED POWER

More than any earlier Eastern-based emperors, Theodosius I had concentrated imperial power, government, military authority, and finally religious jurisdiction (except for the Bishop of Rome) in the single capital of Constantinople. Power all flowed from that city, as it had once flowed from Rome. For many years the official symbols, on coins and effigies, continued to proclaim the twin centres of the Roman empire, the twin guardian spirits of Rome and Constantinople. In the political reality of the fifth century, there was now only one.[1]

The power centres in the West had been radically divided for half a century of invasions and crises. First Rome, then Milan, had been abandoned as imperial capitals. Ravenna, selected by Stilicho when Italy itself was in peril, was a secluded imperial refuge, not a centre of rule. Actual power was located in the largest army group, wherever it happened to be, commanded by its generalissimo. He moved forces, made appointments, and routinely issued laws in the name of the secluded emperor. When Constantius, successful general and Roman by origin, tried in 421 to recombine these two roles by assuming the imperial authority himself, he allegedly found the atmosphere of Ravenna and the court stultifying and politically paralysing with its weary ceremonial and empty intrigues. Power lay in the midst of the largely barbarian armies. Imperial legitimacy, necessary but impotent, lay elsewhere, at a protected, cloistered Ravenna. This political and geographical split became permanent. The next great general, Aetius, also a Roman, might have made himself emperor in the earlier manner, but did not even try. He did seek a marriage alliance with the imperial family, but this was aimed at extending his influence and getting a more pliant figure on the throne rather than at imperial ambition per se.[2]

As well as being an impregnable fortress in a crucial strategic position, Constantinople was in every sense the capital of an empire. Here was emperor and palace, an expanding Senate, a bureaucracy and all the machinery of centralised government, including the two military commanders of the Praesental armies permanently stationed in the emperor's vicinity, which meant, in practice, close to Constantinople. These were not bodyguards or elite palace corps (who had a separate command), but full fighting army groups. Their nearby presence ensured that all major strategic planning and decisions would happen in the capital, in the company of emperor and government. The fact that they were two, not one, derived from the political caution of Theodosius I in dividing the highest military commands.[3]

Constantine had spared no effort or expense on his new capital, but already in less than a century it had doubled in size and population. The external suburbs had multiplied westward at such a rate that Anthemius' new belt of walls were located a mile to the west of those of Constantine. By the mid-fifth century, the population was in the region of 500,000 or more. Artificially, Constantine had tried to make the city resemble old Rome, identifying seven hills and dividing the area into fourteen districts. He even introduced the extravagance of a corn dole for the idle mob. There were two conspicuous differences. Although there was a great Hippodrome, modelled on the Circus Maximus at Rome, there was no amphitheatre. Gladiatorial fights had never been as popular in the Greek East, were strongly condemned by the Christians, and were finally abolished in the West in the reign of Honorius.[4] By the end of the fourth century the only pagan temples left were no longer places of worship but museums, or they had been put to other uses. Instead, the city was adorned with numerous splendid churches great and small, whose number continually multiplied.[5]

The heart of the capital was the huge complex of buildings at the eastern end of the peninsula, almost a city within a city. It contained the great imperial palace, on the site of the present Topkapi, overlooking the Sea of Marmora. The private quarters were connected to the throne room, great banqueting hall, chapels, and the Consistory chamber. Close to these were the offices of the ministries and the quarters of the Scholarian guards and the elite *Candidati*. In the east was the Senate house and to the north the original Church of the Holy Wisdom, the principal church of the city. Immediately to the southwest was the great Hippodrome, which itself contained an extension of the palace in the Kathisma, originally simply the emperor's box but now a small imperial building in itself, dominating the scene. The famous four horses of Lysippus, which now stand over St Mark's in Venice, once adorned the Kathisma.

From the central area, the main street ran westwards past the Praetorium (law courts) to the Forum of Constantine and the Forum of Theodosius, then forked northwest and southwest. One branch led to the great Church of the Apostles, built by Constantine and containing his mausoleum and those of successive emperors, and thence out to the Gate of Charisius, one of the five imposing civilian gateways in the walls. The other led, via the Forum of Arcadius, to the Golden Gate and the Hebdomon Palace, close to the Campus Martius where troops were reviewed, and where every new emperor was acclaimed by the army. At the opposite end of the walls was another imperial palace, the Blachernai, and the foremost of many churches to the Mother of God (map, p. 170).

The city's districts were generally allocated to the different markets, warehouses and workshops of the trade guilds. The main harbour was in the Golden Horn, but there were three subsidiary harbours on the Propontis by the Sea of Marmora. The winds and tides in fact made navigation around the peninsula very difficult for much of the year, an inconvenience for trade but in the last resort an extra defensive advantage against attack from the sea.

The main machinery of government was essentially that devised by Diocletian and Constantine, with a few important additions. The Senate was not in any sense a legislature but a hereditary social order and honorific assembly of nobles, whose members originally achieved their status through imperial government service, including military service, not just family or landed wealth. Having held one of the great offices of state, including *Magister Militum*, was the primary qualification. During the fourth and fifth centuries, senatorial rank was bestowed widely with the tenure of senior positions. The seven commanders of the Scholarian guard units, as well as the elite *Candidati* in Constantinople, all held it as a matter of course. So, probably, did many of the guards officers, as well as senior military officers in the regional armies – the *Duces* and *Comites* – either in service or on retirement. By the end of the fifth century the Senate's membership had swollen to about 2,000 and encompassed not just the families of leading magnates but a wide spectrum of wealth and position. It was divided into four orders or grades of importance; the fourth grade included men of quite modest means. Libanius mentions a military *Dux* who possessed only one farm and eleven slaves. In the upper grades were men of much greater or inherited wealth, but even they were nowhere as rich as the leading senators in the West. They were mostly the descendants of men of middling fortunes who had started on the service ladder at Constantinople during the fourth century, whereas the great senatorial families of the West had been accumulating and consolidating their wealth for five centuries or more.[6]

The Senate's upper members (*illustres*) lived in the capital and represented the collective attitudes of the civil bureaucracy, whether or not they were in office. Occasionally it could cautiously discuss proposed laws or policies, and occasionally the emperor sought (and was granted) its ratification, usually over some unpopular or risky measure for which he wanted to share public responsibility, or declare his intentions with special emphasis. An important feature of this service aristocracy, notoriously absent in the senatorial order in the West, was that its leading members, at least, could not be permanently divorced in their interests from the management of government. Their wealth, power and social position stemmed ultimately from their offices, not vice versa. Of course, they used their office to enrich themselves, legally or otherwise. But outstanding ministers such as Anthemius, Aurelian, Antiochus, Cyrus, Marinus, Celer, were ready to put aside the interests of their own class – especially in the matter of taxation, where their measures frequently antagonised the richer senators.

Central government proper lay with the emperor himself and his individually chosen ministers, but this was partially formalised in a small Council of State, the Sacred Consistory, where he took advice from his senior ministers and generals, and anyone else who might be invited, including other influential members of the imperial family. Although the meetings were entirely at his discretion, the practice seems to have grown up of regular Consistory meetings to discuss serious policy issues.

Otherwise, civil and military chains of authority were separate at the higher levels. The lower levels of the civil bureaucracy, the lesser officials, legal advocates, clerks and accountants, were permanent employees with a career for life, and might move about from the staffs of Prefects to those of military commanders. The ministers and higher generals were usually appointed to their posts by the emperor for relatively short periods, mainly to allow others the chance to occupy these dignities. There were several top ministerial posts. The Praetorian Prefect, supreme head of the civil administration, outranked everyone except the emperor himself, and could even issue minor laws in his own name. The old empire was divided into four giant Prefectures, each geographically far larger than modern nation-states: Gaul, Italy, Illyricum and the Orient. Each was divided into more manageable dioceses, and subdivided in turn into smaller provinces. In practice, the Prefect of the Orient, resident in the capital, was now senior. There were two finance ministers, for the public revenues (*Comes sacrarum largitionum*) and the emperor's private estates (*Comes rei privatae*), but in practice funds could be moved between the two. The cumbersome system of assessment, taxation and disbursement was controlled by the Prefect, who had his own treasuries.[7]

Within the palace, an important figure was the Grand Chamberlain (*Praepositus sacri cubiculi*) simply by virtue of his constant attendance on the emperor. He was nearly always a eunuch, and this, together with his unofficial power behind the scenes, routinely made him highly unpopular in the ruling circles and automatically with the wider population, as Eutropius and Chrysaphius witness. The many more honest, competent and loyal eunuch officials generally go unsung and unremembered. The Oriental practice of castration, adopted by late Rome for palace purposes, is something we generally deplore. It was a similar measure to Claudius' high promotion of freedmen, who because of their lowly status would depend on him alone. Perhaps it also had a reflection in the rule of celibacy for the higher clergy, who would not then put natural dynastic ambitions before service to God and the church. Deprived of these more normal and approved satisfactions, it is hardly surprising that some high eunuchs valued personal power and amassed personal treasures, as if the genitally intact did not do the same.

There was a supreme legal minister (a *libellis*) who managed the drafting of all laws and the huge flow of rescripts and other imperial legal decisions. A further minister who became increasingly powerful was one for whom there is no modern counterpart (except possibly the White House Chief-of-Staff): the Master of Offices (*Magister Officiorum*), often a newcomer from a relatively lowly background. He originally supervised the permanent officialdom both at the capital and in the provinces. As manager of state ceremonies he dealt with all audiences and embassies, and hence controlled the official channels of access to the emperor. As a result he received foreign delegations and gradually developed into the role of a foreign minister, a post otherwise conspicuously absent in all previous Roman government. He also controlled – though not commanded – the 3,500-strong *scholae*, the imperial guard in the capital. He ran the imperial postal service, and the network of *agentes in rebus* who were the pervasive government system of security, information, oversight and special duties (though not, as some modern writers have suggested, a secret police). Later, the Master of Offices came to represent the emperor in Church councils. In this way, from the apparently routine management of detail, the office accumulated multiple powers that in practice approached those of the Prefect.[8]

There was not the strict modern distinction between executive and administrative branches of government, nor between executive and judiciary, although there were, of course, specialists among the permanent staffs. The only great division was between civil and military skills and duties. It was expected that anyone in the upper senatorial classes, with the usual education and suitable experience, could manage finances, draft and issue instructions, or preside over a court. In fact, this gentlemanly generalism was supported by a growing professionalism among the permanent staffs. The relatively fluid, open nature of the service senatorial order meant that proven men from the lower bureaucracy could, with suitable patronage, rise to the higher mandarin posts. The great financial reforms of Anastasius, described below, were devised and carried out by men – Marinus, Polycarp and John – who had originally been lowly accountants but rose to occupy the great ministries of state.

Even more important was the simple fact of geographical concentration of most of this officialdom in one central capital. At a time of slow communication and uncertain record-keeping, this made a very great difference. When emperors had been continually on the move between one imperial capital and another, the detailed machinery of government had to travel with them and its personnel distributed among the different centres, and tended to stay there, jealous of one another. Now it was possible to draw on the accumulated experience and skills of several generations of permanent officials in every post and over many reigns. The total number of officials in this great reservoir of expertise made a gradual but lasting difference to the continued running of the government machine in periods of both stability and crisis in the fifth century. There were about 3,000 permanent officials in

Constantinople, and some 10,000 in the provincial bureaucracy. Each diocese of the empire had a staff of about 300, with fairly small staffs at a lower level. The military establishment also maintained a significant administration, with each *Magister Militum* having a staff of 300, another forty in the *officia* of the numerous frontier *Duces*, and others, probably totalling another 2,500 to 3,000. Under Diocletian, the imperial administration probably numbered some 30,000 in total, and so with a steady increase after him there must have been a total of well over 15,000 in the East by the fifth century.[9]

The senior ministers, the Praesental army commanders and, to a lesser extent, the Patriarch of Constantinople were in close physical proximity and, in conjunction, formed an establishment of power. It was not, of course, an acknowledged counterweight to the emperor, for legally there was emphatically no separation of powers. But it could in practice sometimes function as a guiding, supporting and tacitly correcting mechanism to the emperor. Especially during the reign of an immature or weak emperor it would be in the Consistory that the main elements of the establishment, military and civil, would come to major decisions, and where its dominant figures, whether the Prefect, Master of Offices or the senior Praesental *Magister*, would make their influence felt. Each of these figures was appointed and dismissed solely by the emperor, and their tenures tended to be short. Important bishops and the Patriarchs held their offices as church appointees, and could only be deposed by church councils; although the emperor could convene and usually control these occasions. Each represented an interest group, a faction, often selfish and venal, in both conflict and collaboration with the others, and often in league with members of the imperial family.

Sometimes, as with Chrysaphius, these conflicts had a bloody resolution. But ever since the violent upheavals of Gainas and Tribigild, each came to recognise that while they might be in ascendancy – as Aspar clearly was after 457 – they alone could not govern all the elements of the state for long. Thus, for the most part, their factional struggles were carried out within a limiting framework, imposed on them by the realities of state power concentrated in the capital. It was an unusual and hazardous move to step outside this framework, by appealing directly to the volatile mob in the Hippodrome, or to the army groups stationed elsewhere in the empire.

Outside the government in the city itself the people had a certain voice to which governments and emperors, however disdainfully, knew they had to listen: rioting could occur very easily, as when the Prefect Monaxius' house had been burnt down when the grain supply failed. The voice was heard in the anonymous roars in the Hippodrome, and especially the organised factions of Blues and Greens. These were far more than just guilds of sports supporters. Their leaders were appointed by government and they were supposed to act as a city militia, and to provide organised labour for repairing the city walls, but they had become virtually autonomous, mutually antagonistic popular forces behind which the people of every large city ranged themselves, and through which all their political and religious rivalries were expressed. The Blues, for example, traditionally supported Orthodoxy while the Greens favoured Monophysitism. They wore distinctive styles of dress, engaged in bloody clashes, and for many people this represented their main loyalty in life. Far from being subservient to the government, they amplified its own conflicts, so that by the mid-fifth century emperors themselves were compelled to favour one faction or the other. Many writers have seen in these organisations a residue of the popular liberties of the ancient cities.[10]

The establishment's tacit power conventions sometimes broke down, as they were later to do drastically in the reign of the emperor Zeno when several external military revolts threatened to sweep him away. Yet, the practices, realities and symbolism of power, focused always on Constantinople, eventually made these anarchic and destructive episodes an exception rather than a rule. The only place where a promising rebel could cash his military support into secure power was in the city. But army power, in the shape of the Praesental commanders and their nearby forces, was already established in the city.

The effect of this unwritten Byzantine establishment of mandarinate and army, as a positive guiding force to the emperor and palace, is reflected sharply in two processes: first, the management of weak or immature emperors such as Arcadius or the young Theodosius II; second, the co-operation of these power groups – predominately the army – in choosing a new emperor when obvious dynastic succession was lacking, as with Marcian, and after him, Leo. Each party had too much to risk by breaking ranks. In the West by contrast, there was a progressive divorce of two geographically separate political centres, the legitimate and symbolic versus the military and effective. This was not allowed to happen in the East, both through the increasingly conscious policy of integrating the army commands into government, and through the geographical constraint of a single undisputed capital. This can hardly be overstressed in an understanding of the East's survival.

If we contrast this with the perpetual bloody power struggles for the purple in the third century, which were terminated by Diocletian and then Constantine, two focal facts stand out. First, among the army, increasingly barbarian in origins, and among the wider population and civil bureaucracy, dynastic loyalty had become the paramount factor in imperial succession. Constantine's dynasty ruled, with or without other colleagues, for seventy years (293–363). The dynasty of Theodosius reigned, if not truly ruled, for seventy-one years (379–450). The days were past when any popular and ambitious general could easily reckon on the personal loyalty of his troops against a dynastically legitimate emperor, man or boy.

Second, by mid-century the role of the emperor no longer required him to be a military commander leading his armies in battle. In the second, third and fourth centuries every emperor had to do this or perish, yet after Theodosius I, with his immature and weak sons, this pattern was broken. This led to very different outcomes in the East and West. Even though several Eastern emperors had military backgrounds, and usually appeared in military dress in their portraits, none of them until after Justinian had to take to the field in person to preserve their authority. Unlike their predecessors, in the days when military prowess was paramount, they could no longer simply carry on their old military careers as emperor. The imperial image and conception had developed further than the Constantinian one, not back to that of civil magistrate, but into that of spiritual overlord and protector. The proportion of actual to symbolic authority the emperor wielded depended largely on his own personal qualities. But at no point did the office itself shrink to being a mere cipher, as it progressively did in the West after the rise of Ricimer in the 450s.

Although there was no legal office of regent during a minority, the Constantinople establishment confidently managed the government in the boy emperor's name, and of course rival factions competed fiercely for dominant influence, as with Anthemius and Pulcheria. Superficially, this might look little different from the West, with its boy emperors Honorius and Valentinian III. The crucial difference was that their tutelage at Ravenna was within a palace and court only, not a real government. They were utterly cloistered from the realities of power, whereas the boy emperors at Constantinople were surrounded by it. They might prefer the seclusion of a palace or to be closeted in it like Theodosius II, but government, army and people were always outside, and looking to them for great decisions. The shell of court ceremonial might insulate an emperor, allow others to use him, delay or blunt the operations of power, but it could not remove actual imperial authority from its role within them. The very intrigues testified to the real potency of this authority, which was not allowed to wither.

When an emperor died without an obvious dynastic successor, the factions fought out their differences behind closed doors, then presented a united front to the people and armies in their unanimous choice. The rule of dynastic transmission was conveniently flexible. Marcian, in reality a newcomer promoted by Aspar, preserved the fiction of continuing the Theodosian dynasty by a nominal marriage to Pulcheria. Later Anastasius, another complete newcomer, married the previous emperor's widow Ariadne as a condition of ruling.

Having chosen, then ceremonially elected and crowned a new emperor, the very diversity of the establishment tended to prevent him from becoming anyone's pliant puppet. It was axiomatic to each of the groups that the figure of the emperor be seen everywhere as the undivided, supreme source of all authority. He therefore had every incentive to act this role to the full and, as far as possible, become it in fact. He stepped into a new and sacred position prepared for him, which now distanced him from conventional political obligations. It is remarkable how the emperors of the later fifth century, often relative nonentities and the apparent creatures of some group or other – the proverbial safe candidate – assumed their new imperial role vigorously and courageously, balanced one part of the establishment against the other, and grew quickly into effective and respected rulers.

Marcian was in part Aspar's nominee, but he was in no sense his mere creature. Leo was even more Aspar's man, but he slowly worked free of the ambitious Gothic military dynasty and eventually rid himself of it in a bloody purge. Zeno, Leo's chosen successor, was highly unpopular with the establishment, yet they grudgingly acquiesced in his election. He had to face a complex succession of conspiracies and revolts, but eventually overcame them all. Anastasius, originally an aged palace official, quickly realised what had to be done, and managed to crush two revolts, wage a victorious war against Persia and overhaul the fiscal system to provide the government with far stronger financial sinews. In the West, when the rare capable emperor, such as Majorian, took his position seriously, leading armies and initiating reforms, he became an embarrassment and a rival to the ruling warlord. Ricimer eliminated Majorian because of his success.[11]

There was thus a strong centralising tendency, a stubborn refusal of emperors, however chosen and whatever their supposed political debts, to allow the imperial position to be diluted. Occasionally revolts occurred, and sometimes succeeded. The constitutional traditions still allowed a successful rebel to be legitimised as emperor by the usual formulae. But this could no longer easily be done, as before, merely by election by an army in the field – it had to be done in the proper place and in the proper way. That place was Constantinople, and that way involved bargaining and agreement with other powers than the purely military, expressed in the evolving succession ceremonies in the capital.

Rome had once been this place, at least until the mid-third century, when the unremitting pressures of alien invaders had forced emperors to locate the effective centres of power closer to the threatened frontiers: Trier, Milan, Aquileia, Sirmium, Salonica and Nicomedia. As they moved from one capital to another the court and ministers moved with them, so that all the imperial functions other than fighting could continue. Large supporting staffs of administrators still had to reside and work permanently in these capitals, with the result that rival bureaucratic centres grew up, unable or unwilling to pool their resources, records, information and experience. As we saw, Constantine's new permanent capital was able, after Theodosius I took up residence in the 380s, to collect all this scattered expertise in a single place, resulting in a far more solid and professional government machinery, which was able to hand on its accumulated experience. In many ways the proverbial Byzantine political and diplomatic craft over the following centuries was the result of this concentration of experience, rather than any inherent Greek subtlety.

It is true that at certain times another powerful establishment figure overshadowed the emperor, gathering most of the reigns of power into his or her hands. Anthemius, heading the senatorial party, was Praetorian Prefect for the East for the unusually long period of nine years, and probably came as close as anyone to being the main power behind the throne. He had the unrivalled confidence of the boy emperor Theodosius II, which was actually enshrined, uniquely, in a legal act allowing him virtually imperial powers of decision, as well as those that actually went with his office. He effectively controlled all appointments and all finances, and both initiated and oversaw major policy at home and abroad. He worked both formally through the emperor's Consistory, and less formally through the palace, and through the vast bureaucratic network, whose members he had mostly appointed himself. His power during those years was perhaps comparable to that of Cardinal Richelieu in seventeenth-century France.

As well as being patriotic and competent, Anthemius was urbane and diplomatic, and his leadership widely accepted by most of the governing class. He seems to have had few enemies. It is highly likely that he had eventual imperial ambitions for his family, not by supplanting Theodosius II but by marrying some younger relative of his to one of the imperial sisters. This was not unusual, but neither in East nor West was there any tendency for the great state positions to become hereditary fiefs in the manner of the Shogunate. Anthemius' family ambition was thwarted either by his death, or by Pulcheria's imposition of pious virginity on all the imperial females, effectively banning male influence from the imperial family. She too wielded considerable power for several years through her almost exclusive influence over the emperor, but unlike Anthemius she could only influence major decisions, not take them herself. Fifty years later Anthemius' grandson of the same name became one of the last emperors in the West.

The power wielded by Aspar was different. He had held *Magister* posts at least four times and was *Magister in Praesenti*, with the rank of Patrician, at Constantinople for fourteen years. He headed a network of family alliances among the Gothic military class and, more distantly and dangerously, the Ostrogothic federates, and secured a *Magister* post for his son Ardaburius. From the time of Marcian's death in 457, it was politically impractical to dismiss Aspar. His concentration of power was perhaps the closest the East ever came to the warlord-generalissimo figure in the Western pattern, but the parallel is limited.

After he secured Leo's election to the purple in 457, Aspar was certainly the dominant military leader in the state, but he was still not the sole commander-in-chief of the armies. There were four other marshals of nominally equal rank, and although Aspar influenced several of their appointments, his control was still limited and indirect. Gothic and Roman generals were still balanced against one another. As a senior member of the Senate and Consistory he had a leading voice in major policies other than military – foreign affairs, for example – and no doubt considerable influence with the emperor in key civil appointments. But he did not directly control civil government, legislation or finance as the Western generalissimos effectively did. Nor did he control the emperor he had set up. Aspar too had vicarious imperial ambitions, and pressurised the emperor Leo into accepting his son Patricius as his nominated successor; a piece of *hubris*, which ultimately led to his downfall.

Aspar's case illustrates the point that in Constantinople military power had become institutionalised. He was senior commander of the Praesental armies and had held one of the highest positions in the government, but he still had to work always in close proximity to the emperor and the rest of the establishment if he was to retain and enlarge his power. Calling on direct military violence or the threat of it – which would involve the Goths – would have risked breaking the whole web of legal power Aspar had built up and perhaps result in losing everything. A despotic and unpopular military rule would have the greatest difficulty surviving in Constantinople, with its half-million riot-prone people, and Aspar knew it. But outside Constantinople, there was nowhere else from which to rule.

Aspar's power, even at its greatest, was probably less than Anthemius', who had almost complete control of all the non-violent levers of government. Neither of these outstanding leaders aspired to the throne himself – Anthemius because he was constitutionally loyal, and Aspar for similar reasons, but also because his Gothic origins and Arian religion counted against him. Both had indirect imperial ambitions for their families. Aspar in particular was involved in bitter rivalries with Leo's other supporters, which were as much personal as political. No-one doubted that the real, enduring source of power was the emperor, and they hoped to make it serve their broad interests. It was the entrenched position of Aspar's Gothic military network, itself no different form the other time-honoured Roman networks of patronage, which allowed him to occupy the foremost position in the state for so many years, and set up two emperors. But it precluded other dangerous military ambitions, and allowed the development of an orderly, ceremonially sanctified method of transferring the imperial power.

The limiting framework, which Aspar's own dominant influence helped to create, eventually proved larger than himself. At a later stage, his political and family ambitions overstepped implicit, barely charted bounds. He tried to put his son into the imperial succession, his kinship with the Ostrogothic tribal federate allies came into play, and something snapped. His murder by the emperor asserted violently and explicitly a new norm of government: the framework within which alone military strength could achieve power and position.

In the West the generalissimo Ricimer was still loyal in his fashion to the idea of Rome, but was finding his puppet emperors an increasing nuisance. He would probably have liked to get rid of the need for them, and instead rule directly himself as the nominal viceroy of the real emperor at Constantinople. His troops were now overwhelmingly new barbarian federates who were often rewarded by gold, pay and piecemeal grants of land, and who had only the haziest sense of being 'Roman'. The native Roman components of the Western armies were already a minority when Aetius had assembled his great coalition against Attila. Now they had dwindled even further, largely because of the chronic inability to pay them. What revenues could still be raised went to pay the federates.[12]

The strategic barrier and concentration of government in Constantinople and the ample supply of wealth from the Oriental provinces were supplemented by other means. Evolving political policies towards enemies and potential enemies, born of hard experience, were deployed as careful adjuncts to military force, and often as temporary substitutes for it – in essence, a more refined diplomacy. Compared with the days of Diocletian, and his aggressive colleagues two centuries earlier, when great military victories were concluded by crushing peace treaties, the East saw little of this. There were few impressive set victories, and several humiliating defeats. Yet it held its state together, except for the Balkans, and retained its identity and polity intact.

Traditionalist opinion, almost always civilian, took a dim view of this. Traditionalists expected great Roman military victories as in the past. Later historians, especially Gibbon, attributed this change to a pusillanimity, a decline in the true Roman martial virtues into 'Greek' craftiness and perfidy. The heroic ages were always before their eyes. Yet in cold fact the very classical heroes they admired – Aemilianus, Marius, Scipio and the rest – had usually overcome the Hellenistic military system by their prudent planning and greatly superior logistics, as much as their valour in the field.

If a commander cannot beat an enemy in a set battle but can split it by promises of gold or new alliances, if he can reduce it by starvation while keeping his own army intact and supplied, then that is what any responsible leader must do, subordinating battlefield glory to the longer interests of his country and state. The Russian general Kutuzov understood this perfectly when he took on himself the odium of abandoning Moscow to Napoleon in 1812. A state cannot rationally be blamed for using the effective weapons it has to hand, and which it is skilled in using. All else is sentimentality and vainglory, not political responsibility.

The East could raise far larger amounts of gold than any of its neighbours, including even Persia, and it put this to constant political use. The most obvious was the hiring of willing barbarian mercenary troops, and except during the embargo imposed by Attila there was never any lack of them. The effects were far wider than simple mercenary transactions. Gold bought considerable prestige and status in a tribal society. Often payments would be made to a king or chieftain for supplying troops on request. In the case of federates, within or outside the empire's frontiers, regular payments were fixed by treaty, which also stipulated certain standing military obligations such as defence of a sector of frontier or the regular supply of soldiers. Occasional dealings with foreign kings often included 'gifts', which were in effect payments for good behaviour or even more bluntly, temporary bribes to buy off one enemy until Roman forces were able to confront him later.

The more regular treaty arrangements tended towards a mutual diplomacy and the search for at least a predictable relationship. The tribal kings wanted both gold and Roman tokens of friendship to maintain their positions among their own nobles and followers, and the internal federates were constantly in need of land and adequate food supplies. The Romans needed troops and stability on a frontier. With Persia, annual payments were normal in support of a treaty, as an earnest of good faith. In every case, both sides were most sensitive about how these transactions were represented domestically. The Romans naturally portrayed them as generous discretionary gifts bestowed on a subdued foreign people as a token of good faith. Attila, and the Persian monarchs also, boasted to their respective peoples that this was submissive Roman 'tribute', acknowledging themselves as overlords.[13]

In its relations with Persia, the only neighbouring state of comparable power and civilisation, the Romans gradually developed a more sophisticated diplomacy, as Blockley's thorough study describes. Both empires had their subordinate allies and common enemies, such as the Huns, and their great military traditions. A Persian great king was always expected by his supporting noble families to fill the role of an aggressive conquering warrior. During the third and fourth centuries there were long periods of stable peace, but they were punctuated by four major wars of territorial aggression. In the 250s the new Sassanid dynasty invaded Syria, took Antioch and destroyed a whole Roman army at Edessa, taking the emperor Valerian captive. In 282–3, the emperor Carus sacked the Persian capital Ctesiphon before his sudden death terminated the expedition. In 296 the new Persian king, Narses, invaded the Roman territories but was utterly defeated by Galerius and Diocletian, who secured a decisive peace treaty heavily in Roman interests. After renewed war in the 350s, Julian's abortive invasion of Persia in 363, in which he was killed, ended in a new treaty which won back for Persia all it had lost sixty years before.

After this, internal problems and external enemies on all sides meant that future clashes, when they occurred, were for more limited objectives. Unlike the more shifting relations with the Hunnic or Germanic peoples, treaties with Rome and Persia were taken very seriously by both sides and could usually be relied on to hold, at least during the lifetimes of their respective rulers. They were increasingly complex affairs, covering many points of concentration – zones of influence, subordinate kingdoms, trade routes, frontier fortifications and even mutual aid against common enemies. They were also subject to renewal and detailed amendment often reflecting some shift in the power balance.

Although there were no permanent ambassadors in either capital in the modern sense, a distinct protocol evolved for the despatch and reception of embassies of appropriate rank and powers. Under the Master of Offices, a form of foreign minister, there grew up a professional corps of translators and in effect, professional career ambassadors. In these ways, through continuous communication between reciprocally recognised empires, there was a mutual understanding of the advantages of avoiding costly and hazardous wars if other methods could resolve disputes. By the fifth century neither power desired serious territorial aggrandisement, whatever their internal propaganda might have represented. At certain junctures, armed conflict did occur, in which the Roman side was usually victorious, but only after all diplomatic resources had been exhausted. Once they were over, relations and negotiations were resumed as usual. War slowly came to be seen as the exception rather than the rule, and with this came a subtly different concept of foreign relations. Treaties and diplomacy were no longer just the formal expression of a military victory or defeat, but an instrument which could actually be a substitute for war. With this emerged an official and ceremonial recognition of each other as equal superpowers and a mutual interest in understanding each other's intentions, in some ways like the stabilisation of American–Soviet relations after 1953. Narses' representative Apharban expressed it as early as 299 (when Persia was the defeated party): the two empires were like the twin eyes of the world, and it would be a sad disfigurement if either were ever to be put out.[14]

This development was in strong contrast to relations with the northern semi-nomadic barbarians such as the Huns, and later the Bulgars, who stood, as it were, at the opposite end of the diplomatic spectrum. Their approach was completely opportunistic, regarding treaties as mere auxiliary tactics towards military gains, to be discarded as soon as chance offered. Unlike the evolving Frankish and Gothic states, anything remotely approaching a civil element in their thinking, which might assess useful alternatives to fighting, was wholly absent.

Foreign policy was also helped by another factor, though this was not its primary intention: Christian missionary activity, which emperors were quick to recognise as a useful if indirect channel of influence. In the fourth century, the Gothic tribes had been converted through their chieftains to Arian Christianity, and many other Germanic peoples followed suit. This did not, of course, stop their depredations and ambitions at the empire's expense, but it did at least offer the possibility of subtle channels of communication, in which bishops played an increasing role. Later, missionary efforts were a conscious form of Roman imperialism, and the conversion of huge and hostile populations such as the Bulgars and Russians was to prove an enormous political gain for the Byzantine state.

During the periods of normal relations with Persia in the fifth century, both empires, each with an exclusive and intolerant state religion, partly signalled their peaceful intentions by tolerating each other's religious minorities: Christian communities in Mesopotamia, Armenia and South Arabia, and a smaller number of Zoroastrians within Roman territories. Of this reciprocity, there is no doubt that Christianity and Constantinople gained more. Of course, both Orthodox church and Zoroastrian priesthood disapproved of such accommodation, but had to defer to the larger interests of the state. Christian churchmen, who were usually able to move freely, developed both diplomatic and medical skills which impressed the Persians, even to the extent of being permitted to found Christian schools, including that at Gundeshapur, which grew into a highly respected centre of medical skills and learning. In these various ways, the overall stability on the Euphrates frontier during the fifth century, despite several short and costly wars, was a main contribution to the stability of the Eastern Empire.[15]

11

THE GOD-PROTECTED STATE

Mercifully, we are beyond the days when Byzantium needed to be defended against the charges of stagnation, unoriginality, lack of dynamic progress but indecent refusal to die. It is now common to see Byzantine civilisation as an unlikely but surprisingly durable blend of Roman law and government, Hellenic monarchy and culture, and fervent Orthodox Christianity. Here we attempt to trace how this remarkable synthesis came about.

Rome, like every successful civilisation or polity, had its sacred symbols, traditions and foundation myths. These were of course invented and reinvented. The earlier myth of Romulus and Remus was supplanted by Virgil's extravagant myth that Aeneas of Troy founded Rome, thus providing a desirable Hellenic ancestry. In the same vein, the new Aztec empire spuriously claimed descent from the ancient Toltecs. But no matter. Having shaken off the cruder elements of rationalism, positivism and functionalism we can perhaps understand these myths and ideologies more justly, as the pioneering sociologist Adam Ferguson did in 1767.[1] We do not need to believe the doctrines of Christianity, nor share the near-alien world of liturgy, icons, relics and miracles, to recognise that it gave expression to very deep and very human aspirations indeed. We have no right to condescend, like Gibbon, for that way we shall fail to understand. It is in this general spirit that we approach this vital aspect of Byzantium.

The essential foundation myth that had shifted from Romulus to Aeneas was now superseded by a new figure: Christ, Jesus of Nazareth, an obscure Jewish rebel executed in the reign of Tiberius. How this great change came about is outside the scope of this book. What matters is that the divine Christ now entered into the role of mythical founder, directing Constantine to establish the New Rome. However profound and dimly-understood the changes, however selective and attenuated the tradition, it was still Rome. It was not a new synthetic state borrowing old garments, like Charlemagne's Holy Roman Empire or the Pahlavi Shah's resurrection of Sassanid Iran.

From the long-distant times of Regulus, Cato and Scipio, to Caesar and Augustus, the recasting of the Republic into a civic monarchy, then Diocletian's transformation into an absolutist state and Constantine's foundation of a new

Christian capital, the threads of tradition were frayed and replaced, but never completely or consciously broken. Popular belief held that Constantine, in founding the city, had actually transferred from Rome the very *arcana* of its power, the Palladium of Troy, and buried it under his monumental column.[2] The Eastern Greeks, even down to 1453, always saw themselves as the proud and legitimate continuation of Rome, because that is what they were. As they prepared to man the walls of Constantinople for the last time against the great cannon of Mehmet II, the emperor Constantine XI exhorted them never to forget that they were the descendants of Greece and Rome and to be worthy of their heroic ancestors. His statue stands proudly in the cathedral square in Athens.[3]

The things men quarrel over among themselves they will also defend fiercely against outsiders. Principles of dissension can also, paradoxically, become principles of a larger unity. Gibbon, for all his insights, was captive to the idealised picture of pagan civic, patriotic virtues his age was brought up to admire so much in Sparta, Athens and Republican Rome, which inspired noble and peasant alike. It excluded the possibility that fractious, otherworldly Christianity might ever become a vehicle for similar loyalties. Yet, stripped of all their later sublimation, their garlands and marble dignities, these virtues had originally been simple, ignorant attachment to a city, a tribe and its gods, and an unthinking willingness to fight for it against despised foreigners. Though in a very different setting, the Byzantine Christian zeal for its icons, its liturgy, its emperor and its God-protected capital contained elements of a similar kind.

In earlier centuries Christianity and Hellenic culture had been strange bedfellows, and perhaps still were. The original inspiration of Christianity was distinctly Jewish, not Greek. As the provocative Tertullian asked, what has Athens to do with Jerusalem? But with Paul's missionary impetus and the spread of Christianity to men and women of higher social rank, a modus vivendi had to be sought. Education was classical education. There was no other. The Hellenistic heritage was almost synonymous with the mind of man. To be ignorant of Homer, the myths and the poets, of Plato and Aristotle, was to be an unlettered rustic.[4]

By the third and fourth centuries Greek philosophy, though still preserving its precious intellectual heritage, had long passed its heroic period. Unlike Aristotle, philosophers no longer enquired into physics, biology and politics. They were no longer really curious about the material world or the political and social world. Like the popular mystery religions and the yearning towards monotheism, they were increasingly concerned with the individual self or soul and its liberation or salvation in an immaterial spiritual realm. Miracle, divination and ascetic disciplines appeared as philosophy. Even at a more rationally educated level its preoccupation was distinctly otherworldly.[5]

Plotinus, who founded the Neoplatonist school, adapted Plato's doctrine of forms to a theory of a transcendent, changeless, supersensible ultimate reality: the One (reminiscent of Parmenides six centuries earlier). The One is without parts, properties, indefinable and indescribable. But it is possible for human minds to know the One, for their souls contain a reflection of the One, if they can rise above bodily and earthly desires.[6] Such views were congenial to a more intellectual Christianity. Clement of Alexandria identified Plato's pure eternal reality with God. He also followed John in identifying the *Logos*, the divine Reason, with Christ. Origen, who studied under the same teacher as Plotinus, took things further, skilfully interweaving biblical and Greek thought. It is in mind and soul, not in the body, that man truly if imperfectly shares in the *Logos*, as he shares in Christ's humanity. It is no exaggeration to say that there could have been no Christian theology without Neoplatonism.

> No-one, whether he is Jew or Gentile, lacks the law which is in men by nature....God implanted in man the faculty of reason which tells him what he must do and what he must avoid, and this faculty is conferred on all men alike...the natural law speaks to all who are subject to it.[7]

Of course, there was still a tension between the traditions, between the Greek idea of soul as mind and intellect, and the Christian emphasis on devotion and grace. Platonic and Stoic arguments could equally be turned against the Christians. Indeed the Neoplatonists, fearing Christianity as a dangerous fifth column within Hellenic culture, had helped to fuel the last great persecution by Diocletian and Galerius in 303. A century after this storm had blown itself out and Christianity had become established, the twin currents of classical culture and Christian faith were combined in the intellectual world of most educated men, and it was almost unthinkable that either could be abandoned.

In a religion which has replaced many gods by one, who walked the earth only once, the precise nature of this incarnation was naturally of central importance. Nevertheless, the Christological arguments over the nature of the Son and his precise relation to the Father were never satisfactorily solved, for the simple reason that they were insoluble. Each more subtle and precise definition only sharpened the contradictions. Today, with a far more discriminating and powerful mathematical logic than Aristotle, the problems of identity, especially personal identity, are notoriously difficult, and it is not at all surprising that the Greek theologians lost their metaphysical way.[8]

The Cyrillian–Nestorian disputes were essentially the successors of the Arian–Athanasian one: was the divine Christ identical and equal to the Father, or subordinate? Once Arianism was rejected and it was firmly accepted that Christ was equal to the Father, the thorny problem arose over the relation between Christ's divine and human natures. As Norman Baynes puts it succinctly, the eirenic compromise creeds adopted at various councils were usually just a restatement of the problem, in no sense a solution. ('The Father incomprehensible, the Son incomprehensible, the Holy Ghost incomprehensible....Yet not three incomprehensibles but one incomprehensible.')[9]

As many have remarked, the exaggerated addiction to metaphysical disputes, which characterised the Eastern Churches far more than the Western, were an overhang of Greek love of argument, and there was no lack of theologians in the marketplace and the baths. But apart from these frivolities, the real issue for the Christian population was how to reconcile the divine *Logos* of the philosophers with the Jesus of the Gospels. Perhaps the two most important outcomes of the Christological controversy were the clear establishment of the very popular cult of the *Theotokos*, Mother of God (not just Christ); and the final assertion of the supremacy of the Patriarchate of Constantinople.

The downfall and banishment of Nestorius had been due to his irascible temper and his direct clash with Pulcheria over the title Mother of God. Although he later changed his views somewhat and agreed that the title could be used, the rancour was not resolved. He had even cast doubt on Pulcheria's virginity, an unpardonable move. Pulcheria's alliance with the Alexandrian bishop Cyril helped pull down Nestorius, but Cyril's own motives and outrageous behaviour – mob violence and bribery on a huge scale – were less to do with theology than with the old struggle for precedence between Constantinople and Alexandria, with the bishop of Rome occasionally intervening.

The formula of the Council of Ephesus, 'two natures in unconfused union', did not settle things for long, and once again, it was Alexandria that fired the first shots. Cyril's successor Dioscorus attacked the two-natures formula, and instead advanced the counter-formula of 'one nature [hypostasis] after the union', whose followers became known as Monophysites. In doing so, he triggered a new conflict at Constantinople. His views were condemned by the Patriarch Flavian, but upheld by his archimandrite Eutyches. Flavian had him condemned, but he appealed to bishop Leo of Rome, and was also supported by Flavian's bitter enemy, the Chamberlain Chrysaphius, who at the time was the dominant influence over the emperor Theodosius II. The conflict generated enough heat and noise for Chrysaphius to persuade the emperor to call a new General Council, which he manipulated, and which met again at Ephesus in 449.[10]

Dioscorus of Alexandria presided. Eutyches was reinstated, Flavian deposed and imprisoned. Bishop Leo of Rome was outmanoeuvred. Voting was heavily influenced by rampaging mobs of Syrian monks, as well as the presence of the imperial officials. The Council adopted the doctrine of one nature. Bishop Leo bitterly denounced the proceedings as the 'Robber Council', but Dioscorus, now triumphant, excommunicated him too.

The whole settlement was abruptly overthrown when in 450 Theodosius died, Chrysaphius was executed and Marcian became emperor with Pulcheria. Despite the menace of Attila, Marcian wanted a way of reconciliation, an end to the overweening pretensions of Alexandria, and a unified structure to the church. He persuaded the bishop of Rome to agree to yet another council, to be held in the East. It met at Chalcedon in October 451, while Attila was embroiled in Gaul. Marcian and Leo together deposed Dioscorus. It was another heavy-handed imperial intervention and influenced the voting as usual, but without employing violent mobs. A new compromise formula was agreed, which became the Orthodox formula of Chalcedon: Christ was perfect God and perfect man, consubstantial with the Father in his godhead and with us in his manhood. He was made known in two natures, without confusion, change, division or separation. The differences between the two natures are not abolished by their union. The properties of each remain intact, and both come to form one person and one hypostasis, whatever that may mean.[11]

Together they had put Alexandria back in its place and reached what, for all its confusions, Marcian regarded as a reasonable compromise settlement, both in doctrine and church jurisdiction. In the 28th canon, Constantinople and Rome were to have equal authority over the various sees of East and West. But Bishop Leo did not see it that way, felt he had been outmanoeuvred again, and refused to ratify the article. Since the previous century the bishops of Rome, beginning with Damasus, had insisted on the primacy of Rome, on the basis that Peter and Paul had been martyred there, and, more important, on the text of Matthew 16, 18: 'Thou art Peter, and upon this rock...'[12] Constantinople, with no apostolic tradition, saw precedence in terms of Roman political and administrative divisions, just as bishoprics corresponded to provinces and dioceses. Constantinople after all was the New, Christian Rome (and by implication, perhaps, God-protected since it had pointedly not been sacked by barbarians). Several other Eastern churches with apostolic claims, such as Antioch where Peter had been bishop, and Ephesus where John was buried, also resented subordination to Constantinople. The new Bishop of Alexandria, Proterius, could only be installed by armed force.

Nonetheless, the Fourth Ecumenical Council imposed a theological Orthodoxy and a unified hierarchical structure, despite strong Monophysite sympathies in Palestine and Egypt. Church organisation now paralleled that of the imperial government, and Chalcedon has been seen as a further step in the subordination of church to state. In fact, this had always been the understood relationship ever since Constantine. The difference was that the see of Rome had only a diminishing Western empire to which to be subordinate, and even this would soon be replaced by a mosaic of new Germanic Christian kingdoms. Not unnaturally, the Bishop of Rome exalted his position to that of their spiritual overlord.

Popular religiosity took strong sides in these theological disputes, much as it took sides between the Blue and Green factions in the Hippodrome: the

Blues supported Chalcedonian Orthodoxy, the Greens Monophysitism. But its real religious fervour was different. The hugely popular cult of the *Theotokos*, so skilfully orchestrated by Pulcheria, perhaps owed something to the older cults of Isis and Horus, or Cybele the Great Mother, but probably less than has been supposed. At all events, it had less to do with the one or two natures of Christ than with the deep need for protection and mediation. One is struck by the growing isomorphism in popular imagination between the imperial order and the heavenly one. The emperor had his ministers and generals, then a hierarchy of lesser officials to whom the humble might address their pleas and petitions – or even, at great expense and difficulty, take them higher to the Prefect or even the emperor himself. God and Christ likewise had a hierarchy, from the archangels, including Michael, Christ's general, and the many lesser angels and saints to whom prayers and offerings for intercession could be addressed.

But Mary, Christ's Mother, stood very high with him. She looked down mercifully and understandingly on suffering, erring, frail humanity and her influence was very powerful. She could work great miracles, and was a special helper and protector of the poor and the humble (a role Hercules had once filled, though never with such ardent devotion). Most importantly, the Virgin, through her supernatural powers, was the special defender of Constantinople, her fortress, her acropolis. In the city her churches outnumbered all others: there was no public place or imperial dwelling, no official's house or even reputable inn without its church or oratory to the Virgin. The cult was not a demotic one only, but shared by all classes. Her favourite was the Church of the Blachernae built by Pulcheria near the Golden Horn, to which so many processions went in times of danger and supplication. In the reign of Leo two relations of the Gothic generals Aspar and Ardaburius discovered the robe (Palladium) of the Holy Virgin in a village near Galilee, stole it, but prayed earnestly to her to forgive the theft. 'It is to your city that the robe is going, the City that is queen of all others, whose first duty is to honour anything of yours.' She answered their prayer approvingly, and so the City placed the holy robe in the church of the Blacharnae. It was later joined by her shroud, her girdle and even the swaddling clothes of the infant Jesus, which still had traces of her breast milk.[13]

It was in such concrete relics, in the holy icons, the Eucharist, the liturgy, that the ordinary person's communal religious devotion and dedication was expressed: the tirelessly repeated picture stories of the Old and New Testaments adorning every church, the ubiquitous images of the Virgin and Child, the hierarchies of saints and, dominating them all, Christ Pantocrator, ruler of the cosmos. Icons were far more than mere man-made representations, they were a living, physical embodiment of spiritual power, a point at which the material and spiritual realm intersected, a small window opening from the earthly world into God's kingdom. Though painted by a human hand, that hand had been supernaturally guided to produce an exact likeness of its subject, and hence copies had to be as unerringly faithful as possible if the spiritual quality was to be preserved and transmitted. Even here there were distant pagan precedents. The *imago* of the emperor, carried at the head of a legion, had a spiritual importance demanding not just homage and respect, but veneration – oaths before it were especially binding. In the Christian East, the power of icons was an active potency akin to the divine presence itself; a power that could work miracles and win battles.

This vernacular religious feeling was becoming closely associated with patriotism. Pagan intellectuals were still tolerated, but for the great mass of people Orthodox Christianity was coming to coincide with Romanness, or *Romanitas*. Their symbols were imperial and holy, their prayers a strength and a shield in adversity. *Kyrie Eleison* became a sacred battlecry among the Greek soldiers. Like Pallas Athene, the Virgin defended Constantinople against all enemies, as she had done against the Visigoths and Huns. Among her many titles was *Theotokos Hodegetria*, Mother of God who leads to victory, whose church was also founded by Pulcheria on the eastern shore of the city.[14] Her own hymn, the *Akathistos*, became the special hymn of victory and deliverance. Her cult as warrior-protectress grew even stronger in later centuries after the city had withstood even more dangerous assaults.

Can this cult really be seen as superstitious or irrational? The fact that we are (mostly) unable to believe such things now is beside the point. To take a modern example: the later Soviet Union of Brezhnev and his gerontocratic Party, tired and threadbare in all its other appeals to its people, fell back on the common achievement of the Great Patriotic War, a triumph in which everyone shared with strong and genuine pride. The Soviet system, it was claimed, was supposedly vindicated by the fact that the Soviet state had withstood and defeated the German Fascist invaders almost alone, whereas in 1916–17 Czarist Russia had collapsed under a similar assault despite a permanent second front in France. Given the Byzantine background of literal belief in the Gospels and their miracles, was it irrational of them to believe that the Virgin was responsible for the city's repeated repulse of Goths, Huns, Avars, Bulgars, Russians, Arabs, some of which victories even we would be inclined to describe with hyperbole as near-miraculous?

Among the governing classes the earlier church prejudices against state service were now eroded. The Brahmanical question of whether a good Christian could serve as a magistrate or soldier without imperilling his soul – especially by shedding blood – had become archaic and academic. He could serve religion by dedicating churches or endowing monasteries. At most, the strong sentiment persisted that the truly holy life was the unworldly one of the monk. But against this, a growing number of bishops in rural towns, especially in the Balkans, were in effect taking over many of the municipal functions of the old town magistrates, the *curiales*. They would contribute to the town's upkeep, help maintain roads and water supplies, provide charitable relief, and in some cases rebuild fortifications and even, in emergencies, organise makeshift military defence.

Perhaps the most potent symbol unifying religion and empire was the great and holy capital of Constantinople itself. This was not Augustine's heavenly City of God, but God's City on Earth, with its emperor, Patriarch, soldiers, palace, harbours, public squares and myriad churches. It was the undisputed strategic, political and religious capital in a way Rome had long ceased to be and Ravenna never was. Though only a few generations old, even by the fifth century the expanding city of Constantinople was becoming, in men's imaginations, more than just the imperial capital: it was also an Idea. After Rome had been sacked twice and pillaged thoroughly, and most of the earlier imperial capitals – Trier, Milan, Sirmium – were either destroyed or in decline, Constantinople stood unequalled and unconquered. This was the New Christian God-protected Rome, which had never been pagan and was unpolluted by sacrifice or idolatry, as they supposed (conveniently ignoring the fact that Constantine had allowed the pagan temples of old Byzantium to continue alongside the new churches). Its strategic impregnability and its divine protection merged into one. As it had been for the first Rome, for Constantinople to fall was the unthinkable disaster: it would both imperil the whole empire and signal that God's favour had been withdrawn. Versions of this sentiment were to grow even stronger in later centuries, when other great cities such as Antioch and Alexandria had fallen to Islam but Byzantium had Christianised its Bulgar and Slav neighbours in the Orthodox faith. To Kievan Russia, though never a province of the empire, Constantinople would always represent the undisputed gravitational source of wealth, power, legitimate authority and above all, Orthodox holiness and all that flowed from it.

The evolving world view of East Rome might be caricatured as medieval, on a strong but inert classical base. For centuries there were painstaking commentaries on Aristotle, for example, but no new ideas, no development of philosophical thought; the intellectual atmosphere for such activity had been slowly stifled. The Christian mould accepted classical thought, but only at the price of emasculating and taming it. Classical literature was prized, but its pagan setting of gods and heroes bowdlerised into harmless literary ornament. Scientific theories of the natural world were bypassed, rather than suppressed: men were more concerned with God's purposes in sending an earthquake than in its immediate physical causes.

None of this, of course, led to the neglect of mathematics, engineering and architecture, especially as applied to fortification and building. But as for speculation on the nature of the universe, a fairly typical view is given by St Basil, who formulated rules for the monastic life. Pagan theories and arguments are profitless, full of error and conflicting opinion. Why are they needed when we have the certainty provided by Moses, who had an excellent academic education under the Egyptians and, more important, met God face to face and was told the truth directly? The Bible is literally true, and if it does not answer certain questions that is because they do not concern us.[15]

Something similar befell Greek political thought. Scholars were well aware of it, but statesmen and lawyers had little contemporary use for it. Certainly, as Baynes, Bury and others have pointed out, East Rome had its coherent political theory, which served it well. The modern objection is that the theory was static and conservative, as indeed it was.

It was a theory of sacred, absolute monarchy (*Autokrator*, *Augustus*, *Basileus*), but tempered by certain constraints – some Greek, some Roman, some Christian. It owed almost nothing to ancient Greek political thought. It had no use for Aristotle's *Politics*, where the respective advantages of monarchy, oligarchy or democracy are dispassionately debated. ('Democracy' seemed to mean something indistinguishable from mob rule by the Blues and Greens, an almost self-contradictory notion.) Its background was rather the great Hellenistic divine monarchies that had established themselves after Alexander – the Seleucids, Ptolemies and Antigonids.

The Alexandrian synthesis of Greek and Oriental political traditions in the East had created large multinational empires ruled by powerful, absolute kings who were automatically accorded divine honours. Ptolemy I, for example, became the successor of the Pharaohs, who not merely ruled but mystically embodied the state. By the time Rome began absorbing these regions, they were already long-established states of a culture and sophistication equal or superior to their conquerors'. It was entirely natural that Pompey, Caesar and then Antony should be honoured as gods in the East, and they would have been unwise to refuse these honours if they wanted to retain their authority. The strong anti-monarchical sentiments at Rome, which Octavius mobilised against Antony even while he was paving the way for a disguised monarchy of his own, had no roots in the Hellenic East at all. The vernacular Greek title for emperor, *Basileos*, has been translated as 'king', but it certainly did not mean king in the Latin sense of *rex*, a title no Roman emperor would have used, and which was reserved for lesser tribal rulers. As with Alexander, it meant monarch over many nations. *Basileos Rhomaion* is accurately rendered as Emperor of the Romans.

Christian emperors were no longer 'divine' in the narrowly conventional pagan sense (Constantine instead made himself the thirteenth apostle, preparing his sarcophagus adjacent to the Church of the Apostles[16]), but they inherited and used all the Oriental regalia and ceremony by which Diocletian and his successors had elevated the imperial image to super-human proportions. The Christian bishop and historian Eusebius, among others, adapted the Hellenistic idea of divine kingship to his own times. The emperor was undoubtedly divinely elected. In his Tricennial oration to Constantine, he skilfully adapted the old pagan *vota* ceremony – anniversary prayers to the gods to protect the emperor – into a Christian one. He also adapted Diocletian's late pagan theology of the earthly emperors mirroring the Olympians, Jove and Hercules in the harmony and justice of their rule – but far more tellingly. Constantine has been chosen by God, he declares, and his earthly rule is an image of God's rule in heaven: 'Thus clothed in the likeness of the Kingdom of Heaven, he pilots affairs on earth with an upward gaze, steering by the original divine form.'[17]

It was a theory and doctrine of absolute monarchy. There was no legitimate way of opposing the monarch's will, once properly known and expressed. But it was not an arbitrary monarchy, like Attila's, where – in Roman eyes – there was no distinction between the monarch's whims and his laws, where everything was charismatic, despotic and personal. It had very clear ideas of what was expected of an emperor. He, like those before him, was author of the laws and ultimate interpreter of them, but within the extremely important framework of Roman legal tradition and jurisprudence, as is so evident in Theodosius II's great project of codification. The emperor was expected to rule according to law. However this ideal might be violated in actual political practice, it was still a violation: treason trials might be fabricated, but they still paid the hypocritical compliment of aping due form and process. An edict of Theodosius in 429 states: 'Our authority depends upon the authority of law. To submit our sovereignty to the laws is truly a greater thing than the imperial power.'

As Gregory the Great put it, the difference between barbarian kings and Roman emperors is that one is lord of slaves, the other lord of free men.[18] Christianity indeed reinforced a roughly parallel sentiment by its frequent quotation of Old Testament strictures on kingship, especially the relation between Samuel the Prophet and David the King.

Legitimate creation of an emperor still depended on the complex formula of 'election' by Senate and army, added to the increasingly strong dynastic backbone and the right of emperors to choose and crown new emperors. In the third and fourth centuries the act could be validly accomplished by an army in the field, and ratified in the capital later. By the fifth century, the old military ceremony of coronation – by the torque and raising on a shield – was supplemented by a civil one, with the diadem, and it was increasingly expected that both be performed in Constantinople. To these were added, by an accretion of custom, the choice of God and the 'acclamation' of the people, as we see in the coronation of Leo after the last vestiges of the Theodosian dynasty had disappeared.

The Patriarch of Constantinople, as the acknowledged senior churchman, came to play a role in the creation of an emperor through the coronation ceremony. This was a further bond between emperor and Patriarch, but the relation was always one of subordination. Unlike the later western medieval kingdoms, coronation did not make an emperor; he was already made. It added to the older components the newer element of the Orthodox Church as a part of the state, through whom God's approval could be properly signalled, spiritually ratifying what had already been done.[19] God's chosen

Vicegerent on earth was not the Patriarch but the correctly elected and crowned emperor.

Even when weak emperors, such as Arcadius and Theodosius II, were succeeded by stronger ones – Marcian, Leo, Zeno, Anastasius, three of whom had been soldiers – the demilitarisation of the monarchy continued, partly because of the steady concentration of other kinds of authority at Constantinople. Publicly they still accorded military victories to themselves, and on their coins they still appeared in conventional military garb, though by no means always. Later, when emperors, such as Heraclius, were occasionally great military leaders in person, this naturally enhanced their prestige, but their essential *Basileia* no longer depended on it as it had done in the third and fourth centuries. In popular imagination at least, the emperor was the nearest earthly being to Christ Pantocrator, ruler and judge of all, whose all-encompassing image dominates the central interior dome of Byzantine churches. In a sense, we might wonder which of them created the other.

We may begin to see the emergence of a self-sufficient, self-conscious empire of East Rome with its distinctive character, not merely half a body with a withered Western limb. Of course the empire was still seen as one, whatever chronic struggles the West was undergoing, but its centre was now Constantinople, and the Asiatic and Oriental provinces were its vital heartland. At this stage it is easy but misleading to retroject the articulated, finished image of Byzantium from about the tenth century back to the formative period. It was still far from being homogeneous politically or culturally. Linguistically Greek was central and dominant, but was still only a surface ruling-class language in the Aramaic and Coptic Orient, and in the Anatolian peninsula it was only slowly replacing the native Phrygian, Lydian, Lycian and Cappadocian. In the Balkan provinces, Latin was still the dominant language superimposed over the local ones. In religion, Chalcedonian Orthodoxy still coexisted uneasily with the Monophysitism in Syria, Palestine and Egypt, as well as the acknowledged Arianism of Gothic generals, soldiers and federates, which did not yield to conversion and could not practically be prohibited.

A huge, anonymous multinational empire defended by a highly paid standing army cannot inspire the same kind of loyalty as a city state or tribal nation. To the great mass of subjects the state and government, as it impinged on their lives, was something they put up with as they had always done. They naturally evaded their taxes where they could, sought protection from influential patrons, and feared few things more than the billeting of soldiers on them. But their local attachments to their cities were of a quite different character. Despite the decline of the curial class, the cities east of the Bosporus were generally thriving, and it is striking that their citizens, sometimes led by their bishops, were willing to defend them in emergencies, rather than to surrender or abandon them, or wait passively for the support of the professional army. Beyond their city and its hinterland, the Roman entity was expressed most simply as the remote, supremely powerful God-given emperor. But just as powerful, and certainly more intimate, were the universal figures of Christ and his Holy Mother. Against Huns or Persians they were the focus of a fierce, common sense of *Romanitas*, a loyalty more spontaneous, more widespread and more deeply felt than Jupiter and Hercules had inspired.

Figure 13 The Barberini ivory of a victorious emperor of the fifth or early sixth century. The identity is uncertain, but it is very possibly Anastasius.

Source: Musée du Louvre

Note: © Photo RMN – Chuzeville

167

Figure 14 Ivory of the Archangel Michael, early sixth century. Michael was to
become the central figure of God's warrior who led the armies to victory.

Note: © The British Museum

Figure 15 Clasp of the *Theotokos* (Mother of God), fifth or early sixth century. The cult was strongly promoted by Pulcheria and became widely popular among the people and armies.

Source: The Metropolitan Museum of Art

Note: Gift of Helen Miller Gould, 1910 (10.130.1522)

Figure 16 Christ Pantocrator, ruler of all. A fifth-century ivory pyxis showing the twelve apostles and the sacrifice of Isaac.

Source: Staatliche Museum, Berlin-Dahlem

Note: © Bildarchiv Preussischer Kulturbesitz, Berlin, 1998; photograph: Jürgen Liepe, 1992

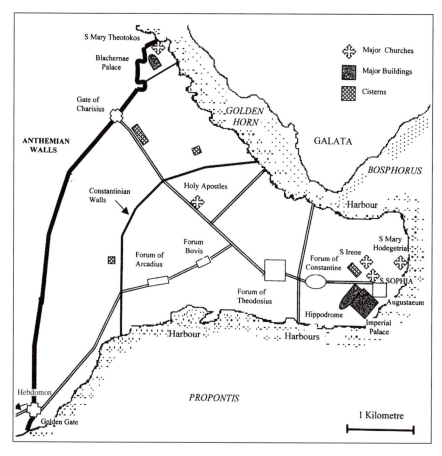

Map 3 Constantinople in the fifth century.

Part 4

THE STRUGGLE FOR STABILITY

12

IMPERIAL CONFLICTS

Pulcheria died in 453, followed by Marcian in 457. With him ended the titular remnants of the Theodosian dynasty in the East, which had reigned, if not actively ruled, for over seventy years. The prestige and loyalties which had accumulated around this imperial house are still remarkable, when we consider that for over half a century the emperors at Constantinople had been, by traditional Roman standards, feeble creatures. Real political power had been wielded by officials or by strong imperial women who, also by traditional Roman standards, had no legitimate authority in their own right.[1]

But some of these traditional standards were beginning to be left behind. As we have seen, it was no longer essential for the emperor to be viewed as a great warrior: he was now a holy being whose piety brought divine favour, and who directed his generals to fight for him as God directed his archangels. It was no longer out of the question for capable imperial women occasionally to exercise their own *Basileia*. Later centuries would see an empress, Irene, actually ruling alone without a consort, a situation unheard of in earlier constitutional law.

The most powerful faction around the court was the Gothic military group, bound by marriage ties and self-protective alliances, and headed by the Praesental *Magister* Aspar, who had held a *Magister* rank for over twenty-five years, in addition to consular and Patrician status, and had played a major role in choosing Marcian.[2] Now that a dynasty had finally ended without an obvious heir, there were no binding precedents. The Senate at Constantinople was one factor in the equation, and had its own favoured candidate. This was the *Magister Militum* Anthemius, grandson of the great Prefect Anthemius, who had served on the Danube frontier respectably if not brilliantly, and been rapidly promoted by Marcian, whose daughter Euphemia he had married. It is possible that Marcian had intended him to succeed, but of this there had been no public signal, such as a court appointment, let alone his elevation to the rank of Caesar, which would have settled the question.[3] In any case, Aspar had different ideas.

After the collapse of the main Hun power, several barbarian groups had established themselves within the empire, either by force – the Gepids and

Ostrogoths in Pannonia – or, soon afterwards, by agreed settlement – a second group of Ostrogoths in the province of Thrace. Marcian, with little other option, had accepted them as federate allies. In Pannonia, the Ostrogoths were under King Valamir of the Amal line, which was later to claim pre-eminence as the Ostrogothic royal house. Valamir had led his people to war under Attila, and had then been first to revolt against his sons. In Thrace, the Ostrogoths were a separate tribal grouping led by Triarius, of less distinguished lineage (or so his rivals later claimed). He was the father of Theoderic Strabo, who was related to Aspar by marriage. Both groups feared Hun domination every bit as much as the Romans did, and both were potential allies and potential dangers. Aspar himself was an astute and powerful politician, and clearly understood two things. First, Gothic military violence, or the threat of it to further his political purposes, would arouse resistance in almost every sector of the population. Second, civil senatorial opinion was strongly opposed to the rise of any overweening military figure in the Western mould, if it could possibly be prevented. Aspar and the other Gothic generals looked over their shoulders to the Ostrogothic federates, but resisted any temptation to repeat the destabilising follies of Gainas by trying to combine forces with them or to bring their influence into the political arena at Constantinople. Aspar's family ambitions were Roman, not tribal. He had by now achieved a very high position in the ruling class. Although he certainly did not have the dictatorial authority of Constantius or Aetius, he was now the most powerful single man in the state.

He needed a pliant and reliable candidate, and Anthemius was certainly not this. Aspar's choice was again a middle-ranking officer who had served under him: Leo, a Dacian by origin and Orthodox in religion.[4] If there was a brief power struggle it was fought out in private and then concealed by an impressive public display of unity. Nor did Anthemius suffer any demotion in consequence; instead he went on to win victories and eventually occupy the tottering throne in the West. The election was a carefully staged performance, one of the earliest examples we have of the new and evolving ceremony of emperor-making. We have a detailed account of it, deriving from a later Byzantine book of ceremonies.[5]

It was performed on the great campus of the Hebdomon on 7 February 457. The palace guards (*scholae*) and units of the Praesental army laid their standards on the ground. The Senate and army called upon Leo, in a litany that was to become, with variants, an increasingly standardised Byzantine ritual:

> Hear O God, we call on you! Hear us, O God who loves mankind! The State demands Leo! The Army demands Leo! The Palace expects Leo! This is the wish of the Palace, the army, the Senate and the People.

He ascended the tribunal, a military torque was placed on his head, the standards were raised again, and all shouted the acclamation, 'Leo Augustus, You have conquered! God gave you, God will keep you! A long reign! God will defend the Christian empire!' The troops closed around him and held locked shields over his head. There then followed, in the palace, a second ceremony of coronation. In the absence of any surviving legitimate member of the imperial family, the diadem was placed on his head and the purple on his shoulders by Anatolius, Patriarch of Constantinople. Leo then reappeared in full imperial regalia, the officials performed the act of adoration (*proskynesis*), then he took up a shield and spear and was re-acclaimed. Through his legal spokesman (*a libellis*) he replied and announced the customary donative of five gold solidi and a pound of silver to each soldier of the army. Those present received it directly from the emperor, the rest by special imperial envoys.[6]

The evolution of the ceremony at Constantinople was politically significant. In earlier centuries an emperor could be properly elevated by the army in the field, away from the capital; it had been a military affair only, to be routinely ratified by the Senate afterwards. In the case of Leo, we still see the distinction between the military ceremony with the torque, and the civil one with the diadem. In later centuries they merged into one. In effect the all-important power of emperor-making ceased to be the prerogative of the soldiers, and required the proper co-operation of army, palace and civil ministers in the capital itself.

Leo, like Marcian before him, was of Balkan origin and took the security of the European provinces seriously. He was also willing to help the fragmented West as far as he could, consistent with more vital priorities. Also like Marcian, he was to show a distinct tendency to pick and fight his battles early, rather than to wait for them to come to him. His military background might be undistinguished, but he stepped into the imperial role determinedly. He was not going to be a mere cipher of Aspar and his faction, if he could find a way to work free of them. But, not coming from within either the old imperial family or the governing establishment he needed to find or create an alternative power base, and did what he could to strengthen his own family through military appointments and marriage arrangements for his daughters Ariadne and Leontia.

Given the traditional nature of the imperial authority, with its enormous powers of patronage gravitating always around the palace and imperial family, he had no alternative but to try and build, from little or nothing, an extended political family of direct personal ties and obligations to himself. The civil bureaucracy, itself interwoven by many family and client networks, was still large and pervasive enough for the values of continuity and state stability to transcend narrow family advantage. But Leo, of obscure origins, uncultured and hitherto undistinguished, was excluded from this polite class. There began an involuntary but insidious rift between emperor and government machinery, in which narrower family and personal loyalties were predominant.

For the next few years Leo was in a weak position and had to temporise, making great concessions. Aspar demanded the position of *Magister Militum per Orientem* for his son Ardaburius, who was a capable general, and this was granted. He also demanded that his other son, Patricius, marry one of Leo's daughters and be given the rank of Caesar – the clear nomination of an imperial succession. Leo was able to evade or defer both these other demands, partly because his daughter was not yet old enough.[7]

He was very soon faced with a revolt by the Ostrogothic allies in Pannonia, who marched into Illyricum. They had some real grievances, which Leo may have provoked. They had served Roman interests by defending Pannonia against Hun attacks, and they wanted the same generous subsidies as were granted to Triarius' Ostrogoths in Thrace. It is very possible that Marcian had agreed a subsidy but Leo clumsily attempted to end it. At all events, after some fighting in which Anthemius distinguished himself, Leo agreed to a treaty. King Valamir was granted 300 pounds of gold annually, an easily affordable sum. In return, his royal nephew Theoderic, son of Theodemir, became an honoured hostage to be brought up at Constantinople.[8]

A more difficult problem was with the Vandal king, Gaiseric, who had been in intermittent war with the West since the deaths of Aetius and Valentinian III, and was now encroaching ever further into what was left of Roman territory in Africa. After his sack of Rome, Gaiseric attempted an invasion of Sicily, but this was heavily defeated in 456 by the *Magister* Ricimer, who soon afterwards made himself generalissimo in Italy in the tradition of Aetius.[9] But the danger was only briefly averted. When Ricimer's nominee, the new emperor Majorian, a soldier for once, spiritedly planned to invade Africa, Gaiseric's fleet anticipated him and crippled his armada off the Spanish coast.[10] The West badly wanted Leo's help. Whether Leo was alive to their dangers, he was inhibited by the attitude of Aspar who, since his own African campaign in the 430s, had favoured a policy of accommodation towards the Vandals, who posed little direct threat to the East.[11]

For the present Leo confined himself to diplomacy, his first concern being to secure the release of the captive family of Valentinian III. A number of embassies were fruitless, until Gaiseric named as his price his son Huneric's marriage to Valentinian's daughter Eudocia, thus securing the connection with the Theodosian house he had long sought. In return for Leo's recognition of the marriage, he then released Valentinian's widow, Eudoxia, and remaining daughter, Placidia, to Constantinople. There were further terms to the treaty, but whatever they were, they did not prevent Gaiseric from continuing to make war on the remnants of the West Roman provinces.[12] He now felt entitled to dabble in imperial dynastic politics, and allegedly claimed that his raids were in support of Placidia's claim to put her husband Olybrius on the Western throne. In fact, they had all the appearance of simple conquest. By about 464 Gaiseric refused even to receive Leo's embassy. Diplomatic relations were broken, and Leo was forced to recognise that only a full-scale invasion could solve the problem, an invasion for which, against Aspar's advice, he now began to prepare.

Aspar, doubtless under the pretext of higher diplomacy, was cultivating the Ostrogothic federates in Thrace, especially his own relative the prince Theoderic Strabo. This was not inherently treasonable, since they were friendly allies. But the new situation that had arisen since the end of Hun dominance could not be ignored. Once again, there were armed federate nations of Goths in the East's territories, as there had been at the time of Theodosius I, capable of putting considerable forces in the field. In particular, and in contrast to Theodosius I, the Thracian settlement seems to have been allowed in agriculturally rich territories well south of the Danube and the Haemus mountains, closer to the European lines of communication with Constantinople – apparently an error of Leo rather than Marcian. Aspar and his Gothic military group might be blamelessly loyal as before, but the fact was that there were now other possible options that had not then existed. Whether or not this apprehension was accentuated by Aspar's obvious dynastic ambitions and whether or not it was widely shared by the senatorial party, Leo now felt it prudent to seek a military counterweight to Aspar and his Gothic power base, preferably one that would be exclusively dependent on himself.

Such a resource was ready to hand. Cautiously, he began to put feelers out to the Isaurian mountain peoples of Asia Minor. Only nominally Roman subjects, these peoples were universally regarded as internal barbarians, and were hated and feared as brigands, which is what they were. One government after another had failed to eliminate their menace. Like most primitive highland peoples, they were excellent fighting material: their troops under Zeno had garrisoned Constantinople against Attila.

Isaurians were highly unpopular in Constantinople, far more so than the Goths, but this was not unhelpful to Leo's purpose and, in any case, he had to balance one risk against another. With lavish promises and much gold he reached a secret agreement with one of their most powerful headmen, Tarasacodissa, to suppress the brigand raiding.[13] In return, Leo promised to recruit Isaurian troops on generous terms, and raise Tarasacodissa to an exalted position. Tarasacodissa accepted readily, the raiding was ended, a rival chief easily suppressed, and Isaurian troops duly recruited. There now began a serious struggle between Aspar's faction and Leo. In 466 Tarasacodissa produced written evidence supposedly showing that Aspar's son Ardaburius was in treasonable correspondence with Persia: Leo produced it in front of the Senate and secured Ardaburius' dismissal. Tarasacodissa was appointed to command a new corps of 300 Isaurian palace guards, the *Excubitores* (the Sentries). He Hellenised his name to Zeno, after the Isaurian who had defended Constantinople, and soon afterwards was raised to new heights. He became *Magister Militum per Thracias*, and married Leo's eldest daughter, Ariadne. Aspar's ambitions were checked and his star in the descendant. But

Leo's choice of a son-in-law must have alienated the senatorial aristocracy still further.

In 467, responding to a request from the West where the throne had been vacant for over a year, Leo appointed as Western emperor Anthemius, the son-in-law of Marcian who had been a possible candidate for his own throne, and could claim at least a distant connection to the house of Theodosius. Anthemius travelled west with a strong military force. The support of Ricimer, the real ruler of Italy, was hopefully secured by a marriage with Anthemius' daughter, Alypia.[14] It was part of a policy of closer co-operation with the West, which had been unable to prevent Vandal raids on Italy and Sicily. It rightly aroused Vandal suspicions, and Gaiseric sent a fleet to raid the Eastern coasts.[15] But in 468, against Aspar's advice and policy, the great invasion of Vandal Africa was ready.

The command was given not to Aspar but to the emperor's brother-in-law Basiliscus, suggesting the influence of the empress Verina, although Aspar was said not to have opposed the appointment.[16] The invasion was a quite enormous, extraordinary effort, drawing on all the military resources the Eastern empire could mobilise, possibly in the order of 100,000 troops of all types, from all sources, including the West. It required stability and peaceful diplomacy on other frontiers. Fortunately, Persia was heavily preoccupied with other enemies, but there was unrest on the lower Danube, over which Leo had to temporise.

The invasion was planned as a three-pronged assault. One prong was under the Western general Marcellinus, who had reoccupied Sicily and managed to expel the Vandal garrison from Sardinia. Basiliscus, with the main army in an armada of over 1,000 ships, would land at a distance from Carthage and link up with a supporting army under Heraclius, advancing from Egypt and Tripolitana (modern Libya). Simultaneously Marcellinus would invade Africa from Sicily with an army of perhaps 10,000 to 20,000 men. The West had agreed to contribute about a quarter of the total cost.[17]

Marcellinus' fleet never sailed, perhaps because of Ricimer's veto. Either he would not spare so many precious troops to get bogged down in Africa and hoped the East would do the job for him, or he resented the military prowess of Marcellinus who aligned himself with the emperor Anthemius, both of them becoming disturbing rivals to himself. But these are pale speculations in the face of the shining fact that here, now, was the one unique opportunity for Ricimer, as ruler of Italy and what was left of the West, to rid himself of Gaiseric and repossess Africa once and for all – an achievement greater than any other he could hope for.[18]

The other two prongs of the invasion made good progress. Heraclius advanced from Tripolitana towards Carthage, while Basiliscus' warships defeated and scattered a Vandal fleet off Sicily, and disembarked the army in Africa. Everything seemed to point, at last, to a crushing victory over the Vandal kingdom. At this point Gaiseric was so alarmed that he evacuated

Carthage while the two Roman armies converged and were set to enter the city. There had been no serious fighting yet. Gaiseric proposed a truce of five days, to negotiate terms of retreat, or an accommodation, or a treaty settlement.

What hopes or blandishments he offered we can only guess, but they worked. Even if Heraclius had not yet arrived, it seemed clear that Gaiseric was in deep trouble and had lost the initiative. With appalling lack of judgement (on the spot, not in hindsight), Basiliscus agreed, at the very moment that a main victory seemed in his grasp and he could entertain possible parleys from the position of conqueror. During the five days, Gaiseric prepared fire-ships that he launched against the anchored Roman fleet, taking it completely by surprise and destroying half of it. In confusion, his supplies cut off, Basiliscus abandoned the attack on Carthage and withdrew with the remnant of the fleet to Sicily to join Marcellinus. But Marcellinus was suddenly murdered, possibly at Ricimer's instigation. Heraclius had no option but to go on the defensive and retreat to Tripolitana, where he held his positions for the next two years until finally recalled.

Basiliscus returned to Constantinople in disgrace, generally reviled. It was said that he had to take refuge from the mob in the Great Church, until the emperor, yielding to his wife's pleas, rescued him and then exiled him. It is a measure of Leo's family loyalties, perhaps his isolation, that Basiliscus did not suffer a worse fate. Leo was forced to agree to a new non-aggression treaty with Gaiseric, who can hardly have believed his good fortune. The shock to Roman prestige was enormous. The invasion had deployed all available Roman strength, yet failed ignominiously, falling to the very same Vandal surprise naval tactics that had defeated Majorian. It seemed that Gaiseric's kingdom had a charmed existence: nothing could destroy him. For the first time, the Eastern imperial treasury actually saw the lining of its pockets. Even had the invasion succeeded, the cost would have been considerable. As it was, it had depleted the reserves by about 65,000 pounds of gold and 700,000 pounds of silver. A year's tax revenue was perhaps a quarter of this.[19]

As with any great disasters, there were fierce recriminations and conspiracy theories. Aspar was believed to be pro-Vandal, and it was therefore naturally put about that he wanted the expedition to fail, and either bribed Basiliscus to sabotage it, or influenced the appointment of Basiliscus, knowing his incompetence. The two stories are not compatible. You do not bribe the incompetent to be incompetent. There is very little plausibility in these charges but the fact remains that Aspar's position was strengthened by the great failure.[20]

The concentration of resources for the African war had exposed other frontiers to trouble that could not immediately be contained. One of the surviving sons of Attila, Dengizich, petitioned Leo demanding subsidies and land for his people, something Leo was in no position to refuse. This soon led to fighting in Thrace, and eventually the Gothic *Magister* Anagast defeated the Huns with the help of the Ostrogoths, killing Dengizich in 469.[21] At the same time a new steppe people, the Avars, were migrating westwards from the Caucasus region, occupying much of the area previously dominated by the Huns. Their immediate effect was to displace the Saraguri, who established friendly relations with the Romans but came into conflict with Persia, over-running Iberia and Persian Armenia. These new tribal movements were probably an indirect cause of the Hun pressures in Thrace.

Relations with Persia worsened in Leo's reign, but hostile moves were confined to the small allied client kingdoms of the two empires. The treaty of 422 was still in force, Persia preoccupied with threats on her northeastern borders, and the overall situation stable enough for Leo to draw off large forces for the African expedition. Into the exposed gap came not the Persians, but the successful and ambitious Arab king, Amorkesos (Imru'al-Qays), formerly an ally of Persia, who had conquered all his neighbours in the Roman frontier province of Arabia Petraea bordering the Red Sea. In the virtual absence of any Roman forces he seized the lucrative trading port of Yotabe in the Gulf of Aqaba and expelled the Roman officials there.

For the present, Leo was unable to prevent this, and amid much criticism invited Amorkesos to Constantinople to negotiate. Amorkesos readily seized the opportunity, ostentatiously converted to Christianity (if he had not done so already) and struck up a fruitful relationship with the emperor. Making the best of the situation, Leo accepted him as *Phylarch*, a recognised Roman allied ruler over the tribes of the region and a counterweight to the client kingdoms of Persia. Amorkesos retained this prosperous position until his death twenty years later, when Rome again reabsorbed the province.[22]

The tensions between Leo and Aspar grew sharper when in 468 Zeno's wife Ariadne gave birth to a son, named Leo after his grandfather. As an Isaurian, Zeno himself had narrowly escaped a mutiny and assassination plot among his European troops, perhaps instigated by Aspar.[23] He had to move to the East, where Leo appointed him *Magister Militum*, and where his Isaurian power base lay. There he quickly expelled the rebel Isaurian Indacus from the key fortress of Papyria. In his absence, Aspar now attempted to cash Leo's earlier promises – if such they were – of a marriage alliance with his son Patricius, and the rank of Caesar. At one point, the sources tell us that it led to open confrontation, in which Leo angrily told Aspar that the wearer of the imperial purple should not be ordered about as if he were a slave. Whatever the truth of the story, if it circulated outside the palace it would not have been lost on those opposed to Aspar's faction.[24]

Without the immediate aid of Zeno, Leo had to give concessions, but he took full advantage of popular anti-Arian feelings at Constantinople. On the news that Patricius was to be nominated Caesar, rioting broke out in the Hippodrome. It was led by Marcellus, leader of the Sleepless Monks. Leo pacified the mob by promising them that Patricius would convert to the Orthodox faith, and only afterwards did he permit the betrothal of his younger daughter, Leontia.[25]

Both factions moved fast, but Leo secured the advantage. Putative evidence emerged of a new plot by Ardaburius. The *Magister* Anagast in Thrace, who had himself come very close to open rebellion, produced 'letters' supposedly proving that Ardaburius had put him up to it. The story is highly suspect, having all the marks of conspiracy, counter-conspiracy and entrapment.[26] Then Zeno also offered evidence that Ardaburius was trying to suborn the guards in the capital. Zeno returned to Constantinople and in 471 Leo took the final drastic, perhaps necessary step. He maintained outwardly friendly relations with Aspar and his family, and invited them to the palace where they were suddenly overwhelmed and massacred by a eunuch bodyguard. Aspar and Ardaburius were killed, but Patricius was only wounded. Strangely, he was allowed to recover and survived, but was stripped of his honours and his imperial marriage was annulled. A third son, Ermenaric, was absent from the capital and escaped into hiding.[27] Leo promptly married his younger daughter Leontia to Marcian, the son of the Western emperor Anthemius, and despite his lack of a military background promoted Marcian to Praesental *Magister*.

Whatever his plotting, Aspar had become a long-accepted and respected leader in Constantinople (popular among other things for his vigorous efforts to organise fire-fighting when a great conflagration broke out in the city). For these murders, Leo earned the widespread nickname of *Makelles*, the butcher. Beyond Aspar's family no proscription of Gothic officers occurred. It had been a family quarrel, not a larger ethnic one. Leo also attempted to check one of the long-standing practices by which Aspar as well as others had built up support, namely the raising of a purely private core of troops – the *bucellarii* – personally dependent on a great general as their patron and loyal to him. Stilicho and a great many others, including landowners who needed the muscle to defend their estates and coerce their tenants, had maintained *bucellarii*. Two laws of Leo attempted both to prohibit civilians from maintaining an armed following, and to prohibit generals from recruiting soldiers outside of the official enlistment channels.[28] They were only partly effective.

After this bloody purge, it was not surprising that an Ostrogothic backlash occurred. Some Ostrogoth troops under Aspar's officer Ostrys even tried to storm the palace, but were cut down by the Isaurian guards. Ostrys escaped to the Ostrogoths in Thrace, who were now headed by Theoderic Strabo, Aspar's relative, who immediately raised a revolt.[29] Leo had neither the forces to quell it nor the money to buy it off. But Strabo was trying to exact concessions, not to overthrow the emperor. He demanded the inheritance and property of Aspar, new grants of land for his troops in Thrace, and the position of Praesental *Magister*, which Aspar had held. It was significant that Strabo now saw this as almost part of a family inheritance, and aspired to play a central role in the government.

Leo evaded or rejected most of these conditions until Strabo besieged and took the city of Arcadiopolis. However, Strabo's own forces were soon starved out, and Leo was able to come to a compromise treaty. He was able to refuse yet further grants of land, but reluctantly agreed to an annual subsidy of 2,000 pounds of gold. Strabo was appointed Praesental *Magister* and was also, at his own demand, recognised as king of *all* the Ostrogoths – a fairly hollow title, which Theodemir must have treated with contempt. In return, Strabo undertook to fight any of the empire's enemies except the Vandals. This exception was not due to any special affinity with them, but rather to the more realistic precaution by Strabo not to release his forces beyond his own control into any new and hazardous maritime adventures.

Leo was alive to the dangers of this combination of federate barbarian king and Roman *Magister Militum*, the dual position Alaric and others had sought. One reason Strabo had been anxious to be acknowledged king of all the Ostrogoths was that the other strong federate settlement of Theodemir's Ostrogoths in Pannonia, separated from him by over 500 miles, had their own ambitions to improve their position relative to the Roman core of the empire. Leo was already attempting to play one against the other, and in about 471 he had returned to the western Ostrogoths the prince Theoderic the Amal, who had grown to manhood in a friendly Constantinople and had been educated in Roman manners.[30] This had not prevented him and his father leading their troops into the Illyrican provinces as far as Macedonia, one of the few highly productive Balkan areas.[31] They were bought off by a series of new and costly land settlements within Macedonia. Shortly after this Theodemir died and the Romanised, but not necessarily pro-Roman Theoderic, succeeded to the kingship.[32] Feeding and supplying his people, rewarding his nobles and maintaining overall unity were still major problems. Others of his followers moved out of Pannonia and took service with the Western emperor.[33]

Leo had little room to manoeuvre. As well as the shortage of money and loss of prestige, the African disaster and the renewed pressure of the Ostrogothic allies had emphasised the dangers of mobilising the bulk of military resources against just one enemy. The ambitions of the two Ostrogoth groups were however different. Theoderic, ruler of the royal house of the Amali, wanted his own permanent, independent kingdom as the Visigoths had achieved in Gaul. Strabo seemed to aim at a powerful military position within the Roman government itself, backed by the external power of his Gothic warriors. But he scarcely realised how very difficult a balance this was to achieve and sustain. He might hold Aspar's old title and command, but Aspar had been a prestigious, long-standing, well-integrated leading member of the Roman establishment, who was part of a network of influence and support, not an outsider. Strabo as Gothic king could hardly base himself at Constantinople in the same way; this was a place where he would be isolated and hated, and where he still had Zeno and Marcian to contend with. The threat of Gothic military violence as a direct lever in government politics was (from 399) an untried, highly dangerous weapon for both parties.

Unlike the emperor Marcian, Leo had been without a distinct power base, and had had to seek allies where he could. His reign had been a series of dangerous crises, improvisations and blunders that left the imperial throne in a weaker position than before. His main accomplishment (whether or not it can be called an achievement) had been the elimination of Aspar's dynastic military faction, which had clearly been aiming at imperial power. This had been essentially a power struggle between two ruling-class families, rather than one between Romans and Goths. Indeed, the fact that Aspar had seen Patricius as a viable candidate, and that the popular obstacle was his Arianism rather than his ethnic origins, indicates that the traditional hostility towards romanised Goths had abated by now. It is uncertain whether the Aspar faction had been seriously plotting with Strabo and the federates, and how far Strabo himself had been led by these contacts into believing he could take Aspar's place. Hence, it is difficult to say if an Aspar dynasty would have been a disaster for Roman interests, as is traditionally assumed. It would doubtless have strained relations with the senatorial classes, and perhaps risked the closer involvement of the Ostrogothic federates in the imperial power. Ironically, both these things happened in any case, despite Aspar's removal.

By this stage, Leo was understandably unpopular with almost all parties. The Vandal war had been a great and humiliating disaster, and to the end of his life he feared, with good reason, that Gaiseric would extend his raiding into Eastern waters. The enormous cost of the whole affair led Leo into ruthless confiscations, which were naturally resented.[34] The civil mandarinate had been merely obedient rather than supportive, and in the capital Zeno and the Isaurian soldiers were hated more than the Goths had been. In place of the old Hun menace were the two external groups of Ostrogothic allies who had extracted many more advantages in land, subsidy and status, and who could only just be managed.

Leo had no surviving son, only a grandson, Leo, the son of Zeno and Ariadne, who was the best he could do in legitimate succession. The boy, a sickly child, was about seven when Leo elevated him to the rank of Caesar, then Augustus, before Leo himself died early in 474. This left Zeno as de facto regent, an extremely precarious position. In yet a further attenuation of the succession, with the crucial backing of the Isaurian guard, he secured the acquiescence of the Senate and the Augusta Verina for a new coronation, in which the boy crowned his father in the Hippodrome within a month of Leo I's death. There was no open resistance, but great resentment. Those of the bureaucracy and the old imperial families of Leo and Anthemius who had supported or accepted Leo for different reasons, felt no such transfer of loyalty to Zeno, the Isaurian.[35]

13

EASTERN CHAOS, WESTERN EXTINCTION

Zeno inherited all of Leo's urgent problems plus several more of his own. Indeed, the combination of enemies and obstacles was so daunting that the odds against him surviving must have seemed overwhelming. Yet survive he did, for seventeen years.

Zeno's infant son, Leo II, died shortly after he had conferred the throne on his father.[1] The treasury was in serious straits, the Ostrogothic federate allies again became troublesome, and Gaiseric, on any pretext or none, again raided the Greek coasts, capturing the city of Nicopolis south of Corfu.[2] As Isaurians, Zeno and his guards were hated by the senatorial class, the population and large sections of the army. Indeed, he was unable to rely steadily even on all of the fragile Isaurian power base, as events quickly demonstrated. As if this were not enough, he was also hated by the dowager empress Verina, who began plotting against him almost immediately with her exiled brother Basiliscus, who had perhaps just as good a dynastic claim to the purple as Zeno did.[3]

Zeno's many detractors have portrayed him as physically ugly and personally cowardly. The record shows him as ruthless, canny and tenacious, yet benign and merciful when he could afford to be.[4] He is said to have been an extremely fast runner. He had successful military experience, and even more experience of political emergencies and isolation. For most of his life he had to live dangerously and, perhaps because of his knife-edge position, was to show remarkable nerve and resilience.

He was fortunate in dealing with Gaiseric – perhaps because the Vandal king was now growing old and more inclined to settle for the best he could. An ambassador, Severus, was sent to Carthage and promoted to Patrician for that purpose – a pointedly higher rank than the Vandals were used to, which had the desired effect. He is said to have impressed Gaiseric by refusing all gifts. The upshot was a 'perpetual' treaty of peace. Gaiseric allowed Roman captives to be redeemed, and ceased his persecution of Catholic churches.[5]

In the present circumstances Zeno had to build on his Isaurian power base, both in the city and in Anatolia. In particular this involved his Isaurian generals: Illus, who had risen under Leo, and Illus' brother, Trocundes.[6] The empress Verina emerges as a compulsive but unskilful plotter, and the whole movement to unseat Zeno is marked by incompetence, personal jealousies and mutual betrayals. Verina wished to replace Zeno not with her brother Basiliscus but with her lover Patricius, formerly a Master of Offices.[7] The plot involved her fomenting opposition in the capital, while Basiliscus secretly bribed or induced Illus and Trocundes, together with the Ostrogoth Theoderic Strabo and his federates in Thrace, to his cause.

The sudden defection of Illus was a severe blow. Zeno, utterly isolated within a year of coming to the throne, was compelled to flee the city eastwards back to his Isaurian homeland, shrewdly taking with him a small band of Isaurians and all that remained in the treasury.[8] The remaining Isaurians in the city were massacred by the mob. This was the first trough in his fortunes. Opposed by almost all, Zeno was besieged in Isauria by Illus and Trocundes, who seized Zeno's brother Longinus as hostage. The chances of his ever returning as emperor seemed remote. Yet Zeno had been here before.

Basiliscus had no intention of playing second fiddle to the empress' lover Patricius. As leader of the revolt he was welcomed by the palace ministers and Senate, dumped Patricius, and entered the city in triumph. He was immediately crowned emperor at the Hebdomon, raised his wife Zenonis to Augusta and his young son Marcus to Caesar, then Augustus.[9] This was not, strictly, an illegal coup – the constitution traditionally allowed Senate and army to confer the purple on a successful rebel, thereby transforming his treason into legitimate rule. But succession by open military revolt, even from within the imperial family, had not occurred in the East for over a century. Zeno was still alive, and Basiliscus, politically incompetent and capricious, soon lost the support of these groups.

Virtually bankrupt, Basiliscus was forced into ruthless tax measures and compelled to auction offices on a far greater scale than usual. He also extorted money from the church through his Prefect, Epinicus, an old favourite of Verina.[10] The bloody massacre of the remaining Isaurians must have strained Illus' loyalty. Basiliscus had already bitterly alienated Verina by betraying Patricius and then executing him. He now alienated Strabo too by irresponsibly appointing as Praesental *Magister* his nephew, the handsome but doubtfully capable dandy Armatus, who was rumoured to be the lover of the empress Zenonis.[11] Having fallen by now under the influence of a Monophysite bishop, Timothy of Alexandria, he also alienated Orthodox opinion by issuing a decree condemning the Council of Chalcedon, and freeing the churches of Asia from the jurisdiction of Constantinople. There was rioting in the city, and the Patriarch Acacius ostentatiously draped the statues and icons of the church of Hagia Sophia in black.[12] Finally, through no fault of his own, Basiliscus earned further odium for a disastrous fire in the city, which devastated several districts and burnt down many prominent public buildings, including the great library of Julian, containing 120,000 volumes.

Zeno, in exile, thus had no monopoly on misfortunes, but his misfortunes were not self-inflicted, and he was soon able to take advantage of Basiliscus' problems. He was quick to see the greed and shallowness of his opponents, including Illus, though he needed to win back Illus' support and was in no position to dispense with him. Basiliscus had ordered Illus to march against Zeno with an army, but by now the civil establishment was so exasperated with Basiliscus that the ministers gave Illus secret signals that they were willing to have Zeno back. This was itself a testimony to the passive power they were conscious of wielding. Zeno soon induced his own countrymen (who had held his brother Longinus hostage as a reinsurance) to change sides, and together they marched on Constantinople.

Alarmed, Basiliscus hastily withdrew the unpopular religious edicts and sent all available forces to resist the advancing Isaurians, but they were commanded by the vain, amateurish Armatus. Zeno had little difficulty in turning him, secretly promising him the post of *Magister* for life, and throwing in the extra transparent bribe of making his young son Caesar. Why Armatus fell for this, we can only conjecture. But he did, and carefully avoided the route by which Zeno was advancing. Basiliscus was lost, and Zeno duly re-entered the capital in August 476.[13]

Basiliscus and his immediate family were exiled and executed. There were no bloody reprisals among the civil establishment, although various changes were made. Armatus was welcomed back and Zeno carefully fulfilled his promise, elevating his son to Caesar at Nicaea. But shortly afterwards Armatus was assassinated, and his son stripped of his imperial rank and forced to take holy orders.[14] Soon after this, Verina was suspected of instigating an attempt to assassinate Illus, whom Zeno needed. She was surrendered to Illus, forced to take the veil and confined in a castle in Isauria. Zeno was certainly not free of enemies and other pressing problems, but at least he had regained what he had lost. Real political power in the Eastern empire was now precariously balanced between Constantinople, the more distant Isaurian power base in Anatolia and, more tenuously, the two separated groups of Ostrogothic federates in Illyricum and Thrace, who at least served to protect the frontier regions against other potential invaders, of whom there were many.

By contrast, the position in the West had reached virtual disintegration. Traditional Roman authority now held sway only in Italy and some fragments of Gaul. Tax resources had dwindled and, partly in consequence, the armies, such as they were, consisted almost wholly of barbarians, either federates or troops hired on an ad hoc basis for their immediate geographical availability, often through concessions of land. Real political power lay always in the acknowledged figure of the military generalissimo holding the title of Patrician, which now meant something very different from its widespread use in the East. This uniquely Western office had been held by Stilicho, Constantius and Aetius. The generalissimo had to control the barbarian troops, deal with the many federate nations as far as possible in

Rome's interests, placate the senatorial nobility, manage a symbolic emperor at Ravenna, and try to keep the confidence of Constantinople, where real imperial power still existed.

Ricimer, like Stilicho, was of barbarian origin, but there was a very great difference.[15] Stilicho had been Roman in loyalties and outlook, and had broken the links with his original Vandal kinsmen, though his intimate knowledge of the barbarians had of course been a great advantage. Ricimer, a grandson of the Visigothic king, Wallia, was closely related by blood or marriage to the royal houses of the Suevi, Visigoths and Burgundians, and used all these connections as a matter of course. He certainly wanted to defend what was left of the Western empire, at least in Italy, but it is probably fair to say that his conception of that empire was no longer the one Stilicho or Aetius had held. He was a ruler spanning two cultures and in his case, unlike his predecessors, it is genuinely difficult for us to say where his true loyalties finally lay. He admired, needed and believed in the prestige and authority of Rome, as did every barbarian king groping towards some settled territorial statehood, in place of predatory wanderings. He accepted naturally that the actual state was not now a set of Roman dioceses and provinces, but a federation of separate Germanic kingdoms, loosely allied to an imperial apex and coexisting with the native Roman populations, with the 'Roman Empire' as a guiding ideal rather than the controlling power. He was on excellent personal terms with almost all the barbarian nations within the empire (except the Vandals) and acquiesced readily in the partition of Gaul between Visigoths and Burgundians, even appointing his brother-in-law Gundioc as *Magister Militum per Gallias*. He did not, therefore, see himself as a traitor to the Roman empire. As several commentators have remarked, he was, perhaps, anticipating the very different imperial idea of the Middle Ages.[16]

In his seventeen-year rule of Italy Ricimer worked through four emperors – Majorian, Severus, Anthemius, and Olybrius – in almost cavalier fashion. Each was simply cast aside when they no longer served his purpose. Indeed Majorian, the last competent military emperor who took his position seriously, was deposed precisely because of this. There were three periods in which no Western emperor reigned at all. All Ricimer's public actions suggest that he found the Western emperor an irrelevant encumbrance, and he would probably have preferred to rule Italy directly in the name of the emperor at Constantinople. He died in 472 and his commanding position passed to his Burgundian nephew, the royal prince (later king) Gundobad. By this time, it was possible and even normal to unite the position of Roman generalissimo with a barbarian king. To quote O'Flynn:

Circumstances in the West demanded the existence of a supreme military commander who had a long record of intimate contact with barbarian troops; by the 470s this virtually meant that he should be a barbarian. If a barbarian was unacceptable on the imperial throne...there had to be a generalissimo to function as a middle-man between the emperor – the impotent figurehead – and the barbarian troops, who represented real power.[17]

The last of the Western generalissimos was Orestes, a Roman who, like Aetius, knew the barbarians intimately (he had been Latin secretary to Attila). He too was careful not to claim the throne himself, but conferred it on his young son, Romulus. He was faced with the demand for permanent Germanic land settlements in Italy, on the same basis of *hospitalitas* which now operated with the Burgundians in Gaul, involving grants of one-third of the land. It was opposed by the Roman senatorial nobles, but Orestes needed these tribal troops in Italy. He wavered. A revolt in August 476 by his own barbarian officer Odovacer, of mixed Hun-Scirian descent, quickly settled the issue.[18] Odovacer was ready to give the barbarian troops the lands. He was himself no tribal ruler but a middle-ranking Roman commander. However the variegated Germanic troops united in proclaiming him their king, the one office they understood, as the best means of gaining and securing their settlements in Italy.[19]

Odovacer defeated and killed Orestes, then deposed and solicitously pensioned off his young imperial son, Romulus Augustulus, no doubt a placatory gesture to the Eastern emperor.[20] He then took the final, logical step of dispensing with a Western emperor, and instead acknowledged himself as subject to Zeno in Constantinople, a move that was clearly necessary to anchor his own legitimacy, to satisfy senatorial and popular opinion, and to assist his position among other barbarian rulers. He represented the position as continuity, not a radical break. His followers might use the title 'king', but the senatorial nobles, forced to acquiesce in the loss of one-third of their ample lands, would not acknowledge it, and his address to Zeno carefully made no use of it.[21]

Accordingly, the Roman Senate despatched the famous embassy to Zeno at the end of 476, together with all the magnificent insignia and regalia of imperial rule. According to the chronicler Malchus, their message was couched, perhaps fittingly, in archaic Republican style.[22] (The apparently vestigial term 'Republic' is still used, though its closest translation is not the entity that died with Brutus and Cassius, but just 'the State'.) It was (to paraphrase): We, the Senate, no longer need nor wish to continue an Imperial succession in Italy. In our opinion, the majesty of a single monarch is enough to govern and protect both East and West. In our name, and the name of the Roman people, we consent that the seat of Universal Empire is transferred from Rome to Constantinople. We relinquish our right to choose our sovereign. We have confidence in the civil and military abilities of Odovacer. We request that you accord him the title of Patrician, and the administration of your Diocese of Italy.

This then was the canonical episode of our introduction, which has been invested with such historical and romantic significance by later ages in Europe, whose picture of the lost Roman Empire was the essentially Western tableau of Cato, Scipio, Caesar, Cicero, Augustus. From the later point of view of Bulgaria or Russia or the Arabs, familiar only with the New Christian Rome, it did not look like that at all. To contemporaries, East or West, whether Italian, Gallic or African senatorial aristocrats, Greek Eastern Romans or Germanic Romans, 476 was only an expected development, a stage in a tortuous but recognisable power shift from Roman to barbarian which had been going on for as long as anyone present could remember.[23]

How this power shift had occurred is of crucial importance. We have traced some of its stages, and attempt to bring the main strands together in later chapters. It is of little use to seek pivotal events, as so many have been tempted to do. The accession of a feeble unmilitary boy after 395 was not itself crucial, for something very similar happened at Constantinople. The unification of military command in the West, as distinct from its deliberate separation in the East, was probably necessary in view of the more exposed frontiers, the longer communications between viable cities, and Stilicho's need to assemble strong mobile field armies very rapidly.

The prioritising of realistically defensible provinces and the abandonment of some, such as Britain, need not have caused mortal damage to the central areas: this had been managed and controlled several times before. Much more destabilising was the progressive and seemingly inescapable reliance on raising either barbarian mercenaries or 'federate' troops on an ad hoc basis; their treaty arrangements, even if adhered to, were now a far cry from the original settlements. Even had the money been available, as it was to some extent after the 420s, Italy and Gaul had ceased to be fertile recruiting grounds for effective native Roman fighting soldiers, despite conscription laws. Their peasant populations had been combed through for centuries, and their descendants no longer wanted military life and traditions. Landlords, needing scarce manpower, colluded with them to evade conscription, offered gold payments in lieu, and often harboured deserters. There was only western Illyricum, which Stilicho had intrigued and fought for, but which had largely been controlled by Alaric and his Visigoths after 397, and which was effectively lost by the 440s. There is no record of conscription even being attempted after Aetius. Barbarian troops and allies, hungry for land and perceiving Roman weakness, were the only readily available reservoir of effective military manpower, if an army was to be kept in being at all. In these conditions, there was no real check on the progressive enlargement of federate kingdoms at the expense of Roman provinces.

The combination of the office of Germanic king with Roman *Magister Militum*, which Theodosius I had strongly and wisely resisted, was a further lurch in the power balance. True, this was also allowed in the East, where both *Magister* and Patrician status were both easily and promiscuously offered in emergencies to buy off troublesome but potentially useful barbarian leaders. The crucial difference in the East was that, although they were accommodated in Roman provinces, and had access to taxable resources in money and men, they never acquired land through grants of *hospitalitas* or as sovereign territory. They were always balanced by other *Magistri*, and could never cash both components of their power in the face of the physical defences and political establishment of Constantinople. No supreme barbarian warlord could establish himself as the head of state.

In the West, supreme military command, and with it effective political power, had long become concentrated traditionally in one man, just as it had been in the great generals at the end of the Republic. If the symbols, authority and legitimacy of the emperors had not been geographically isolated in the impotent court at Ravenna, but been always at the centre of the ever-mobile armies, some central concentration and perhaps stability of Roman power and authority, however attenuated, might have been retained – as it might have been if Constantius had continued to rule as emperor. As it was, however patriotic and loyal individual supreme commanders might have been, there was no longer any barrier to prevent a barbarian warlord/king stepping into the ready-made office of generalissimo. After that, the arrangements of political power fell into a new, rational pattern. Whatever the symbols, Latin titles, Christian leavening and genuinely civilised accommodations, it was a Germanic pattern, not a Roman one.

Zeno had only just regained his throne. He was in no position at all to interfere in the West, and had far more pressing concerns. He acquiesced in Odovacer's effective control in Italy, but there was an awkward difficulty in the shape of a surviving but exiled emperor, Julius Nepos, in Dalmatia. Nepos was a relative of Verina, whom he had previously recognised, and public abandonment of him would be impolitic. Nepos also sent him an embassy, requesting his restoration as Western emperor. It is doubtful whether he seriously expected any help. At all events, after an outburst of quite synthetic indignation against the ambassadors of Odovacer, Zeno compromised by asking the Roman Senate to receive Nepos back, but at the same time pointedly addressed Odovacer as 'Patrician' and did not return the imperial insignia.[24]

Odovacer had essentially what he wanted and of course did nothing to restore Nepos, who died or was murdered in 480. Now almost all the former Western empire, including Italy, was ruled by young Germanic kingdoms, superimposed with varying degrees of accommodation or oppression on the far larger Roman populations and institutions: Ostrogoths in Pannonia, Franks, Alemanni, Burgundians and Visigoths in Gaul, Visigoths and Suevi in Spain, Vandals in Africa. Only in northwest Gaul did a small independent Roman state still function, ruled by one Syagrius and based at Soissons.[25] For most of the populations, inured for generations to insecurity and crushing exploitation, the change was hardly a disaster.

Odovacer's recognition by Zeno was minimal and grudging, and he increasingly used the title *Rex*, like others among his fellow barbarian kings. But he conciliated the Roman nobility, and maintained their consulates, Prefectures and other dignities and ministerial offices, which indeed he could hardly rule without. He was also able to negotiate with the aged Gaiseric for the return of Sicily in exchange for an annual payment.

Zeno's position was still very insecure. The western federate Ostrogoths under Theoderic the Amal had migrated once more from Macedonia to Lower Moesia, a tribal move that could not be prevented. Theoderic, who had been brought up at Constantinople and had supported Zeno in the recent civil conflict, was formally recognised as an ally with enhanced status: Zeno appointed him Patrician and adopted him as son-in-arms in the Germanic fashion – both inexpensive gestures, little more.[26] The eastern group of federates under Strabo was still hostile and dangerously close. They advanced from Thrace towards Constantinople, encouraged by rumours of a new plot in the capital, a plot which had been inspired as usual by Verina. Strabo offered to negotiate, but Zeno rejected his terms. By the end of 477, many of Theoderic's followers were deserting to join Strabo, who was poised for a move against Constantinople. Theoderic affirmed his loyalty. Zeno also needed, but did not trust, his Isaurian general Illus.

The next twelve years were, politically, a turmoil of semi-serious wars, feints, intrigues, attempted coups, treaties, betrayals and counter-betrayals, in which for a long period there was paralysis and insecurity among the governing classes because no one faction could achieve ascendancy. It was one of the most anarchic and dangerous periods for the East, a low point for its fortunes. The incessant power struggles were now fought out openly, outside of the central controlling institutions of the political capital – even when there was armed conflict in the streets of Constantinople itself. The civil bureaucracy could not bring its weight to bear, and Strabo's Ostrogothic forces increasingly became a new and destabilising factor in the power game. Imperial authority and continuity were weakened, and many of the European provinces were in danger of being lost.

The two groups of Ostrogothic federate allies could not be expelled or resisted by direct military force. Their total combined available strength, with the usual very high ratio of warriors to total population, was probably as great as the Roman army of Thrace or Illyricum – in the order of perhaps 30,000 men. They were not yet firmly established states within the empire, but had the potential to become such. Unlike Attila, they were always amenable to rational negotiation and they had no wish to destroy the empire on which they depended, but they were drawn unavoidably or willingly into its own internal political conflicts. Theoderic the Amal's immediate aims were larger lands and subsidies, and eventually a permanent independent kingdom. Strabo's aims were a decisive and dominant place at the Roman top table, backed by Ostrogothic arms – eventually perhaps even eclipsing the existing armies by Gothic ones as the main support of the Roman emperors. Also unlike Attila, once they were securely settled the Ostrogoths were not going to go away. There was now the serious possibility that, as in the West, effective Roman power might be steadily eroded west of the Bosporus, in Illyricum, Thrace, Macedonia, and replaced by new Germanic kingdoms.

The settlement agreements with these allies under Marcian, Leo and now Zeno were generally reluctant expedients, and meant as much or as little as the respective pressures on each side could effect at any one time. Leo, for example, had initially sided with the Sciri in a war against Theodemir's Pannonian Ostrogoths, and only when the latter were decisively victorious and had become the dominant barbarian force in the middle Danube, had he cultivated their alliance seriously. The territorial boundaries were vague and shifting in this largely mountainous region, and although this apparently advertised Roman weakness, it may well have suited emperors' purposes. The primary value of the land was of course as a food supply, which presented recurrent problems for the Goths and an incentive to migration or negotiation, a fact which the Roman government, with its more organised, city-based network of warehouses and granaries, exploited fully. A stable food supply and a flow of tangible rewards for the nobility and their subclans was absolutely necessary to hold the loose tribal confederations together. For all their royal lineage, titles and the substructure of nobles, leaders such as Theoderic possessed no coercive state apparatus. If they failed to deliver victories and goods their armed followers could shift their allegiance elsewhere.

This instability clearly suited the government. Although some elements of native Roman populations were no doubt displaced from the land, none of the emperors had any intention of granting the Ostrogoths a *hospitalitas* settlement of the kind that operated in the West, and involved legally transferring a proportion of lands and all their assets from Roman proprietors. This was the very type of status Theoderic wanted, and it would have set a virtually permanent seal on his statehood. Also, of course, the barrier of Constantinople and the eastern provinces could still be held, given properly led and supplied troops. But even the regular Roman core of the armies, not to mention the barbarian units, were divided in their loyalties towards Zeno. Throughout his whole reign he never could never depend securely on the allegiance of all his armies, a drastic handicap which neither Marcian nor Leo had suffered, and which explains much of his devious and opportunistic manoeuvring. His finances were utterly precarious, and relations with Persia were deteriorating.

The long, convoluted power struggle has been described by a number of writers.[27] Its players were: first, Zeno at Constantinople, determined not to go on his travels again; second, Illus and a strong section of the Isaurians, nominally loyal to Zeno but as before, capable of changing sides; third, the two Ostrogothic nations with their distinct ambitions, the followers volatile, the leaders mutually distrustful but equally wary of being played off against each other by the emperor. Fourth, there were the disaffected parties around the throne, anti-Isaurian relatives or protégés of Verina, looking for every opportunity to unseat Zeno. Desperately, Zeno made frequent changes of military command and scattered abundant promises: Patriciates, *Magister* posts, gold, subsidies, and imperial marriage alliances. Larger loyalties and proper political ambitions fragmented into personal ties and advantage. Yet, out of this general bear pit, viciously and clumsily there eventually emerged a greater stability, not just as a result of the final conquest of all others by one, but as a result of a war of manoeuvre that led in the long run to new and more stable power adjustments.

To counter the threat of Strabo to the capital, Zeno in 477–8 called on Theoderic's alliance, and mustered his own forces. Their reliability was in some doubt, and the Praesental *Magister* Martinianus, Zeno's brother-in-law, had been unable to maintain discipline. Theoderic, knowing very well that Zeno's negotiations with Strabo had broken down, insisted wisely that Zeno choose clearly between the two groups of Ostrogoths, and the result was a solemn oath by emperor and Senate that they would never make peace with Strabo. Accordingly, a great combined operation against him was planned in which the whole army of Thrace was promised, to join forces with Theoderic at a rendezvous in the Haemus mountains. The assembled Roman forces failed to arrive, probably because Zeno could not trust them. Whatever the real reason, it was a critically lost opportunity, which weakened his standing and prolonged the whole period of confusion.[28]

When the two Ostrogothic armies met, Theoderic was in a weak position. His own followers virtually compelled him to make peace with Strabo. Both Theorderic and Strabo accepted that they had been tricked by the usual Roman perfidy, and joined forces. To persuade him to continue the war Zeno offered Theoderic even more lavish promises of gold and a marriage connection with some lady of imperial standing, perhaps a daughter of Placidia, but to no avail. He then threatened war on him, undertaking to lead the assembled Roman army in person, but the soldiers' mood was close to mutiny and on Martinianus' advice he had to disperse them. This was one of the episodes in which his detractors alleged his personal cowardice.

Zeno then offered generous terms to Strabo, with greater success, including the rank of *Magister Militum* and, most dangerously, command of two *scholae* of the imperial guards in Constantinople (1,000 men). Strabo was also promised pay and supplies for 13,000 of his own military following. The terms were readily accepted, as well they might be: Strabo was now a great stride closer to achieving his ambition of power broker. Theoderic withdrew his forces in disgust, ravaging Macedonia and Greece, harassed by Roman forces who starved him of supplies, until he put out feelers for a new alliance with Zeno, but negotiations broke down and fighting went on until 481.

Simultaneously, Verina's anti-Zeno party found a leader in Marcian, son of the Western emperor Anthemius and son-in-law of Leo. Despite the promotion and favours he had received, he resented Zeno's treatment of Verina, and became persuaded that he had a better legal claim to the purple than Zeno. Verina, from her imprisonment, again made contact with Strabo and persuaded him to support them in a coup, though his motives are obscure.[29] With the help of Strabo's two *scholae* of guards in Constantinople, Marcian, his brother Procopius and their supporters suddenly seized the key points in the city, including the palace; Zeno narrowly escaped capture. The city mobs mobilised in favour of Marcian, and those guards loyal to Zeno and Illus were showered with stones from the rooftops. Yet at the crucial moment, when Marcian could have occupied the palace and been proclaimed emperor, he faltered. That night Illus arrived with Isaurian troops in a daring dash across the Bosporus from Chalcedon, and crushed the coup decisively.

Marcian and Procopius fled to Strabo, who was still approaching from Thrace. Zeno stripped him of his generalship and called on a newly arrived Altaic horse people, the Bulgars, to attack him, but he repelled them. Strabo again marched on Constantinople but was repulsed and withdrew into Greece, where he was accidentally killed, falling off his horse on to a spear.[30] His son Recitach lost control of most of his followers, who naturally drifted over to Theoderic. Unlike Theoderic, Strabo had not been of noble or 'royal' Gothic lineage, hence his anxiety for Roman recognition of his kingship and his need to buttress his position by other means, such as a central role in the government. His death and the collapse of his following removed one very dangerous threat to Zeno's position, brought Thrace back under Roman control, and at least simplified the problem of the federate allies.

Zeno now clearly had to make terms with a more powerful Theoderic. In a new treaty of 483 Theoderic was recognised as undisputed king of the whole Ostrogoth nation, confirmed in all his extensive lands along the Danube including Dacia Ripensis and Lower Moesia, appointed *Magister Militum in Praesenti*, and given a consulship. With Zeno's approval he murdered Recitach, son of Strabo. The treaty did not repair relations for long.

Relations with Persia had slowly worsened, as a result of Arab raiding in Mesopotamia and what was perceived as Zoroastrian persecution of the Christians in Persian Armenia, which in 481 broke into open rebellion. However reluctant Zeno might be, there was pressure on the Roman side to intervene. Fortunately, the Persian King Peroz was heavily preoccupied with the attacks of the Hephthalites in the Caucasus region, who were at least nominally enemies of Rome also. Peroz appealed to Zeno for help in some form, and Zeno initially supplied funds for the Persians' campaigns. But as the Persians began to lose the war Zeno stopped his payments and even offered subsidies to the Huns. In 484 Peroz' army suffered a shattering defeat in which the king himself was killed. His successor Valash was forced to buy peace with very heavy concessions and were no longer in any position to demand renewed Roman assistance. The Christian revolt in Armenia was finally ended and Persian Armenia recognised as a Christian nation.

At Constantinople, relations between Zeno and Illus were strained. Illus had quarrelled bitterly with the empress Ariadne, allegedly over the continued imprisonment of her mother Verina. An attempt (not the first) was made on Illus' life, in which one ear was cut off, and no disclaimers by Zeno could now dispel Illus' suspicions of him. Illus went east with a new military command, and the loyalties of the Isaurians gravitated into the two rival camps of Zeno and Illus. At Antioch Illus consolidated his power base and dabbled in even more exaggerated global politics, trying to enlist the help of the Persian King Peroz, the Armenian satrapies, as well as Odovacer in Italy. Only the satraps responded. Illus then shamelessly courted an alliance with his arch-enemy Verina, whom he had imprisoned, and together they set up a rival emperor, the general Leontius, at Tarsus. Verina crowned him, and publicly claimed that as Augusta the empire was in her gift: she had conferred it on Zeno and she now legally dethroned Zeno and trans-ferred it to Leontius.[31] The rebels were recognised at Antioch and some other places, but lasted only a few months of 484. Zeno was unable to crush it alone, and once again he called on Theoderic, and a mixed force of Romans, Ostrogoths and Rugians completely broke the army of Leontius and Illus. Verina died soon afterwards, removing another dangerous variable from the equation. Illus and Leontius retreated to the mountain redoubts in Isauria, as Zeno had done before him.

Now Theoderic remained to be placated or managed somehow. Dissatisfied with his insufficient Danube lands he marched on Constantinople, but as usual did not capture it and perhaps did not try – a large sum of gold persuaded him to raise the siege. At about this stage, with only two contenders, the confused struggle began to assume a more predictable shape.

Zeno and Theoderic struck yet another new bargain in secret. Zeno, knowing what Theoderic really wanted, invited him to invade Italy and, if he could overthrow Odovacer, rule in his place as Zeno's viceroy. It was an attractive prospect to Theoderic, and it was significant of the moral authority that the East exerted that he still needed the emperor's invitation to such an adventure. For him it promised a self-sufficient Ostrogothic kingdom instead of perpetual shortages, and fighting on another's behalf or simply in order to extract gold or favour from the wily emperor. To Zeno it was a heaven-sent opportunity to rid the Balkans of the Ostrogothic proto-state for good.

The conquest of Italy was not easy. In August 490 Theoderic defeated Odovacer at the battle of the Addua near Milan, but the war dragged on for another three years, in which town after fortified town had to be taken, and the bloody massacres of Odovacer's garrisons prolonged the desperate resistance. Theoderic, with his upbringing in Roman ways, courted and gained the overall support of the senatorial nobles. After Addua had tipped the balance, the Senate sent their *Princeps*, Festus, to seek Zeno's public recognition for Theoderic as his Patrician and viceroy in Italy. This was a major historic step in the larger survival of the East. A shifting warlike population, groping towards more settled statehood, had conquered and occupied a stable national territory.

Having eliminated all his enemies in Italy Theoderic ruled well for an unprecedented thirty-six years. There were no reprisals against Romans; most of Odovacer's Roman civil officials continued in their posts. Relations between Romans and Goths were explicitly regulated, with separate territories and legal codes, and a clear division of political authority between Goths, who alone comprised the armies, and Romans, who alone manned and occupied the civil bureaucracy. This continuity of office served him well in constructing the more secure and organised kingdom he needed, and in signalling friendly messages to Constantinople. After a false start in which he tried to adopt the imperial title but was rebuffed,[32] he used the title *Rex*, conveying his sovereignty over both communities, but was equally careful to preserve all the titular fictions of still being part of the Roman empire. There was toleration between Arian and Catholic. His state was slowly growing into a durable partnership between the Roman and Gothic cultures, as Athaulf had once envisaged. The Franks and Visigoths, as well as Odovacer, had also partly achieved this. Politically he saw this as an investment both against the neighbouring Germanic kingdoms, with whom he contracted many marriage alliances, and potentially against Constantinople, which might in future intrigue against him.

In the same year that Theoderic had been persuaded to invade Italy, Zeno's forces under John the Scythian finally reduced Papyria, the last Isaurian stronghold of Illus and Leontius. Against all odds, Zeno had survived every peril and every enemy.

In religion Zeno, following Basiliscus' blunders and faced with stubborn Monophysite loyalties in Egypt and Syria, naturally sought unity. He was lucky in a mild and moderate Patriarch, Acacius. Together they produced another compromise encyclical, the Henotikon, aimed at healing wounds. It wisely did not try yet again to redefine the two natures of Christ, but neither did it explicitly endorse the Orthodoxy of Chalcedon, although its doctrines were practically identical. However, through adroit wording and judicious references it allowed Monophysites to believe it was a real departure from Chalcedon. The discreet, hair-splitting differences enabled all politicians who wanted lay or churchmen, to achieve a working compromise. All but the utterly doctrinaire Monophysite bishops were prepared to live with it, as they chose to interpret it. It alienated Bishop Felix of Rome, mainly (as usual) because it implicitly accorded the emperor the right to pronounce on Christian doctrine, on a level with ecumenical councils. But Zeno paid little attention to this. It bought an uneasy peace between the

Chalcedonian and Monophysite blocs, provided that all the parties were careful to avoid any symbolic acts which might rekindle popular animosities.[33]

These naturally lived on just below the surface. One of the most potent symbols was in the litany of the Trisagion; 'Holy, Holy, Holy, Lord God of Hosts!' At Monophysite Antioch this was chanted with the significant addition '...who was crucified for us!' Around these rival banners yet new conflicts would erupt in the next decades.

Zeno had inherited serious financial problems not of his own making, and in all his wars and power struggles had been forced to pay and promise gold recklessly to buy off a pressing emergency. His financial policies were utterly hand-to-mouth, nor was he at the best of times a good financial manager, apart from being shrewd enough to take the treasury with him into exile. It is said to his credit, that although he naturally confiscated the property of rebels he defeated, he would not revert to the vile old practice of fabricating treason charges against the rich for the sole reason of seizing their estates. The very fact that this was a government fiscal option testifies to the scale of wealth that some individuals possessed. He proposed to increase taxation, but this was so bitterly unpopular that his Praetorian Prefect Erythrius bravely resigned in protest.[34] It was a sign of Zeno's clemency, or perhaps insecurity, that such a public gesture could be made. In 476, the new Prefect Sebastianus dealt with the problem briskly, by a far more public and comprehensive system of the simony that had always occurred. Public appointments were all openly tariffed at official prices (*suffragium*). The office holders in turn hoped to recoup their outlay by passing the burden of bribery further down the line.

By the time the Italian embassy from Theoderic arrived at Constantinople Zeno had died, in April 491, leaving the empire in a distinctly more stable state than he had found it. In the circumstances, his achievements were all the greater for having laboured under near-universal anti-Isaurian sentiments, which served to blacken his name in Byzantine annals. These sentiments now surfaced immediately in the capital.

Zeno left no son. His nearest male relative was his brother, Longinus, whom the Isaurian guards rather naively expected to succeed. The Senate and the majority of the Praesental armies were determined to thwart this, and moved quickly. They very publicly called on Zeno's widow, the Augusta Ariadne, to choose (and marry) a successor, and she played her role admirably. Time was crucial and whatever bargaining went on, we have the distinct impression that almost anyone would do, provided he was Orthodox and above all, came from within the traditional civil governing class. In the first days Ariadne stepped into the imperial ceremonial role, obviously enjoying it, and was saluted by army and people in the Hippodrome with the standard litany, imploring her to select an Orthodox emperor.[35]

The choice was the elderly, middle-ranking palace official, Anastasius, who had no military background but a wide reputation for uprightness, ability and concern for religion, although his beliefs were not entirely Orthodox, tending towards the Monophysites; at one point he had been a candidate for the see of Antioch.[36] A now familiar pattern emerged. The Constantinople establishment of imperial family, army, Senate and Patriarch wanted a safe candidate: no creature of a faction, nor a spineless cipher, nor yet a great overbearing hero. They had had enough of unpredictable outsiders; now they had a clean slate. The one dissident was the Patriarch Euphemius who had long been hostile to Anastasius, suspecting him of Manichean leanings. But the other groups overruled him and instead had Anastasius declare solemnly in writing his full Orthodox faith, which of course he did. After this, the ceremonial went as before: he appeared before the lowered military standards, was raised on a shield and crowned with a torque and acclaimed by the troops. The Patriarch crowned him with the diadem, he put on the purple cloak and red boots, then made his public speech and gave the standard donations to the army. For a man of about sixty-one this could have been a little unusual and even fatiguing, but the padlock of power was closed.

With all help from his friends, Anastasius stepped confidently into the exalted role. The choice was in fact wiser than they knew. He may not have been at the front rank of imperial government, but he had served and observed it for many years. It was his talent as an honest, trusted and very sound administrator that gave him widespread support, and provided the empire with the more efficient government it badly needed. After the turmoils of Zeno, Anastasius, in a remarkably long reign of twenty-seven years, would have his share of wars and political crises. But he began with more solid advantages, and the enemies and obstacles he faced, though formidable, were neither so multiple nor so complex. Anastasius would prove to be an emperor most suited to the times.

Indeed, the more we learn about his reign, the more he emerges as an outstanding ruler, who has not received the full recognition he deserves. Gibbon passes over him in a few sentences as an aged nonentity. Later historians acknowledge his important contribution in reforming the empire's finances. In fact, his achievements were wider than that. This aged nonentity used new financial muscle to strengthen and expand the armies, revive urban economies, restore many ruined cities and invest in a great programme of strategic fortification. Much of the military and civil rebuilding traditionally attributed to Justinian we now know was the earlier work of Anastasius.[37]

His first, eagerly awaited task was to suppress the Isaurian faction in the city, and this was done quickly. A brief popular tumult, whether inspired by the Isaurians or deliberately provoked, gave him the excuse to crush the mob with anti-Isaurian troops, then purge the Excubitors of Isaurians and expel them from Constantinople. Their leader, Longinus, was not executed but – a growing Christian practice – made to take holy orders and then banished to the Thebaid in Egypt. This removed Isaurian power from the capital only, not the empire. Again the Isaurians regrouped in their native territories as Zeno, Illus and others had done before. They were met in a set battle at Cotyaeum in Phrygia (southern Asia Minor) by an imperial army including Goth and Hun contingents, and heavily defeated.[38] This marked the end of the Isaurians as an effective power bloc, but it was to be another five years before their mountain strongholds were taken, and then systematically demolished.

Part 5

STABILITY ATTAINED

14

THE ACHIEVEMENTS OF
ANASTASIUS

Zeno's final removal of the Ostrogothic federates had been a great political gain. For decades they had been a source of chronic instability in the empire, able to put into the field armies of up to 15,000 men for whatever purpose they chose. These were forces too powerful for the main Roman armies to defeat, except possibly as a result of an unacceptable weakening of other main frontiers. Zeno's success also ended the disturbing possibility that the Ostrogoths might carve out permanent kingdoms from the Eastern empire, as they had in the West. Henceforth the position of Gothic soldiers and commanders in the empire became easier, as the suspicions of divided loyalties died away.

The gain, however, was at high cost and a sharp reminder of the unending pressures of peoples beyond the northern frontier. The Bulgars, a nomad steppe people, had now become the dominant tribal group in the central territories north of the Danube formerly ruled by Attila, and included many of the Huns remaining there in their new, loose tribal confederation. Formerly, Strabo's Ostrogothic federates in Thrace had kept them in check (despite Zeno's unprincipled attempt to lever them against him), but now they began raiding deep into Roman territory with a ferocity not seen since Attila.[1] Any hope on Anastasius' part that the Danube frontier might now be stabilised and fortified in the traditional manner evaporated. Indeed, in the short run the Ostrogothic federates, menacing though they were, had offered rather more protection to these regions than was now possible. In 493, an imperial army under Julian, the *Magister per Thracias*, met the invading Bulgars in a set battle and was heavily defeated; Julian himself was killed.[2]

Like the Huns, the Bulgars wanted plunder, bribes, and glory, but not territory, though they were never as organised as Attila's great kingdom had been at its height. Apart from the Roman military defeat of 493, we have few details of the first Bulgar incursion. For the unfortunate inhabitants of the Thracian areas it no doubt threatened a return to the terrible days of the Huns, and for several years it was.

By 498, after a prolonged war of sieges in their near-impregnable mountain regions, the armies of Anastasius finally reduced the rebel Isaurians.

The last of their main leaders, Longinus of Cardala, had been captured, tortured and beheaded in 497.[3] The fortresses were systematically demolished, and the surviving Isaurian warriors resettled in large numbers in Thrace, in the hope perhaps that they would provide some obedient buffer against the Bulgars, or at least a useful reservoir of troops for the expanded army, on the reform of which Anastasius was now embarking.

It was in 498 that Anastasius began his great overhaul of the tax system, which we have already described in Chapter 9. Here more than anywhere, his skills and experience as a middle-ranking bureaucrat were called upon. He knew well the intricate machinery of collecting and spending the revenues, understood all its clumsiness, inefficiency and the endless opportunities for evasion and corruption, and brought to the task a patient, tireless attention to detail rare among emperors. He was supported by three talented financial advisers. Marinus the Syrian had begun as a lowly *Scriniarius* or tax accountant in the Prefecture of the Orient – a post traditionally held in disdain by the main civil service, since it did not require a classical education.[4] However, these practical skills were in high demand by the government and the corps of accountants grew steadily. In a long career, Marinus became Anastasius' chief financial adviser and eventually Praetorian Prefect. Polycarp, another *Scriniarius* who had risen to high rank through financial ability, was Prefect of the Orient in 498, and John of Paphlagonia was appointed *Comes Sacrarum Largitionum*, the public finance minister.[5]

All of them knew the wasteful and precarious state of the imperial finances, and that the problem was not the volume of taxable wealth, but of getting it to its intended destination where it could be effective. Perhaps the most important measure, long overdue, was widely to replace tax payments in kind by payments in gold.[6] Taxes in kind, the *annona*, dated from the military emergencies of the third and early fourth centuries, when inflation had wrecked the currency and other means were urgently needed to pay and supply the constantly mobile armies. In lieu of worthless silver coinage and crude military seizures Diocletian and his successors had imposed a comprehensive tariff of abstract tax units based notionally on a soldier's annual needs, but convertible into whatever kinds of goods or services were wanted at any point: food, clothing, transport, skilled or unskilled labour, and so on. Officers had been paid in multiples of soldiers' rations and equipment, which had to be traded; official receipts to taxpayers had likewise been traded, and become a form of currency.[7]

This rough and ready system had not only served its emergency purpose, but also equipped the state with the more powerful fiscal machine of a calculated annual budget. Now, two centuries later, there was a stable and more plentiful gold currency, soldiers were nearly all billeted in or around cities, and the shackling effect on an exchange nexus was obvious. By now, all large private transactions were in gold, as well as many taxes and higher state salaries. But soldiers and officers in cities still had to juggle clumsily with their actual or notional wages in kind, plus a small addition of copper.

Anastasius swept almost all of this away. All land taxes except those needed for immediate army supply were commuted to gold, as well as the pay of soldiers of every rank. Gold solidi, not dubious paper or cumbersome records now flowed to and from the Prefects' accounting offices as well as army quartermasters, at town, provincial and treasury level. Since army pay was the main means of putting money into circulation, the release of such purchasing power into the cities and garrison areas gave a great stimulus to their economies.[8] Liquidity was greatly increased by a parallel measure, initiated by John of Paphlagonia, to reform the chaotic copper currency used in the millions of small transactions and provide proper convertibility to gold. A new larger copper coinage, with clearly marked face values in four denominations, was issued at a fixed rate to the gold solidus. Its value fluctuated slightly, but henceforth there was once again a coherent, working currency.[9]

The military advantages appeared very quickly. The gold payments to the army, the major proportion of total state spending, were set at generous levels, more than equivalent to the old *annona*. Raising willing recruits from native Roman populations suddenly ceased to be a problem, so much so that in a few years it was possible for Anastasius to allow the earlier conscription laws, dating from Diocletian, to lapse.[10]

This allowed the 'Roman' core of the army to be strengthened numerically, although by this time, as we have indicated in Chapter 8, this Roman/barbarian distinction in the army no longer had the same political significance as before. Isaurians, after all, were legally Roman subjects, yet were not only widely hated and distrusted, but at one stage had formed a distinct military power bloc which had endangered the ruling establishment at Constantinople as much as any 'barbarians', until they were finally crushed. The removal of the Ostrogothic federates from the east Roman provinces had deprived the barbarian army units of national political territories within the empire. They were now recruited and sometimes settled on various terms and conditions, but within an overall imperial framework. Although the old name persisted, the large 'federate' class of soldiers frequently mentioned in the late fifth and sixth centuries refers generically to the many foreign troops serving in the Roman army on whatever basis, as distinct from the *comitatenses* and *limitanei*. These federates were no longer the distinct national armies supplied under treaty by self-contained 'allied' nations settled within the empire. The one exception to this was the system of allied Arab phylarchies, many of whom occupied frontier lands within imperial territory and fought as distinct tribal units within the overall Roman military structure. They fought only on the eastern frontiers, often against traditional Arab enemies and had neither the interest nor the strength to engage in political intrigues as the German federates had done. The danger was not that they would threaten the government at Constantinople, but that they might opt for the Persian side instead. As a result, the potentially destabilising effect of foreign troops under

Anastasius was probably smaller than at any other time in the fifth century. The total size of the army at the end of Anastasius' reign has been estimated at 300,000 men of all types, but with all the usual qualifications about under-strength units, etc.

At the tax delivery end, Anastasius increased real yields by a more systematic attack on the many forms of evasion, profiteering and outright corruption. Where army supplies were short, the old resort of compulsory purchase (*coemptio*) was severely limited, requiring special authorisation, and had to be justified in detail. Regular and accurate returns of roster levels and rations were demanded of army units, and strenuous efforts were made to prevent officers and quartermasters defrauding soldiers of their pay, as they had habitually done. In practice, these widespread abuses could at best be limited and regulated but never completely abolished.

By far the most important change was proposed by Marinus and this was to check the almost universal evasions by the *curiales*, the land-owning town councils who were responsible for collecting the assessed land taxes that constituted the great bulk of the state's revenues. A new class of imperial official, the *vindex*, was created under the Praetorian Prefect to supervise the tax collection and delivery of each city, and to control the municipal finances in tandem with the imperial fiscal system. Where disputes arose over the level of assessments, as they naturally did, the government official despatched to resolve them, the *Compulsor*, had his costs paid directly out of the municipal funds as supervised by the *vindex*, and was no longer passed down to the poorer and weaker taxpayers. Needless to say, the *vindices* were highly unpopular with the *curiales*, but the new system undoubtedly raised far higher revenues, as even a bitter opponent, John Lydus, had to admit.[11]

The aim of all these measures, whether achieved or not, was to place the burden more squarely on those most able to pay. The dramatic revival in the revenues made it possible to abolish one of the most unpopular gold taxes, the *Collatio Lustralis* (*Chrysargyron*), on merchants and small craftsmen. This tax was originally introduced by Constantine and was both a harsh burden and an inhibition on trade and exchange. The amount it yielded was now disproportionate to its political cost, even in an absolutist state. It was a concession Anastasius could afford, making up the shortfall from the impe-rial private estates, and his propaganda made the most of it in promoting his popularity. He was supposed to have had all the tax records burnt, so that the tax could never be revived. At Edessa (Urfa), according to John Stylites, there was great public rejoicing; the citizens dressed in white and went in procession to the church to celebrate the Eucharist, then had a week-long festival of thanksgiving.[12]

In 499 the Bulgars returned in a larger and more dangerous expedition. This time Anastasius was able to mobilise a large field army (the sources say 15,000 to 16,000 men) commanded by the *Magister per Illyricum*, Aristus.[13] But again, in a battle in the Thracian triangle approaching Constantinople the Romans were severely defeated: Aristus was said to have lost a quarter of his army. The bulk of these seem to have been Illyrians, whose countrymen had filled the armies for several centuries, for the contemporary chronicler Marcellinus lamented that this battle marked the end of the long Illyrian martial traditions.[14] It seems likely that the Bulgar battle tactics were near identical to those of the Huns, combining fast, disciplined cavalry manoeuvre with lethal archery, and that the Romans had still not found an effective counter to them. Apart from the bloody clash with Aetius' coalition and the battle of Nedao, a large well-commanded Hun army had very rarely been defeated in a set battle where cavalry could manoeuvre.

It seemed that this was a repeat of the great scourge of Attila but, in practice, it was to prove less damaging, though certainly severe enough. The records are very fragmentary, but it does not appear that the Bulgar rulers imposed or sought the humbling yet logical victory terms with the Romans that Attila had done. Nor did they rule such a coherent hierarchy of subject warrior peoples. On the Roman side, the lesson had long been learnt that so long as the gateway of Constantinople was firmly shut, whole areas of the Balkans could be temporarily lost to Roman control without it mortally wounding the empire. This of course was little comfort to the hapless peoples of these provinces, who had had to endure one invader after another for most of living memory.

Difficulties with the Arab allies on the Mesopotamian frontier now erupted into several major revolts in the Syrian, Palestinian and Arabian provinces. The Persian King Kavad, recently restored to his throne after a brief civil war, with the help of the warlike Hephthalites, wanted to adopt a more visibly aggressive foreign policy. He probably encouraged his allies, the Lakhmid Arabs, to attack the Roman frontier province of Euphratensis, on the northeastern edge of present Syria.

To the south a rebellion broke out among a new group of tribes led by the Ghassanids, who had recently been settled as Roman allies in Palestine and Arabia. This was probably set off by Anastasius' own policy, which was to end the Arab phylarchy based on the important trading city of Yotabe in the Gulf of Aqaba, an arrangement that had been forced on Leo twenty years earlier. The old Arab chief Amorkesos had died in 498, and Anastasius, determined to rebuild the empire's financial resources, wanted to regain this significant source of revenue. He therefore refused to renew the treaty of alliance, and revolt followed. Under their leader Jabala, who also commanded tribes of the Kindite and Salihite confederations, nominally Roman allies, they overran areas of Palestine until decisively defeated by the *Dux* Romanus, who went on to capture Yotabe and restore it to Roman merchants.[15] It was several more years before the Kindites and Salihites were reduced and new treaties established, which effectively left the Ghassanids as the major allied confederacy on the Arabian frontier.

The fighting in the north turned in Roman favour with the eventual defeat of the Lakhmids by the *Dux* Eugenius, but all the signs confirmed Persian hostility.[16] Relations had been bad ever since Anastasius' accession, when Kavad had abandoned the tolerant stance towards Christians in his empire, and repeatedly demanded, in haughty terms, Roman payments allegedly towards the defence of the Caspian Gates. Anastasius repeatedly refused, at one point even making a counter-demand for the return of the city of Nisibis (Nusyabin), which had been ceded by the Romans for 120 years in the treaty of 363, and hence in strict legality should have been returned in 483, although no Roman emperor seriously expected this.[17]

Although the Arab revolts in the Orient had been effectively suppressed, Kavad continued to prepare for eventual war. There had been no open war between the two empires for half a century and, in terms of either's vital interests, there was no real cause for one now. But Kavad's position at home, depending heavily on his powerful Hephthalite allies, was still insecure and he wanted the prestige of a victory to hold their allegiance and to impress his own Persian nobility. He offered the Christian Armenians toleration in return for their support, and succeeded in bringing several Arab nations on to his side. Anastasius might possibly have avoided war by agreeing to payments, but saw no reason to climb down. A subsidy to Persia would have been affordable, but not in the diplomatically humiliating form in which it was being demanded: in one exchange, Anastasius pointedly returned the insult by offering the Great King a loan. Also, Anastasius had ceased to see the defence of the Caspian Gates as a mutual advantage to both empires. On the contrary, it was distinctly useful to have menacing enemies on Persia's northern borders, and they were occasionally encouraged to cause trouble. It is therefore all the more surprising that when war did come, the Roman side was militarily unprepared.

In 502, there came a third invasion of the Bulgars, and in August of that year Kavad seized the opportunity to launch his war against the Roman Orient. Assailed on two frontiers, Anastasius this time made no attempt to halt the Bulgars militarily, although he did begin longer-term defensive plans. But for the present their raiding went unopposed, and the Danube provinces had to fend as best they could with what fortified refuges they had. Yet even in the East, garrison forces were under-strength, and the defences of the forts and cities were in poor repair. The Arab allies were still smarting from the recent revolts, and some of the persecuted Jewish communities were willing to help the Persians. It is possible, as Blockley suggests, that the Romans did not expect war so soon and that Kavad, having quietened his own Armenian population, marched quickly into Roman Armenia without warning or declaration of war. Certainly, he seems to have taken Anastasius by surprise. On learning of the Persian invasion, Anastasius hastily sent an envoy, Rufinus, to negotiate, but Kavad simply arrested him.[18]

In the first offensive, the Persians captured several cities in Roman Armenia.

Theodosiopolis (Carana) was betrayed by its commander Constantinus, who had some bitter grievance against Anastasius that led him to change sides. Martyropolis (near Sint) fell soon afterwards, while the Persians laid siege to the great fortress of Amida, on the Tigris (Diyarbakir), whose defences were under strength. In January 503 the fortress fell, and many of its people were massacred.[19]

For 503, a large Roman army was assembled under three commands, in the manner of the Isaurian campaigns. Here Anastasius showed an uncertain management of strategic affairs. There was not only poor co-ordination between commanders but also rivalry among them. One of the commanders was Hypatius,[20] a nephew of Anastasius who lacked experience. The army under Areobindus had some initial success around Nisibis, but Hypatius and Patricius, the two Praesental commanders with far larger forces, sat down to besiege Amida and refused to send Areobindus the supporting forces promised him. Worse, their great force was surprised by the Persians and suffered a defeat which caused them to retreat across the Euphrates.[21] Areobindus, isolated, retreated to Edessa, which Kavad besieged. Inspired by its holy legend that Jesus Christ himself had once promised that the city would never fall, the garrison and people held out energetically until Kavad was forced to withdraw. Except for some raiding of Persian Arab territories by Roman Arabs, the only checks to Persia in this year were, as in Edessa, the result of the courage and patriotism of the city populations, who were often led by their bishops.

Next year these mistakes were rectified by removing Hypatius and uniting the armies under a single overall commander. This was Celer, not a military man but Master of Offices. Anastasius probably appointed him because of his organising talents and his ability to co-ordinate a very large force commanded by several professional generals while remaining unaffected by their rivalries.[22] The army of 504 is reported to have been as large as 80,000, a quite exceptional size for this period. Whatever its actual figure, there is no doubt that by now Anastasius was able on occasion to deploy considerably larger forces than hitherto.[23]

The scales were quickly turned. Patricius renewed the siege of Amida. In separate offensives, Areobindus invaded Persian Armenia, and Celer marched through Callinicum, retaking several cities and then invading Persian Arzanene, which his forces devastated and plundered thoroughly. Amida's Persian garrison held out very stubbornly through the winter of 504 until provisions were exhausted and the remaining Roman inhabitants were starving and said to have been reduced to cannibalism. By early 505, at the latest, negotiations had begun with the Persians. Confirming Anastasius' perception of the usefulness of Persia's northern enemies, Kavad was now faced with new attacks from the Huns throughout the Caucasus and, as a result of this in combination with his reverses and their effect on his allies, he was forced to send envoys of peace to Celer.

The immediate outcome was the Persian evacuation of Amida in exchange for a payment of 1,000 pounds of gold, but on other points the negotiations dragged on, with the Persians objecting to many of the terms, until finally Celer pressed the Roman military ascendancy by concentrating his army at Edessa, then moving it forward to Dara near the Mesopotamian frontier.[24] The resulting treaty was distinctly in Roman interests, though by no means a crushing one. Anastasius' far greater financial resources allowed him both to keep the menacing army assembled for almost a year, and lubricate the treaty by granting the financially straitened Kavad an annual 'gift' (not a tribute) of 500 pounds of gold for seven years, which was in effect a compromise over the Caspian Gates issue.

The initial failures in the war prompted an inquiry, and led to a considerable overhaul of the whole Eastern defence system. Even while negotiations were going on, work was begun on strengthening the defences and resources of cities such as Edessa, Batnae, Virtha and Europus. The sacrifices and successful self-defence by the civil populations of key cities in the absence of a main Roman army was amply recognised. The taxes of Amida and Edessa were reduced or remitted altogether, and measures were taken throughout all the frontier provinces to improve the cities' water supplies, magazines and overall capacity both to withstand siege themselves and support Roman armies operating in the region. As well as tax concessions, city bishops were given a leading role in organising the reconstruction and resupply.

Anastasius was also persuaded by his generals of the difficulty of operating in Mesopotamia without a strong strategic base close to the frontier, in the manner of Nisibis before it passed into Persian hands. He therefore took advantage of Kavad's preoccupation with the invading Huns to invest in a new fortress at Dara, confronting Nisibis. Skilled labour was drafted in from Syria at very high rates of pay, and what had been a small town was quickly transformed into a large, heavily fortified city with granaries, cisterns, arms magazines, baths, churches and all that was needed to sustain it and supply an army. It was completed in a few years and renamed Anastasiopolis; the ruins of its fortifications are still impressive today.[25] Kavad protested that this was a violation of a previous treaty, and protested likewise at the refortification of Theodosiopolis, but there was little he could do about it.

To limit the danger from the Bulgars, and in effect acknowledging the fragility of much the Danube frontier, Anastasius embarked on an even more ambitious fortification project. About forty miles west of Constantinople a new sea-to-sea forward defence line was built across the neck of the Thracian peninsula, from the Black Sea to the Sea of Marmora, corresponding to the Turkish Chatalja line in the Bulgarian war of 1912–13. Known as the Long Walls of Thrace or the Anastasian Wall, it was about twenty-six miles long with projecting towers, and only recently (1997) began to be systematically surveyed. The structure that is emerging suggests different periods of construction, with projecting towers of various shapes and dimensions, and numerous forts and fortlets. The spacing of the towers is not uniform, but more closely grouped in the vulnerable sectors, especially the south, where they faced the main approach road from the west. Large polygonal projecting towers are located at points where the alignment of the wall changes, with smaller rectangular towers in between. In front of the curtain wall was a lower, outer wall, and on some sectors there was also a ditch beyond the wall system. A twin military and civil administrative structure was set up for a new district of the Long Wall, intended to supply and defend this outer ring of fortification of Constantinople and its immediate hinterland.[26]

Built between 502 and 505, the wall marked a new determination to defend the vital approaches to the capital in the wake of heavy and humiliating defeats in the field. By 505 it appears that some kind of arrangement had been reached with the Bulgars, or at least some of them, since their troops are found serving in the Roman army in the same manner as Hun contingents. There are no reports of new Bulgar incursions for the next fifteen years, but this may reflect the unsettled state of their dominion over subject tribes north of the Danube rather than any accommodation with Constantinople.

The creation of the Long Walls did not imply any abandonment of the Balkan provinces, although for the immediate future it was unrealistic to expect field armies to defend these areas against serious Bulgar invasions. At least in the middle and lower Danube, many forts and cities that had been partially destroyed or abandoned during the Bulgar depredations and before were being restored and reoccupied. But it was usually on a modest scale with a smaller fortified citadel in place of generous city walls. This could at least support a local military presence and a civil administration, which in practice often meant the local bishop and church. Strenuous efforts were made to reclaim and refortify most of those towns where there seemed some chance of recovery. City authorities were encouraged to repair or rebuild the defensive walls, and people were encouraged by good building wages, tax concessions and similar incentives to reoccupy the surrounding lands and townships. This was a distinct moral signal to a beleaguered, but still tough, and resourceful peasant population of continued imperial support and investment in a future. There is recent evidence, usually from brick or tile stamps, of rebuilding at many sites during the Anastasian period: at Istros, Dinogetia, Tomi, Histria and Sucidava. Tomi (Constanza) yielded an inscription imploring God to protect the restored city.[27]

Anastasius did not formally recognise Theoderic as his viceroy (Patrician) in Italy until 497.[28] Relations remained cordial until 504–5 when the Gepids, who had occupied the upper Danube region around Sirmium beyond the effective control of Constantinople, came into conflict with Theoderic. In the course of this the Ostrogoths conquered lower Pannonia and then invaded Upper Moesia, which was east Roman territory, in the process defeating a Roman force which included Bulgar mercenaries.

Anastasius retaliated first by sending a fleet to raid the south Italian coast, which the Vandals of Africa did nothing to hinder. More effectively, he encouraged the territorial ambitions of the Germanic kingdoms who rivalled Theoderic, especially those of the expansionist Franks, now converted to Orthodox Christianity, who were coming to dominate most of Gaul. After a crushing victory over the Visigoths, the Frankish king, Chlodovech (Clovis), was handsomely recognised by Anastasius with an honorary consulship. Gold, presents and symbolism all underlined this prestigious diplomatic relationship.[29] The Lombard attack on Theoderic's allies, the Heruli, may well have been encouraged by Anastasius. Although the Frankish kingdom was not yet at war with Theoderic, it was by now enough of a threat on his northern borders to cause him to pull his horns in, and come to an agreement with Anastasius in about 510, in which the disputed areas of Pannonia were recognised as belonging to the Eastern empire. The rivalry did not stop however, and a few years later we have Anastasius conferring the title of Patrician on the Orthodox Burgundian King Sigismund, an obvious opponent of the Ostrogoths. Although he had originally been provoked, Anastasius clearly took up the tradition of the right of the Eastern emperor to interfere in the West as their ultimate overlord.

It is possible to trace some pattern in the overall defensive strategy of Anastasius, which perhaps represents a clearer recognition of the realistic territorial limits to the empire and the ways of defending them. The Eastern frontiers were secured, as far as possible, by investment in the strategic cities and the infrastructure for supporting field armies, as well as a reconstructed system of allied Arab phylarchies whose pay, maintenance, leaders and obligations were at least broadly under Roman control. After the victorious war of 504–5, both empires had a clear interest in a period of peace, and Anastasius showed no concern about later disturbances beyond the defensible limits that might otherwise have been exploited in Roman interests.

In the Balkans, the loss of Roman military ascendancy over much of the region was temporarily acquiesced in, in the hope that these provinces might once again be fully reclaimed as far west as Sirmium. The message was that the Long Walls did not in any way imply abandonment of these populations, who remained firmly Roman in their loyalties and institutions and whose towns were still linked by an imperial administration, though they relied increasingly on self-help. Further west, the African Vandal kingdom was in decline after Gaiseric and had ceased to challenge Rome at sea. The dangers of Ostrogothic encroachment into the lower Danube could be counteracted, as we saw, by diplomatic moves to encourage their powerful neighbours, especially the Franks, to keep them occupied in western Europe.[30]

A distinction was clearly drawn between those provinces temporarily undefended against the Bulgars or other powerful enemies, and those of the West, temporarily ruled by Germanic kings on behalf of the emperor. There was never any question that these areas, including Vandal Africa, were still seen as part of the Roman empire, the *Orbis Romanus* or *Oikoumene*, the natural and eternal order of things, with the emperor as *de jure* ruler. Nor was all this, the carefully styled embassies and bestowal of Roman titles, merely an impotent legal ceremonial. The German kings were all acutely conscious of the great emperor at Constantinople, and needed the prestige of the Roman name. Among their peers, the title of Patrician carried far more weight than mere *Rex*, which every petty local ruler could claim. Theoderic, for example, still carried the emperor's name and image on his coins. In evolving their own states, laws, political frameworks and kingly authority the only model they had was Rome, visible not in ancient archives but in the remaining civil structures and the palpable power and authority of the New Rome with its ambassadors and symbols. In this way the East, far more than the Papacy, was developing a distinct form of diplomacy towards evolving Christian states which were independent militarily but not ideologically. To be a properly constituted state was, in part, just to be recognised as one by Rome, with the appropriate adoption of its values and apparatus, especially the *leges Barbarorum*. The elaborate, finely tuned Byzantine ceremonials, presents, carefully graded levels of recognition – including even imperial marriage alliances – were being used to persuade the new kingdoms into the dignity of respected allies and partners, and away from the status of barbarians who had troops for hire and chieftains to placate with gold. The ultimate basis of such a relationship, hopefully, was a shared outlook which was both Roman and Christian.

It was during the long reign of Anastasius that there began to appear a self-conscious reservoir of foreign diplomatic skills that could be organised and handed on, and which was centred on the department of the Master of Offices. Envoys, military or civilian, with a good record in negotiations and a specialist knowledge of some foreign people – Persians, Arabs, Ostrogoths, Vandals – were retained, valued, and used again, instead of each situation being met by an ad hoc response using whoever was at hand and happened to know something of the terrain. The multinational character of the armies, including commanders of foreign origin themselves, helped this development. A corps of translators emerged; intelligence gathering, through traders, Christian missionaries and bishops, and other routes, became more serious. This more careful attention to foreign affairs, its professionalisation as a continuing activity and source of careers, reflected a sober recognition of the costliness of wars, of the de facto territorial limits to the empire, and of the desirability of peace as a normal condition if it could be obtained. Diplomacy became more able to anticipate and shape events rather than simply react to them, and thus became seen as a proper parallel arm to military strategy and not just a rationalisation of it.[31]

Ethnic attitudes and hostilities did not disappear, but to a growing extent balanced each other as Constantinople and its hinterland became steadily cosmopolitan in soldiers and civilians. The traditional Hellenic anti-barbarian feelings were still there, but now, especially after the Isaurians had been neutralised, there was no one single threatening group against which they could define themselves as they had against the Goths at the beginning of the fifth century. The hostility between Orthodox, Arian and Monophysite was as sharp or sharper than between ethnic groups. The Ostrogoths had ceased to be a menace within imperial territories. Germanic peoples – usually soldiers – and people with Germanic ancestry suffered from fewer social handicaps; this was now merely one more nationality among many that made up the empire. At a vernacular level, Romanness, a many-sided and ill-defined concept, was more associated with baptism and Christianity than geographical origin.

For most of his reign, Anastasius wisely tried to avoid the religious conflicts which always simmered below the surface. This mostly depended on moderate bishops occupying the crucial sees of Constantinople, Antioch and Alexandria. As a responsible emperor Anastasius publicly adhered to Zeno's compromise formula of the Henotikon, and demanded that others do likewise, although his own personal sympathies were with the Monophysites. The follies of Basiliscus twenty years earlier were not lost on him. Yet, Anastasius himself was unusually devout for an emperor. His sense of Christian duty led him to forbid wild beast fights (whether or not the ban was effective) as well as the surviving pagan celebrations of the Brytae, one of the popular dance festivals of the East. Neither measure endeared him to the capital's crowds.[32] Perhaps it is not surprising that towards the end of his life his true religious loyalties emerged more openly. Unfortunately, this helped to fuel a prolonged and costly rebellion that the East could well have done without.

For five years, Anastasius tolerated the bitter antagonism and intrigues of the Patriarch Euphemius, who did not hesitate to appeal to Pope Felix III for support in deposing the Monophysite bishop of Alexandria. Eventually Anastasius, exasperated, convened a council in 496 which deposed Euphemius, who was then banished.[33] Otherwise, he took care not to upset the difficult balance between Chalcedonians and Monophysites, insisting simply on the Janus-like Henotikon as the touchstone for acceptability. This entailed that both Nestorians and Eutychians, on each extreme wing, were heretical, beyond the pale. At Jerusalem and Antioch, the new bishops were discreetly or openly Chalcedonian, as was Euphemius' successor at Constantinople, Macedonius.

What sober spirits had hoped would be a reconciling or at least a balancing formula, proved to be neither. Adroitly and sensitively drafted, the eirenic Henotikon was in the final resort what it was intended to be, a political and ecclesiastical compromise, and not a (*per impossibile*) theological solution. Those who opposed it did so virulently, whereas its supporters were pragmatists and accommodators. Had Anastasius been as relaxed about religious questions as his three predecessors had been, these conflicts might have been at least contained. But he was at bottom deeply religious, and in earlier life had even preached his own unorthodox views in the church of Hagia Sophia, until his enemy, Bishop Euphemius had banned him. He now felt the balance tilting ominously against the Monophysites, even in Palestine and Syria. At length, at an advanced age, he fell under the influence of two subtle Monophysite theologians, Philoxenus and Severus, and steadily abandoned his official neutrality.

He decided to get rid of Macedonius, but the Patriarch was popular and every legitimate device had to be put to use. In July 511, the twentieth anniversary of his reign, Anastasius carefully administered the oath of allegiance to guards and army and paid the donative, equivalent to a year's pay, to the troops (above, p. 135). He then accused Macedonius in the Consistory of preaching Nestorian heresies, producing 'evidence' that he had not only slandered the emperor but was even plotting rebellion. All the same it was no easy task, and at one point required Anastasius' impassioned protestations in the Consistory of his own Orthodoxy, followed by tearful demonstrations of loyalty. Finally the Senate obediently tried and condemned Macedonius, who was deposed and exiled.[34] At Antioch the moderately Chalcedonian Patriarch Flavian was also deposed and replaced by the Monophysite Severus, one of the inspirers of Anastasius' new policies.

Purging Macedonius had been difficult enough, but Anastasius' next step was virtual folly, explicable only by his own devoted belief in what he saw as the true Christian path. The population of Constantinople was overwhelmingly Chalcedonian in loyalty, with a small Monophysite minority mainly identified with the Green circus faction. Macedonius' successor, Timothy, was an open Monophysite, prepared to champion the cause publicly with the support of Anastasius and his Monophysite Prefect, Marinus. On a Sunday in 512 in the great church of Hagia Sophia, Timothy introduced into the sacred liturgy of the Trisagion the inflammatory Monophysite addition '...who was crucified for us'. The result was predictable: the liturgy was drowned by an angry congregation, and rioting followed.

The Prefects deployed some troops who temporarily dispersed the mob, with some bloodshed.[35] The fire did not blow out, but instead grew to explosive proportions not seen in the turbulent capital in living memory. Two days later huge Orthodox crowds reassembled in the Forum of Constantine, and their sense of sheer numbers and collective visceral emotions produced the results they commonly do. Leaders emerged. Vociferous protest boiled over into outright revolt. Buildings were set on fire, and Anastasius' statues smashed – the standard gesture of open rebellion. The mob, or parts of it, impulsively tried to proclaim as emperor the retired general Areobindus, hero of the Persian war. He was very distantly connected to the Theodosian dynasty, and his presumed Orthodoxy clearly outweighed his Gothic origins. They marched to the house of his wife, Juliana, but he had wisely gone into hiding.[36]

There were troops in the city, but as usual only palace guards or token ceremonial units, insufficient to quell a movement of this scale; the main Praesental forces were some distance away. The Praesental commander, Patricius, and the Master of Offices, Celer, vainly tried to pacify the great mob, but were stoned. The house of Marinus, the Monophysite Prefect and a special target for their hatred, was burnt down. But with Areobindus unavailable the mob had little coherent plan of revolution, and it is very possible few of them seriously wanted to overthrow Anastasius.

Anastasius was clearly alarmed at the crisis but, with great presence of mind, he announced that he would address the crowds in person. Perhaps its was his last chance of riding out the storm. Perhaps, indeed, at his advanced age he was calmly resigned to the possibility of ending his reign. He appeared in the Hippodrome without his imperial diadem. Ignoring the shouts that the two Prefects be thrown to the wild beasts, he calmed the mob and solemnly offered to abdicate if he no longer enjoyed their loyalty. This had a sobering effect. The mood changed, the revolutionary fury evaporated. The crowds signalled their loyalty and agreed to disperse peacefully. But it had been a very close thing.

Whatever concessions might have been made or promised, the conflict could not now be contained as before, and the following year the banners of Orthodoxy were taken up by a serious military revolt. The rebel was Vitalian, who held the middle-ranking position of count of the multinational federate troops in Thrace, and who succeeded in knitting several grievances together.[37] The troops complained that their agreed pay and supplies had been stopped, and turned their anger against Vitalian's immediate superior, the *Magister* for Thrace, Hypatius. This may well have been a consequence of Anastasius' tax reforms. The discontent spread easily to the peasant population of the region, who had long suffered from insecurity, were used to taking their own measures of self-defence, and had traditionally provided ready recruits for the armies. Other commanders and their troops joined the revolt, which Vitalian advertised as a holy Orthodox crusade to rid the empire of the Monophysite heresy, to secure justice for the deposed Patriarchs Macedonius and Flavian, and to restore the revered Trisagion to its true purity.[38]

How important the religious motive was in Vitalian's own ambitions may be argued, but there is no doubt that his movement could ever have achieved such size and importance without this rallying theme. Hypatius fled, and Vitalian's large, motley force of Thracian troops, federates and peasants advanced on Constantinople without opposition, and encamped outside the walls. So far, there had been no armed clash: it was not yet full civil war. Vitalian took care not to present himself as a rebel intent on overthrowing Anastasius but presented himself only as the redresser of popular grievances, and for the moment it was prudent of the emperor to treat him in this light. Vitalian warily sent his chief officers into the city to negotiate, and they were persuaded by such gifts and promises that Vitalian had little option but to agree, or declare outright rebellion. The pay and supplies were restored, Hypatius removed, and it was promised that the theological dispute would be submitted to the Pope, Hormisdas, for arbitration – a dangerous concession that Anastasius hardly intended seriously. But the movement was temporarily defused, and Vitalian's army withdrew to Lower Moesia.[39]

The truce did not last. After Hypatius' successor Cyril had been assassinated, Anastasius had Vitalian declared a public enemy and despatched a powerful army against him. The expedition misfired badly, the army was defeated, and Vitalian's prestige and war coffers were greatly strengthened. He occupied the fortified cities of Moesia and Scythia, and the next year advanced again on Constantinople.

Vitalian's ambitions were unusual for a Roman general. He was a capable military leader and had a strong base of support in the federates and the Thracian population who had long borne the brunt of invasions and suffered neglect, as they saw it, by the imperial government. Knowing the risks of attempting to overthrow and replace the emperor, Vitalian's position became that of a regional warlord, similar to the earlier opportunist Ostrogothic kings. He could menace the capital, extract heavy concessions, and now foment discontent and try to destabilise Anastasius by posing as the great champion of Orthodoxy. But beyond Orthodox sentiments he had no concrete power base outside the Balkans. Anastasius implicitly acknowledged the position when, worried by the spread of anti-Monophysite feeling, he hurriedly mollified the Asian and Oriental provinces by further tax concessions.

With Vitalian's forces once more facing Constantinople, Anastasius had to accept his terms, which included the post of *Magister Militum* of Thrace, restoration of the expelled bishops, and a General Council to be held at Heraclea close to the capital, attended by the Pope's representatives. For many months, Vitalian kept his army assembled in the region of the capital. In correspondence, the Pope's conditions for a settlement were quite uncompromising, and the council never met. Feeling betrayed, Vitalian again moved his army against the city, occupying the northern shore of Galata and assembling a strong fleet of ships at the mouth of the Golden Horn.

It is doubtful if Vitalian intended a direct assault on Constantinople; more likely he planned a blockade by which he could impose his conditions. But his objectives were ambivalent. Anastasius' promises were worthless, but unless Vitalian's pressure could induce a revolt in his favour inside the city, he could make little more headway than perhaps to extort payments. Like so many other besiegers, time was not on his side. Vitalian was probably having difficulty holding his varied forces together for such a long period. During the interval, the defence had been able to organise itself.[40]

There was probably some religious sympathy with Vitalian in the city, or at least a reluctance to fight him and his followers. The two Praesental *Magistri*, it is said, were personally known to Vitalian and asked to be excused the command, which went instead to the civilian Prefect, Marinus, the staunch Monophysite supporter of Anastasius. This may have seemed a risky appointment, but in the event it was very successful. In a battle at the mouth of the Golden Horn, Marinus' ships completely defeated Vitalian's fleet. One account is that they used a new chemical fire-throwing weapon, anticipating the fearsome Greek fire centuries later. Marinus' troops landed on the northern shore and routed the rebels, after which Vitalian's forces collapsed quickly. Several of his commanders were captured and executed, and he himself fled back to Thrace with his remaining followers, where he went into hiding, only to reappear several years later, after Anastasius' death.[41]

There were solemn ceremonies of thanksgiving, in which the Archangel Michael was specially honoured as the city's deliverer. But the military effort and the long distractions of the Thracian army in the civil war once more, in 517, allowed a deep Bulgar invasion which was able to plunder in Greece and Macedonia with little or no resistance.

Anastasius finally died in 518, at the remarkable age of eighty-eight. His religious policy, by any standards of statesmanship, was something of an aberration, inspired only by his own pious belief in the One Nature. For the empire it was a dead end. The majority of the East, apart from Egypt and sections of Palestine and Syria, was firmly and aggressively Chalcedonian-Orthodox. Almost immediately after the emperor's death the religious regime was reversed, and communion with Rome, which had lapsed since Zeno's Henotikon, was re-established. Vitalian, emerging from rebellion, was welcomed at Constantinople and given a Praesental post, but soon suspected of treachery and assassinated, allegedly by Justinian.

In all other respects, Anastasius' long reign had been one of considerable achievement – fiscal, administrative and strategic – and had put the East on a more sound basis than it had been since the first half of the fifth century, before the great shock of Attila's Huns. It is true that territorial control had been lost in some areas, notably the Western Balkans, but a great deal had been invested in limiting the damage and providing strongpoint defences against a wayward enemy, who might be worn down and neutralised by adroit combinations of resistance and diplomacy, and creating an enhanced barrier against military threats to Constantinople itself. In the Orient, with the reorganisation of the frontier system, the empire's defences were now better entrenched, and supported increased security and growing agricultural prosperity in the provinces of Syria, Palestine and Arabia.

The fiscal achievements, which left an unprecedented 320,000 pounds of gold in the treasury (twenty-two million solidi) were inseparable from Anastasius' constant attention to the administrative machine.[42] Having risen through this machine, he knew it intimately, and chose other capable administrators with skill and success, as even his detractors had conceded. Over his reign of twenty-seven years a more effective, professional corps of bureaucrats was trained and put to work. Apart from the creation of the *vindices*, the fiscal system was not radically reorganised, but made to operate far more effectively. Anastasius' reign amply demonstrated that, provided that they were protected by Roman arms, the Eastern provinces continued to be a great source of taxable wealth, as long as it could be gathered and redirected honestly and competently. In this period, in contrast with the financially disastrous African expedition of Leo and the near-anarchy of Zeno's reign, ambitious fortification projects were completed and manned, army pay was raised and significantly larger numbers of first-class troops, both Roman and foreign, were recruited to serve within the established command structure, which had now excluded alien bases of military power. With so much of the empire's flexible strategy and diplomacy dependent on cash, there was, in addition to all of this, an enormous reserve of money. Except for his religious dissensions, Anastasius bequeathed to his successors at Constantinople great, well-organised reserves of power for prosperity and survival. It remained to be seen what they did with them.

At his death in 518, Anastasius left neither an heir nor a nominated successor, nor an Augusta who could mediate a transition. Once again the powers in Constantinople bargained and bluffed with proposed candidates, this time in a more open fashion. The army was represented, for all practical purposes, by the rival groups of guards, the Scholarians and the Excubitors. Neither would support a candidate from the other, and their fierce arguments were carried on among great crowds in the Hippodrome. The other group was composed of the ministers, Senate and Patriarch gathered in the great hall of the palace and holding all the ceremonial regalia necessary for election and coronation. Anastasius' Master of Offices, Celer, urged them to decide quickly, before others forced someone on them. After a series of false manoeuvres in which several unlikely candidates were proposed by the soldiers and people, only to be rejected, the palace party finally threw their weight behind the commander of the Excubitors, Justin.[43] The whole wrangle was very possibly a devious stratagem from the first to have Justin elected. At any event, this settled the matter without bloodshed or disorders, even though the Scholarians were definitely the larger military force. In effect, bloc votes replaced swords.

Justin was duly enthroned with all ceremony. He was sixty-six, an experienced soldier of lowly Illyrian peasant origins who had served in Anastasius' Persian and Isaurian wars and distinguished himself in the suppression of Vitalian. His most important act was the clear re-establishment of Chalcedonian Orthodoxy and communion with Rome, which was accompanied by the rehabilitation of the dangerous figure Vitalian, who was given a Praesental *Magister* post.

While commanding the Excubitors Justin had advanced his elder nephew, Peter Sabbatius, given him an education at Constantinople which he himself had lacked, and enrolled him in the *Candidati*. He was adopted as Justin's son and took the name Justinian. Within two years of Justin's election he was created a Praesental *Magister*, and soon afterwards arranged the murder of his rival Vitalian. Justinian's formal powers and outstanding personal abilities left little doubt that he was the destined successor, and during the remaining years of Justin's reign he was increasingly the power behind the throne. In 527 the aged Justin fell ill, and formally adopted Justinian as his imperial colleague. By August of that year Justin had died, and Justinian became sole ruler at the age of forty-five.

Figure 17 Theoderic, the Ostrogothic king of Italy, 493–526. He was persuaded by Zeno to move West and rule Italy as the emperor's nominal viceroy.

Source: Museo del Terme, Rome; Deutsches Archäologisches Institut, Rome.

Figure 18 Leo I, 457–74. He purged the Gothic military dynasty of Aspar, but failed disastrously in the great expedition to retake Africa from the Vandals.

Note: © The British Museum

Figure 19 Zeno, 474–91. The Isaurian emperor, during whose reign the East was convulsed by internal wars and in danger of disintegrating. He eventually emerged victorious, and rid the East of the Ostrogothic federate nations.

Note: © The British Museum

Figure 20 Anastasius I, 491–518. He restored the East's finances, expanded the armies and fortifications, crushed the Isaurians and fought a victorious war against Persia.

Note: © The British Museum

Figure 21 The empress Ariadne, 474–515. Wife of Zeno, she secured the smooth succession of Anastasius by marrying him. Ivory diptych.

Source: Museo del Bargello, Florence; Archivi Alinari/Anderson

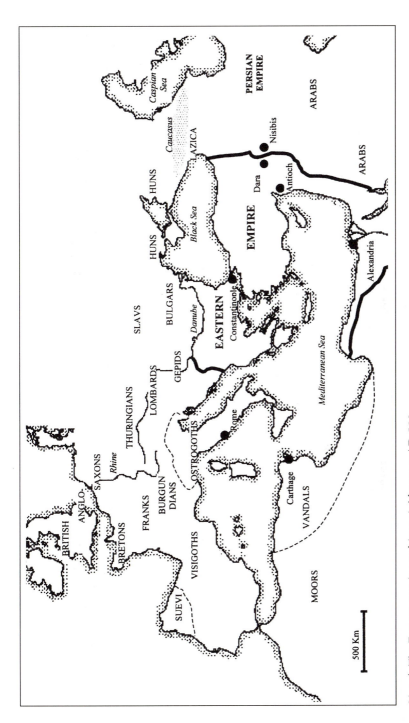

Map 4 The Eastern empire and its neighbours *c.* AD 500.

15

THE SURVIVAL AND
RENEWAL OF THE EAST

Our narrative ends as Justinian, that dominating figure of early Byzantine history, is about to make his appearance. His seemingly great achievements were only made possible by the huge fiscal and military resources bequeathed to him by Anastasius, and the underlying political stability provided by the tenacious, self-renewing institutions of the Constantinople establishment which had emerged, strengthened and self-conscious, through the crises of the fifth century. Justinian's dramatic reconquests of Africa, Italy and Illyricum, so widely admired then and today, were achieved only at enormous cost to the empire's total resources and proved to be short-lived. However militarily and diplomatically impressive they were to other states, they badly overstretched the East's deployable strength and steadily evaporated after Justinian's death. The old Roman empire could not be restored in this way, or indeed any other way.

Explaining both the disintegration of the West and the survival of the East in the fifth century are finally not two issues, but one. Both halves of the empire were faced, at the beginning, with an array of similar prominent problems: immature or ineffective emperors, barbarian invaders, an unruly soldiery and dangerous settlements of armed barbarian federates. From Montesquieu and Gibbon onwards, there have been very many studies devoted to the disintegration of the West, and until quite recently a Western European viewpoint, and a steady focus on the high empire of the first and second centuries, have attempted to persuade us that the Roman Empire, for all intents and purposes, was what fell apart and was extinguished in Italy in the fifth century. Anything after that was something different.

As to the question of the East, the survival of the 'something different', even modern histories tend to concentrate on the later ebb and flow of Byzantium's fortunes and its remarkable resilience down the centuries, rather than on its consolidation in the critical early years. The student sometimes receives the impression that, given the wisdom and foresight of Constantine I in founding his new capital at the time and place he did, and the undoubtedly greater wealth of the Eastern provinces, the Eastern empire's continuation was unproblematic, only to be expected. It is presented almost as if the two halves

of the empire neatly decoupled themselves in 395 and went their own insu-
lated ways, the East wisely leaving the West to sink or swim, as if winding
down the unsuccessful component of a business venture.

This is not just a very superficial picture but a fundamentally false one.
There are several obvious examples. In the 370s, the arrival of the Huns
began a process that wrecked the whole fourth-century defensive system and
frontier policy on the eastern Danube. This was the greatest single cause of
the destabilisation and military crises that followed in the fifth century.
After the great disaster of Adrianople there was chronic insecurity in the
East for several years, in which the Visigoths could not be defeated in the
field, and could barely be prevented from moving and plundering where
they wished. A citizen of Trier or Paris could feel distinctly more secure than
one in Athens or Serdica.

Similarly, in the years after 395 the East was temporarily defenceless, and
gravely threatened first by Alaric's Visigoths, and then by Gainas and the
Ostrogothic federates who occupied Constantinople and held the government to ransom by military violence. In retrospect, these may appear to have
been transitory crises; but at the time, there was no guarantee that ambitious generals would not continue to destabilise the government with their
armies; or that the Gothic federates would not remain on imperial territory
indefinitely in their doubtful role as defenders of the frontiers, extending
their power at the expense of the imperial government. Later, something of
this did begin to happen with the new Ostrogothic federates in the critical
years of Leo and Zeno.

That these dangers were averted was due to more than military geography
and gold. The East certainly had important inherent advantages, but it still
required the ability and willingness of its many rulers, often in conflict with
each other, to utilise them. It had to develop the skills of controlling and
using military force for its proper purposes; of finding other means of
defence when its armies were repeatedly defeated in the field by the Huns; of
ensuring that the great potential wealth was tapped and deployed effectively
at the real points of application; of maintaining a stable state in the reign of
immature or weak emperors; of managing the orderly transfer of power in
the difficult periods of dynastic breaks; and of managing and mobilising the
new patterns of religious loyalties. None of these things came automatically
or naturally in the radically changed conditions.

Constantinople was indeed an undisputed centre of imperial power and
authority, ideally planned strategically and soon fortified to make it near-
impregnable by land or sea. Most importantly, it was also the centre in
which there could develop a new kind of ruling class around the emperors.
Its backbone was civilian rather than military, but it soon learnt to become
more comprehensive, drawing the different levers of power – palace, Senate,
ministers and army (and to a degree, church) – into a single effective institution of a centralised state, an establishment of power and authority. Because

it was essentially bureaucratic and impersonal it could survive the deaths of emperors, or the purges of this or that faction, and continue functioning after violent civil wars had decided in favour of one or other candidate. Because it was geographically concentrated in one capital it could reach authoritative decisions quickly, and resolve most of its internal conflicts without them spreading into the wider empire. The emergence of any viable functioning rival power centre was correspondingly very difficult.

This was certainly not achieved quickly or effortlessly, but grew in an atmosphere of often poisonous rivalries around the weak unmilitary emperors Arcadius and Theodosius II. Some writers have talked easily about the 'demilitarisation' of the Eastern government after Theodosius I, but this is apt to suggest both a drastic change and an almost deliberate policy, whereas, like many profound political developments, by the time it had become a clear and conscious policy it had already come about. To displace or dethrone the power of the generals was, after all, an extremely difficult goal that might previously have seemed near-impossible, rather like Synesius' fantastic proposals to expel or enslave all barbarians.

In fact of course, the Eastern armies with their large and indispensable barbarian components, were always a mainstay of the state. They rightly consumed the bulk of its huge fiscal deliveries, and were deliberately expanded under Anastasius as he enlarged these. What was achieved in the fifth century was not a weakening or demotion of the military power, but its institutionalisation within a centralised state structure that included the inseparable civil components. The army was never firmly subordinated as the mere instrument of civil power, as it was in Britain after the end of Cromwell's Protectorate, or in the American states from their very beginning. East Roman generals, whether Roman or barbarian in origin, were by right equal members of the upper ruling circles, members of the Consistory and senior members of the Senate.

The career of Aspar illustrates this most clearly. For many years he was the most important single man below the emperor in the state, and his influence prevailed in choosing two other emperors, Marcian and Leo, as well as contributing to many of the highest government decisions. For all that, he was still *primus inter pares*. He and other ambitious *Magistri*, who had held their posts for long periods and cultivated the loyalties of the armies, were faced with a choice and a temptation. They might call on external military force to dominate, by indirect threat, the government at Constantinople – and perhaps make themselves effective dictators over a weak imperial incumbent, as Constantius, Aetius and Ricimer did in the West. Alternatively, they could utilise their leverage and their indispensability within the established central power structure, where there was now a proper place for them.

Gainas in the crisis of 399 to 400 attempted the first of these two options in a confused way. He was out of his depth, confronted by a loose front of civil ministers, primarily Eutropius. They both denied him the *Magister* position he felt was his due and implicitly isolated him, with the background menace of the treason charge and judicial murder by which Rufinus and then Eutropius had destroyed several other Eastern generals. However glad they were that he had rid them of Rufinus, they were as concerned as Rufinus had been to keep ambitious generals out of the inner circles of power. There was at that time no 'proper place' for the military, consonant with its real power. Deadly personal rivalries did not prevent the mandarins sharing a common interest as a class, but at that stage it probably did not go beyond that. Gainas was not only seen as an ambitious Gothic general but also as an outsider, a dangerous agent of the Western dictator Stilicho, their greater enemy. At this stage, their crude policy of 'demilitarisation' was little more than the response of one entrenched faction to a perceived threat from the West. It certainly did not extend in any farsighted way to a workable accommodation with the military, which would integrate it as a proper component of government. That began to emerge only at the earliest with Anthemius and his successors during the ascendancy of Pulcheria.

However, the occupation of Constantinople, the expulsion of the Goths and the overthrow of Gainas, were all very traumatic and formative experiences, reinforcing the wisdom or prejudice against unbridled generals. Only when Alaric had been removed westward and Gainas had been destroyed could ministers once again appreciate the indispensability of capable, professional commanders, especially the 'barbarian' ones, provided they were severed from a tribal federate power base. Theodosius I had promoted very many of them, and their patronage in turn had advanced many others up the rungs of military careers, creating a reserve of skill and experience. The clear separation from tribal blocs made these commanders respectable again, and the threats from Persia, the Huns and the new challenge of Vandal Africa made them necessary.

By the 420s *Magistri* such as Plintha, Ardaburius, Areobindus and their relatives and colleagues were rising to occupy top commands again, often for extended periods. The Theodosian fivefold division of these commands undoubtedly checked any overweening concentration of military power, as did the military geography of the East. In the West, Theodosius had himself helped to create the basis for a more united command, which with Stilicho meant a single pre-eminent commander-in-chief who controlled all the subordinate appointments.

A catalyst to the consolidation of civil power in the East was the accident of immature and unmilitary boy emperors. Again, the pivotal years were 395 to 408, when the two halves of the empire were in a state of cold war. In terms of the military/civilian balance, the responses to the problem were diametrically opposed in East and West.

For almost two centuries, it had been axiomatic that the ruling emperor should be commander-in-chief of the armies in both name and fact, directing them in battle in person. Valens had died with his soldiers at Adrianople. In the West, Gratian, though he inherited the purple at only sixteen, had already been taught by his ferocious father Valentinian I to fight and command armies. It is true that Diocletian and Constantine, both of whom had fought their way to supreme power through civil war, worked to elevate the status and image of the emperor above that of a mere general to a semi-divine ruler commanding both soldiers and civilians alike. This was part of the necessary measures to break the destructive cycle of opportunist civil wars, something which was largely accomplished. In the fourth century, there were far fewer civil wars over the throne (or one of the two thrones) and these were mainly between members of the same imperial dynasty.

Still, the emperors had to be great warriors and the armies had to be placated, flattered and well paid, and their high status and privileges had to be confirmed and renewed. 'Our most noble soldiers' was a standard imperial style of reference. Even Julian, a just and conscientious emperor with high-minded traditional civic values was driven to sacrifice the life of his finance minister Ursicinus to appease the wrath of the army: Ursicinus' only crime had been to protest too publicly that the army's pay was bankrupting the treasury. The army of the fourth century, with its strong dynastic feelings towards blood and kin, looked up loyally to emperors if they were proper warlords. If they were not, the bond of affection and allegiance was more tenuous. Julian, on his elevation to Caesar in the West by his imperial cousin, Constantius II, was initially regarded slightly, as a bookish Greek youth – until to everyone's surprise he turned out to be a superb general, winning great victories and earning the devoted loyalty of his troops.

Theodosius represented a break with the dynasty of Valentinian and its martial Pannonian traditions. When he died suddenly in 395, neither of his sons had embarked on an apprenticeship in war, and it is perhaps unlikely that they would have benefited from it in any case. Still, Arcadius was about seventeen and it is surprising that Theodosius had not initiated a training so necessary for an imperial future, as had been the case for Gratian at that age. Thus in 395 the Prefect Rufinus was the undoubted regent figure in the East. For the moment, there was no adequate army to deter Alaric, and when the Eastern army returned with Gainas much of it soon proved unreliable. The civil rulers had expected the victorious Theodosius to return and call them to obedience. Whatever the personal animosities within the ruling circle it was natural that they would close ranks around Arcadius and the palace, and fill this sudden power vacuum themselves.

The crises of these years were successfully averted, and the succession of an even younger boy emperor in 408 only confirmed and reinforced the wisdom of this policy. The army may have expected that on coming of age Theodosius II would be trained in arms or at least initiated into the military world as its commander. But by then the link with his grandfather's military background was a distant one, and the civilian ministers had no intention of renewing it.

The ascendancy of Pulcheria altered the balance within the government, with the court – that is, Pulcheria herself – securing the dominant influence over the weak emperor. As she was effective regent, there were important differences between her policies and those of the Anthemian tradition, but for all her piety she was a naturally shrewd politician, who knew the indispensability of both the bureaucracy and army, and co-operated rationally with them. She also had every intention of keeping the emperor unwarlike – not a very difficult task – and took the process a step further by providing it with a rationale. Theodosius became a kind of spiritual commander whose prayers, devotions and special invocation of the saints gave the armies victory. Certainly, his images on coins and statues continued to wear the military garb, but it was now accompanied by the cross and his religious contributions were emphasised. Everyone now knew him as commander-in-chief in title but not in fact. Both Marcian and Leo had been soldiers of middling rank, but by then it was no longer necessary to take the field as emperors. Both were protégés of Aspar who clearly did not intend to erect an actual commander above himself. Zeno did take the field himself, but only because he was compelled to fight for his throne and survival.

In the West, the response to the same problem was different: an unmilitary emperor meant a strong military figure ruling on his behalf. From 395, Stilicho had enjoyed extraordinary powers, which he used to unify all military authority under himself. Very soon, the mounting dangers of Alaric, Radagaisus and the multiple Rhine invasions demonstrated the imperative need for such a generalissimo. As the East rid itself of such military threats and entered a period of relative stability, the West reeled under multiple emergencies and a military dictatorship was a natural response to them, as it had been long ago in the Republic. But now it could not be legitimately institutionalised. The legal office of Dictator had been formally abolished by Mark Antony after Julius Caesar's assassination, and all proper strands of earlier Republican authority had been carefully combined in the single office of Princeps, Augustus.

This was not just a legal nicety. Opponents of the generalissimo could and did seek to replace his influence with the emperor, and why should they not? Despite the new title of Patrician and all the oblique, special honours such as three consulships and special connections with the imperial house, the generalissimo had no acknowledged position of power beyond his monopoly of military force, and no means of transferring his authority to a successor. Constantius, the next such figure after Stilicho and so obviously needed, had to intrigue or fight his way to dominant power, sometimes even against the opposition of the emperor. Unavoidably, generalissimos came to depend more and more on their personal prestige and popularity among the soldiers, many of whom they had recruited with promises, rather than their impersonal institutional command which could in theory be withdrawn at any time. This meant a political crisis of greater or lesser severity whenever, and in whatever circumstances, such a generalissimo died.

Not only was there a separation between real power and imperial legal authority. After the Western court's migration to Ravenna it was a geographical separation too, with all its consequences in an age of slow communications. The logical step would have been to reunite these two elements, as Constantius eventually tried to do by becoming co-emperor with Honorius (although his elevation was pointedly not recognised in the East). Constantius died very soon afterwards and we cannot say what he would have done had he lived and ruled. At that stage order had been successfully restored in Gaul and Spain by federate settlements, and it is not implausible that Constantius might have achieved a consolidation of what was left of Roman power and authority in the West.

However that may be, the move was not repeated by Aetius (a Roman), who faced the hostility of the dynasty and would have been even less acceptable in the East. Warlord and monarch remained separate. What had begun with Stilicho, as an expedient during a minority reign, had turned into permanent military rule. After the end of the Theodosian dynasty with the death of Valentinian III, the balance swung even further away from the emperor. Up to that time, the generalissimo, such as Aetius, still needed his formal position confirmed by imperial appointment, however grudging that was and however irremovable he might be in practice. (Stilicho had obeyed his emperor to the last, and gone calmly to his own execution.) With the new figure, Ricimer, it was on the contrary the generalissimo who appointed the emperor. When an untypically energetic Western emperor, Majorian, attempted to reclaim real imperial power, he became an embarrassment and a rival to the generalissimo and was duly eliminated. By then, the emperor's role had to be symbolic only.

In the East, too, there was separation of real power and imperial authority during the reign of Arcadius, the minority of Theodosius II and arguably well after that. At times power flowed through the hands of one individual: Rufinus, Eutropius, Anthemius and, of course, Pulcheria. Yet, there were very significant differences from the situation in the West. First was the relative security from outside invaders, at least for a decade or more, and freedom from a state of near-permanent war in which generals naturally thrive. Equally important was the geographical location of all the elements of power around the emperor in one single capital. The emperor might be a puppet, but the puppet master, for example Rufinus, had to operate through a complex and closely communicating machinery of government, which included other ministers, nominally, his peers. He had to work by patronage, faction, bribery, spying, intrigue and the ultimate fear of ruin by political trial. Unlike the great Western generalissimos he could not in the last resort tap the sword-hilt, and call in military force to tip the balance of opinion and interest. Most importantly, unlike them, he was never indispensable to the state. His formal position was simply one of the great appointments of state, which might be withdrawn at will.

Others were always in competition because access to the emperor and imperial authority, however exercised or exploited, could not be removed from the capital, could not be sent to wither in some secluded Ravenna. The potency of competition was always present, Constantinople hummed with faction and intrigue, and the tenure of a dominant figure was always being tested.

An individual emperor might be a puppet, but the office itself never shrank to that, as it eventually did in the West. In the West, the fiction of imperial authority was in the end a mere encumbrance to the real barbarian military rulers, and if the incumbent happened to be capable, like Majorian, it was an even greater one. At Constantinople, imperial authority was a sacred source. The civil mandarinate drew their lifeblood from it and were committed to maintaining it at all costs.

This shared imperative, especially during the reigns of Arcadius and the minority of Theodosius II, drew the mandarinate together, for all their bitter individual hostilities, into a common establishment which could fill the power vacuum, keep the military at a distance, and protect their own career ladders, privileges and family ambitions precisely by preserving and strengthening the government machinery. Soon the military were again cautiously and successfully integrated into the topmost circles of power. The accretion of experience, skills, and the political wisdom that goes with a single bureaucracy in a single location, provided a strong underlying continuity to the institution. Its maturity and emergence as an entity greater than the sum of its venal parts is shown in several important ways.

The mandarinate was able to incorporate or at least deal with the court, and carry on competent government even when it was partly excluded from close access to imperial decision-making, as in the periods of Pulcheria and Chrysaphius. It could prevent these most serious struggles and rivalries from spilling out into the public arena. It could join forces effectively and quickly to select a new emperor when a dynasty ended, resolving the conflicts behind closed doors and then enacting a great public ceremony of unity and coronation, ritually and legally satisfying all the significant sections of the empire, of which Constantinople was supposed to contain a microcosm. In distinct contrast to the West after the end of the Theodosian dynasty, it allowed a respectably capable emperor such as Marcian or Leo, however he owed his election, to reclaim the proper power and functions of an emperor which weak predecessors had allowed to slip into other hands.

A destabilising element in both East and West was the presence of new Germanic federate allies. Despite the common term these are of course to be contrasted with the 'old' federates such as the Arab tribes and phylarchies on the extensive frontiers with Persia. Given generous regular Roman subsidies and appointments for their chieftains and kings, they willingly acted as efficient buffer states on the very edge of the Roman provinces proper, and with a few exceptions did not have territorial ambitions on these provinces. Along other main frontiers too, treaties had been made with tribes and small kingdoms that had played a well-defined role in the empire's defences. Sometimes – as earlier in the low countries around the Rhine mouth – they were granted land for settlement and the actual Roman frontier pulled back to a new defensive line. The central point was that they remained on the fringes of imperial territory.

The new Germanic federates were quite different. They had all more or less forced their way deep into Roman provincial territory and could not be expelled – their treaty relations with the empire were closer to being agreements between equals. Emperors and statesmen from Theodosius I onwards no doubt hoped, or wanted to believe, that these barbarians could be slowly assimilated into the overall fabric of the empire and their national loyalties diluted by Romanisation as so many others had been. Since they could not be crushed militarily this was the only palatable alternative.

The large German federate blocs generally kept their side of the treaties, or believed that they did. They fought the empire's enemies and defended its nominal territories, which they now saw as really their territory, although they would naturally seek to enlarge it at imperial expense if they could. They looked to the empire for subsidies and supplies, high military posts and special honours, and they were happy to allow Roman law and administration to continue among the civil populace since they had nothing to replace it with. They looked up to their image of Rome, adopting many of its imperial manners and styles, and later imitating its coinage and legal code. Relations between the two sides were cordial, depending mainly on the personal rapport between leaders.

The one thing no longer possible was assimilation. The earlier *laeti* settlements of barbarians, though often of considerable numbers, had been made in the mutually acknowledged recognition of Roman military superiority. The immigrants were largely disarmed and lived under Roman administration; their recruits were trained in the standard manner and paid as regular soldiers. None of these constraints applied to the new *foederati*. Far from becoming diluted and Romanised, their relations with the empire and their new fixed territories had actively encouraged their evolution into self-conscious ethnic national states with noble hierarchies and hereditary kingships.

The West's federate problems turned out to be insoluble whereas the East was able, in the early part of the century, to shake off the menace, partly by exporting it westward. The plains of Pannonia and the flat lands of Gaul could easily feed far greater populations. As we saw, the East was in a perilous position immediately after 395. Rufinus and, later, Eutropius were able to bribe and manoeuvre Alaric's marauding Visigoths into leaving

Greece and the eastern territories. The succeeding civil government was able to disrupt and finally crush the chaotic Ostrogoth rebellion of Tribigild and Gainas.

Then, for thirteen years, Alaric became the main destabilising force in the West. The most damaging single development in this turbulent time was the mass invasion across the virtually undefended, frozen Rhine at the end of 406. By the time the Visigoths were eventually granted a permanent home in Aquitaine and the West was enjoying a short period of relative order, its whole political map had been altered beyond recognition, with several powerful warlike nations occupying much of Gaul and Spain. There was now no possibility of weaning them back to the earlier federate status that had operated under Theodosius I, the status of loyal subordinate allied groups in the service of the empire. They could still be diplomatically managed more or less, as Constantius and Aetius did with great skill – witness the successful great coalition that for the first time actually stopped Attila in open battle. However, they could not be prevented from developing into independent kingdoms, who were aware of Roman military weakness, encroached on its territory, and dealt with the empire from an undisguised position of growing strength.

Apart from the Arab phylarchies and a limited settlement of Goths in Thrace in the 420s (intended, unsuccessfully, as a shield against Hun raiding), the East had avoided a policy of new federate settlements until the final break-up of Attila's conglomeration of subject peoples. At this point, large numbers of these were settled, or simply settled themselves, in various parts of the Balkans, very willing to serve in or alongside the Roman armies. These regions were so ravaged and diminished in productive or martial populations that it was not practical for Marcian to try to restore the old exclusive Danube frontier. Instead he made the best defensive arrangements he could using the new federates. Of the many new groups, the largest were the Ostrogoths in Pannonia (Illyricum) and Thrace. Each could field forces able to challenge one whole Roman field army. The presence of the federates strengthened the already powerful position of Aspar, himself related to the Ostrogothic noble houses.

The Ostrogothic federates became a problem in the reign of Leo. For reasons that are not clear, the Thracian settlement seems to have got out of hand, and established itself geographically too close to Constantinople. By the time of Zeno, they were a serious menace to the empire's stability. The whole period was aggravated by the further problems of imperial insecurity and the rise of the Isaurians. Both Leo and Zeno were dynastic newcomers and attempted to work free of the close constraints and entrenched family interests of the central establishment, mainly by promoting their own close relatives to high civil and military positions, whether they were capable of holding them or not. Power and loyalty tended towards the narrowly personal, with all the fragmentary consequences of this. Leo was alarmed at

Aspar's great family ambitions and also, no doubt, at his links with the Ostrogothic federates.

There is no evidence that Aspar planned to mobilise the federates and forfeit the very powerful institutional position he had built. But Leo, unless he was content to remain a creature of Aspar, could only create a counterpart to him by calling up the dangerous genie of the Isaurians, who became in effect a third kind of federate force. Though nominally Roman subjects, they were regarded as the 'internal barbarians' and tended to live up to the name. Despite Zeno's Isaurian national origin, even he could not consistently rely on them. The murder of Aspar had triggered off the first serious revolt by the Thracian Goths, staking a semi-coherent claim to inherit his position in government. As a result Theoderic Strabo, Aspar's relative, had extracted the concession of a Praesental *Magister* post, but had been unable or unwilling to base it at Constantinople, as Aspar had naturally done. In Zeno's confused reign there reappeared that perilous and destructive development which the East had overcome seventy years earlier: external military violence, based both in the Gothic federates and the Isaurians and using ephemeral rebels in the imperial family, which attempted to dominate and dictate to the government in Constantinople.

In the capital these family factional intrigues, narrow and petty, mirrored and encouraged the conflicting forces outside. Stable centralised power was temporarily lost, but the emperor in Constantinople still had some advantages, which Zeno used effectively. Strabo was not, like the other Theoderic, an acknowledged and established king of the Goths, and he wanted imperial recognition of this status. He also wanted what Aspar had enjoyed: a *Magister* post and with it a seat at the top table of government, which would secure the dominant position of his federates and his own exclusive – personal and tribal – leadership of them. His ambition could hardly have been more transparent than in his demand for command of the two *scholae* of guards in Constantinople. When this ambition erupted in the attempted coup in alliance with Verina, it led to fighting in the capital itself and was only crushed by the timely arrival of Illus' Isaurians.

Theoderic's ambitions were different. His *Magister* appointment was welcome for the prestige and subsidies rather than a central position in the government. What he wanted was a strong and secure territorial kingdom. The sudden accidental death (or murder) of Strabo opened the way for that by giving him undisputed rule over all the Ostrogoths. This great increase in his power was deflected from the empire by Zeno's master-stroke of sending him to conquer Italy from Odovacer.

During this dangerous period, the conservative establishment temporarily lost control, but it was far from powerless, having several very distinct advantages. There was always a strong bloc of regular Roman troops to balance the federates, and they continued to be steadily recruited. Each group of federates might be too formidable to be defeated directly, but they in turn were hardly strong enough to take on the combined Roman field armies. Added to this was their problem of supply. With their limited agricultural base, and still relatively primitive systems of distribution and administration they suffered periodic, destabilising shortages of food and other necessities, which their casual plunder of other regions did not make good for long, and which the imperial government was quick to exploit. Moreover, every soldier, whether Gothic federate or Roman regular, could only be paid from the central treasuries which the bureaucracy controlled. Timely payments of gold or the promises of such payments, were always used as levers on their good behaviour.

At critical times it seemed that the Gothic federates, in their shifting combinations, had a virtual stranglehold on Zeno. Yet his apparently reckless, ad hoc concessions to them at no time included full endorsement of their territorial kingdoms, and never included the legal transfer of fixed proportions of land on the *hospitalitas* basis, whereby the Germanic nations were stably settled in the West. The relative depopulation of the Balkans made this easier to resist. At most, Leo and Zeno would 'confirm' them in their well-entrenched landholdings, but would withhold imperial recognition of other territories they might temporarily occupy. The network of connections between multiple towns and cities, despite the severe disruption, allowed Roman control to be reasserted at intervals.

At no point could any of the federate leaders — notably Strabo — successfully combine the rank of Praesental *Magister*, advising the emperor in Consistory, with tribal king. Aspar, their model, had not done it, since his power had rested on his long and trusted integration within the establishment — a thing his Ostrogothic relatives did not fully understand. Never did any military leader, Roman or federate, gather in his hands the centralised power of the generalissimos in the West.

After Theoderic had migrated to conquer Italy the days of an independent Isaurian bloc were clearly numbered, and Zeno could safely employ strong regular Roman armies to break the last resistance of the rebels Illus and Leontius in Isauria. After this, his imperial position was secure and, although loyal Isaurians continued in the palace guards and the government, the conservative establishment of Constantinople steadily reasserted itself, as it did so confidently after Zeno's death. The naive presumption of Zeno's Isaurian brother Longinus that he might step into the imperial place by hereditary right by then betrayed a quite mistaken idea of where power lay and how it operated. It was left to Anastasius finally to crush the Isaurians as an independent political force.

The East was certainly more fortunate in its frontier geography. The Danube was always the great defensive line protecting what we have loosely called the Balkan provinces — that is, all the present territory between Belgrade and Istanbul. Apart from occasional Vandal maritime threats to the Greek coasts and islands, it was to the north that the main enemies lay. After

Alaric had led his Visigothic federates out of Thrace and into western Europe, after the first Hun incursion had been defeated and the Ostrogoth revolt broken, the Eastern government, principally Anthemius and those after him, sought to restore the Danube as a preclusive cordon frontier. Forts were repaired and garrisoned and a new patrol flotilla built, but the strategic position before the 370s could not be restored. Then, the defensive system had included manageable treaty relations with many of the tribes with lands immediately beyond the Danube, tribes who had, with suitable incentives, functioned as a further barrier to others and whose mutual antagonisms could be exploited by Roman diplomacy where necessary. Now, these tribes had been either displaced or absorbed into the greater entity that the Huns were assembling. Across the Danube the empire faced a single power.

In 422, when much of the army had been sent east for the Persian war, the Huns under Rua first punctured the defences, raided in strength into Thrace and briefly threatened Constantinople itself. The far greater invasions of Attila in 441–2 tore a great breach in the Danube defences, wrecking many of the strategic cities. During the interval before 447, attempts were made to restore defences, but there can have been little hope that these would stop another full-scale invasion by Attila. Nevertheless, they served the function of preventing low-level threats, and of placing a system of obstacles in the way of a larger invasion. Their usefulness in this role is evident from the fact that Attila later insisted on complete Roman evacuation of an area five days' march south of the Danube.

The repeated defeats of the Roman armies by Attila but his inability to take Constantinople brought home to the government the great lesson that, provided this gate was firmly shut, it was possible even to lose Greece and the Balkans for a time without fatally damaging the empire. (By contrast, the loss of the far richer Anatolia many centuries later was to prove crippling.) In fact, these regions were not 'lost' in the way that Britain or Africa had been lost. What was lost for extended periods was overall military control. There were cities that the Huns could sack and plunder, but otherwise most of this mountainous area was not attractive territory for nomadic plains pastoralists such as the Huns or, later, the Bulgars. The people, of course, suffered greatly in the prolonged insecurity but, as soon as the plundering invaders had left, Roman armies and garrisons would reoccupy the strategic points.

The Balkans were not so much a lost or abandoned territory as a permanent war zone. The pastoralist invaders could penetrate deeply but not occupy large areas for very long. Nor were they seeking, at this stage, permanent territories for settlement. They were already in possession of extensive home lands north of the Danube, and saw the Roman provinces wholly as sources of plunder or extortion. At the same time their domination of their homeland area, and of many Germanic tribes, acted as a check on other barbarian pressures to conquer and settle south of the Danube.

When Attila's edifice was eventually demolished these pressures were let loose again. By comparison, the fertile Western provinces of Gaul, Spain and Africa were very attractive to migrating Germanic tribes who were intent on occupation and settlement, and who had no other permanent homelands. The period of Anastasius shows a concerted effort to reclaim the Balkan provinces as the Bulgar menace receded.

On the 1,400-mile Euphrates frontier from the Caucasus to Arabia, Persia had always been a different kind of enemy. Both sides knew each other of old, and both used many intermediaries – federate Arab phylarchies, buffer kingdoms and satrapies – to conduct the continuous military and diplomatic chess moves, short of outright war, against each other. The Arab federates were indispensable to Roman security in this theatre and, since they did not usually have ambitions for imperial territory, their loyalty was well worth paying for.

Full-scale wars occurred only at long intervals, but when they did they were very expensive. Competently led, a Roman army could usually win in set battle, but at huge logistic costs and for questionable gains. Throughout most of the fifth century, it was still this frontier that received most consideration, resources and military commitment. The fear was not so much that Persia would launch a direct aggressive war to take the Roman provinces, as they had rashly attempted to do in the third century. It was rather that they might disrupt or unravel the careful system of Arab alliances that were the first line of defence, and compel the empire to a huge commitment of its own forces, which must imperil all other defensive frontiers. Persia, of course, knew this, and was always well-informed of the empire's difficulties elsewhere.

There were three serious wars with Persia in the fifth century, but unlike those of the third and fourth centuries, none ended in large territorial alterations. The first, in the 420s, was partly a product of Pulcherian religious zeal and ended in a draw, which both sides advertised to their peoples as victory. The second, in 441 was again a stalemate that altered little. The third, more serious, came almost a century later and ended in a Roman victory. In the interval, two developments had occurred which contributed importantly to the East's stability. For most of the fifth century Persian temptation to take advantages of the empire's severe problems with the Huns and Vandals was severely checked by Persia's own northern enemies, the Hephthalite horse peoples, who caused grave damage and were tacitly encouraged by Constantinople. Only when the Persian Great King Kavad secured the military support of the Hephthalites did he venture to risk a third war with the empire. By then the empire's other great problems, the Ostrogoths and Isaurians, had been dealt with and the Bulgars gone. Anastasius, his defences stable and his coffers full, was able to accept the challenge and win the war.

The second development was shown in the resulting peace treaty. This was not one of territorial aggrandisement but restoration of the previous position, which was used by Anastasius to strengthen considerably the Roman military defences, but within definite limits. Whatever the traditional martial messages they might broadcast to their subjects, both sides had in practice been forced to recognise the advantages of avoiding these costly and ultimately unrewarding wars if local conflicts could be resolved and honour satisfied by other means. In a region such as this there was never any lack of combustible issues, but it suited both sides to prevent these getting beyond their control, which meant a diplomatic strategy in parallel with, and perhaps as important as, the military one. We have already seen the deliberate cultivation of diplomatic skills and experience under the Master of Offices, especially during the reign of Anastasius. All this was of course greatly assisted by the empire's far greater available resources of gold.

By any measure, there is no doubt that the Eastern empire was the wealthier half, as we have seen in Chapter 9 and as Constantine implicitly recognised in the historic location of his new capital. He had come at the end of a long period of bad times in which the economy had been strained to breaking-point in many regions. The imperial recovery, which he had brought to completion, involved the imposition of Diocletian's new, comprehensive and far more effective budgetary and tax system on to every corner of the empire. The periodic estimation of the state's total 'needs' (*indictio*) – from which the very detailed tax assessments for each locality and productive unit were calculated – was naturally revised upwards in times of emergency. The results of this during the fourth century were, among many other things, an accentuation in the regional disparities of prosperity, as well as an increasing social polarisation of wealth, most especially in the West.

Overall the tax system was crudely uniform, not progressive, and it could only be enforced approximately, given the slowness of ancient communications and an officially stratified society of distinct social ranks. Its obligations were generally collective – on a city or an estate or a trade guild, rather than the individuals composing it. The general result was of course that the wealthy and influential evaded much of their taxes or achieved exemption from them, passing the burdens further down to the poorer and humbler. They in turn passed them yet further down if they could. Peasant smallholders in debt to the treasury would be bought up or 'protected' by larger, richer landowners and turned into landless tied tenants, *coloni*. The remaining curials in those cities had to shoulder the extra civic burden unless they too could find ways of escaping it. Those at the bottom, the unfree *coloni*, could barely afford to raise children. In Gaul and elsewhere brigandage and peasant revolts increased.

It was in the West that all these effects were much more pronounced, well before the early fifth century when territorial losses and enforced barbarian federate settlements took much land out of the tax base. In the West the cities were historically recent introductions superimposed on an agrarian economy, consuming but not producing. Traditionally they had been kept alive only by the generous civic spending of the rich local land-owning aristocracy. By the late fourth century many of the very wealthy had migrated to their distant estates where they tried to achieve regional self-sufficiency, in some cases even creating their own private militia. Because their landholdings were so large, the economic effect on the cities was correspondingly more drastic. In Britain for example there were many very wealthy villa estates flourishing in the southeastern countryside in the late fourth century, while almost all cities except London were in decay.

The Western senatorial aristocracy, systematically excluded from the top levels of government by Diocletian, had consolidated and increased its family wealth on a huge scale during the fourth century, partly through networks of intermarriages combined with a low birth rate. By the fifth century the average income of a senatorial noble was perhaps five times what it had been in the early empire: most of the land in Gaul and Italy was owned by about twenty extended aristocratic clans with estates dispersed over many regions. To them, a Prefecture or other magistracy was simply the honour due to their birth and social rank, not a responsibility to be shouldered. At a time when the imperial treasury was desperately in need of money to pay for defence, the great senatorial landowners managed to evade their taxes on a massive scale – witness the extreme difficulties Stilicho had in raising money from them to pay his armies. Imperial laws could do little to stop this since the very officials responsible for implementing them were either members or clients of the same class as the offenders.

The East of course had a richer tax base, and the Balkan areas that were ravaged by war were in any case far less productive than the securer regions of Anatolia, Syria, Palestine and Egypt, which continued in and even increased their prosperity in the fifth century. But this alone did not account for the great fiscal disparities between East and West. There were far more cities in the East, dating from pre-Roman times, and their relationship with the surrounding land was stronger and more intimate. The attached landholdings were far more numerous than in the West, with a wider distribution of size and wealth: many were owned by modest gentry and peasant smallholders with no estates elsewhere. At the same time, as we have seen, there was a new growth of networks of 'villages' in areas such as Syria, reflecting a rise in cultivation and population. These were in fact an alternative kind of township, without city status but rivalling many cities in prosperity, usually based around church and bishop rather than curials. Even at the upper levels of the new nobility and bureaucracy, there was nowhere near the concentration of wealth that the Western aristocracy enjoyed, but a more gradual spread with even the richest seeming modest by Western standards. Overall, the middle levels of wealth survived to a much greater extent in the East.

Most important was the sharp distinction in the governing classes themselves. In the East, the great mass of those who filled Constantine's new bureaucracy and enlarged senate were gentry of modest income and limited local power who had no family traditions of government office. This was the first time their class of people had entered imperial service. At the top of the mandarinate, just as at the lower levels, the great Prefects and *Magistri* owed their careers and social positions not to independent noble birth or great wealth, but almost entirely to the government machine. These men had a far greater loyalty to the imperial state and a vested interest in managing and preserving it. One important result was that the great tax machine in the East, though clumsy and approximate, was more responsibly operated and far less distorted by corruption and venality. A far greater proportion of the taxable wealth was raised, and a far greater proportion actually reached the treasury and the uses for which it was intended. We saw in Chapter 9 how the Prefect Antiochus, faced with Attila's demands, was prepared to levy extra taxes on his own wealthy senatorial class despite their storm of opposition. We saw too how the officially accepted level of 'fees' which the tax collectors could collect from the taxpayers was set in the West at forty-eight times, then sixty times, the level in the East. Equally, the creation of the *vindices* by bureaucrats from the same provincial strata as those it was aimed at indicates clearly where the priorities lay.

There are other, less tangible reasons for what can be recognised, though with caution, as a higher level of patriotism and loyalty among many sections of the Greek East. The new senatorial mandarin class was free, not only from its Western counterpart's snobbery over ancient family lineage, but also from the affected Republican nostalgia which caused it to look with disdain on the uncultured military emperors. Western senatorial sentimentality about the lost Republic runs as a persistent theme for centuries, through even the best of the historians, such as Tacitus and Cassius Dio, and is still echoed in the lesser works, such as those of Aurelius Victor and Eutropius, over three centuries after Brutus and Philippi. The rule of one man and the loss of 'liberty' was seen at best as a necessary evil for the sake of order; naturally the best emperors were those who respected the Senate and its ancient privileges. In Italy the senatorial nobles settled down easily enough to the extinction of the emperors and the rule of a Gothic king, provided they could go on enjoying their ancient 'Republican' family honours of the consulships and praetorships as before.

Among the new Constantinople Senate and the wider city aristocracy these sentiments found almost no echo at all. Loyalty to a divine absolute monarch personifying and embodying the state went far back to Hellenistic times, and seemed the natural order of things. From pre-Roman times, they were used to a centralised royal bureaucracy. What Roman rule had added, importantly, was a developed and articulated legal system which served in turn, especially since Diocletian and Constantine, to define the ranks and powers of the bureaucracy and turn it into a more functional and impersonal machine. This ruling class had never had an interest in the oligarchical struggles of the late Republic, when Pompey, Caesar, Brutus and Antony had treated then as little more than conquered provinces to be plundered. Roman 'liberty' to them meant simply freedom under the law, with the emperor as the only proper lawgiver. The notion of sovereign rule by the Senate – let alone the 'People' – seemed to them as remote and unworldly as, conversely, the divine right of kings seems to us. This strong tradition has to be remembered in understanding why they unhesitatingly worked to preserve the office of emperor when the actual incumbent was weak or immature.

In the wider territories of the East, with their many cities, the same allegiances existed but their object was remote. The emperor was their natural ruler, but that of course did not prevent them from heartily resenting his tax-collectors and unruly soldiers consuming their resources. Very occasionally cities surrendered to the barbarians on favourable terms. Skilled Greeks were willing to serve Attila. Many Goths settled as *laeti* or living as slaves fled to join Fritigern, Alaric or Tribigild. A comparison with the West in the same period, with its repeated peasant uprisings, growing brigandage and the (oft-quoted) secession of Armorica, is difficult. Absence of perceived imperial power will of course let loose other forces: but this does not imply that resentment and disaffection are absent when these forces are firmly in control.

What stands out is not so much the rarity of manifest unrest in the East, but rather a tenacious loyalty on the part of the people to their native cities in invasions and emergencies, a loyalty which, one suspects, had older roots than that towards the imperial Roman *civitas*. Beset by enemies and with imperial forces temporarily unable to help them, we might expect the rich to flee or attempt to bribe their way to safety. Yet in many cases the citizens manned their walls in remarkable solidarity, endured great hardships and co-operated energetically in mounting a stiff resistance, which was sometimes inspired or led by their bishops. As at Edessa, their special saints, their miracles and icons became a powerful focus of resistance and the will to survive.

In this book we have addressed a question which is still strangely neglected, despite the great upsurge of interest in Byzantium in recent decades. While fully recognising the inherent advantages enjoyed by the East, we have pointed to the appropriate skills and policies that were needed to make use of them. In the fifth century East there emerged a distinct pattern of practices and formative institutions to meet the urgent problems and crises of the period.

Unlike the West, the East enjoyed several decades of relative peace and stability until it experienced the full brunt of the Hun expansion. This was because its people had resolutely rid themselves of Gothic federates and other destabilising military elements during the struggles of 395 to 400. In contrast with the West, they had much more ready gold to pay armies and buy off opponents. This was because, as well as having a much richer tax base, they operated a more efficient, honest fiscal machine. Unlike their counterparts in the West, those in the East would not allow the imperial authority to be diminished or marginalised. This was because of the greater solidarity and purpose of their ruling class, which accomplished the difficult task of integrating the military power into a lasting establishment around the emperors.

Final questions arise: how far was the survival of the East at the expense of the West? Did the East succeed in exporting its most serious problems westward? Again, perhaps the most critical period is the cold war between the two halves in 395 to 408. The basis of central military control in the West by Stilicho had already been laid by Theodosius I, in contrast with his reorganisation of the Eastern armies into five distinct army groups, principally for defending the respective frontiers but also as a check on military ambitions. There is little doubt that Stilicho was resented and feared by the Eastern government, but it is equally true that his sincere but quixotic claim to the guardianship of Arcadius as well as Honorius fuelled these fears. Eutropius' bribe to Alaric to propel him and his Visigoths westwards was a rational response to the threat, and the one blatant example of transferring a dangerous problem westward. After 408 when cordial relations were ostensibly restored, the Eastern government generally attempted to help the West when and where it could.

The old relation, however, was disrupted irreparably by realities rather than sentiments. With the striking exception of the expeditions against Vandal Africa, Eastern military intervention was concerned with upholding the claims of the imperial dynasty, or fragments of it, especially in installing Valentinian III and later, Anthemius. It did not try to prevent the progressive marginalising of the imperial authority under the generalissimos – indeed, it even hastened the process, as in its refusal to recognise Constantius' elevation to the purple.

In any case, for the East to throw its military weight in any way decisively into the unstable power relations of the West was now simply beyond its strength. Theodosius I in his time had marched west twice to crush usurpers to the throne, at very great cost, and in a period when the Rhine frontier was, if not secure, then at least holding. Even so, the political and military arrangements he had left behind in the West had not proved durable. However devoutly Theodosius II or Pulcheria might believe in a united empire, such a crusade was not feasible in the period of Western federate kingdoms and Roman warlords.

After the end of the Theodosian dynasty at Constantinople there was less incentive. The great abortive expedition against Gaiseric in 368 was as much to remove the menace of Vandal sea power as to help the West, and it is perhaps significant that Ricimer took no part in it. By the time Zeno wisely despatched Theoderic to claim the throne of Italy, the Western empire had ceased to exist. After that, the pretensions to a single empire of course continued, and Eastern emperors continued to meddle in the politics of Popes and Western kings, nominally their viceroys. But in reality, Justinian's belated glories notwithstanding, the East was on its own.

APPENDIX I

List of emperors
(*Usurpers in brackets*)

West		East	
Valentinian I	364–375	Valens	364–378
Gratian	367–383		
(Maximus)	383–388	Theodosius I	379–395
Valentinian II	375–392		
(Eugenius)	392–394		
Theodosius I	394–395		
Honorius	395–423	Arcadius	395–408
(Constantine III)	407–411	Theodosius II	408–450
Constantius III	421		
(John)	423–425		
Valentinian III	425–455	Marcian	450–457
(Petronius Maximus)	455		
Avitus	455–456		
Majorian	457–461	Leo I	457–474
Libius Severus	461–465	Leo II	473–474
Anthemius	467–472		
Olybrius	472		
Glycerius	473–474		
Julius Nepos	473–475 (480)	Zeno	474–491
Romulus Augustulus	475–476	(Basiliscus)	475–476
		Anastasius	491–518
		Justin I	518–527
		Justinian	527–565

APPENDIX II

The Theodosian dynasty

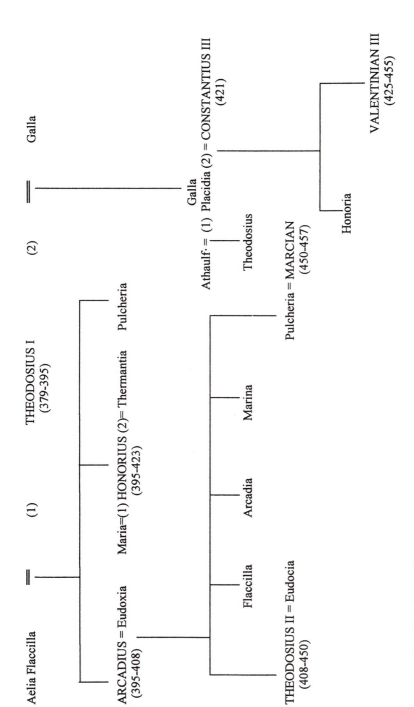

Figure 22 The Theodosian dynasty

NOTES

1 CRISIS AND PARTITION

1 Theodosius, *PLRE*, I, 904 for full classical sources. For his reign, Williams and Friell, *Theodosius*; Lippold, *Theodosius der Grosse und seine Zeit*; Matthews, *Western Aristocracies and Imperial Court*; Cameron, 'Theodosius the Great and the Regency of Stilicho'; Jones, *LRE*, ch. 6 and *passim*. For the battle, Ammianus Marcellinus, *Rerum Gestarum*, XXXI, 12–13. Also an extensive discussion in Williams and Friell, *Theodosius*, app. I.

2 The Visigoths (*Tervingi*) originally split over the issue of entry into the empire. The minority under Athanaric finally petitioned for admission in 381. For Gothic tribal names and movements, Wolfram, *History of the Goths*; Heather, *Goths and Romans*.

3 Themistius, *Orationes* 16. For a discussion of reactions to the treaty, Liebeschuetz, *Barbarians and Bishops*, ch. 3. More generally, Williams and Friell, *Theodosius*, chs 2 and 7.

4 Wolfram, *History*, 73–4.

5 Stilicho, *PLRE*, I, 853. See Bury, *History of the Later Roman Empire*, ch. 5; Mazzarino, *Stilicone*; O'Flynn, *Generalissimos of the Western Roman Empire*; Cameron, *Claudian*; Williams and Friell, *Theodosius*, ch.11.

6 Rufinus, *PLRE*, I, 778.

7 *Chronica Minora*, I, 650; Claudian, 'In Rufinum', II.

8 Gainas, *PLRE*, I, 379. Eutropius, *PLRE*, II, 440.

9 Africa alone was outside Stilicho's control at this time. For numbers, see ch. 8.

10 Claudian, 'In Eutropium', I.

11 They were comparatively few in numbers, and the fear the revolt inspired seems exaggerated. It is perhaps to be understood in terms of the recent ravages of the Visigoths before 382, or even memories of the great Gothic raids of the third century since when Asia Minor had been relatively peaceful.

12 Synesius, *de Regno*. But in *de Providentia seu Aegyptius*, Synesius took care to distance his views from those of the Prefect Aurelian – probably because Aurelian was by then trying, unsuccessfully, to co-operate with Gainas. Liebeschuetz, *Barbarians*, ch. 9.

13 Eudoxia, *PLRE*, II, 410. Bauto, *PLRE*, I, 159.

14 Fravitta, *PLRE*, I, 372. For the Gainas revolt, Zosimus, *Historia Nova*, V; Liebeschuetz, *Barbarians*, chs 9 and 10. Gainas was, of course, a bitter enemy of Eutropius from the outset, but did he see his revolt as acting in Stilicho's interests? The most we can say is that, if so, it was extremely inept.

15 Eunapius, *Fr.*, 71–2, 85. He accused the finance minister, John, of sowing dissension between the thrones of Honorius and Arcadius, but John, a favourite of the empress Eudoxia, secured his execution.

16 Eutychianus, *PLRE*, I, 319. Anthemius, *PLRE*, I, 93.

17 Lampadius, formerly a supporter of Stilicho. For this comment, Zosimus, V, 29.

18 Zosimus, V, 31–4 for the main events in Stilicho's downfall.

19 Orosius, Rutilius and Jerome (*Epistulae*) took the official line and damned Stilicho as a barbarian traitor. In modern times, Bury and Seeck, but not Gibbon, have largely accepted this view. He has been rehabilitated by, among others, Cameron (*Claudian*) and O'Flynn.

2 THE FOURTH-CENTURY BACKGROUND

1 The multiple crises of the third century and their resolution in a new type of state are described in the standard sources: Jones, *LRE*; Alföldi, Ensslin *et al.* in the *CAH*; Pauly Wissowa, *Real-Encyclopädie*. Also MacMullen, *The Roman Government's Response to Crisis*; Williams, *Diocletian and the Roman Recovery*.

2 Williams, *Diocletian*; Seston, *Dioclétien et la tetrarchie*; Kolbe, *Diocletian und die Erste Tetrarchie*.

3 See ch. 8, below.

4 Frontier defensive systems naturally varied according to the terrain and peoples faced, and military measures were closely combined with diplomatic ones. In many cases it is probably more correct to think of a frontier zone rather than a firm linear barrier: a frontier territory might be settled with a foreign people under treaty obligations, giving Rome definite rights such as the power to nominate their ruler. Whether this counted as part of the empire is almost a semantic question; see Whittaker, *Frontiers of the Roman Empire*. Among the many studies a most useful overview is Millar, *Emperors, Frontiers and Foreign Relations*.

5 Williams and Friell, *Theodosius*, chs 1, 2, app. I; Heather, *Goths and Romans*, 146–7; Ammianus Marcellinus, XXXI, 12–13. Hoffman, *Das spätrömische Bewegungsheer und die Notitia Dignitatum*; Wolfram, *History*, 124 for suggested higher casualties.

3 FORTUNES OF EAST AND WEST

1 For the great invasions, Olympiodorus *Fr.*, 9; Zosimus, V, 26; Orosius, *Historiarum adversos paganos*, VII, 37; Augustine, *de Civitate Dei*, V, 23; Paulinus, *Vita S Ambrosii*, 50.

2 The number claimed is 30,000, which seems extremely high. Zosimus, V, 35–42.

3 Olympius, *PLRE*, II, 801. The two new *magistri* were Varanes and Turpilio. The first returned to the East shortly afterwards, and the second was murdered after the fall of Olympius.

4 Olympiodorus 3–13; Zosimus, V, 36, 44–51; Philostorgius, *Historia Ecclesiastica*, XII, 3; Orosius, VII.

5 Zosimus, V, 40.

6 Zosimus, V, 35–42.

7 Zosimus, V, 44–51.

8 Attalus, *PLRE*, II, 18. Zosimus, VI, 6–13; Sozomen, *Historia Ecclesiastica*, IX, 8–9.

9 Athaulf, *PLRE*, II, 176–8.

10 Heraclian, *PLRE*, II, 539; Constans, *PLRE*, II, 310.

11 Bury, *History*, I, 183 discusses the likely chronology of the events between spring 409 and August 410.

12 For the supposed treachery Sozomen IX, 9; Procopius, III, ii, 14–24. For the sack, Zosimus, VI, 6; Sozomen, *op cit.*; Orosius, II and VII; Augustine, I, 7; Jerome, *Epistulae* 127–30; Marcellinus comes, *Chronicon* 410.

13 Death of Alaric, Jordanes, *Getica*, 156–8; Olympiodorus, *Fr.*, 10; Philostorgius, XII, 3.

14 He had been elevated to Augustus by his father in 402. Anthemius, *PLRE*, II, 93–5

15 Eudoxia, *PLRE*, II, 410.

16 *C.Th.*, XII, xii, 14.

17 John Chrysostom, *Epistulae* 147.

18 Marcellinus comes, 409; *Chronicon Paschale*, 407.

19 *C.Th.*, XIII, v, 32 and XIV, vi, 1.

20 Sozomen, 9, 5; *C.Th.*, V, vi, 3.

21 Ammianus Marcellinus, XIV, 2, 1–20 on the long-standing Isaurian menace. For the raids of the early 400s, Zosimus, V, 25; Rouge in *Revue des études anciennes*. Arbazaicus, *PLRE*, II, 127.

22 *CJ*, IV, lxiii, 4. See especially the discussion by Blockley, *East Roman Foreign Policy*, 48–55.

23 *C.Th.*, VII, xvii, 1.

24 *C.Th.*, XV, i, 51. Van Millingen, *Byzantine Constantinople*. Meyer-Plath and Schneider, *Die Landmauern von Konstantinopel*, and Schneider, *Die Bevölkerung Konstantinopels im XV Jahrhundert*. There is still considerable uncertainty about the main phases of construction of the Anthemian wall, beyond the clear archaeological evidence of different styles of towers. It is accepted that the City Prefect Cyrus added sea walls in *c.* 439–41, but were these the full circuit that existed later? In 447, after the great earthquake, Constantinus repaired the walls in record time (below, ch. 7). Some present writers such as Thompson and Liebeschuetz follow Van Millingen in the belief that Constantinus not only repaired the existing walls but added the second outer belt as well. Since the whole work was completed in three months, this seems barely credible. Until new archaeological or epigraphic evidence throws light on this issue, it seems more plausible to assume that they were part of the original Anthemian construction.

25 Pulcheria, *PLRE*, II, 929.

26 Sozomen, IX, 1; Theophanes, *Chronographia*, AM 5901. A very valuable discussion is given by Holum, *Theodosian Empresses*, ch. 3.

27 Marcellinus comes, 414; *Chron. Pasch.*, 414.

28 *C.Th.*, XVI, viii, 22.

29 Hypatia, *PLRE*, II 575. Socrates, *Historia Ecclesiastica*, 7, 15; Philostorgius, 8, 9; Theophanes, AM 5906. The later constitution was in 418: *C.Th.*, XVI, ii, 43.

30 Plintha, *PLRE*, II 892. Ardaburius, *PLRE*, II, 137.

31 *CJ*, VII, xviii, 7.

32 The identification of Anatolius is problematic: see Blockley, *East Roman Foreign Policy*, 57 and notes.

33 For the war, Socrates, 7, 20; Procopius, I, ii, 11–15; Malchus, *Fr.*, 1; Theophanes, AM 5921. See the discussion of Stein, *Histoire du Bas-empire*, 1, 281, and more recently, Blockley *East Roman Foreign Policy*, 56–9.

34 Priscus, *Fr.*, 2. See also Croke, 'Evidence for the Hun Invasion of Thrace in AD 422', on the chronology.

4 THE WESTERN WARLORDS

1 Constantius III Augustus, *PLRE*, II, 321. Ulfila, *PLRE*, II, 1181.
2 Olympiodorus, *Fr.*, 24; Philostorgius, XII, 4; Orosius, VII.
3 Orosius, VII.
4 See esp. O'Flynn, *Generalissimos*, 65ff.
5 Wallia, *PLRE*, II, 1147.
6 Orosius, VII, 43; Olympiodorus, *Fr.*, 31; Hydatius, *Chronica*, 60–7.
7 Though other settlements following this were less generous to the barbarians, involving transfer of only a third of the land, doubtless reflecting their smaller numbers and political leverage. Prosper Tiro, *Epitoma Chronicon*, 419; Jordanes, *Getica*, 173; Hydatius, 69.
8 For the settlements, Stein, *Histoire du Bas-empire* 1, 267 ff. Demougeot, *De l'unité à la division de l'empire romain*, 502 ff. Wolfram, *History*. Thompson, 'The Settlement of the Barbarians in Southern Gaul' and 'The Visigoths from Fritigern to Euric'. Goffart, *Barbarians and Romans*, has argued that the settlement was based on apportioning tax revenues and not property as such. See Heather, *Goths and Romans*, 221–2 for the arguments.
9 Olympiodorus, *Fr.*, 34; Philostorgius, XII, 12; Sozomen, 9, 16; Hydatius, 62.
10 Valentinian III Augustus, *PLRE*, II, 1138.
11 Olympiodorus, *Fr.*, 34; Theophanes, AM 5913. See esp. O'Flynn, *Generalissimos*, ch. 5.
12 Castinus, *PLRE*, II, 269; John, *PLRE*, II, 594.
13 Aetius, *PLRE*, II, 21–9.
14 Olympiodorus, *Fr.*, 41; Prosper Tiro, 423–5; Hydatius, 83–4; 'Chronica Gallica' in *Chron. Min.*, n.d. 423.
15 Felix, *PLRE*, II, 461. Boniface, *PLRE*, II, 237.
16 He became *Magister Utriusque* in 433, but did not achieve Patrician rank until 435.

5 A CHANGING STATE

1 Helion, *PLRE*, II, 533.
2 *C.Th.*, XVI, x, 21.
3 Eunapius, *Fr.*, 87.
4 Asclepiodotus, in AD 423: *C.Th.*, XVI, v, 60 and VIII, xxvii, 10.
5 For a thorough discussion of Pulcheria's new role, Holum, *Theodosian Empresses*, is invaluable, and we are indebted to him in much of this chapter.
6 Sozomen, IX 1, 6–7.
7 Theophanes, AM 5941.
8 Holum, *Theodosian Empresses*, ch. 5. See also Cameron, 'The Theotokos in 6th Century Constantinople'.
9 *Lettre a Cosme* 8, cf. Holum, *Theodosian Empresses*, 153 n. 35.
10 *Book of Heraclides*, quoted in Bury, *History*, I, 353 n. 1.
11 *Acta Conciliorum Oecumenicorum* 1.
12 Synesius, *de Regno*.
13 Cf. Demangel's rendering of the victory inscription, and Holum's translation, *Theodosian Empresses*, 110. See the solidi of Pulcheria, Constantinople 420–22 (Dumbarton Oaks).
14 Kaegi, *Byzantium and the Decline of Rome*, 229–31. Blockley, *The Fragmentary Classicising Historians*, 1983, for new translations.
15 *C.Th.*, XIV, ix, 3.

16 Cf esp. Honoré, *Emperors and Lawyers*, for an extensive discussion of the compilations of Diocletian's time and afterwards.

17 Antiochus, *PLRE, II, 102*, Mommsen, in his edition of the *Codex Theodosianus*, and Seeck, *Regesten der Kaiser und Päpste*, examine the sources of the Code.

18 Theodosius II *Novellae* 1, as quoted in Bury, *History*, 233–4. See also Harries and Wood, *The Theodosian Code*.

19 Jones *LRE*, 476.

20 Gaiseric, *PLRE*, II, 496–8.

21 Hydatius, 90; Jordanes, *Getica*, 167; Prosper Tiro, n.d. 427; Theophanes, AM 5931. Victor Vitensis, *Historia persecutionis Africae provinciae*. The figure of 80,000, derived from the head-count needed to allot the necessary shipping, is one of the more reliable manpower figures in the ancient sources. Boniface's role in this, treasonous or not, has been questioned: see Jones, *LRE*, 190 n. 40, for the crossing as an opportunistic invasion.

22 Aspar, *PLRE*, II, 164–9.

23 Priscus, *Fr.*, 2.

24 In early 435. Prosper Tiro, n.d. 435; *Chron. Min.* II, 297.

6 THE SHOCK OF ATTILA

1 There is some disagreement over whether this was a joint kingship or dual kingship over separate tribes. Maenchen-Helfen, *The World of the Huns*, 85 argues for the second. Priscus can be read either way. The treaty was with both brothers. Perhaps it is a mistake to look for a fixed and formalised jurisdiction here.

2 *Chron. Min.* I, 660; Socrates, VII, 43; Theoderet, *Historia Ecclesiastica*, V, 37; John of Nikiu, *Chronicle*. LXXXIV; Ezekiel. XXXVIII, 2 and 22.

3 *Chron. Pasch*, n.d. 439. Whether these were a full wall circuit, or merely faced the Golden Horn, is uncertain. Some writers such as Mango place them at a later date.

4 A short bow whose laminated construction, made of several materials, gave it a similar power and lethal range to the later English longbow. Maenchen-Helfen, *World*, 221ff.

5 Ammianus Marcellinus, XXXI, 2, 1.

6 Valentinian III, *Nov.*, IX, 24, June 440.

7 Bury, *History*.

8 Details of this brief Persian war are sparse, and there may have been some confusion by Theodoret V, 37 with the war of 421. For the arguments, *ERFP*, 60–1 nn. 17–21.

9 An ordinary reader who even glances at the main modern works on Attila and the Huns – Bury, Thompson, Maenchen-Helfen, say – is soon struck by the fact that, while the broad outlines of the main invasions and their consequences are agreed, the details and chronologies are full of gaps, uncertainties and disagreements. The broad picture is one of increasing Hun victories and Roman defeats, with Attila ravaging the Balkans and being bought off with ever-larger concessions until, repeatedly blocked by the barrier of Constantinople, he moves westward. Exactly when he invaded, which cities he captured and sacked, whether he demolished them, where and when the battles were fought and, most important, which treaties followed which defeats and what diplomatic shifts they represented – these are all subjects of close scholarly argument which, given the fragmentary nature of the evidence, may never be resolved.

In all this we have broadly followed the interpretation of Bury, Thompson and Jones, as against Maenchen-Helfen, Blockley and others. For the sake of a readable narrative we have kept the qualifications and reservations to the notes, but of course this is not the only narrative that could be retailed.

10 Priscus, *Fr.*, 6, 1; Marcellinus comes, n.d. 441, 442; *Chron. Pasch*, n.d. 442.

11 Procopius, *Buildings*. IV, v; Priscus *op. cit.*

12 Gren, 61, quoted in Thompson, *The Huns*, 89, n. 69.

13 Attila's siegecraft. Attila took so many fortified cities so quickly that some explanation is needed. No other barbarians had done this, and they were probably incapable of it. True, some towns were ungarrisoned, others fell by treachery, and others may have been taken by surprise, given Attila's unexpected speed of movement and co-ordination. But such a lightning run of successes can hardly be explained in these piecemeal ways. We see no good reason to disbelieve Priscus, *Fr.*, 6, 7, describing the storming of Naissus, that Attila enlisted skilled siege engineers just as he enlisted many other skilled men. He gives a most vivid description of the elaborate and well-organised assault, using siege towers with protected archers, and battering rams and scaling ladders simultaneously at different points. The possibility that Priscus' unusually detailed descriptions of the siege engines may well have been borrowed from Thucydides does not at all impugn his report that siege machinery of some kind was used. Cf. Blockley's translation of Priscus in *FCHLRE*, vol. 2. Also Jordanes, *Getica*, 222 on the later siege of Aquileia.

14 Priscus, *Fr.*, 6, 1.To what extent were any of these cities physically destroyed as distinct from being sacked thoroughly, perhaps depopulated, then wrecked sufficiently to be unviable as defensive points or barriers in Attila's way? Only archaeology is likely to help us here. See, e.g., Velkov, *Cities in Thrace and Dacia in Late Antinquity*.

15 Theophanes, AM 5942.

16 Procopius, V, v, 13; Marcellinus comes, n.d. 441.

17 Priscus, *op. cit.*; Alföldi, *Der Untergang der Römerherrschaft in Pannonien*, II, 96; Mirkovic, *Sirmium*, I.

18 Marcellinus comes, n.d. 441.

19 Priscus, *Fr.*, 13, 1.

20 Some modern writers may have tried to discern a greater rationality and profound strategy in Attila's war aims than is actually justified. Certainly he was a very great military leader and an astute, highly successful political figure in Hun terms; but for all his new-found wealth, diplomatic ambitions and the more centralised and hierarchic character of his rule, the fundamental values of a steppe warrior society can hardly be expected to have changed in such a short time.

21 Valentinian III, *Nov.*, 33 and 18. The treaty was with the West only, not with Theodosius: Clover, *The Late Roman West and the Vandals*, 84–7. It is Bury's reasonable assumption that the 'tribute' of grain was now a purchased import: *History*, I, 255–7.

22 Clover, *passim*.

23 There was at the time a power struggle going on in the topmost military circles, which led to the murder of John, the Vandal *Magister* for Thrace; he was replaced by Arnegisclus, a Gothic colleague of Aspar and Areobindus. It is generally thought that the latter murdered him. Possibly his Vandal origins were used against him when war was launched against Gaiseric. John, *PLRE*, II, 597.

24 Priscus, *Fr.*, 9, 1.

25 Priscus, *Fr.*, 11, 2.

26 Priscus, *Fr.*, 9, 3; Theophanes, AM 5942.

27 Priscus, *ibid.*

28 For the treaty Priscus, *ibid.* and Theophanes, *ibid.*, assuming our chronological assumptions are correct. See also the appendices in the 1996 edition of Thompson, *The Huns*.

29 *ERFP*, 64 n. 42.

30 This was probably Apollonius, *PLRE*, II, 121.

31 Priscus *ibid.*; Theodosius II, *Nov.*, 26. A strong example of fiscal rigour over tax exemptions and arrears had already been provided by the Prefect Antiochus in 430, and his measures were specifically reaffirmed. See *LRE*, 206.

32 Valentinian III, *Nov.*, 6, 3, 444.

33 See above, ch. 5.

34 Eudocia, *PLRE*, II, 408.

35 On the conjecture of a possible son who died in infancy, *PLRE*, II, 130.

36 *PLRE*, II, 295–6. The figure of the sly eunuch Chamberlain is a stock one, and a strong prejudice among chroniclers can be assumed.

37 Theophanes, AM 5940. He wrongly attributes the event to 447.

38 Theophanes, *ibid.*

39 For the fanciful 'apple of discord' story, John Malalas, *Chronographia*, XIV. Bury, *History*, 229–31.

40 *Chron. Pasch.*, n.d. 444.

41 Theodosius II, *Nov.*, 24, 1. See also ch. 8, below. As Blockley points out, it was unusual for the Master of Offices to be given such a task, although his powers and influence were steadily increasing during the century. In addition to the substantial measures themselves, this may well have also been an attempt to gain a more accurate and reliable understanding of their real defensive strength, a task for which the Master of Offices was well qualified.

42 Cyrus, *PLRE*, II, 336–9. Sources for his building works, introduction of street lighting and adoption of Greek as an official language are given in the PLRE entry.

43 Gildas, *de excidio et conquestu Britanniae*, 20; *LRE*, 191 and n. 42; Salway, *Roman Britain*, 479; all referring to the 'lamentations of the Britons', sent to Aetius in the late 440s and seeking aid against barbarian aggressors.

44 Marcellinus comes, n.d. 443–6.

45 Prosper Tiro, n.d. 444; Marcellinus comes, n.d. 445; Jordanes, *Getica*, 181: Theophanes, AM 5942.

46 For the sources and arguments about this massacre, and Aetius' attitude to it, O'Flynn, *Generalissimos*, 89 and notes.

47 With Thompson and others, *contra* Maenchen-Helfen, we place the non-payments of gold, which then had been made good by a payment of 6,000 pounds, in the period before 443.

48 Marcellinus comes, n.d. 447; Jordanes, *Romana*, 331.

7 RESISTANCE AND RECOVERY

1 Arnegisclus, *PLRE*, II, 151.

2 There was one Hunnic raid which took this route, in 395; Maenchen-Helfen, *World*, 51ff.

3 Ammianus Marcellinus, XVII, 7.

4 Croke, 'Two Early Byzantine Earthquakes' in *Christian Chronicles and Byzantine History*.

5 Evagrius, *Historia Ecclesiastica*, II, 14; Marcellinus comes, n.d. 447; Theophanes, AM 5930.

6 Attila invaded in the spring. Even if he had not yet begun to move at the end of January, it is reasonable to suppose that news or rumour of his preparations would be common knowledge, and that he in turn would soon have heard of the disaster and be on the move during the two-month period of rebuilding. Constantinople's awareness of its peril is borne out by Nestorius, quoted in Maenchen-Helfen, *The World of the Huns*, 121ff.

7 Constantinus, *PLRE*, I, 317.

8 Zeno, *PLRE*, II, 1199.

9 Jordanes, *Romana*, 331; Marcellinus comes, n.d. 447; *Chron. Pasch*, n.d. 447.

10 Dessau, *Inscriptiones Latinae Selectae*, 823. Thompson, *The Huns*, 91. As we point out in ch. 3 above, Thompson believes that Constantinus added the second line of walls with their forward bastions. Since the one attested fact is that he repaired the walls in the record time of sixty days, this seems most implausible.

11 Marcellinus comes, n.d. 447; Callinicus, *Vita S Hypatii*, 104.

12 Priscus, *Fr.*, 9, 3 and 11, 1.

13 Priscus, *Fr.*, 11, 1.

14 For a discussion of its location, *FCHLRE*, Priscus, n. 43.

15 Priscus, *Fr.*, 12–14.

16 Priscus, *Fr.*, 15, 2. Orestes was to be father of the last emperor in the West, ch. 13, below.

17 Priscus, *Fr.*, 15, 3.

18 Priscus, *Fr.*, 15, 4; John of Antioch, *Fr.*, 199.

19 John of Antioch, *ibid.*; Jordanes, *Getica*, 224.

20 Priscus, *Fr.*, 20, 1; Jordanes, *Getica*, 184. On this question, see Clover, 'Gaiseric and Attila'.

21 Prosper Tiro, n.d. 451; John of Antioch, *Fr.*, 199.

22 *Chron. Pasch*, n.d 450; Evagrius, I, 22; Theophanes, AM 5942; John Malalas, *Chronographia*, 366.

23 He was handed over to the son of one of his many victims. The chronology of these events is confused and uncertain, and it is possible that Theodosius had already exiled Chrysaphius, and that Pulcheria had returned to power soon afterwards, before Theodosius' death. See Holum, *Theodosian Empresses*, 207 ff.

24 Marcian, *PLRE*, II, 715. There are less plausible versions concerning his elevation. John Malalas claims that he was crowned by the Senate, while Simeon the Logothete says it was done by the Patriarch Anatolius. The story that Theodosius had bequeathed the throne to Marcian is from Marcellinus comes and *Chron. Pasch*, n.d. 450. See *PLRE* above, and Bury, *History*, 236.

25 Priscus, *Fr.*, 20.

26 Priscus, *Fr.*, 20, 3.

27 Jordanes, *Getica*, 35–6.

28 Bury, *History*, 291–2; Thompson, *The Huns*, ch. 6.

29 Prosper Tiro, n.d. 451; Jordanes, *Getica*, 197–213; Sidonius Apollinaris, *Epistulae*, 8; Hydatius, 150; Gregory of Tours, *Historia Francorum* 117; *Chron. Gall.*, 452.

30 Prosper Tiro, n.d. 452.

31 See the discussion of O'Flynn, *Generalissimos*, 99–100.

32 Prosper Tiro, n.d. 452; Jordanes, *Getica*, 42, 2; Procopius, III, iv, 29–35.

33 Prosper Tiro, n.d. 452.

34 Seeck, *Geschichte des Untergangs der antiken Welt*, 301.

35 Prosper Tiro, n.d. 452; Priscus, *Fr.*, 22; Jordanes, *Getica*, 42, 220–4; Hydatius, 153.

36 Prosper Tiro, n.d. 453; Marcellinus comes, n.d. 454; Jordanes, *Getica*, 49, 254–5; Hydatius, 154; Cassiodorus, *Variae*, n.d. 453.
37 Prosper Tiro, n.d. 453; Victor Tonnennensis, *Chronicle*, n.d. 453.
38 Jordanes, *Getica*, 50; Ellac, *PLRE*, II, 391.
39 Walamir, *PLRE*, II, 1135.
40 Jordanes, *Getica*, 268–9; Thompson, *A History of Attila and the Huns*, 168–9.
41 Jordanes, *Getica*, 263–8. See esp. *ERFP* ch. 2, 10.
42 John of Antioch, *Fr.*, 201; Prosper Tiro, n.d. 454; Hydatius, 160; Gregory of Tours, II, 8; Sidonius Apollinaris, *Carmina*, 5–7; *PLRE*, II, 28 for the full references.
43 John of Antioch, *ibid.*; Priscus, *Fr.*, 31, 1; Jordanes, *Getica*, 235; John Malalas, *Chronographia*, 365–6; Theophanes, AM 5947. Full refs in *PLRE*, II, 1138.

8 MILITARY DEVELOPMENTS, EAST AND WEST

1 Jones, *LRE*, 607, 654, viewed this period as one of significant change for the Eastern army, despite acknowledging a general continuity; Elton, *Warfare in Roman Europe*, 265, and especially Treadgold, *Byzantium and its Army*, 284–1081, 13, consider it a period of strong continuity and little structural change. Dixon and Southern, *The Late Roman Army*, largely ignore the fifth century. Although some administrative reform and gradual development can be seen in our period, the significant changes which led to the late sixth-century army described in the *Strategicon* (see Treadgold, *passim*, for details) must be largely the responsibility of Justinian, and his immediate successors.
2 Hoffman, *Das spätrömische Bewegungsheer und die Notitia Dignitatum*, 490–516, for the transfer. On the army between 378 and 395, see Williams and Friell, *Theodosius*, ch. 6; *LRE*, 156–60, 607–86.
3 The 'Huns of Thrace' mentioned serving under Theodosius, in Eunapius, *Fr.*, 60, do seem to have been settled within the empire; according to Zosimus, in 395 Rufinus had a Hunnic bodyguard, possibly drawn from the same source.
4 Elton, *Warfare*, 145–52 and app.2 for barbarian origins, and 132 for this reference to barbarian settlements by Constantius I. Barbarian groups did feature in the armies, with Gratian's use of Alans in the 380s being well known; but they may only have been a bodyguard or similar contingent. Many units with barbarian names appear in the *Notitia*, but these were regular units, even if their initial complement was of barbarian origin as individuals.
5 Zosimus, 4, 17 for the command of Theodosius' campaign army. Also *LRE*, 159–60, 174–5; Liebeschuetz, *Barbarians*, 30–1. For Stilicho generally, see Mazzarino, *Stilicone*, and Williams and Friell, *Theodosius*, esp. ch. 11.
6 Doubts are often expressed about the efficiency of these troops, based on their perceived lack of success against major barbarian incursions. However, they probably achieved their objectives against lower-level threats, and were valued as part of the Roman military establishment. They do not feature in our sources because,

> Besides these battles [in Gaul in the 360s] many others less worthy of mention were fought...which it would be superfluous to describe, both because their results led to nothing worth while, and because it is not fitting to spin out a history with insignificant details.
>
> (Ammianus Marcellinus, XXVII, 2, 11)

The *Peri Strategikes*, probably sixth-century in date, gives the role of frontier forts and their garrisons as: observing the enemy, receiving deserters from the enemy, holding back fugitives from the empire, and facilitating raids and reconnaissance – Dennis, *Three Byzantine Military Treatises*.

7 The *Notitia* is an essential source for the size and composition of the late Roman army, although it must be used with caution. No army has ever borne a direct resemblance to its official registers, and despite its 'theoretical' nature as an account of real military strengths, it does reflect a contemporary official view of the army. See *LRE*, app. II; Williams and Friell, *Theodosius*, ch. 6 and app. II; Goodburn and Bartholomew, *Aspects of the Notitia Dignitatum*; Treadgold, *Byzantium*, 46–57. For more hostile views of the *Notitia* and its usefulness, see Liebeschuetz, *Barbarians*, 40–2, and MacMullen, *Corruption and the Decline of Rome*, esp. 183.

8 Liebeschuetz, *Barbarians*, ch. 4; Elton, *Warfare*; LRE. For a specific example, Zosimus, 4, 30–1 for barbarian recruitment under Theodosius I.

9 *LRE*, 196 n. 55 for the figures in contemporary sources.

10 See Whitby, 'Recruitment in Roman Armies from Justinian to Heraclius' in Cameron, *The Byzantine and Early Islamic Near East*; Elton, *Warfare*, 128ff. and *LRE*, 614–19 for a summary of the recruitment system, and detailed references. Taking an equal age distribution across the army, and standard length of service, the army of the whole empire would require 25,000 to 30,000 recruits annually just to replace retired veterans, never mind casualties.

11 Zosimus, 5, 33–5, 42 for numbers in Stilicho's and Alaric's forces. Also *LRE*, app. 2, table 6 for pre- and post-395 units in these armies.

12 Olympiodorus, *Fr.*, 4, 7 refers to federates in Italy under Stilicho as 'diverse and mixed bodies of men', and to *bucellarii* of Romans and Goths. Liebeschuetz, *Barbarians*, 43–5, suggests that these refer to barbarians recruited as individuals to form federate units, rather than en masse, and to the emergence for generals of bodyguard units who were regular units and soldiers, but with an obviously close tie to their patron. Procopius, III, xi, 1–5 also describes how in the sixth century federates were both Roman and barbarian, although 'formerly' they were recruited exclusively from barbarians who had entered the empire as free men, i.e. not as captives or defeated enemies. This passage implies two things: one, that even by the 530s federates were not part of the regular army structure – although they may have been almost permanently available for service; and two, that barbarians entering the empire under any other terms seem not to have entered the federate system, and so may have been recruited into regular army units.

13 *LRE*, app. 2, tables 6, 7, 14, 15.

14 Valentinian III's financial difficulty, *Nov.*, 444.

15 Gregory of Tours, II, 18, 27.

16 Procopius, V, xii, 16–19.

17 Isaac, *The Limits of Empire*, suggests that the army in Palestine was mainly concerned with the control of internal unrest and banditry. He is too dismissive of Arab threats, and see Parker, *Romans and Saracens* and Shahid, *Byzantium and the Arabs* (3 vols, on the fourth, fifth and sixth centuries) for an opposing view. Mountain tribes in Asia Minor had been a long-standing problem – see Tacitus *Annals* 12, 55 for a first century example. See Treadgold, *Byzantium*, 50–3 and Table 8.1 for a breakdown of these figures, based on *LRE*, app. II.

18 Cheesman, *The Auxilia of the Roman Imperial Army*, app. I. The trend of high cavalry numbers in the frontier forces (*auxilia* or *limitanei*) was established by the second century at the latest.

19 Shahid, *Byzantium*, describes successive tribes fulfilling this role from the fourth to the sixth centuries.

20 Abundantius and Timasius, both probably *Magistri Praesentales*, were removed from office and exiled, following which Eutropius took command himself rather than trust Gainas or any others – an insult to the army he was to regret. *LRE*, 181 for the lack of Germanic names. Liebeschuetz, *Barbarians*, 105–6 for doubts as to the genuine nature of the anti-German camp at Constantinople, and 122–30 for the political nature of the fall of Fravitta.

21 Liebeschuetz, *Barbarians*, ch. 10, implies that the greater part of the Eastern army was Gothic/Germanic, much of it on a federate basis. Even if we assume Gainas' total force was Gothic it was still much the lesser part of the army. Synesius, *de Providentia*, ii, 2 for the 7,000 losses, reported as one-fifth of Gainas' forces, in Constantinople.

22 There is legislation promoting the fortification of cities, recruitment of regulars, billeting of troops, keeping units up to strength and collection of taxes in lieu of recruits dating to the period of Eutropius' supremacy. Liebeschuetz, *Barbarians*, 97–8 for references.

23 *LRE*, ch. XVII, nn. 50, 108 and 109 for references. Another indication of growing administrative control by central authority was the capping of the *officia* of *Magistri* in 441 – they were limited to a staff of 300 each. Provincial military staffs were probably also capped at this stage, later recorded as forty-one per *Dux limitis*.

24 See Lee, *Information and Frontiers*, for an assessment of this problem.

25 Although it is difficult to tie down exact dates for rebuilding, archaeological evidence shows renewed activity at almost all sites in the Balkans after destruction in the mid-fifth century. Much of this is Anastasian (Dinogetia, Istros, Tomi and others have numerous brick stamps, and inscriptions, of his reign) but some re-occupation must have occurred under Marcian and his immediate successors. Scorpan, *Limes Scythiae*, esp. 123; Velkov, *Cities*, esp. 272; Rich, *The City in Late Antiquity*; John Malalas, *Chronographia*, XVI, for Anastasian rebuilding. Jordanes, *Getica*, 267 for the settlement of Harnac, son of Attila, and his followers in the Dobruja as federates.

26 Procopius, II, vi; Treadgold, *Byzantium*, 189–92, for the expedition of 468.

27 The Goths had also discovered painfully in their progress through Illyricum in 479, described by Malchus, that they could only take fortified cities when they had been abandoned by their populations or were not defended; a garrison of 2,000 in Epidamnus was enough to prevent the whole Gothic army from taking the city. Denied access to Roman supplies they found great difficulty in living off the land.

28 *CJ*, XII.35.17 for the legislation on *probatoria*.

29 Procopius, I, viii, 3 records Gothic warrior nobles, Godidisclus and Bessas, and their followers who had not gone to Italy with Theoderic, and presumably remained in the Balkan provinces; I, xii, 6–7 and II, x, 23 for the continued use of Huns.

30 Marcellinus comes, 493, 499.

31 Howard-Johnston, 'The Two Great Powers in Late Antiquity'. *LRE*, 629 and n. 45 for the supply of the army. There were over 52,000 in the army in 503, according to the contemporary witness Joshua Stylites, and the supplies suggest at least a third again in 504.

32 Procopius, I, viii, 3 records the complete lack of co-ordination of the divisions of the Roman army in 503.

33 Crow and Ricci, 'The Anastasian Long Wall', and Procopius, IV, ix, 6–8. Also n. 25, above. The value of fortification was demonstrated by the people of Amida, who held out against the whole Persian royal army for eighty days despite having no resident garrison – Procopius, I, vii, 3–4, 12–29, and *passim* for Anastasius' efforts to fortify Eastern cities/military bases.

34 See ch. 9 for details of these financial changes.

35 Frank, *Scholae Palatinae*. It is likely that not all, and perhaps only one, of the *scholae*, along with the *candidati*, was resident in Constantinople. The importance of the *Comes Domesticorum* is shown by Stilicho's tenure of the post under Theodosius, when he had power over the *Magistri* on campaign as the emperor's deputy.

9 IMPERIAL WEALTH AND EXPENDITURE

1 *LRE*, chs 18 and 19 for a general survey of urban development. This study still provides the most useful and comprehensive historical survey of the Roman economy in general. See also Greene, *The Archaeology of the Roman Economy*; Hendy, *Studies in the Byzantine Monetary Economy c.300–1450*; Cameron, *The Mediterranean World in Late Antiquity*; Whittaker, *Frontiers of the Roman Empire*.

2 For example, Aphrodisias, where significant archaeological discoveries, especially epigraphic material, have demonstrated a strong and sophisticated urban life; *JRS* Monograph Series; Liebeschuetz, Poulter in Rich, *The City*. *LRE*, ch. 19 for numbers of cities.

3 Loseby, 'Marseille', for an example. Even where Eastern cities suffered from barbarian attacks, esp. in the Balkans in the fifth century, there is strong evidence for re-occupation and rebuilding, although sometimes at a reduced level; see ch. 8, n. 25.

4 See Greene, *Archaeology*; Hendy, *Studies*, 157; Cameron, *The Mediterranean World*, ch. 4.

5 From Leo's *Tactica*, quoted in Toynbee, *Constantine Porphyrogenitus and his World*, 33.

6 See ch. 8 for the size of the two armies.

7 Hendy, *Studies*, 620; *LRE*, 830–4; Procopius, *SH*, XXX, 1–11 for a description of the post, and the disastrous effect of Justinian's restriction of it.

8 See the various papers on this region in Liebeschuetz, *From Diocletian to the Arab Conquest*; Hendy, *Studies*; and Greene, *Archaeology*, for this pattern in Syria and Palestine. Cameron, *The Mediterranean World*, 177ff.

9 Even in Egypt marginal land might not be exploited due to failures in the irrigation system, poor returns on lets or efforts invested, or localised exactions through the rent and taxation systems (although what was considered marginal land in Egypt might have been thought quite productive in other areas). At Aphrodito, in 525/6, 30 per cent of the land was not under cultivation due to poor irrigation; Bagnall, 'Landholding in Late Roman Egypt', 135. *LRE*, 469, 819–23, for tax and profitability.

10 For population levels generally, see McEvedy and Jones, *Atlas of World Population History*, and Treadgold, *Byzantium*, 159–62. For Constantinople, Grant, *The Emperor Constantine*, 116–22, and Cameron, *The Mediterranean World*, 12–15. *LRE*, ch. 18 for Rome and Constantinople. Salway, *Roman Britain*, 542ff. for the figure of *c.* two million. Haas, *Alexandria in Late Antiquity*. Liebeschuetz and Kennedy, 'Antioch and the Villages of North Syria in the Fifth and Sixth Centuries AD'. Procopius, II, xiv, 6 claims 300,000 were killed in Antioch by the earthquake of 526.

11 Hendy, *Studies*, for a review of the problem, and Procopius, *Buildings passim*, for the remedies of (Anastasius and) Justinian.

12 For the currency and relationship to the economy in general, see: Hendy, *Studies*; Harl, *Coinage in the Roman Economy*; *LRE*, ch. 13.

13 *LRE*, 624.

14 Incidence of taxation under Anastasius, and his generosity: *LRE*, 236–7.

15 Personal wealth: *LRE*, esp. ch. 15; Hendy, *Studies*, 201–20; MacMullen, *Corruption*, for a very negative view of personal prosperity.

16 Tax rebates and remission: Jones, *LRE*, 467.

17 Valentinian III, *Nov.*, X, 3, 441. Jones, *LRE*, 205 and nn. 75 and 76.

18 Jones, *LRE*, 396–401 and 467–8.

19 During the nine-year reign of Justin I, 400,000 pounds of gold (28.8 million *solidi*) are described by Procopius as being raised from 'illegal means', implying an annual revenue of 3,200,000 *solidi*. The sources of the revenue are not clear, and it may not represent the total raised. If the Egyptian grain supply, and similar levies from elsewhere, are added to this figure then the lower figure suggested above, of seven to eight million *solidi*, may be close to the revenue available in the early sixth century; but if only a part of imperial revenue is described then the higher revenue figure above is more likely. Procopius was keen to portray Justinian in a bad light, and may only have referred to particular measures seen as harsh or extravagant: *SH*, 19, 8. Treadgold, *Byzantium*, Tables 12 and 13 for budgetary estimates. See n. 23 for supporting figures.

20 John Lydus, *de Magistratibus*, III, 43 for reserves under Theodosius II and Marcian; III, 44 for the financial ruin of the empire after 468.

21 A large part of the Western contribution probably represented Anthemius' accessional donative, so additional campaign funding was very limited.

22 The Western contribution to the Vandal expedition in 468 must have represented only a part of the total imperial treasury. Even if some came from reserves, income must have been sufficient to allow these to accumulate, and so was presumably still in excess of two million *solidi*. Potential Western revenues may have been around four million solidi, before the loss of most of Africa. In 445 Numidia was assessed at 9,800 *solidi*, and Sitifensis at 5,200 *solidi*; these figures are based on the reduced levels allowed to recover from the Vandal invasion, and so before 429 between them these two provinces should have yielded *c.* 125,000 *solidi*. The territories ceded to the Vandals were much wealthier, and so total African tax revenues may have been in the order of 500,000 to 600,000, plus the grain supply. See Jones, *LRE*, 462–3 and 468–9.

23 From *de Rebus Bellicis* and *Peri Strategikes* respectively; quoted in Hendy, *Studies*, 157ff.

24 Procopius, *SH*, 17, 5; Jones, *LRE*, 447–8; Treadgold, *Byzantium*, 118–19. A population of *c.* twenty million, and subsistence levels of *c.* two *solidi* per annum, suggests a minimum product of forty million *solidi*. Jones, *LRE*, 469 claims Justinianic revenue was one-third of gross land yield, which lends support to the budget figures suggested above.

25 Zacharias of Mitylene, *Chron.*, 511; Hendy, *Studies*, 189.

26 *C. Th.*, VII. iv. 28, 406; iv. 31, 409 for the East. *C. Th.*, VII. v. 1 for the West. Annual rations for a soldier cost *c.* five *solidi*: Jones, *LRE*, 447–8.

27 Treadgold, *Byzantium*, ch. 4 for the arguments on pay rates.

28 Based on the troop numbers set out in ch. 8 (*c.* 100,000 *comitatenses* and 200,000 *limitanei*, rising to as many as 150,000 in Justinian's field army).

29 Procopius, *Buildings* esp. I, i, 27ff., iii, 1–2, viii, 5.

30 Treadgold, *Byzantium*, 192–3 and nn. for a summary of non-military costs, and further references.

10 CENTRALISED POWER

1 As in the ivory diptych, *c.* 470, in the Kunsthistorisches Museum, Vienna.
2 Above, chs 3 and 4.
3 Most of the essential reference sources in this descriptive chapter are to be found in the two comprehensive volumes of Jones, *LRE*, 284–602.
4 *C. Th.*, XV, xii, 1. They were not abolished in the West until allegedly after a monk, Telemachus, had leapt into the arena to separate the combatants, and was himself killed by the mob: Theoderet, *Historia Ecclesiastica*, 5, 26.
5 Of the many descriptions of the City, cf. Mango and Dagron, *Constantinople and its Hinterland*; Jones, *LRE*, ch. 18; Cameron, *The Mediterranean World*, 12–16. Also Bury, *History*, ch. 3.
6 Jones, *LRE*, chs 11, 12, 15, 16.
7 For the accumulation of powers in the office of Praetorian Prefect, Howe, *The Praetorian Prefect from Commodus to Diocletian*.
8 Boak, *The Master of Offices in the Later Roman and Byzantine Empires*; Dunlap, *The Office of Grand Chamberlain in the Later Roman and Byzantine Empires*; Hopkins *Eunuchs and Politics in the Later Roman Empire*.
9 Jones, *LRE*, 1057 for numbers.
10 Cf. Ostrogorsky, *History of the Byzantine State*, 66–7; also Cameron, *Circus Factions*.
11 It is generally claimed that Majorian's naval failure, preparing to invade Africa, was the reason for his downfall, but there is good evidence that Ricimer resented his ability and independence and used this as an occasion to depose him. See esp. O'Flynn, *Generalissimos*, 109–11.
12 See O'Flynn, *Generalissimos*, ch. 8.
13 *ERFP, passim.*
14 *Ibid.*, esp. III, 1 and IV, 2–3.
15 Brock, 'Christians in the Sassanian Empire'.

11 THE GOD-PROTECTED STATE

1 Adam Ferguson, *An Essay on the History of Civil Society*, 1767. In contrast to Gibbon and most Enlightenment writers, he emphasises strongly the essentially social character of human thought and motivation, rejecting as virtually nonsensical all ideas of a rude and solitary State of Nature. Also in contrast to them, Ferguson does not necessarily see warfare as barbaric or religion and myth as superstitious: on the contrary competitive war, tribal and national myths are often positive forces for cohesion, identity and progress in mankind.
2 Grant, *The Emperor Constantine*, 119, n. 4.
3 Runciman, *Byzantine Civilisation*, ch. 9. Of course there are endless and sometimes sterile taxonomical discussions about where 'Roman' civilisation ends and 'Byzantine' begins, and of course there are convenient historical dividing points such as 395, 602 and so on. Our point here is not to enter into such essentialist arguments, but to stress only the fact of conscious continuity.
4 On the relation between Greek and Christian thought, a good introduction and reference book is Shiel, *Greek Thought and the Rise of Christianity*. See also Niebuhr, *Christ and Culture*; Hatch, *The Influence of Greek Ideas on Christianity*;

Armstrong and Markus, *Christian Faith and Greek Philosophy*; Jaeger, *Early Christianity and Greek Paideia*.

5 For the change in both philosophy and popular religion, Nock, Baynes, Alföldi in *CAH*; Ferguson, *The Religions of the Roman Empire*; Vogt, *The Decline of Rome*; Cumont, *The Oriental Religions and Roman Paganism*; Brown, *The World of Late Antiquity*; Dodds, *Pagan and Christian in an Age of Anxiety*; Liebeschuetz, *Continuity and Change in Roman Religion*; Lane Fox, *Pagans and Christians*.

6 Plotinus' main works are the Enneads, in 64 books. (Dean W. R. Inge *The Philosophy of Plotinus*, London 1918). He taught at Rome and was favoured by the emperor Gallienus (253–68) even to the extent of a quixotic proposal to found Plato's Republic in the form of a new city, Platonopolis, in Campania. The empire was fighting for its life at that time and the scheme came to nothing. His most important disciple was Porphyry, who published all his works and later wrote a comprehensive and influential polemic, *Against the Christians*.

7 Origen, commentary on Romans, 3.6.

8 Williams and Friell, *Theodosius*, ch. 4, and notes. Since Kripke's seminal work in 1970 even more esoteric metaphysical programmes have emerged, such as David Lewis' Modal Realism: Lewis, *On the Plurality of Worlds,* Oxford 1986.

9 Baynes, *The Thought World of East Rome*.

10 There is very extensive church literature on the two councils of Ephesus. See esp. Norris, *Manhood and Christ*; Sellers, *The Council of Chalcedon*; Sarkissian, *The Council of Chalcedon and the Armenian Church*.

11 Understand it who can. Hypostasis, as distinct from personhood, may not be a very intelligible or useful concept now. But was it even then? At least Aristotle's concepts such as Essence (*Ousia*) are logically clear. But as philosophers are still arguing sharply even about what personhood is, perhaps we should not press the question.

12 The title and office of Pope involves an accretion of claims beginning with that of Bishop Damasus (Theoderet, *Historia Ecclesiastica*, V, 10) and culminating perhaps in the special claims of papal infallibility at the First Vatican Council in 1870. The most Byzantium would concede, until its very last desperate period, was co-equal authority between Constantinople and Rome, never the supremacy of Rome. Because of its connotations and because this is a history of the East, we have avoided the title Pope throughout.

13 Baynes, 'The Supernatural Defenders of Constantinople'.

14 Bury, *History*, I, 238. Nicephorus Callistus 14. Cameron, 'The Theotokos in 6th Century Constantinople' and *Images of Authority*.

15 Mango, *Byzantium*, ch. 8.

16 Bury, *History*, I, 77. Cameron, *The Mediterranean World*, 13 and n. 2.

17 Eusebius, *de vita Constantini*, 3, 1.

18 *CJ*, I, xiv, 4; Gregory of Tours, *Epistulae*, XI, 4.

19 On accession and coronation, see ch. 11 below. Also Baynes, *The Thought-World of East Rome*; McCormack, *Art and Ceremony in Late Antiquity*; Bury, *History*, ch. 1; Charanis, *Byzantion* 1940–41.

12   IMPERIAL CONFLICTS

1 Holum, *Theodosian Empresses*, chs 1–3 and *passim*.

2 Aspar, *PLRE*, II, 164. See chs 5 to 7 above. He is attested as *Magister* in 424–5 when he went on the expedition to crush the usurper John in the West, and

again in 431–4 on the African expedition. In 441, and perhaps far earlier, he was *Magister Utriusque*, but the specific commands are not known for certain. He may not have been a Praesental *Magister* until 457.

3 Anthemius, *PLRE*, II, 96. An intended imperial future seems a possibility, but much of this may be based on senatorial hopes as well as his later career. Sidonius Apollinaris, *Carmina* 2 suggests he was reluctant to take the purple, which is most implausible.

4 Leo, *PLRE*, II, 663. He was born in Thrace but also said to be from the province of Dacia in the Diocese of Moesia. He had a son in 463, who died the same year. In 457, he was *Comes et Tribunis Mattiariorum*.

5 *de Ceremoniis*, by the emperor Constantine VII Porphyrogenitus. See Bury, *History* I, 316, n. 1, and especially the excellent commentary of McCormack, *Art and Ceremony*, 242–7. Constantine's writers derived the description from an earlier ceremonial book by Peter the Patrician in the sixth century.

6 This is a slightly abbreviated version; see McCormack.

7 Candidus, *Fr.*, 1; Jordanes, *Getica*, 239; Marcellinus comes, n.d. 471. Theophanes, AM 5961 for the later encashment of the supposed promise.

8 The sequence of events is uncertain. For recent surveys of the evidence Blockley, *ERFP*, 72; Jones, *LRE*, 221; Stein, *Histoire du Bas-empire*, 1, 356. The date is generally thought to be 459 (Jones, Wolfram). Blockley, *op. cit.*, considers that the revolt may have broken out under Marcian but been ended by Leo.

9 Ricimer, *PLRE*, II, 924, of noble Vandal-Suevic ancestry. With his military colleague Majorian (his nominee for emperor), he overthrew the Western emperor Avitus in October of that year.

10 Majorian, *PLRE*, II, 703. He was soon afterwards deposed by Ricimer and executed.

11 This reluctance to fight the Vandals appears as a tradition among later Gothic military leaders. The reasons probably have less to do with any Goth-Vandal affinity, than the very reasonable Gothic dislike of distant military adventures, especially maritime ones with all their hazards – an attitude amply borne out by events.

12 Priscus, *Fr.*, 39, 53; Blockley, *ERFP*, 72; Clover, *The Late Roman West*, 191. We are told that Gaiseric refused even to admit a Roman embassy to his territories.

13 *PLRE*, II, 120. The name is variously rendered: Tarasicodissa, Codisseus, Trascalissaeus.

14 Sidonius Apollinaris, *Carmina*, 2; John of Antioch, *Fr.*, 209.

15 Priscus, *Fr.*, 52; *Vita S. Danielis Stylitae*, 56.

16 Basiliscus, *PLRE*, II, 212–4.

17 Heraclius, *PLRE*, II, 541. Candidus, *Fr.*, 2; Procopius, III, vi, 1ff.; Theophanes, AM 5961.

18 Marcellinus, *PLRE*, II, 708–10. See Clover, *The Late Roman West*, 192–4. The puzzle of why Ricimer refused to co-operate remains.

19 Jones, *LRE*, 224, 462. This has to be a crude guess, based on John Lydus and Candidus for the cost of the expedition, and Procopius that the annual revenue in Justin's time was 2.8 million *solidi* or nearly 39,000 pounds of gold. In general, the resulting financial strains may have been exaggerated. As the later reforms of Anastasius showed, the problems arose as much from inefficiency and corruption in the fiscal chain as from an absolute depletion of wealth. But see ch. 9.

20 There have been many post mortems on the African failure. The idea that Basiliscus was bribed by the Vandals can be discounted. One rumour was that Aspar's bribe was a promise to make him emperor, and is almost as implausible. All that is fairly certain is that Aspar wanted friendly relations with the Vandals

and opposed the expedition, and that he wanted to regain his influence in government. Whether Basiliscus was quite as incompetent as alleged may be doubted. Priscus suggests that as *Magister Militum per Thracias* he had several successes against both Goths and Huns. Was Aspar prepared to have Leo murdered or foment a revolt? On general showing, both seem unlikely. It is possible that Basiliscus' fatal agreement to the truce with Gaiseric was partly a move to favour Aspar and achieve a compromise peace with the Vandals. But of course there are infinitely more variants.

21 *Chron. Pasch*, n.d. 468. Anagast, *PLRE*, II, 75. Dengizich, *PLRE*, II, 354.
22 Amorkesos, *PLRE*, II, 73. Malchus, *Fr.*, 1. Sartre, *Trois etudes sur l'Arabie romaine et byzantine.*
23 Theophanes, AM 5961.
24 Zonaras 14, 1.
25 *Vita Marcelli*, Symeon Metaphrastes, *S. Demetrii Miracula*, PG 116, 74.
26 John of Antioch, 206. For the attempt to seduce the Isaurians, Candidus, *Fr.*, 1.
27 For the full references to the murder, Aspar, *PLRE*, II, 168.
28 *CJ*, 9, 12, 10.
29 Theoderic Strabo, *PLRE*, II, 1073–6.
30 Theoderic the Amal, *PLRE*, II, 1077–84.
31 Wolfram, *History*, 265–9; Blockley, *ERFP*, 77–8. The Goths originally attacked a Sarmatian group around Singidunum, which the Romans treated as a hostile act.
32 Jordanes, *Getica*, 283–7. They were said to have been settled in seven Macedonian cities.
33 Glycerius, Western emperor 473–4., *PLRE*, II, 514.
34 Malchus, *Fr.*, 2.
35 Full references in Zeno, *PLRE*, II, 1202.

13 EASTERN CHAOS, WESTERN EXTINCTION

1 See above, ch. 11.
2 Malchus, *Fr.*, 5. Possibly Zacynthus was taken too. Blockley, *ERFP*, 79
3 *PLRE*, II, 213. Candidus, *Fr.*, I; John of Antioch, 210; *Vita S. Danielis Stylitae*, 68–9; Malchus, *Fr.*, 7, 8.
4 Evagrius, III, 1; Malchus, *Fr.*, 16; John Lydus, iii, 45, who says, ridiculously, that he could not even bear the picture of a battle when it was presented to him. For a discussion of his many detractors, Lanaido in *BMGS* 1991.
5 Procopius, III, vii, 26; Malchus, *Fr.*, 3; Blockley, *ERFP*, 79 suggests that the treaty may have been supplemented by an agreed mechanism for settling disputes, cf. Malchus, *Fr.*, 17.
6 Illus, *PLRE*, II, 586. Trocundes, *PLRE*, II, 1127.
7 Verina, *PLRE*, II, 1156. Patricius, *PLRE*, II, 838.
8 For the Basiliscus coup, Candidus 1; John of Antioch, 210; *Vita S. Danielis Stylitae*, 68–9; Malchus, *Fr.*, 7, 8; Theophanes, AM 5967.
9 Evagrius, III, 4.
10 Epinicus, *PLRE*, II, 397. On his extortions, Malchus, *Fr.*, 7; Suidas *Lexicon* 2424; Bury *History*, 393–4. He was later dismissed in disgrace.
11 Armatus, *PLRE*, II, 148–9. Zenonis, *PLRE*, II, 1203.
12 Evagrius, III, 4; *Vita S. Danielis Stylitae*, 70–85.
13 For Zeno's restoration, Evagrius, III, 7; *Vita S. Danielis Stylitae*, 69; Anonymous Valesianus, 9, 42–4.
14 Malchus, *Fr.*, 8; John Malalas, *Chronographia*, 381–2.

15 Ricimer, *PLRE*, II, 942. He was of mixed Sueve and Visigoth ancestry, both parents being of royal houses. His sister married the Burgundian king Gundioc.

16 O'Flynn, *Generalissimos*, 127–8.

17 *Ibid*. 132

18 Odovacer, *PLRE*, II, 791. His father was the Hun Edeco. He is referred to as Scirian through his mother, but this has been disputed. He co-operated with the Franks under Childeric I to defeat the Alemanni in Italy. Gregory of Tours, ii 19.

19 Procopius, V, I, 4–8 ; Jordanes, *Getica*, 242; *Chron. Min.*, I; Evagrius, II, 16. Anon. Val., 10, 45. He was variously styled *Rex Herulorum, Rex Gothorum*.

20 Procopius, V, I, 7–8; Anon. Val., 8, 38.

21 The question of barbarian settlement and *hospitalitas* has been addressed elsewhere: see ch. 4, n. 8.

22 Malchus, *Fr.*, 10–14. The precise date the embassy arrived is uncertain: either winter 476 or early 477.

23 Cf. the discussions of Kaegi, *Byzantium*, and his major references.

24 Nepos, *PLRE*, II, 777. Malchus, *Fr.*, 10.

25 Syagrius, *PLRE*, II, 1041. He ruled from 465 to 486 and was styled 'King of the Romans'.

26 Malchus, *Fr.*, 18; Anon. Val., 11, 49; Jordanes, *Getica*, 289.

27 Classical sources: Malchus; Candidus, *Fr.*; John of Antioch, *Fr.*; *Vita S. Danielis Stylitae*; Theophanes; also Bury, *History*, I, ch. 12; Jones, *LRE*, I, 224–30.

28 Malchus, *Fr.*, 18. With so little evidence it is still difficult to explain this crucial failure in what had been a solemnly advertised major military effort.

29 Marcian, *PLRE*, II, 717.

30 Marcellinus comes, n.d. 481; Jordanes, *Romana*, 346; Evagrius, III, 25.

31 Leontius, *PLRE*, II, 670.

32 Jones, *LRE*, 244.

33 Evagrius, III, 14.

34 Malchus, *Fr.*, 6–9.

35 Ariadne, *PLRE*, II, 140. Her role in the succession, Constantine VII Porphyrogenitus *de ceremoniis* I, 92; Evagrius, III, 29–32; Theophanes, AM 5983; John Malalas, *Chronographia*, 392.

36 Anastasius, *PLRE*, II, 78.

37 See ch. 8, esp. nn. 25 and 33.

38 Bury, *History*, I, 432–3.

14 THE ACHIVEMENTS OF ANASTASIUS

1 Marcellinus comes, 493, 499, 502; Theophanes, AM 5994. Stein, *Histoire du Bas-empire*, 89–90.

2 Julian, *PLRE*, II, 639. The location of the battle is unknown.

3 John Malalas, *Chronographia*, 393; Theophanes, AM 5988; Longinus, *PLRE*, II, 688. Not to be confused with Zeno's brother, who died in exile in the Thebaid. Yet another Longinus, of Selinus, was a minor leader in the revolt, captured about the same time, taken to Constantinople for public exhibition, then beheaded at Nicea after brutal torture. Marcellinus comes, n.d. 498; Evagrius, III, 35.

4 Marinus, *PLRE*, II, 726. John Lydus, III; John Malalas, *Chronographia*, 400.

5 Polycarp, *PLRE*, II, 895–6; John, *PLRE*, II, 604–5. John Lydus, III; John Malalas, *Chronographia*, 400.

6 For the commutation of *annona*, a gradual accretion of measures in the fourth and fifth centuries, comprehensive references are given in Jones, *LRE*, ch. 13,

461–9 and notes. The principal sources are *C. Th.*, 11; *CJ*, 10; John Malalas, *Chronographia*, 394; Evagrius, III, 42.

7 For an account of the Diocletianic system, Jones, *LRE*, ch. 12, and his collection, *The Roman Economy*; MacMullen, *The Roman Government's Response*, chs 5–7; Seston, *Dioclétien*, Part II; Williams, *Diocletian*, ch. 9.

8 Cf. Jones, *LRE*, 235–7, 460–1; *CJ*, 10, 27, 1; *CJ*, 12, 37, 16; *CJ*, 1, 42, 1–2.

9 Jones, *LRE*, 443–4. John copied the copper coinage already operating in the Ostrogothic kingdom of Italy. See ch. 9 for more discussion.

10 See above, ch. 8.

11 John Lydus, III 46, 49. John Malalas, *Chronographia*, 400. There is a detailed scheme reorganising the civic finances of Alexandria by the *Vindex* Potamo. Justinian, *Edicta* 13, 15.

12 Joshua Stylites, *Chronicle*, 31. Edessa had raised 140 pounds of gold every four years, Evagrius, III, 39. He also makes the point that the church strongly opposed the tax (though most clergy were exempt from it), less for its economic hardship than because it included prostitutes as taxpayers and hence condoned sinful earnings. This may be connected with the pious and decorous form of the celebrations.

13 Aristus, *PLRE*, II, 147.

14 Marcellinus comes, n.d. 499; Jordanes, *Romana*, 356.

15 Shahid, *Byzantium*, for these conflicts; Sartre, *Trois études*; Theophanes, AM 5990, 5994, 5995; Evagrius, III, 36; Romanus, *PLRE*, II, 948.

16 Eugenius, *PLRE*, II, 417.

17 Joshua Stylites, 18–23. Blockley, *ERFP*, 88–9, doubts whether the Persian demand for money was concerned with the Caspian Gates.

18 Procopius, I, vii, 1–5; Theophanes, AM 5996; Joshua Stylites, 50. Blockley, *ERFP*, 87–9 n. 25; Liebeschuetz, 'The Defences of Syria in the Sixth Century'.

19 Joshua Stylites, 48 and 53; Theophanes, AM 5996; Zacharias, 7, 3; Procopius, I, vii.

20 Hypatius, *PLRE*, II, 577–80.

21 John Lydus, III; Patricius, *PLRE*, II, 840–2.

22 Celer, *PLRE*, II, 275.

23 The figure is calculated from the records of wheat needed to supply the army. See ch. 8 above.

24 Joshua Stylites, 57–95; Theophanes, AM 5998; Zacharias, 7; Procopius, I, viii; John Lydus, III.

25 Joshua Stylites, 89; Procopius, I, x; Zacharias, 7. On the development of Dara and the Justinianic contribution, Croke and Crow, 'Procopius and Dara'.

26 Crow, 'The Long Walls of Thrace' in Mango and Dagron (eds), *Constantinople and its Hinterland*. An earlier study, defending the Anastasian, not Justinianic origin of the wall is Croke, 'The Date of the "Anastasian Long Wall in Thrace"'. Procopius, VII, xl, 43, and *Buildings* IV, ix, 5–13.

27 Ch. 8, nn. 25 and 33.

28 Anon. Val., 12, 64.

29 Marcellinus comes, n.d. 505 and 508; Jordanes, *Getica*, 300–1 and *Romana*, 356. Chlodovec, *PLRE*, II, 288–90; his consulship Gregory of Tours, II, 38.

30 See Blockley's very useful ch. II, 13 in *ERFP*.

31 See the collection *Byzantine Diplomacy*, ed. Shepherd and Franklin, especially the papers by Kazhdan, Chrysos and Antonopoulos.

32 In 499. Priscian of Caesarea, *Panegyricus*, 223; Procopius of Gaza, *Panegyricus*, 15. For the *Brytae*, John of Antioch, *Fr.*, 103; Joshua Stylites, 35; John Malalas, *Chronographia*, 16. See Bury, *History*, notes to pp. 437–8. The festival was often

an occasion for riots and disorders, culminating in a particularly bloody tumult in 501.

33 Zacharias, 7.
34 Zacharias, 7
35 Zacharias, 7; Marcellinus comes, n.d. 512.
36 *Chron. Min.*, II, 97–8; John Malalas, *Chronographia*, 407–8.
37 Vitalian, *PLRE*, II, 1171–76. John of Antioch, *Fr.*, 214; Jordanes, *Romana*, 357–8; Zacharias, 7.
38 Theophanes, AM 6005–6.
39 Marcellinus comes, n.d. 514; Zacharias, 7; as above, full references in, *PLRE*.
40 John of Antioch, *Fr.*, 214; Marcellinus comes, n.d. 515; John of Nikiu, 89; John Malalas, *Chronographia*, 403; Evagrius, III; Theophanes, AM 6007.
41 As above. For Vitalian's later reappearance, Jordanes, *Romana*, 361; Zacharias, 8; Evagrius, IV; Marcellinus comes, n.d. 519; John Malalas, *Chronographia* 411.
42 Procopius, *SH*, xix, 7.
43 Justin, *PLRE*, II, 648.

BIBLIOGRAPHY

The bibliography includes all the works referred to in the text, and a range of other sources used in researching this volume as starting points for further reading.

Alföldi, A. (1926) *Der Untergang der Römerherrschaft in Pannonien* Budapest.

Alföldy, G. (1974) *Noricum.* trans. Birley, A. London.

Altheim, F. (1959) *Geschichte der Hunnen* Berlin.

Anderson, P. (1974) *Passages from Antiquity to Feudalism* London.

Armstrong, A. and Markus, R.A. (1960) *Christian Faith and Greek Philosophy* London.

Arnheim, M. (1972) *The Senatorial Aristocracy in the Late Roman Empire* Oxford.

Bagnall, R.S. (1992) 'Landholding in Late Roman Egypt: The Distribution of Wealth' *JRS* 82, 28–49.

Bagnall, R.S., Cameron, A., Schwartz, S.R. and Worp, K.A. (1987) *Consuls of the Later Roman Empire* Atlanta.

Barth, W. (1894) *Kaiser Zeno* Basle.

Baynes, N. (1955a) *Byzantine Studies and Other Essays* London.

—— (1955b) 'The Thought-World of East Rome' in *Byzantine Studies and Other Essays.*

—— (1955c) 'The Supernatural Defenders of Constantinople' in *Byzantine Studies and Other Essays.*

Baynes, N. and Moss, H. (eds) (1948) *Byzantium* Oxford.

Blockley, R.C. (1981, 1983) *The Fragmentary Classicising Historians of the Late Roman Empire*, 2 vols, Liverpool.

—— (1992) *East Roman Foreign Policy* New York.

Boak, A.E.R. (1919) *The Master of Offices in the Later Roman and Byzantine Empires* New York.

Bregman, J. (1982) *Synesius of Cyrene: Philosopher-Bishop* London.

Brock, S. (1982) 'Christians in the Sassanian Empire: A Case of Divided Loyalty' in Mews, S. *Religion and National Identity.*

Brooks, E.W. (1893) 'The Emperor Zenon and the Isaurians' *Eng. Hist. Rev..*

Brown, P. (1971a) *The World of Late Antiquity* London.

—— (1971b) 'The Rise and Function of the Holy Man in Late Antiquity' in *JRS* 61.

—— (1972) *Religion and Society in the Age of St Augustine* London.

—— (1981) *The Cult of the Saints: Its Rise and Function in Latin Christianity* London.

Brunt, P. (ed.) (1974) *The Roman Economy* Oxford.

Burgess, W.D. (1965) *The Isaurians in the 5th Century AD*, Dissertation, Madison, Wisconsin.

Burns, T.S. (1984) *A History of the Ostrogoths* Bloomington, Indiana.

Bury, J.B. (1939) *Cambridge Ancient History*, 12 vols, Cambridge.

—— (1958) *History of the Later Roman Empire*, 2 vols, New York.

Cameron, Averil (1978) 'The Theotokos in 6th Century Constantinople' *J Th S*.

—— (1979) 'Images of Authority: Élites and Icons in Late Sixth-century Byzantium' *Past and Present* 84, 3–35.

—— (1993) *The Mediterranean World in Late Antiquity, AD 395–600* London.

—— (ed.) (1995) *The Byzantine and Early Islamic Near East III: States, Resources and Armies* Princeton.

Cameron, Alan (1969) 'Theodosius the Great and the Regency of Stilicho' *Harvard Studies in Classical Philology* 73, 247–80.

—— (1970) *Claudian: Poetry and Propaganda at the Court of Honorius* Oxford.

—— (1976) *Circus Factions: Blues and Greens at Rome and Byzantium* Oxford.

—— (1981) 'The Empress and the Poet: Paganism and Politics at the Court of Theodosius II' *Yale Class Studies* 27, 272.

Chadwick, H. (1967) *The Early Church* London.

Charanis, P. (1972) *Studies in the Demography of the Byzantine Empire* London.

Cheesman, G.L. (1914) *The Auxilia of the Roman Imperial Army* London.

Christie, N. and Loseby, S.T. (eds) (1996) *Towns in Transition. Urban Evolution in Late Antiquity and the Early Middle Ages* Aldershot.

Clover, F. (1973) 'Geiseric and Attila' *Historia* 22, 104ff.

—— (1993) *The Late Roman West and the Vandals* Aldershot.

Croke, B. (1977) 'Evidence for the Hun Invasion of Thrace' *GRBS* 18, 347–67.

—— (1982) 'The Date of the "Anastasian Long Wall" in Thrace' *GRBS* 23, 59–78.

—— (1983) 'AD 476: The Manufacture of a Turning Point' *Chiron* 13, 81–119.

—— (1992) *Christian Chronicles and Byzantine History, 5th–6th centuries* Aldershot.

Croke, B. and Crow, J. (1983) 'Procopius and Dara' *JRS*, 73.

Crow, J. (1995) 'The Long Walls of Thrace' in Mango, C. and Dagron, G. (eds) *Constantinople and its Hinterland*.

Crow, J. and Ricci, A. (1997) 'The Anastasian Long Wall' *JRA* 10.

Cumont, F. (1911) *The Oriental Religions and Roman Paganism* Chicago.

Dagron, G. (1974) *Naissance d'une capitale. Constantinople et ses institutions de 330 à 451*, Paris.

Demandt, A. (1990) *Der Spätantike Romische Geschichte von Diocletian bis Justinian 284–565* Munich.

Demouget, E. (1951) *De l'unité à la division de l'empire romain 395–410* Paris.

Dennis, G.T. (1984) *Maurice's Strategikon* Philadelphia.

—— (ed.) (1985) *Three Byzantine Military Treatises* Washington DC.

Dessau, H. (1916) *Inscriptiones Latinae Selectae* Berlin.

De St Croix, G.E.M. (1981) *The Class Struggle in the Ancient Greek World* Oxford.

Dixon, K.R. and Southern, P. (1996) *The Late Roman Army* London.

Dodds, E.R. (1965) *Pagan and Christian in an Age of Anxiety* Cambridge.

Drinkwater, J. and Elton, H. (eds) (1992) *Fifth Century Gaul: A Crisis of Identity?* Cambridge.

Duncan-Jones, R.P. (1978) 'Pay and Numbers in Diocletian's Army 541–608' *Chiron* 8, 541–60.

—— (1990) *Structure and Scale in the Roman Economy* Cambridge.

Dunlap, J.E. (1924) *The Office of Grand Chamberlain in the Later Roman and Byzantine Empires* New York.

Durliat, J. (1990) *De la ville antique à la ville byzantine* Paris.

Dvornik, F. (1966) *Early Christian and Byzantine Political Philosophy* Washington DC.

Elton, H. (1996a) *Warfare in Roman Europe, AD 350–425* Oxford.

—— (1996b) *Frontiers of the Roman Empire* London.

Ferguson, A. (1966) *An Essay on the History of Civil Society* Edinburgh.

Ferguson, J. (1970) *The Religions of the Roman Empire* London.

Ferril, A. (1986) *The Fall of the Roman Empire: The Military Explanation* London.

Foss, C. (1996) *Cities, Fortresses, Villages of Byzantine Asia Minor* Aldershot.

Fowden, G. (1993) *Empire to Commonwealth: Consequences of Monotheism in Late Antiquity* Princeton.

Frank, R.I. (1969) *Scholae Palatinae: The Palace Guards of the Later Roman Empire* Rome.

Freeman, P. and Kennedy, D. (eds) (1986) *The Defence of the Roman and Byzantine East* BAR Oxford.

French, D.H. and Lightfoot, C.S. (eds) (1989) *The Eastern Frontier of the Roman Empire* BAR Oxford.

Frend, W.H.C. (1972) *The Rise of the Monophysite Movement* Cambridge.

Gibbon, E. (1910) *The History of the Decline and Fall of the Roman Empire* Everyman, London.

Goffart, W. (1980) *Barbarians and Romans AD 418–584: Techniques of Accommodation* Princeton.

Goodburn, R. and Bartholomew, P. (eds) (1976) *Aspects of the Notitia Dignitatum* BAR Oxford.

Grant, M. (1993) *The Emperor Constantine* London.

Greene, K. (1986) *The Archaeology of the Roman Economy* London.

Grillmeier, A. and Bacht, H. (eds) (1951) *Das Konzil von Chalkedon* Würzburg.

Groenman-van Waatering, W. (ed.) (1997) *Roman Frontier Studies 18* Oxford.

Haas, C. (1997) *Alexandria in Late Antiquity* Baltimore.

Haldon, J.F. (1979) *Recruitment and Conscription in the Byzantine Army c.550–950* Sitzungsberichte der Osterreichischen Akademie der Wissenschaften, Vienna.

Harl, K.W. (1997) *Coinage in the Roman Economy 300 BC to AD 700* Baltimore.

Harries, J. and Wood, I. (1993) *The Theodosian Code* London.

Hassall, M.W.C. and Ireland, R.I. (1979) *De Rebus Bellicis* BAR Oxford.

—— (1994) 'Theodosius II and Fifth Century Constantinople' in Magdalino, P. (ed.) *New Constantines*.

Heather, P. (1991) *Goths and Romans: 332–489* Oxford.

—— (1994) 'New Men for New Constantines? Creating an Imperial Elite in the Eastern Mediterranean' in Magdalino, P. (ed.) *New Constantines*.

Hendy, M.F. (1985) *Studies in the Byzantine Monetary Economy c. 300–1450* Cambridge.

Hoffman, D. (1969, 1970) *Das spätrömische Bewegungsheer und die Notitia Dignitatum*, 2 vols, Düsselfdorf.

Holum, K.G. (1982) *Theodosian Empresses: Women and Imperial Dominion in Late Antiquity* Berkeley.

—— (1977) 'Pulcheria's Crusade' *GRBS*, 18.

Honoré, T. (1981) *Emperors and Lawyers* London.

Hopkins, M.K. (1963) 'Eunuchs and Politics in the Later Roman Empire' *Camb. Philol. Soc.*

Howard-Johnston, J. (1995) 'The Two Great Powers in Late Antiquity: A Comparison' in Cameron, A. *The Byzantine and Early Islamic Near East III*, 157–226.

Howe, L. (1942) *The Praetorian Prefect from Commodus to Diocletian* Chicago.

Inge, D.W.R. (1918) *The Philosophy of Plotinus* London.

Isaac, B. (1992) *The Limits of Empire: The Roman Army in the East* Oxford.

—— (1995) 'The Army in the Late Roman East: The Persian Wars and the Defence of the Byzantine Provinces' in Cameron, A. *The Byzantine and Early Islamic Near East III*, 125–55.

Jaeger, W. (1962) *Early Christianity and Greek Paideia* Harvard.

Jones, A.H.M. (1971) *The Cities of the Eastern Roman Provinces* Oxford

—— (1974) *The Roman Economy* Oxford.

—— (1990) *The Later Roman Empire, 284–602* Oxford.

Kaegi, W.E. (1968) *Byzantium and the Decline of Rome* Princeton.

—— (1981) *Byzantine Military Unrest 471–843: An Interpretation* Amsterdam.

Kazhdan, A. (ed.) (1991) *Oxford Dictionary of Byzantium* New York.

Kennedy, D. and Riley, D. (1990) *Rome's Desert Frontier from the Air* London.

Kidd, B.J.(1922) *A History of the Church to AD 461*, vol. 3, Oxford.

King, C.E. (ed.) (1980) *Imperial Revenue, Expenditure and Monetary Policy in the Fourth Century AD BAR* Oxford.

Kolbe (1987) *Diocletian und die Erste Tetrarchie* Berlin.

Lanaido, A. (1991) 'Some Problems in the Sources for the Reign of the Emperor Zeno' *BMGS*.

Lane Fox, R. (1986) *Pagans and Christians* London.

Lee, A.D. (1993) *Information and Frontiers: Roman Foreign Relations in Late Antiquity* Cambridge.

Lengyel, A. and Radan, G.T.B. (1980) *The Archaeology of Roman Pannonia* Budapest.

Liebeschuetz, J.H.W.G. (1977) 'The Defences of Syria in the Sixth Century' in *Akten des X Internationalen Limes Kongress* Cologne.

—— (1979) *Continuity and Change in Roman Religion* Oxford.

—— (1990) *From Diocletian to the Arab Conquest* London.

—— (1991) *Barbarians and Bishops: Army, Church and State in the Age of Arcadius and Chrysostom* Oxford.

—— (1992) 'Alaric's Goths: Nation or Army?' in Drinkwater, J. and Elton, H. (eds), 75–83.

Liebeschuetz, J.H.W.G. and Kennedy, D. 'Antioch and the Villages of North Syria in the Fifth and Sixth Centuries AD: Trends and Problems' in Liebeschuetz, J.H.W.G. *From Diocletian to the Arab Conquest.*

Lippold, A. (1980) *Theodosius der Grosse und seine Zeit* Munich.

Loofs, F. (1913) *Nestorius and his place in the history of Christian Doctrine* Cambridge.

Loseby, S.T. (1992) 'Marseille: A Late Antique Success Story?' *JRS* 82, 165–85.

Luibheid, C. (1965) 'Theodosius II and Heresy' *J. Eccl. Hist.*.

MacCormack, S. (1981) *Art and Ceremony in Late Antiquity* Berkeley.

McCormick, M. (1977) 'Odovacer, Emperor Zeno and the Rugian Victory Legation' *Byzantion* 47.

—— (1986) *Eternal Victory: Triumphal Rulership in Late Antiquity, Byzantium and the Early Medieval West* Cambridge.

McEvedy, C. and Jones, R. (1978) *Atlas of World Population History* London.

MacMullen, R. (1976) *The Roman Government's Response to Crisis* New Haven.

—— (1980) 'How Big was the Late Roman Army?' *Klio* 62, 451–60.

—— (1988) *Corruption and the Decline of Rome* New Haven.

Maenchen-Helfen, O.J. (1973) *The World of the Huns* Berkeley.

Magdalino, P. (1992, 1994) *New Constantines: The Rhythm of Imperial Renewal in Byzantium, 4th–13th Centuries* Papers from the 26th Spring Symposium of Byzantine Studies, St Andrews, March, Aldershot.

Mango, C. (1980) *Byzantium. The Empire of the New Rome* London.

Mango, C. and Dagron, G. (eds) (1995) *Constantinople and its Hinterland* Aldershot.

Martindale, J. (ed.) (1980) *Prosopography of the Later Roman Empire II* Cambridge.

Matthews, J. (1990) *Western Aristocracies and Imperial Court, AD 364–425* Oxford.

Mattingley, D.J. (1995) *Tripolitania* London.

Mazzarino, S. (1942) *Stilicone* Rome.

Mews, S. (1982) *Religion and National Identity* Oxford.

Meyer-Plath, P. and Schneider, A.M. (1943) *Die Landmauern von Konstantinopel* Berlin.

Millar, F. (1982) 'Emperors, Frontiers and Foreign Relations, 31BC to AD 378' *Britannia* 1–23.

—— (1992) *The Emperor in the Roman World* London.

Mircovic, M. (1976) *Sirmium* Belgrade.

Mitchell, S. (1983) *Armies and Frontiers in Roman and Byzantine Anatolia BAR* Oxford.

Mocsy, A. (1974) *Pannonia and Upper Moesia* London.

Mommsen, T. (1905) *Codex Theodosianus* Berlin.

Morrison C. and Lefort, J. (1989) *Hommes et richesses dans l'empire byzantine Ive–VIIe siècle* Paris.

Moravcsik, G. (1963) *Principles and Methods of Byzantine Diplomacy* Belgrade.

Norris, R.A. (1963) *Manhood and Christ: A Study in the Christology of Theodore of Mopsuestia* Oxford.

Norwich, J.J. (1988) *Byzantium* London.

O'Flynn, J.M. (1983) *Generalissimos of the Western Roman Empire* Edmonton.

Oost, S.I. (1968) *Galla Placidia Augusta* London.

Ostrogorsky, G. (1940) *History of the Byzantine State* Munich.

Parker, S.T. (1986) *Romans and Saracens: A History of the Arabian Frontier* Winona Lake.

—— 'Geography and Strategy on the Southeastern Frontier in the Late Roman Period' in *Roman Frontier Studies (1995)* Oxford (1997).

Potter, T. (1995) *Towns in Late Antiquity* Sheffield.

Rich, J. (1992) *The City in Late Antiquity* London.

Richardson, C.C. (1958) *The Doctrine of the Trinity* London.

Rou22é, C. (1989) *Aphrodisias in Late Antiquity* London.

Rougé, J. (1966) 'L'Histoire Auguste et l'Isaurie au Ive siècle', *Revue des études anciennes* 68, 282–315.

Runciman, S. (1933) *Byzantine Civilisation* London.

Salway, P. (1981) *Roman Britain* Oxford.

Sarkissian, K. (1965) *The Council of Chalcedon and the Armenian Church* London.

Sartre, M. (1982) *Trois études sur l'Arabie romaine et byzantine* Brussels.

Schneider, A.M. (1949) *Die Bevolkung Konstantinopels im XV Jahrhundert* Gottingen.

Scorpan, C. (1980) *Limes Scythiae* BAR Oxford.

Scott, L.R. (1976) 'Aspar and the Burden of the Barbarian Heritage' *Byzantine Studies* 3, 59–69.

Seeck, O. (1876) *Notitia Dignitatum* Berlin.

—— (1919) *Regesten der Kaiser und Päpste* Stuttgart.

—— (1920) *Geschichte des Untergangs der antiken Welt* Stuttgart.

Sellers, R.V. (1953) *The Council of Chalcedon* London.

Seston (1946) *Dioclétien et la tetrarchie* Paris.

Shahid, I. (1984) *Rome and the Arabs* Washington DC.

—— (1984/1990/1995) *Byzantium and the Arabs in the Fourth/Fifth/Sixth Century*, 3 vols, Washington DC.

Shepherd, J. and Franklin, S. (eds) (1992) *Byzantine Diplomacy* Aldershot.

Shiel, J. (1968) *Greek Thought and the Rise of Christianity* London.

Soproni, S. (1985) *Die letzten Jahrzehnte des Pannonischen Limes* Munich.

Starr, C. (1982) *The Roman Empire, 27BC–AD476: A Study in Survival* New York.

Stein, E. (1949) *Histoire du Bas-Empire* Paris.

Teall, J.L. (1965) 'The barbarians in Justinian's armies' *Speculum* 40, 294–322.

Thompson, E.A. (1948) *A History of Attila and the Huns* Oxford.

—— (1950) 'The Foreign Policies of Theodosius II and Marcian' *Hermathena*.

—— (1956) 'The Settlement of the Barbarians in Southern Gaul' *JRS* 46, 65ff.

—— (1963) 'The Visigoths from Fritigern to Euric' *Historia* 12, 105ff.

—— (1996) *The Huns* Oxford.

Tomlin, R. (1987) 'The Army of the Late Empire' in Wacher (ed.) *The Roman World*, 107–35.

Toynbee, A. (1973) *Constantine Porphyrogenitus and his World* London.

Treadgold, W. (1995) *Byzantium and its Army: 284–1081* Stanford.

Tsangadas, B.C.P. (1980) *The Fortifications and Defence of Constantinople* East European Monographs 71, New York.

Van Milligan (1899) *A Byzantine Constantinople: The Walls of the City* London.

Vasiliev, A.A. (1952) *History of the Byzantine Empire* Madison, Wisconsin.

Velkov, V. (1977) *Cities in Thrace and Dacia in Late Antiquity* Amsterdam.

—— (1980) *Roman Cities in Bulgaria: Collected Studies* Amsterdam.

Vogt, J. (1993) *The Decline of Rome* London.

Wacher, J. (1987) (ed.) *The Roman World* London.

Webster, L. and Brown, M. (eds) (1997) *The Transformation of the Roman World AD 400–900* London.

Whitby, L.M. (1985) 'The Long Walls of Constantinople' *Byzantion* 55, 560–83.

Whitby, M. (1995) 'Recruitment in Roman Armies from Justinian to Heraclius' in Cameron, A. *The Byzantine and Early Islamic Near East III.*

Whittaker, C.R. (1995) *Frontiers of the Roman Empire: A Social and Economic Study* Baltimore.

Whittow, M. (1990) 'Ruling the Late Roman and Early Byzantine City: A Continuous History' *Past and Present* 129, 3–29.

Wickham, C. (1988) 'Marx, Sherlock Holmes and the Late Roman Economy' *JRS* 78, 183–93.

Williams, S. (1985) *Diocletian and the Roman Recovery* London.

Williams, S. and Friell, G. (1994) *Theodosius: The Empire at Bay* London.

Wissowa, P. (1894) *Real-Encyclopädie der klassischen Altertumswissenschaften* Stuttgart.

Wolfram, H. (1988) *History of the Goths* Berkeley.

Wormald, P. (1976) 'The Decline of the Roman Empire and the Survival of its Aristocracy' *JRS* 66, 217–26.

Classical sources

Acta Conciliorum Oecumenicorum

Ammianus Marcellinus *Rerum Gestarum*

Anonymus Valesianus

Augustine *de Civitate Dei*

Callinicus *Vita S. Hypatii*

Candidus *Fragments*

Cassiodorus *Variae*

Chronica Minora

Chronicon Paschale

Claudian *Carmina*

Codex Justinianus

Codex Theodosianus

Constantine VII Porphyrogenitus *de ceremoniis aulae Byzantinae*

Eunapius *Fragments*

Eusebius *de vita Constantini*

—— *Historia Ecclesiastica*

Eutropius *Breviarium*

Evagrius *Historia Ecclesiastica*

Gildas *de excidio et conquestu Britanniae*

Gregory I (Pope) *Epistulae*

Gregory of Tours *Historia Francorum*

Hydatius *Chronica*

Jerome *Chronicle*

—— *Epistulae*

John Chrysostom *Epistulae*

John Lydus *de Magistratibus populi Romani*

John Malalas *Chronographia*

—— *Exerpta de Insidiis*

John of Antioch *Fragments*

John of Nikiu *Chronicle*
Jordanes *Getica*
—— *Romana*
Joshua Stylites *Chronicle*
Justinian *Edicta*
Malchus *Fragments*
Marcellinus comes *Chronicon*
Olympiodorus of Thebes *Fragments*
Origen *Commentaries*
Orosius *Historiarum adversus paganos*
Paulinus *Vita S. Ambrosii*
Philostorgius *Historia Ecclesiastica*
Priscian of Caesaria *Panegyricus*
Priscus of Panium *Fragments*
Procopius of Caesarea *Buildings*
—— *History of the Wars*
—— *Secret History*
Procopius of Gaza *Epistulae*
—— *Panegyricus*
Prosper Tiro *Epitoma*
—— *Chronicon*
Rutilius *de redito suo*
Severus of Antioch *Epistulae*
Sidonius Apollinaris *Carmina*
—— *Epistulae*
Socrates *Historia Ecclesiastica*
Sozomen *Historia Ecclesiastica*
Suidas *Lexicon*
Symeon Metaphrastes *S. Demetrii Miracula*
Synesius *Catastaseis*
—— *Epistulae*
—— *de Providentia seu Aegyptius*
—— *de Regno*
Tacitus *Annals*
Themistius *Orationes*
Theodoret *Epistulae*
—— *Historia Ecclesiastica*
—— *Historia Religiosa*
Theodore Lector *Excerpta Historiae Ecclesiasticae*
Theodosius II *Novellae*
Theophanes of Byzantium *Fragments*
Theophylactus Simocatta *Historiae*
Theophanes *Chronographia*
Valentinian III *Novellae*
Vegetius *Epitoma rei militaris*
Victor Tonnennensis *Chronicle*
Vita et conversatio S. Marcelli

273

Vita S. Danielis Stylitae
Zacharias of Mytilene *Chronicle*
Zonaras *Epitome Historiarum*
Zosimus *Historia Nova*
Zosimas (Pope) *Epistulae*

INDEX